The Old Woman Who Lived in a Shoe

A pantomime

Norman Robbins

Samuel French — London

New York - Toronto - Hollywood

CHARACTERS

Calumnia, an evil witch
Mother Goose, an immortal
The Squire of Tumbledown, Sir Hugo Hepatitis
Boy Blue, a villager
Bo-Peep, a shepherdess
Wrack } the Squire's bailiffs
Ruin }
Corydon, Dame Dallymore's son
Dame Dallymore, mother to multitudes
Princess Marigold of Entertainia
Giggles, the Court Jester
Old King Cole, Ruler of Entertainia
Tapioca, a shoe-maker
Chorus of **Villagers**, **Children**, **Tourists**, etc.

COPYRIGHT INFORMATION

(See also page ii)

SYNOPSIS OF SCENES

ACT I

ACT II

MUSICAL NUMBERS

ACT I

1	**Song**	Villagers
2	**Song**	Corydon, Boy Blue, Bo-Peep and Children
3	**Song**	Mother Goose and Company
4	**Song**	Princess and Corydon
5	**Song**	Corydon and Princess
6	**Dance**	Juniors
7	**Song**	Dame and King
8	**Song**	Princess
9	**Song**	Corydon

ACT II

10	**Song**	Villagers
11	**Song**	Giggles and Dame
12	**Song**	Wrack and Ruin
13	**Dance**	Mushrooms/Babes
14	**Dance** (Reprise)	Mushrooms/Babes
15	**Song/Dance**	Villagers
16	**Song**	Corydon and Princess
17	**Song**	Party Guests
18	**Song**	Full company
19	**Song**	Giggles

SONG SUGGESTIONS

For Norman Robbins' list of song suggestions, please contact the Librarian, c/o Samuel French Ltd, 52 Fitzroy Street, London W1T 5JR.

AUTHOR'S NOTE

It was during a pantomime seminar last year that the President of an amateur pantomime society mentioned that although they'd staged *most* of my scripts, they were unable to manage *Humpty Dumpty, Jack and the Beanstalk* and *Puss in Boots* because their small stage could not accommodate a Giant. "Was it not possible", he asked, "to write a pantomime that normally featured such a character, yet could be staged without it?" Other representatives complained that the cost of hiring a "Giant" was often too expensive for church hall groups and restricted their choice of yearly subject. I had to confess I hadn't given it much thought, but promised I'd try to come up with a solution. *The Old Woman Who Lived in a Shoe* is my answer. Another almost forgotten Victorian pantomime, it proved very popular with audiences until the Second World War and I remember seeing a small-scale version of it at the Castleford Theatre Royal sometime in the 1940s. Its origin as a pantomime subject is not too clear, but William H. Holland, Manager of the Surrey Theatre in London wrote a version of it in 1878 entitled *The House That Jack Built; or Harlequin Dame Trott, the Little Old Woman Who Lived in a Shoe*, and ten years earlier, it had played to record houses at the Old Bowery Theatre, New York. As most pantomimes presented in the USA at that time were based on London productions, it clearly indicates the pantomime was well known in Britain by the second half of the 19th century. In the version I saw (alas, the one and only) the Giant appeared in the opening scene then vanished for good. Using this as a basis, I have omitted the Giant from the cast list, but as you will see, still allow him to play a big part (ouch) in the story. Apart from this, the rest is a truly traditional pantomime, stuffed with corny jokes, well-tried routines and a host of zany characters. If the pace is kept brisk, it should prove a joy to audience and performer alike.

Norman Robbins

For Amanda Smith

My editor and friend for more years
than I care to remember

Other pantomimes by Norman Robbins
published by Samuel French Ltd

Aladdin
Ali Baba and the Forty Thieves
Babes in the Wood
Cinderella
Dick Whittington
The Grand Old Duke of York
Hickory Dickory Dock
Humpty Dumpty
Jack and the Beanstalk
Puss in Boots
Red Riding Hood
Rumpelstiltzkin
Sing a Song of Sixpence
The Sleeping Beauty
Snow White
Tom, The Piper's Son
The Wonderful Story of Mother Goose
The White Cat

Plays by Norman Robbins
published by Samuel French Ltd

The Late Mrs Early
Nightmare
Pull the Other One
Slaughterhouse
Tiptoe Through the Tombstones
Tomb With a View
Wedding of the Year

ACT I

The Witch's Cave

Mysterious chords play

The CURTAIN *rises to reveal a lane backdrop depicting the interior of a vast cavern, in which great stalactites and stalagmites can be seen, bathed in a mixture of green, blue and red light. This is the lair of Calumnia, the witch*

Calumnia stands C, *her back to the audience, peering intently into her crystal ball. As the chords end, she swiftly turns to face the auditorium*

Calumnia (*suspiciously*) Who's there? (*She realizes and sneers*)
   Well, well. An *audience*. No doubt on pleasure bent.
   All smiling faces, fancy clothes, and cash on sickly sweeties spent.
   (*Harshly*) Well, *tough*. You'll find no solace here and that I guarantee.
   For all that happens from now on will be controlled by *me*.
   Clear off. You're only wasting time with hopes of "happy ending".
   (*Gleefully*) Disaster, misery and woe are more what *I'm* intending.
   To Entertainia's happiness, I mean to be the hitch,
   And all shall tremble at my name — Calumnia , the witch. (*She cackles*)

Mother Goose enters R *in a white follow-spot. She is a cheery, elderly lady in clothes resembling the Welsh National costume, and carries a wooden spoon which she uses as a wand*

Mother Goose (*beaming*) So *this* is where you're lurking?
   And on mischief bent, no doubt ...
   Well, mark my words, you cannot hide
   If Mother Goose should seek you out. (*She curtsies*)
   With magic spoon (*she displays it*) your plots I'll foil
   And bring about your fall.
   For in the Land of Nursery Rhymes
   I'm Fairy Guardian to *all*.
Calumnia (*savagely*) Begone, you foolish creature and consider your
      position ...
   'Gainst me, you're twice as useless as a British politician.

By ev'ry witch that's ever lived, I'm hailed the greatest rotter.
Not one has powers to equal *mine*. Not even Harry Potter.
With evil spells and wicked deeds, *disaster* I shall bring
To all in Entertainia — from commoner to king.

Mother Goose (*cheerily*) I see. Then as for punishment you *really* seem to yearn,
It's patently quite clear a lesson *hard* you'll have to learn.
Oh, well … You've had your warning. That's a fact you can't deny.
So do your worst, but rest assured, we'll meet again each time you try.

Calumnia Such confidence. Yet all the same, you'll find it counts for naught.
Just interfere in *my* concerns, and lessons sharp I'll see *you* taught.
But morning comes. It's time to leave. There's mischief to be done.
(*She smirks*) In ever-happy Tumbledown, I mean to start my fun.
So fare thee well, my fairy friend, and 'ware the witch's curse —
Attempt to foil me and I'll make their troubles *ten times worse*.
(*She cackles with glee*)

Calumnia exits L

Mother Goose (*amused*) Oh, dear. I fear a nasty shock awaits that scheming crone.
I've no intention — as she'll find — of letting *her* go there alone.
(*Brightly*) So join us in old Tumbledown, where peasantry prepare
To greet their day with dance and song upon the village square.

Mother Goose flourishes her wooden spoon and exits R

Black-out

Scene 1

The Village of Tumbledown

A full set. A typical pantomime village of ancient cottages set against a backdrop of hills and trees. The village inn is UR, *and Tumbledown Orphanage is* UL. *The orphanage is simply a decrepit-looking thatched cottage with a hand-painted sign fastened to the wall and a practical door. Other quaint buildings* DS *conceal entrances and exits*

When the scene begins, it is a bright and sunny morning, and the Villagers, led by Boy Blue and Bo-Peep, are singing and dancing

Song 1 (*Villagers*)

Sir Hugo Hepatitis, the unpleasant Squire of Tumbledown, enters DL *holding a large envelope affixed with a wax seal*

The Villagers fall back

Squire (*as he enters*) Out of the way. Out of the way. (*He swaggers* DC) Make room for a man of importance.

The Villagers look around excitedly

Boy Blue (*eagerly*) Who *is* it? Where is he?
Squire (*in irritation*) It's *me*, you impertinent peasant. Sir Hugo Hepatitis. Richest man in all Entertainia, and Squire of Tumbledown village. (*He adopts a superior pose*)

The Villagers groan in disappointment

Bo-Peep (*pointedly*) We thought you said a man of *importance*.
Squire (*sharply*) Well? Aren't *I* important? (*He glowers at Bo-Peep*)
Boy Blue (*incredulously*) You? *You're* just a nasty old miser who wouldn't give a *penny* to last year's carol singers.

The Villagers agree

Squire (*hotly*) And why should I? (*Sneering*) There wasn't a decent voice amongst them.
Bo-Peep (*scornfully*) How would *you* know?
Squire (*smugly*) Because, young lady, I was once a singer *myself*. (*He preens*)

Everyone looks incredulous

Many's the time I've sung at the Royal Opera House. And the minute my name was announced, the entire audience clapped their hands.
Boy Blue Yes. Over their ears.

The others laugh

Squire Bah. Clear off, you tawdry tatterdemalions. Another word and I'll have you *all* in the village stocks.

The Villagers jeer and exit variously

(*Muttering*) Neighbourhood's going to the dogs. It's worse than (*local district*). Still — now I'm rid of *that* lot, there'll be no-one around to see my *next* bit of dirty dealing. (*Scowling*) That flannel-faced old faggot Dame Dallymore's been using her cottage as an orphanage without permission *and* hasn't paid a penny of the rent she owes. (*Smirking*) So — as Chairman of the Planning Department, I've given myself permission to throw her out and turn the place into Tumbledown's first cyber-café. (*Chortling*) As soon as I'm rid of *her*, I can rake in millions from the Internet. (*Glancing around in annoyance*) Now where are those stupid Bailiffs of mine, Wrack and Ruin?

Jangly music plays

Wrack and Ruin shamble on to the stage UC *and move* DS *to the Squire. They are dressed in badly-fitting and shabby clothes with soft felt hats, and their beaming faces conceal their almost total lack of intelligence*

Wrack   (*cheerfully*) Here we are, Boss. Wrack and Ruin, at your service.
Squire   (*glaring at Wrack and Ruin*) And about time. I distinctly told you to meet me here at nine o'clock.
Ruin   We know, but first thing this morning we saw Little Jack Horner making his friends laugh by pretending to be *you*.
Squire   (*annoyed*) What? Then I hope you did something *about* it?
Wrack   Course we *did*. We told him to stop acting like an idiot.
Squire   Bah. You haven't the brains you were born with. (*Firmly*) Now stop wasting time and get inside the orphanage. I want every stick of furniture thrown into the street.
Ruin   (*surprised*) You mean — Dame Dallymore's orphanage?
Squire   I certainly *do*. She hasn't paid her rent for the last ten years, so out she goes.
Wrack   (*aghast*) But what about the poor little orphans?
Squire   (*harshly*) Who cares? They're just as big a nuisance as *she* is. Now get to work and let me know the minute you've finished. I'm off to (*local travel agency*) to complain about that terrible holiday I had in Switzerland. They told me the scenery there was the finest in the world.
Ruin   And didn't you like it?
Squire   (*savagely*) Like it? I didn't even *see* it. Everywhere I looked there were *mountains* in the way.

The Squire exits DR

Wrack   (*grimacing*) Oooh, I don't know why we work for *him*. He's always moaning about *something*.
Ruin   (*surprised*) *You've* some need to talk. Look at the moaning *you* did yesterday, when you went to get your car insured.

Wrack (*defensively*) That was different. I wanted to insure it against *theft* and the stupid feller at (*local insurance office*) wouldn't let me.

Ruin Of course he wouldn't. You can't insure your car just against *theft*. You have to insure it against *fire* and theft.

Wrack (*protesting*) But that's *daft*. Who'd pinch a burning car?

Ruin (*pushing Wrack*) You know what *your* trouble is, don't you? You're a *moron*. It's no wonder you can't get yourself a decent job.

Wrack (*stung*) I could if I wanted. (*Proudly*) They offered me one at the Town Hall last week. Asked if I'd like to be a Borough Surveyor. (*He smirks*)

Ruin (*in disbelief*) Borough Surveyor? (*With curiosity*) So why didn't you take it?

Wrack I'm too *big* to get down rabbit holes. (*Concerned*) But never mind *that*. What are we going to do about Dame Dallymore? We can't throw *her* out. Not with all those *children*.

Ruin I know. Nobody'd speak to us again. (*Worried*) But if we *don't* do it, that rotten old Squire'll give *us* the sack.

Wrack Tell you what. Let's have a sit down and see if we can think if a plan. I know somewhere we can eat dirt cheap.

Ruin (*grimacing*) Oooh, I don't fancy that. Who wants to eat *dirt*?

Wrack beats Ruin over the head with his soft cap and they exit DR

The music of "Boys and Girls come out to play" is heard

Children of all ages, shabbily dressed but clean, pour out of the orphanage and into the square; they mill around chasing, shouting, laughing, fighting, skipping or playing games. It is bedlam

Bo-Peep and Boy Blue enter R *and chat with a pair of the older children*

Corydon enters UR *and moves* DC. *He is a handsome youth in a patched and worn tunic, shirt and tights, and carries a bundle of twigs for the fire*

Corydon (*with mock severity*) And what's happening *here*, if you don't mind my asking?

The commotion ceases abruptly and the children look guilty

I could hear you at the other end of the village.

Bo-Peep (*pleading*) Oh, don't be *cross*, Corydon. It's far too nice to be *inside* the orphanage. Look how the sun's shining. It's a perfect day for enjoying themselves.

The children agree with nods and murmurs

Corydon That's all very well. But they really ought to be helping Mother with the housework.

Older boy (*brightly*) Well we *would* if she was anywhere about, but she's *not*. She's out shopping and won't be back for ages. (*Scowling*) Besides — I don't see why *we* should have to work, anyway. It's so *boring*, all that dusting and cleaning.

The others agree with nods and murmurs

Small Girl We'd *much* rather be having fun.

Corydon (*wryly*) Wouldn't we *all*? (*Seriously*) But you can't expect *her* to do everything. She's up before anyone else is, cooks, washes, irons *and* mends, looks after the ones who are poorly, and *rarely* gets to bed till after midnight. She's the poorest person in Tumbledown, but never turns anyone away who knocks on the orphanage door.

Boy Blue (*grinning*) Except Sir Hugo when he comes for the rent.

Corydon (*amused*) That's true. But as he won't do any of the repairs he promised to do, I'm not surprised she won't pay. It's so run down, a good *sneeze* would make it collapse. (*He sighs deeply*) Oh, if only I were rich. I'd buy us the best house in the kingdom and the Squire would be welcome to have his creaking old ruin back.

Bo-Peep (*surprised*) Do you *mean* that, Corydon? Really and truly?

Corydon (*lightly*) I certainly *do*. And if you've a minute or two to spare, I'll tell you the reason why. (*He puts his bundle of sticks down*)

Song 2 (*Corydon, Boy Blue, Bo-Peep and Children*)

As the song approaches the end, the children exit into the orphanage, still singing. Bo-Peep and Boy Blue exit R, leaving Corydon to pick up his bundle of sticks, exit into the orphanage and close the door

Dame Dallymore is heard off UR and cheerful music signals her entrance

Dame (*off*) Are you there, children? Yoo-hoo? Aunty's home.

Dame Dallymore enters UR and moves UC. She is a lady of indeterminate years, outrageously dressed à la Oxfam, and carries a battered old shopping basket

You'll never guess what I found in … (*She notices the audience and lets out a startled gasp*) Oh, I *say* … (*She gapes at the audience in concern as she moves DC*) You're not *more* orphans, are you? I don't think I've enough *beds*. (*She begins to count the audience*) One … two … three … four …

five … (*Reeling*) It must be a coach-load. It's that or they've come through the Channel Tunnel. (*She thinks*) Er … Voolay-voo commen dans le tunnel … Er … Er … (*She peers again then sighs with relief*) Oh, no … You're not foreign at all, are you? I recognize the lady from the Post Office. (*Confidentially*) She was in the Clic shop (*or local charity shop*) yesterday looking for a low cut dress. (*Calling out cheerfully*) I see you *found* one, dear? (*Admiringly*) Oh, and doesn't it *suit* you? It's one of those "Trouble" dresses, isn't it? (*To the audience generally*) Oh, yes. It's definitely a "Trouble" dress. You can *see* her trying to wriggle her way out of it. (*She chortles; then realization dawns*) Just a *minute*, though. You're the *audience*, aren't you? Of course you are. I'd heard you were coming *tonight*. Nothing decent on the telly, then? (*Beaming*) Still — never mind. You'll enjoy yourselves here. We're ever so friendly. Well — all except the Squire. *He* can be a bit peculiar. (*Confidentially*) Comes of being *spoiled*, you see. Well … they were very *rich*, his family. Bought him anything he wanted when he was a boy. His dad asked him what he'd like for Christmas, once, and you'll never guess what he said? A *Mickey Mouse* outfit. (*Amazed*) Can you believe it? A Mickey Mouse outfit for a sixteen-year-old. But he *got* one. Oh, yes. His dad bought him the Labour Party. (*She chortles*) Here — but listen to me going on, and you don't even know who I am, do you? (*Beaming*) Well, Dallymore's the name. Diphtheria Dallymore. Mother to multitudes and widow of this parish. (*She curtsies*) Here, and I'll tell you *this*, fellers — it's not easy looking after little ones. There's always *one* of them feeling poorly and needing a doctor. Isn't that right, girls? Look at Polly Flinders. Had to be rushed into hospital last week through eating half a bag of daffodil bulbs in mistake for onions. "Oooh, Doctor" , I said, "is she going to be all right?" "Of course she is," he said. "We'll pop her into a bed and she'll be out again in the Spring." (*Fondly*) They do a wonderful job, don't they? Doctors and nurses. But it's terrible they way the government's running the Health Service. Especially at (*local hospital*). The last time *I* was in there, one of the nurses asked me if I wanted a *bedpan*. "Good heavens", I said, "I know you're short-staffed, but I didn't realize we'd to cook our own meals."

Corydon enters from the orphanage

Corydon (*seeing the Dame*) So *there* you are, Mother. (*He moves to her*) Where on earth have you *been*?

Dame Down in the Oxfam shop. (*Excitedly*) Oooh, and just *wait* till you see what I found there. (*Pulling a battered book out of her shopping basket*) Look at this. It's called "How to Become a *Millionaire*". (*She hands the book to Corydon and chortles happily*)

Corydon (*examining the book*) But — half the pages are missing.

Dame So what's wrong with *half* a million? (*Blissfully*) Oooh, just think of it. We'll be able to move into one of those posh houses in (*local area*) and I can have a nice little bedroom where the neighbours don't bang on the walls at half-past two every morning.

Corydon (*surprised*) Bang on the walls? You've never mentioned *that* before.

Dame (*sheepishly*) Well ... I didn't like saying. But it was so bad last night, I nearly went round and complained.

Corydon (*indignantly*) I should think so, too. They shouldn't be waking you up at half-past two in the morning.

Dame Oh, they don't wake me *up* — it just breaks me concentration when I'm practising me bagpipes.

Corydon (*laughing*) Oh, Mother. You *do* make me laugh. (*Sighing*) But I'm afraid we'll never get rich by reading *this* book. (*He hands the book back to the Dame*) What we *really* need is a marvellous stroke of *luck*.

Dame Well ... There's a lot of it about. Look at the feller at number seven. Bought a raffle ticket on Tuesday and won *first prize*. Did the Lottery on Wednesday and got twenty thousand pounds. Backed a horse on Friday and won two hundred, and *Saturday* night, there's a feller knocking on the front door from *Littlewoods*.

Corydon (*astonished*) To say he'd won the football pools?

Dame No. No. They'd picked his wife up for shoplifting.

Corydon (*amused*) Well, thank goodness you're home again. Everyone's *starving*, as usual, and can't *wait* for you to start lunch.

Dame (*dismayed*) They've hardly had time to finish their *breakfast*. (*Sighing*) Oh, well, back to the kitchen sink.

Corydon (*kindly*) Don't worry, Mother. I'll give you a hand.

Corydon takes the Dame's basket and they exit UL

The Lights dim

Calumnia enters DL *in a green follow spot*

Calumnia (*sneering*) Such puerile, nauseating chat.
　　I'll quickly put a stop to *that*
　　And from their faces wipe those smiles
　　With nasty spells and witch's wiles.
　　(*Thoughtfully*) Now let me see. I must be brief.
　　Which plan will cause the greatest grief?
　　(*Deciding*) Ah, *yes*. From distant lands I'll call
　　A giant, twenty metres tall,
　　Whose mighty feet shall crush and pound

Their fragile cottage to the ground.
(*Proudly*) A plan that's bound to work a treat.
And leave them homeless in the street.
(*She cackles with glee*)

Calumnia exits DL. *The follow spot is extinguished and the Lights return to normal*

Princess Marigold enters UR. *She is every inch a fairytale princess in a beautiful gown; she wears a small crown. Gazing around curiously, she moves* DC

Princess (*amused*) What a quaint little village. It's like something from a nursery-story book. And to think, if a wheel on the Royal Coach hadn't broken, I'd never have known it was *here*.
Giggles (*off* R, *calling; anxiously*) Princess? Princess *Marigold*? Where *are* you?

Giggles, the Court Jester, hurries on breathlessly, UR. *He is a zany character, who normally bubbles with good humour. He is dressed in traditional jester's costume, and has a hopsack bag bearing the Royal Insignia hanging from one shoulder*

The Princess turns to face him

(*Relieved*) Ohhh, thank goodness you're all right. You really *mustn't* go wandering off on your own. Something *terrible* might have happened.
Princess (*puzzled*) Like what, for instance?
Giggles (*at a loss*) Well — like *anything*. I mean — we've not been to *this* part of the kingdom before and it could be *dangerous*. (*He glances around fearfully*)
Princess (*amused*) But it's the most charming place I've ever seen.
Giggles (*darkly*) Maybe it is. But if you ask *me*, there's something very *strange* about villages where *animals* can read.
Princess (*baffled*) What on earth are you talking about?
Giggles Somebody's written "Wet Paint" in front of a lamp-post back there (*he indicates the way he came*) ... and a fat little sausage-dog has done it.
Princess (*laughing*) Oh, Giggles. You *are* funny. (*Kindly*) But there's no need to worry. I'm perfectly safe. Now stop following me and let me explore while the coach-driver's fixing the wheel. I'm sure there's *lots* of interesting places in a village like this. (*She glances around*)
Giggles (*worried*) Oh, come back to the coach with me. Please. If anything happens to you, your dad'll have my head chopped off.

Princess (*amused*) Don't be silly, Giggles. No-one has their head chopped off *these* days.

Giggles Oh, yes they *do*. They did it to Anne Boleyn.

Princess (*in disbelief*) Where did they do *that*?

Giggles (*seriously*) Just under her chin.

Princess (*laughing*) All right, Giggles. I won't go far. I'll just look in the old antique shop over there (*she indicates off* L) and be back in a few minutes.

Giggles (*doubtfully*) Well, if I *do* let you out of my sight, you've got to promise you won't *buy* anything.

Princess (*puzzled*) Why ever not?

Giggles Because my Auntie Aggie bought something from an antique shop once and it gave her a really nasty shock.

Princess (*wide-eyed*) What was it?

Giggles A great big desk full of secret drawers and sliding panels.

Princess Really?

Giggles Yes. And as soon as she got it home, she heard this awful shouting coming from inside it. (*Demonstrating*) "Help. Help. Somebody *help* us." So quick as a flash she opened one of the panels and found dozens and dozens of people trapped inside that nob'dy had seen for years and years and *years*.

Princess (*amazed*) What kind of desk was *that*?

Giggles A missing persons bureau.

Princess (*laughing*) Giggles.

Giggles (*relenting*) Oh, all right. Go on then. I'll give you *ten* minutes. But you'd better leave your crown with *me* or everybody'll know who you are.

Marigold takes off her crown and hands it to him

And don't be *late* or we'll *both* be in trouble. I'll wait here and talk to the audience. They look as though they need waking up.

The Princess kisses him lightly and exits L

(*Putting the crown inside his hopsack bag and beaming at the audience*) Hallo.

Audience reaction

(*His face dropping in dismay*) Oooh. Is that the best you can do? (*Mockingly*) Hallo. (*Reprovingly*) You're supposed to *shout* and *scream*. Go absolutely *crackers*. You can't just sit there looking like *this*. (*He pulls a glum face*) You're not at the *dentist's*. (*Brightly*) Come on. Let's have another go. *I'll* shout "Hallo, everybody", and *you* shout back "Hallo, Giggles" as loud as you can. Are you ready? (*Shouting*) Hallo, everybody.

Audience response

That's *better*. Well now we've got *that* out of the way, I'd better introduce meself, hadn't I? My name's Giggles the Court Jester and I live in the palace with all the other posh folks. Mind you ... I might not be there much longer 'cos I'm a bit nervous, and when I went into the ballroom last night, I found a *ghost* sitting at the piano. Playing all the songs from *Phantom of the Opera*. Oooh. I was scared stiff. "Who are *you*?" I said — and it gave a loud moan like this (*he gives a dramatic moan*) and said "I am the ghost of the famous composer Ludwig van Beethoven". Well ... I thought he was *joking*, so I said, (*scornfully*) "Give over. You don't look a *bit* like Beethoven". (*Shocked*) *Well* — you've never seen anybody get in such a *temper*. "I *am* Beethoven," he shouted. "I am. I am. I *am*". "All right," I said, "all right. If you're the ghost of Beethoven, *prove* it. Do his last movement for me." (*Awed*) And he *did*. He fell off the piano stool. (*He chortles*)

The Squire enters DR, *still clutching the envelope*

Squire   (*spotting Giggles*) Bah. *Another* layabout cluttering up the streets. I'll soon get rid of *him*. (*He crosses to Giggles and clears his throat*) A-hem.

Giggles turns to the Squire

(*Snootily*) In case you're *unaware* of it, beggars are unwelcome in Tumbledown village.
Giggles   (*indignantly*) Here, who are *you* calling a beggar? I'm the Court Jester, I am.
Squire   (*scornfully*) A likely story. What would a Court Jester be doing here?
Giggles   Well, if you *must* know — I'm looking for eight musical idiots.
Squire   (*taken aback*) Musical idiots?
Giggles   That's right. Do, Re, Fa, Sol, La, Ti and Do.
Squire   Do, Re, Fa, Sol, La, Ti, Do? (*He realizes one is missing*) Haven't you forgotten *Mi*?
Giggles   Course not. You're here already. (*He chortles*)
Squire   (*annoyed*) That *done* it. (*Calling*) Bailiffs. *Bailiffs*.

Wrack and Ruin enter hurriedly UR

Arrest this individual at *once*.

Wrack and Ruin hurry down and seize Giggles

Giggles (*startled*) Hang on a *minute*. You can't arrest *me*. (*Struggling*) Gerroff. Gerroff. (*Calling*) Help. *Help*. (*He continues to struggle during the following*)

Villagers enter L *and* R, *and children from the orphanage*

All What's happening? What's going on? (*Etc.*)
Squire (*scowling*) Mind your own business. As Squire of Tumbledown, I'm having this repulsive-looking ruffian locked in the village stocks.
Giggles (*dismayed*) Eh?
Boy Blue (*firmly*) Don't worry, Mr Jester. *No-one* can be locked in the stocks if the villagers object to it. (*He glares at the Squire*)

Everyone agrees

Squire (*sneering*) And who'll do *that*, eh? (*With menace*) If one of you breathes a word, I'll raise the Council Tax ten times higher than (*local authority*) did. (*He sniggers in triumph*) Now then — does anyone *still* wish to object? (*He polishes his fingernails on his lapel*)

Corydon enters from the orphanage

Corydon (*firmly*) Yes. (*He moves* DC) They most certainly *do*. (*To Wrack and Ruin, firmly*) Release that man at once.

Wrack and Ruin hastily release Giggles, who brushes himself down

Squire (*annoyed*) Fools. Dolts. Idiots. You don't have to listen to *him*. He doesn't even *live* here any more.

The Villagers react. Wrack and Ruin quickly grab Giggles again

Corydon (*amused*) I *beg* your pardon?
Squire (*nastily*) By lunchtime today, he and his mother and all those scruffy orphans of theirs will be out of my beautiful cottage and far away.
Corydon (*laughing*) Says who? *We're* not going *anywhere*.
Squire (*smirking*) That's what *you* think. Just wait till you read this *letter*. (*He thrusts the letter at Corydon*) From this minute on, you're out on the streets, and there's the document to *prove* it. You can give it to that flea-bitten mother of yours and tell her I said "good riddance".

Everyone looks shocked

Corydon (*stunned*) But where will we go?
Squire (*smirking*) That's not *my* problem. (*To Wrack and Ruin*) And in the meantime, *you* can take *him* (*indicating Giggles*) to the stocks.

Wrack and Ruin drag the protesting Giggles away towards the exit. The Villagers and Children jeer and boo loudly

Princess Marigold enters DL, *and takes in the scene*

Princess (*surprised*) What's happening? (*She takes in the situation*) Take your hands off my jester *at once*.

Everyone stares at her

Squire (*grandly*) And who might *you* be, pray? (*He glares at Marigold*)
Princess (*firmly*) Princess Marigold of Entertainia.

All but the Squire and Giggles react

Squire (*dismissively*) Nonsense and tarradiddle. If you *were* a princess, you'd be wearing a *crown*.

Giggles breaks free, quickly produces the crown from his bag and hurries to the Princess's side

Giggles (*handing the crown to the Princess*) Here you are, Princess.
Princess (*to Squire*) You were *saying* …? (*She puts her crown on*)

All but the Squire and Giggles gasp and quickly curtsy or bow to the Princess

There is a muffled thud from the bass drum; the Lights dim during the following

Squire (*annoyed*) It's a *trick*. She's not a real princess at all. (*To Wrack and Ruin*) Throw *her* in the stocks, as well.
Corydon (*moving forwards*) Take one step, and you'll answer to *me*.
Giggles And me. (*He shows his fists*) I might be only a jester, but I'll punch your lights out.

There is a second muffled thud, but slightly louder

Wrack (*frowning*) Here. And talking of lights: it's getting a bit *dark*, isn't it?

Ruin (*looking downwards*) *And* the ground's starting to shake.

There is a third thud, no longer muffled. Everyone staggers. The Lights dim further

Squire (*looking around wildly*) What's happening?
Corydon (*looking up* L *and pointing*) It's a *giant*. (*Horrified*) And he's heading in this direction.

The Dame hurries out of her cottage to join the others

The thuds grow louder and faster. Everyone cries out in panic

The stage plunges into total darkness. Everyone cries out in panic. There is a great crash. Everyone cowers or falls to the floor. Corydon moves to protect the Princess, Ruin faints and has to be supported by Wrack, and Giggles jumps into the Squire's arms. The orphanage vanishes from view, and in its place arrives an enormous, buckled shoe. The Lights begin to come up again. All react as the sound of the Giant's footsteps fades into the distance

Wrack (*gaping*) It's the Giant's shoe.

Wrack drops Ruin who then staggers to his feet

Squire (*dropping Giggles*) And it's flattened *my* cottage.
Dame (*horrified*) What are we going to do? Where will we live? (*She sobs*)
Princess (*hurrying to comfort the Dame*) Don't worry. I'm sure my father will help.

   Mother Goose enters R

Mother Goose Well, here's a pretty how d'y'do.
      Made homeless by a giant's shoe.
      But dry those tears and never fear.
      Your guardian, Mother Goose, is here.

Everyone stares at Mother Goose in astonishment

      With fairy spell I'll wax quite clever, making, from that piece of leather,
      Such a home, I do declare, that folks will come from ev'rywhere
      To marvel at and wonder who resides inside a giant's shoe.
      A prospect sure to make you grin, for tourists bring the money in.

Everyone but the Squire reacts with delight

      So come. Let lightness fill your heart

Whilst I, with magic, make a start
To build a home of rare design —
Imposing, free of rent, and fine.
It's *just* the spell that's right for you …
(*She waves her spoon*)
So bibbidy, bibbidy, bobbidy, boo.

Song 3 (*Mother Goose and Company*)

The Squire slinks out during the song

Black-out

SCENE 2

A Quiet Street

A lane scene depicting a high stone wall, above which can be seen the tops of cottages, etc., and trees

When the scene begins it is dark. A green follow spot comes UL

Calumnia, gleeful, enters L *into the spot*

Calumnia The deed is done. That mighty giant's earthquake-causing tread
Has crushed the orphanage to dust, exactly as I said.
What *tears* they must be shedding, now;
With joy my heart is filled.
I've shown that foolish Mother Goose,
That never was a witch so skilled.
(*Smirking*) But now *another* way I'll spread some miasmatic gloom —
And Tumbledown will meet, I vow, its well-deservéd doom.
(*She cackles with laughter*)

Calumnia exits L

The green follow spot vanishes and the Lights come up to a normal setting

Giggles enters R *and moves* C

Giggles (*calling*) Hallo, everybody.

Audience response

Here, I say — what do you think to *that*, eh? Fancy Mother Goose changing the Giant's shoe into a house so they'll all have somewhere to live. Isn't it *fantastic*? But best of all — they're having a great big *celebration party* and everybody in the village has been invited to it — even me and the Princess. There'll be all sorts of entertainment. Singing. Dancing. Fireworks. (*Remembering*) Oooh, hey. And a feller's coming from that hospital series on television — you know — *Casualty* (*or similar*) to give a talk about heart, lung, liver and kidney transplants. (*He pulls a face*) Mind you, I shan't be listening to *that*. I'm not keen on *organ recitals*. (*He chortles*) I'll tell you what, though, I can't wait for it to start. I'm absolutely *starving* and I haven't a penny to buy anything. (*He glances around*) I wonder if there's anybody who'll *give* me some money? (*He peers off* L)

The Dame enters R, *in a new outfit*

Dame (*seeing Giggles*) Oh, I say — it's that good-looking jester again. I wonder what *he's* doing here? (*Calling*) Coo-ee.

Giggles (*turning and seeing the Dame*) Dame Dallymore. Oh, I'm really glad to see *you*, 'cos now you've got a new house and everything, I was wondering if you had a pound coin you didn't want?

Dame (*beaming*) Well, of course I have. (*She gets out her purse and gives Giggles a pound coin*) Here you are.

Giggles (*delightedly*) Oh, thanks. (*He looks at the coin*) Just a minute. This is a *fake* pound coin.

Dame Yes, I know. It's the one I don't want.

Giggles (*upset*) Ohhhh. I should have *known* I was wasting my time. It's full of *daft* people, this place.

Dame (*surprised*) Daft people? What are you talking about? They're all as sane as I am. (*She puts her purse away*)

Giggles (*resentfully*) Well what about that feller I was talking to five minutes ago? Every time I asked him a question, he shook his head and told me the time.

Dame Well, of course he did. He's the Neighbourhood Watch.

Giggles (*helplessly*) You see? You see?

Dame (*taking pity on him*) Oh, cheer up. I was only pulling your leg. To tell you the truth, I haven't any money meself. I've spent it all on tonight's party. And talk about rising prices. Have you been to (*local supermarket*) lately? I couldn't believe my eyes. The food there's gone up by two pounds a bottle. But don't worry. I *do* know how we can raise a few pounds.

Giggles (*eagerly*) How's that?

Dame We'll tell folks there's a mysterious *echo* round here — then charge 'em something to listen to it.

Giggles But how can we do that if there isn't one?

Dame It's dead simple. *You'll* be the echo. (*Explaining*) All you've got to do is hide over there (*she indicates* L) where nobody can see you and repeat everything I say.

Giggles (*puzzled*) Everything you say?

Dame (*nodding*) And just to make sure nothing goes wrong, we'll have a little practice first. Off you go.

Giggles hurries off L

(*To the audience*) Oooh, we're going to make a fortune with this. (*She chortles. Calling* L) Can you hear me, Giggles?

Giggles enters

Giggles 'Course I can. I'm not *deaf*, you know.

Dame No, no, no. You don't come back *on*. You stay over there so they can't see you. It's no use saying it if they *can* see you, is it?

Giggles (*realizing*) Oh, no. No. Sorry. We'll do it again, eh?

Giggles exits

Dame (*calling*) Can you hear me?

Giggles (*off*) Yes, thanks.

Dame No, no, no, no, no. You mustn't say *yes*.

Giggles enters

Giggles What?

Dame I said you mustn't say "yes" when I ask if you can *hear* me.

Giggles Well you didn't *tell* me that, did you? I didn't *know*. We'd better have another go.

Giggles exits

Dame (*trying again*) Can you hear me *now*?

Giggles (*off*) No.

Dame (*puzzled*) What do you mean, no? Of *course* you can hear me.

Giggles enters

Giggles I know I can, but you've just told me I'd not to say "yes".

Dame (*grimly*) If brains were made of wood, *you'd* have death-watch beetle. (*Patiently*) Listen. You don't say yes and you don't say no. You just say exactly what *I* say. Understand? Exactly what *I* say.

Giggles (*nodding*) All right. All right. I'll get it right next time.

Giggles exits

Dame (*to the audience*) Another few minutes of this lot and I'll be as cracked as the pavement in (*local street*).
Giggles (*off*) Exactly what *I* say.
Dame (*after a reaction*) Are you ready?
Giggles (*off*) Are you ready?
Dame (*calling*) Yes, I am.
Giggles (*off*) Yes, I am.
Dame (*delightedly*) That's it. That's it. We've finally *got* it.

Giggles enters quickly

Giggles Where's my share, then? (*He holds out his hand*)
Dame No, no, no, no, no. I don't mean the *money*. I mean we've got it *right*. Now we can start *earning*. (*She glances off* R) Quick. Hide. There's somebody coming. And don't forget what I told you. Everything I say, you say the same.

Giggles gives a thumbs up sign and exits L

The Squire enters R, *scowling*

Squire Confound that interfering Mother Goose. Now she's turned that giant's shoe into a brand new orphanage, I'll never be able to build my cyber-café. I've a good mind to … (*He sees the Dame and sneers*) Well, well, well. If it isn't that old faggot Dame Dallymore. I wonder what *she's* doing in this part of the village?
Dame (*to him*) Oh, I say. Fancy you coming along. Especially after last night. I dreamt I saw the most wonderful sight outside your house.
Squire (*puzzled*) What was that?
Dame A "Sold" notice and a removal van. (*She chortles*)

The Squire reacts

Anyway — I'm glad you're still around because if you weren't, you'd have missed the most *amazing* thing.
Squire (*disdainfully*) Really?
Dame Yes. Here I was, stood standing in the middle of the road, minding my own business and waiting for a 47 bus, when suddenly — I *heard* it. (*Dramatically*) An echo.
Squire Don't be ridiculous. There's not an echo round here for *miles*.

Dame Oh, yes, there is. And I can *prove* it to you.

Squire (*scornfully*) Salmon-paste and codswallop. I bet you five pounds you *can't*.

Dame (*excitedly*) Five *pounds*? (*Aside*) Oooh, I can't wait to get started.

Giggles (*off; delightedly*) Neither can I.

Squire (*reacting and gazing around suspiciously*) What was that?

Dame (*hastily*) Must have been a sedan chair back-firing. (*She beams*) All right, then. You put your five pounds down and I'll get my voice warmed up. (*She practises*) Mi-mi-mi-mi-mi.

The Squire gets five pounds out and places it on the floor

Now then. Just listen to this. (*Calling daintily*) Mr Echo.

Giggles (*off*) Mr Echo.

Dame (*calling*) Can you hear me?

Giggles (*off*) Can you hear me?

Dame (*to the Squire*) You see? I said there was an echo. (*She bends to get the money*)

Squire (*suspiciously*) Just a minute. Just a minute. Let *me* try this. (*He crosses to her. Calling*) Mr Echo?

There is no reply

Dame (*calling hastily*) Mr Echo?

There is still no reply

Hallo. (*Louder*) Hallo.

Giggles (*singing, off*) Who's your lady friend? Who's the little girlie by your side? Avabanana.

The Dame and the Squire react

Dame (*to the Squire*) Must be interference on the Internet. (*She simpers*) Have another go.

Squire (*calling reluctantly*) Mr Echo?

Giggles (*off*) Mr Echo?

Squire (*calling*) Are you ready?

Giggles (*off*) Fire away.

Squire (*after a reaction*) Umpa-umpa.

Giggles (*off*) Stick it up your jumpah.

The Squire and the Dame react

Squire (*suspiciously*) I think I'll try something a little more *difficult*. (*Calling in a sing-song manner*) Coughs and sneezes.
Giggles (*off*) Spread diseases.
Squire (*calling*) Rumpelstiltzkin.
Giggles (*off*) Rumpelstiltzkin
Squire (*calling*) Supercalifragilisticexpialidocious.
Giggles (*off*) You must be *joking*.

The Squire and the Dame react

   All right. All right. (*Attempting it*) Soup and cauli, old elastic, eggs and halitosis.
Squire (*realizing he is being tricked*) Hmmm. (*He calls temptingly*) Are you *hungry*?
Giggles (*off*) Hungry? I'm absolutely *starving*.
Squire (*calling*) Well, I know where ——
Giggles (*off*) I know where ——
Squire (*calling*) Roast beef dinners ——
Giggles (*off*) Roast beef dinners ——
Squire (*calling*) Cost you nothing.

Giggles dashes on

Giggles Cost me nothing? Where's that, then?

The Squire reacts in triumph

   The Dame snatches up the fiver and dashes off R. *The Squire sees the Dame dash off and chases her in fury, followed by Giggles*

Corydon and the Princess enter L, *holding hands*

Corydon And here we are — almost back where we started.
Princess Oh, Corydon. It's the most beautiful village in Entertainia. No wonder you love it so much.
Corydon It'll be nicer *still* now we've somewhere better to live. (*Impressed*) And of all the amazing *houses*. There can't be another family in the *world* who live inside a giant's shoe.
Princess (*happily*) I know. And I've sent a message to Father telling him all about it. I can't *wait* to see his face when he arrives.

Corydon (*startled*) You mean — he's coming *here*? To Tumbledown village?

Princess (*amused*) It won't surprise *me* if he brings the entire Court with him.

Corydon (*dazedly*) Now I *know* I'm dreaming. Only this morning we'd no idea where our next meal would be coming from — and now we've got the most extraordinary house in the whole world, the King of Entertainia's coming to visit us, and *I've* walked down the village street with a real live *princess* on my arm. (*Pleading*) Oh, please. Don't let anyone try to wake me.

Princess (*laughing*) You're not the only one enjoying yourself. You'd never believe the fun *I've* had being away from the palace and all that bowing and scraping. It's been the most wonderful day of my *life*. A coach-ride in the country — a narrow escape from a giant — watching Mother Goose working her magic — and being escorted round a fairytale village by the handsomest man I've ever met.

Corydon (*stunned*) Do you really *mean* that?

Princess (*smiling*) Do you really need to *ask*?

Song 4 (*Princess and Corydon*)

The Princess and Corydon exit R

The Lights fade to Black-out

SCENE 3

Inside the Shoe House

The backdrop depicts the cottage-like interior of the Giant's shoe, with mullioned windows and chintz curtains, etc. An easel stands UC *facing front, a large blackboard resting on it. Into the blackboard, a few inches below its top, a nail has been hammered then painted black so as to be invisible to the audience. On the easel is a piece of white chalk and a duster, or eraser. The teacher's desk (or a lectern) is* L, *and on the* DS *side of this a slapstick hangs. Two or three long benches are positioned* R, *at an angle to the audience, and in front of these is a shorter bench with only two supports (one in the middle and the other at one end); if anyone sits on the unsupported end and the other end is unoccupied, the bench will tip*

When the scene begins, lively music plays

The Dame enters UL *in a new outfit. She moves* DC

Dame (*to the audience, delightedly*) Ooh, I say — have you ever seen anything like it? My own little class-room, tucked away in the toe-cap of the Giant's shoe. (*Explaining*) Well — we haven't had a school in the village for *years* so I asked Mother Goose to fix it all up for me. (*Beaming*) I can't *wait* to see the children's faces when they find out about it. And as *I'm* going to be their teacher, it means I can make quite sure that they all know how to *read*. 'Cos it doesn't matter *what* the know-alls tell us, does it girls? Television will *never* replace a decent newspaper. I mean — how often do you get your fish and chips wrapped in a TV set? Anyway, I mustn't stand gossiping all morning. I've to find where the little rascals have hidden themselves and get things started. But don't worry. I'll see you all later. (*Calling off*) Are you there, children? It's time for school.

The Dame exits DL. *The Squire enters* DR

Squire (*glowering*) So *that's* what the flannel-faced old faggot is planning. To run a private school with herself as the headmistress. (*Smirking*) How fortunate I managed to sneak inside and overhear. (*Scowling*) If this news gets out, there'll be *hordes* of parents wanting their nasty little brats to be educated. And the more they *learn*, the less chance *I'll* have of swindling them out of their money. I've got to *stop* her. But *how*?

Wrack and Ruin enter hastily DR

Wrack (*to the Squire*) Quick. Quick. It's just been on (*local radio station*). Old King Cole's heard about the shoe-house orphanage and he's heading this way to see it for himself.
Squire (*startled*) What?
Ruin He'll be here in the next few minutes.
Squire (*annoyed*) Corkscrews and coconuts. Once *he's* been here, it'll be worse than Disneyland Paris (*or similar theme park*). The whole *world'll* be wanting to visit. Before we know it, Dame Dallymore'll be rolling in cash and I'll be left with *nothing*. (*Glowering*) We've got to make sure that something goes amiss. (*He thinks furiously*) I *have* it. (*Smirking*) We'll make King Cole so *angry* with her that he'll give *her* the push and turn the shoe-house over to *me*.
Wrack (*puzzled*) How do we do *that*?
Squire (*smirking*) Just walk this way and I'll explain *everything*.

The Squire slinks off DR. *Wrack and Ruin watch him doubtfully, shrug, then exit after him, imitating his walk*

There is a commotion, off, and a snowstorm of crumpled paper balls, paper aeroplanes, etc., heralds the entry of the Children, who shriek, yell, race around and generally create havoc. Boy Blue and Bo-Peep follow them on.

Bo-Peep seizes the chalk from the easel and scrawls on the blackboard "All teechers iz stewpid", then replaces the chalk and joins Boy Blue again, giggling. The mêlée continues

> *Dame Dallymore enters* UL, *now wearing a university cap and gown and ringing a large hand-bell*

There is a mad scramble for places on the benches, but the small bench is left unoccupied

Dame (*beaming*) Good-morning, children. (*She puts the bell down on the desk*)
Children (*brightly*) Good-morning, Aunt Dallymore.
Dame (*reprovingly*) Oh, no, no, no, no, no, no, no, no, *no*, children. You mustn't call me Aunty at *school*. You have to call me "Miss". We'll try again, shall we? (*She beams*) Good-morning, children.
Children (*brightly*) Good-morning, Miss.
Dame (*pleased*) That's better. Now as you all know, today is the first day of my new school and just to make sure we all enjoy ourselves …
Boy Blue (*sneezing loudly*) Achooo.

The other Children laugh and react

Dame (*startled*) Who did *that*?
Boy Blue (*standing*) Be Biss. (*He sniffles miserably*) I think I'b got a cold.
Dame (*reprovingly*) Yes. And you've probably given it to everybody *else*, now. Why don't you show your broughtings up and do what *I* do when *I'm* going to sneeze?
Boy Blue (*sniffling*) What's that, Biss?
Dame (*primly*) I put me hand in front of me mouth like *this*. (*She demonstrates*) Now — does anybody know why I *do* that?

All the Children eagerly raise a hand. The Dame indicates Bo-Peep

Bo-Peep (*standing*) To catch your false teeth, Miss.

The Dame reacts and everyone rocks with laughter. Boy Blue and Bo-Peep sit down again

Dame (*recovering herself*) We … Er … We'd better get on with some lessons. Right. Can everybody see the blackboard? (*She spots the writing and reacts*) Who wrote *that*? (*She indicates the writing*)
Bo-Peep (*standing; guiltily*) Me, Miss.

Dame (*glowering*) You ought to be *ashamed* of yourself, Bo-Peep. What would an OFSTED Inspecticator think if *he* saw that and knew how to read? Sit down.

Bo-Peep sits. The Dame moves to the blackboard, rubs out the word "iz", replaces it with "are" and underlines it

All teachers *are* stupid. (*She puts the chalk down and moves away triumphantly*)

All the Children laugh

The Dame realizes her mistake, hastily returns to the board and erases all the words

(*Trying again*) Now, children. Can anybody tell me why it's very important for children to come to my beautiful new school?

All the Children look blank

Well, I'll *tell* you. (*With great vigour*) It's because thanks to *this* terrible government, education is a total mess. Forty per cent of children today can't *read*. Forty percent can't *write*. And the other thirty per cent can't add up properly. (*Proudly*) Well I'm just the woman to change all that, so we're starting lessons this very *minute*. You'll have GCSEs, DVDs, ABCs, ITVs, A levels, S levels ——
Boy Blue (*interrupting*) What's an S level, Miss?
Dame An S level is a *spirit* level. You get it for *Woodwork*. (*Briskly*) Now what shall we start with? (*She decides*) I know. Some good old-fashioned *English*. (*She beams in satisfaction*)

The Children pull faces and groan loudly

(*Sharply*) Silence in class. (*Beaming*) Now then — who can give me a sentence that contains the word "fascinate"?
Bo-Peep (*putting her hand up*) Me, Miss. Me, Miss. *I* can.

All the others react

Dame (*pleasantly surprised*) Well *there's* a clever girl. (*She beams at her*) Off you go, then, dear.
Bo-Peep (*standing and reciting*) My best coat's got ten little buttons on it ... but I can only fasten eight.

The Dame reacts. The Children laugh and applaud. Bo-Peep smugly sits again

   Giggles enters L

Giggles (*to the audience*) Hallo, everybody.

Audience response

Dame (*turning to him indignantly*) Never mind "Hallo, everybody". (*She recognizes Giggles*) Giggles? What are *you* doing here?
Giggles I've come to learn *French.*
Dame (*puzzled*) French?
Giggles Yes. My sister's adopted a French baby, and we all want to know what he's saying when he's old enough to talk.

The others all laugh and fall about

Dame (*after a reaction*) Go and sit down — and take your hat off.
Giggles (*removing his hat*) I'll hang it on the hook, shall I?
Dame (*puzzled*) Which hook?
Giggles This one. (*He draws a hook on the blackboard, its point ending where the black painted nail is situated, and hangs his hat on it*)

The Dame gapes and the others laugh. Giggles moves to the small bench and sits on the "safe" end

Dame Now then — does everybody know the *alphabet?*

Everybody noisily assents

   (*Muttering*) Well, that's a relief. (*To the class*) Stand up Tommy Tittlemouse and let's hear you recite it for us.
Tommy (*rising unhappily*) Er ... Er ... A.
Dame (*encouragingly*) A.
Tommy B?
Dame (*nodding*) B.

Tommy flounders helplessly

   Come along. Come along. What's after B?
Tommy (*unhappily*) I don't know, Miss.
Dame (*surprised*) You don't *know*? (*Annoyed*) Well, you *should* know. (*Helpfully*) I'll give you a little *hint*, shall I? What is it I do with my *eyes*?

Giggles (*calling out*) Squint. (*He chortles merrily*)

Everybody laughs and falls about

Dame (*crossly*) Who said that?
Children (*loudly*) Giggles.
Dame (*glaring at Giggles*) Come out here at once. (*She grabs the slapstick*)

Giggles rises and moves to the Dame

   Do you know what *this* is? (*She displays the slapstick*)
Giggles (*baffled*) A stick of liquorice?
Dame (*grimly*) No, it *isn't*. It's a nice big cane for punishing naughty boys.
   And *you're* the first one I'm going to give it to.
Giggles (*pleased*) Oooh, smashing. Who do you want me to hit with it?
Dame (*after a reaction*) Bend over.

*Puzzled, Giggles bends. The Dame wallops him on the buttocks with the
slapstick*

Giggles (*pained*) Owwwww. (*He jumps up*)

The Children laugh

Dame Now go sit down and behave yourself.
Giggles (*pained*) I'll behave myself, but I can't sit down. (*He rubs his bottom
   and sits on the short bench*)
Dame (*replacing the slapstick and recovering herself*) Now then. As I was
   about to pontificate …

*Wrack and Ruin enter L. Wrack is dressed in a large, frilly frock and curly-
haired wig, etc.; he looks like a giant doll. He carries a large sugar lollipop.
Ruin is dressed as a very unlikely schoolboy complete with large catapult*

Wrack (*waving camply at the pupils*) Ooo-oooh.

All the boys wolf-whistle and cat-call, etc. The Dame restores order

Dame Who are *you*?
Wrack (*simpering*) Daisy Dumpling, Miss. And I've brought *this* for you.
   (*He hands the lollipop to the Dame*)
Dame (*pleased*) Oh, I say. A lovely big lollipop. I've not had one of these
   for years. (*She takes the lollipop*)
Wrack (*wide-eyed*) It goes all different colours when you lick it.

Dame (*delightedly*) Does it really? (*She licks rapidly*) Oh, yes I can see it
changing now. (*She licks at the lollipop again and chortles happily*)
Wrack (*simpering*) I've never seen another one *like* it.
Dame Neither have I. (*She licks it again*) Where did you get it from?
Wrack On the floor in the lavatory.

The Dame reacts. The others laugh. She hastily places the lollipop on the desk

Ruin (*to Dame*) And I'm *Fred* Dumpling. Her little brother. (*Proudly*) *I*
know all about *animals*.
Dame (*surprised*) Oh. Well in that case, you can tell all the boys and girls
which family the *crocodile* belongs to.
Ruin Nobody in *our* street. They've all got cats or dogs.

The others laugh heartily

Dame (*defeatedly*) Go and sit down.

*Wrack minces to the short bench and sits next to Giggles, batting "her"
lashes at him. He nervously slides to the "unsafe" end and Wrack slides to
the centre. Ruin sits next to Wrack*

(*Gathering herself*) Right. Now if we're all settled, we'll have questions
on General Knowledge. (*Sweetly*) Can anybody tell me what Moses did
after he'd crossed the Red Sea?
Giggles (*calling out*) Dried himself. (*He chortles*)

Everyone but the Dame laughs

Dame (*crossly*) Who said that?
Children⎫
Wrack   ⎬ (*together*) Giggles. (*They indicate him*)
Ruin   ⎭
Giggles (*alarmed*) No, I *didn't*.
Wrack ⎫ (*together; jumping up*) Yes he *did*.
Ruin ⎭

The bench tips and Giggles falls to the floor. The Children laugh

Dame (*to Giggles*) Come out here. (*She gets the slapstick again*)

Giggles gets to his feet and moves C. Wrack and Ruin re-set the bench and sit

Bend over.

Giggles bends over reluctantly and she wallops him

Giggles Owwwwwww. (*He returns to the bench, glowering at Wrack and Ruin and gingerly sits again*)

Dame (*replacing the slapstick*) Now then — when you score in football, you get goals. When you score in cricket, you get runs. Who can tell me what you get in bowls?

Wrack   (*calling out*) Goldfish. (*He smirks*)

Everybody laughs

Dame (*annoyed*) Who said that?

Wrack
Ruin   } (*together; indicating Giggles*) Giggles.
Children

Giggles (*aghast*) I didn't. I didn't.

Wrack
Ruin   } (*together; standing*) He did. He did.

Giggles is pitched to the floor again

Dame Come out here. (*She gets the slapstick again*)

Protesting his innocence, Giggles is punished again to the amusement of all

Giggles (*returning to his seat; muttering*) I'll be glad when this scene's over.

Dame (*replacing the slapstick*) Right. We'll move on to a bit of *History*.

Everybody groans unhappily

First of all we had the *Ice* Age. Then came the *Stone* Age, the *Bronze* Age and the *Iron* Age. So what came after that?

Wrack   (*calling*) The Saus-Age.

Everybody laughs

Dame Who said that?

Wrack
Ruin   } (*together; indicating Giggles*) Giggles.
Children

Giggles (*protesting*) I didn't. I didn't.

Wrack
Ruin   } (*together; standing*) He did. He did.

Giggles is pitched on to the floor again and all laugh

Dame (*grabbing the slapstick*) Come out here.

Giggles reluctantly moves to the Dame. Wrack and Ruin right the bench

This is going to hurt me far more than it'll hurt you.
Giggles (*hopefully*) Can *I* wallop *you*, then?
Dame Bend over.

Giggles bends over, is walloped again and painfully returns to his seat. The Dame replaces the slapstick

Now then. What do we call the outside of a tree?

Everyone looks blank

(*Exasperated*) Bark, you silly things. *Bark.*

Everyone begins barking loudly

> *The Squire enters* L, *followed by Old King Cole, an elderly and kind individual in full royal regalia*

Squire (*loudly*) How *dare* you greet His Royal Majesty with this terrible commotion?

All fall silent. The Dame looks mortified

(*To the King*) What did I *tell* you, Sire? She isn't *fit* to look after an orphanage, let alone run a village school.
King (*sadly*) Oh dear, oh dear. I'm afraid you're right, Sir Hugo. We can't have this sort of thing in Entertainia.
Squire (*smirking*) If you'll take *my* advice, Sire, you'll banish her from the Kingdom and turn the shoe-house over to *me.*
Giggles (*jumping up indignantly*) Just a minute. Just a minute.
King (*surprised*) Giggles? What are *you* doing here?
Giggles You can't give the shoe-house to *him.* He's nothing but a double-crossing twister.
King Really? (*He looks at the Squire*)
Wrack
Ruin } (*together; jumping up*) Oh, no he isn't.
Children
Dame } (*together*) Oh, yes he is.

Squire (*savagely*) Silence, you repulsive ragamuffins.

Giggles, Wrack and Ruin sit again

(*To the King*) Give me just *five seconds*, Your Majesty, and I'll *prove* this
old faggot's a terrible teacher.
King (*frowning*) You will? But how?
Squire I'll ask these children one simple question — something even a five
year-old should know — and if they give me the wrong answer, Dame
Dallymore gets the push and the shoe-house belongs to *me*.

Everyone reacts

King (*deciding*) Sounds fair enough to me.
Squire (*smirking*) Now who shall I ask? (*He indicates Wrack*) The little girl
there. *She* seems quite intelligent.

Wrack stands, simpering

Tell me, my dear — what are seven thirteens? (*He winks broadly*)
Wrack Seven thirteens are — twenty-eight. (*He sits again, smirking*)

The Dame and the Children look dismayed

Squire (*joyfully*) Wrong. Wrong. She's got it wrong. The shoe-house is
mine.
Giggles (*jumping up*) Just a minute. Just a minute. What do you mean, she's
wrong? Seven thirteens *are* twenty-eight.
Squire (*snarling*) Don't be so *stupid*. How can seven thirteens be twenty-
eight?
Giggles (*firmly*) I'll show you. (*He hurries to the blackboard, puts on his
jester hat, rubs out the hook then writes the number 13 in large figures,
placing a 7 beneath the 3. Multiplying*) Seven threes are twenty-one. (*He
writes it down*) Seven ones are seven. (*He writes this down*) And twenty-
one and seven makes twenty-eight. (*He writes it down*) Seven thirteens are
twenty-eight. (*He puts the chalk down*)

All but the Squire, Wrack and Ruin applaud and cheer

Squire (*annoyed*) But that's ridiculous. He's done it all wrong. (*Firmly*)
Divide twenty-eight by seven, and you *see* the answer can't be thirteen.
Giggles (*caught out*) Ooo-er.

Dame (*quickly*) Oh, yes it *can*. Let *me* show you. (*She rubs out the figures on the board and writes a 7, an old-style division sign, and 28*) Now then … Seven into two won't go — so we'll put the two over here for a minute. (*She writes the 2 on the left of the board*) Seven into eight goes once (*she writes 1 above the line of the division sign*) and one's left over. (*She writes the 1 below the 2*) And one and two makes three. (*She writes the 3 next to the 1 above the line of the division sign*) So 28 divided by 7 is 13. (*She puts the chalk down in triumph*)

Everyone but Wrack, Ruin and the Squire applaud and cheer

Squire (*storming* R, *protesting*) It's all *wrong*. She's pulling a fast one. I demand an immediate re-count.

King (*doubtfully*) It seemed right to *me*. (*Deciding*) But you're quite correct, Sir Hugo. We mustn't have any doubt. We'll try it one more way and *this* time we'll *add* it up. (*He moves to the board, rubs out the sum, then writes 13 down seven times in a column*) And to make sure there's no trickery, I'll do it myself then everyone else — including the audience — can add it up with me.

Squire (*smirking*) Good idea, Sire. (*He sits next to Wrack, rubbing his hands*)

King (*adding up the 3s with the audience*) Three, six, nine, twelve, fifteen, eighteen, twenty-one. (*He counts the 1s*) Twenty-two, twenty-three, twenty-four, twenty-five, twenty-six, twenty-seven, twenty-eight. (*Surprised*) There's no mistake at all. Dame Dallymore keeps the shoe-house.

Everyone but the Squire, Wrack and Ruin cheer. Wrack and Ruin jump up to protest and the Squire is tipped to the ground. The others react joyfully

The Lights fade rapidly

Scene 4

Down by the Duckpond

A lane scene. Full lighting

Mother Goose enters R

Mother Goose (*beaming*) With dented pride and egg on face
    Once more the Squire's put in his place,
    Whilst round the kingdom – as I said ——
    The fame of shoe-house starts to spread.

From city, town and village too
In *thousands* people come to view
To gaze in wonder, point or laugh,
And paint, or sketch or photograph.
Then gladly pay admission fees
And purchase lemonade or teas.
In short — Dame Dallymore, it's plain,
Will nevermore be poor again.

Calumnia enters L, *in a green follow spot*

Calumnia   (*snarling*) Enough. This time you've crossed the line.
You've *dared* to match your skills with mine.
On you the blame must squarely fall
When doom I bring to one and all.
Mother Goose (*shaking her head*) The times that empty threat I've heard.
It's laughable — and quite absurd.
No matter what *your* kind intend,
Good always triumphs in the end.
Calumnia   (*to the audience*) But not *this* time. I hereby vow
To me the Kingdom soon shall bow,
And though you fret and plead or frown,
On *tears* I'll bring your curtain down.
(*She cackles nastily*)

Calumnia exits

The green follow spot is extinguished

Mother Goose (*to the audience*) She'll quickly sing another tune
When faced with magic from *my* spoon,
And learn that lesson known to all —
"Pride *always* comes before a fall".

Mother Goose waves her spoon and exits

Corydon and Princess enter L, *hand in hand*

Corydon (*heading* C) I can't *tell* you how nervous I am. Going to meet your
father for the very first time.
Princess   (*amused*) He won't bite, you know. He's the kindest man in the
whole wide world.
Corydon All the same. He *is* the King of Entertainia, and *I'm* just a
commoner.

Princess (*laughing*) Well, *that* won't worry him. He was a commoner
   himself, before they crowned him. He used to be the Court Chamberlain
   and only became King when the *real* heir to the throne went missing and
   no-one could find him.
Corydon (*surprised*) Why was that?
Princess He was ordered to marry a princess he didn't love, and rather than
   do it, simply ran away and vanished.
Corydon (*wonderingly*) And no-one's seen him since?

The Princess shakes her head

   (*Kindly*) Poor prince. I know just how he must have felt. If someone
   stopped me marrying *you*, I wouldn't want to marry *anyone*.
Princess And I feel exactly the same.

Song 5 (*Corydon and Princess*)

   They exit R

The Lights fade rapidly

SCENE 5

The Gardens of the Shoe-house

A glorious semi-formal garden with the shoe-house UC. *This is a wonderful
and imaginative home, obviously fashioned from a giant-sized shoe. The roof
is thatched and a crooked chimney-stack is in evidence. A practical door
leads into the house. There is a tiny porch over this and climbing roses of
various colours cascade around it. A large water-butt is situated by the
porch. Several windows, boasting brightly painted wooden and decorative
exterior shutters, have been added and flower filled window-boxes are on
every sill. Flower beds, shrubs and trees mask entrances and exits* L *and* R

*When the scene begins, the full stage is warmly lit. Junior Children are
performing a dance for the entertainment of Visitors, who also move around
admiring the shoe-house and grounds*

Dance (*Juniors*)

The visitors applaud and the Children exit L *and* R. *The Visitors resume their
sightseeing and gradually move off* L *and* R

   Dame Dallymore enters UL, *in an outrageously over-the-top gown*

Dame (*moving* DC) Oh, boys and girls. Thank goodness it's nearly closing time. We've had people knocking on the door all afternoon, wanting to look round the shoe-house and buy refreshments. (*Delightedly*) Still — I've taken so much money, we'll never go hungry again.

King Cole enters R

King (*beaming*) Dame Dallymore. So *there* you are. I've been looking for you everywhere. Not only is your house a National Treasure, the garden is simply *amazing*. I've never *seen* so many flowers.

Dame (*modestly*) Well — they brighten the place up, don't they? And my late husband *loved* 'em, so every week I put a nice big bunch on top of his grave.

King Ah. So he's buried in the local cemetery?

Dame Certainly not. (*Proudly*) He was a *forester*, my Marmaduke. Worked in the forest all his life and *that's* where he wanted to be buried. Even picked his own spot.

King (*fascinated*) Really?

Dame (*remembering*) There he was — lying on his deathbed and filling in his Lottery numbers, when suddenly he looked up at me and said (*with great drama*) "Diphtheria. I want you to open the bedroom window so I can see my beloved forest for the last time, then fetch me my old bow and arrow. The place that arrow lands is where I want to be buried." So I *did* it, and he fired it, and *that's* where I buried him.

King In the middle of the great forest?

Dame No. On top of the *wardrobe*. He couldn't shoot straight to save his life. Mind you — he wasn't sorry to *go*. He had terrible headaches after the doctor took his temperature.

King (*puzzled*) Why was that?

Dame The thermometer broke and he swallowed all that silver stuff inside it. Every time the sun came out, he bashed his head on the ceiling.

King (*after a reaction*) And you've never thought of marrying again?

Dame (*off-handedly*) Well — I did *once*. I was engaged to a famous *artist* but when I found out he never used brushes and painted everything with his finger, I changed my mind.

King Whatever for?

Dame He'd have taken a year to do the kitchen cupboards.

King (*after a reaction*) So now you run the local *orphanage*. You must be *very* busy looking after all those children.

Dame Oh, I am. But I've still got time for my favourite hobbies. Knitting and swimming. (*She beams proudly*)

King (*puzzled*) Doesn't the wool get wet?

Dame (*pushing the King playfully*) Saucebox. (*She chortles*) Well, now you've had a look round, why don't we sashay to the summerhouse and have a little *tête-à-tête*?

King   (*startled*) I *beg* your pardon?

Dame   (*coyly*) Well — you're a *widower* and I'm a *widow*. Couldn't you fancy a woman like me? (*She simpers at him*)

King   (*doubtfully*) I suppose so. Providing she wasn't *too* much like you.

Dame   (*to the audience, delightedly*) Oooh, isn't he gorgeous, girls? Just the kind of feller that attracts me. Still breathing.

Song 6 (Dame and King)

The Dame and the King exit DL. *The Squire enters* UR, *scowling, and moves* C

Squire   (*fuming*) Corkscrews and counterweights. You can hardly *move* for tourists coming to gape at this stupid-looking house. The old faggot's making a fortune *and* even has that idiotic king eating out of her hand. (*Glowering*) There must be *some* way of turning the tables.

Calumnia enters L *in a green follow spot, cackling*

Calumnia   Indeed there *is*. And with my aid
    Her hopes and dreams will quickly fade.
    So if her fall you long to see,
    Draw near, and place your trust in me.

Squire   (*approaching suspiciously*) You're not Anne Robinson, (*or other supposedly fearsome female*) are you?

Calumnia hisses furiously and Squire steps back hastily

    I only asked. (*Recovering himself*) So who *are* you?

Calumnia   (*dismissively*) No matter. Just suffice to say
    I'm here to help you win the day.
    (*She glances round suspiciously*)
    But so none *close* can overhear,
    My plan I'll whisper in your ear.
    (*She whispers to the Squire*)

The Squire's eyes grow large

    (*Aloud*) Now go. The course I've clearly shown.
    Your message send by text or phone,
    By e-mail, fax or any way that
    Guarantees us no delay.
    Then stand aside, my new-found friend
    And watch these celebrations end.
    (*She cackles triumphantly*)

Calumnia exits L

The follow spot fades

Squire (*delightedly*) Well, I don't know who *she* was, but she's certainly done me a favour. I'll send a message at once. (*Looking round*) And as for those bungling bailiffs — they've let me down once too often. I can sack them at the self-same time.

The Squire exits DR. *Giggles enters* UR, *followed by the Princess, who looks anxious*

Giggles (*to the audience*) Hallo, everybody.

The audience responds

Princess (*anxiously*) And you're quite sure we won't be going home before the party begins? Even though the coach has been repaired?
Giggles Absolutely positive. As soon as they'd finished fixing it, I took it in for a service.
Princess But *that* won't delay us long.
Giggles Yes it will. I got it stuck in the church doorway. (*He chortles*)
Princess (*dreamily*) Oh, Giggles. Now I've met Corydon, I don't think I'll *ever* want to go home.
Giggles (*concerned*) Here. Don't say things like *that*, Princess. If *you* weren't there, I'd be so miserable, I'd run away and be a soldier in the Foreign Legion.
Princess (*alarmed*) But what if you got *hurt*?
Giggles (*amused*) Who'd want to hurt *me*?
Princess Well, the *enemy*, of course.
Giggles (*stunned*) Oh. Well in that case, I *won't* join the Foreign Legion. I'll be the enemy instead.
Princess (*amused*) Oh, Giggles. You *do* make me laugh. But there's nothing to worry about. Of course I'll be going home when the party's over. Only *this* time it's to let everyone know that very shortly I'll be marrying the most wonderful man in the world.

Song 7 (*Princess*)

The Princess exits into the shoe-house

Wrack and Ruin hurry on UR *in a panic. Wrack holds a piece of paper with something written on it*

Wrack (*calling towards the house*) Dame Dallymore. Dame Dallymore.
Giggles The Squire's men again. Up to some *more* dirty tricks.

Wrack and Ruin see Giggles and hurry to him

Ruin Quick. Quick. Where's Dame Dallymore? We've got to see her.

Giggles (*thinking quickly*) She — er — she's just gone to the lavatory.

Wrack (*urgently*) Well, in that case, you'd better give her *this*. (*He thrusts the message at Giggles*)

Giggles (*scornfully*) Don't be daft. She's got a toilet roll.

Ruin No, no. You don't understand. The Squire's sent the Giant a text message telling him where to look for his missing shoe.

Wrack And any minute now he'll be coming to collect it.

Giggles (*firmly*) No he won't. You're just trying to get rid of her again. That stupid old Giant'll never come back.

There is a heavy drum-thud. Wrack, Ruin and Giggles stagger. The Lights fade during the following

Wrack (*in a panic*) It's *him*.

Ruin Oooh.

Ruin jumps into Wrack's arms and clings on

There is another loud thud

Anxious Visitors and Children hurry on, gazing up

Chorus (*ad-libbing; fearfully*) The Giant. He's coming back. Somebody help us. (*Etc.*)

Corydon hurries on R

Corydon (*alarmed*) What is it?

The Princess appears in the doorway of the cottage and the Dame and King hurry on. The Dame wears the Royal Crown and the King's face is covered with lipstick kisses

All gaze upwards in horror

Look out, everybody. Look out.

The crowd scatters with cries of fear and exits

The stage is plunged into darkness once more. There are further cries from the company

The shoe-house is removed, leaving only the water-butt behind. The Dame and the King cower DL. *Corydon sprawls on the ground* UR. *Wrack and Ruin fall in a heap* DR, *and Giggles jumps into the water-butt and disappears from view*

The Lights come up again. Everyone gets to their feet, gazing at the spot once occupied by the house

Dame (*stricken*) My house. My beautiful house. It's gone.

The Visitors and Children enter cautiously

Corydon (*looking around anxiously*) Is everyone safe?
Wrack (*looking around*) Where's Giggles?

Everyone glances round anxiously. Giggles slowly emerges from the water-butt and expels a mouthful of water

Giggles (*weakly*) Hallo, everybody.

Audience response

The Chorus crowd round and assist Giggles to get out of the water-butt

King (*anxiously*) And where's Marigold? What's happened to *her*?

Everyone looks around

Mother Goose enters DR

Mother Goose   Alas, I'm very sad to say,
　　　　By now she's *many* miles away.
　　　　Though rest assured, she's safe. It's true.
　　　　Just carried off inside the shoe;
　　　　Its owner simply unaware,
　　　　That anybody's hiding there.

Everyone reacts

Corydon (*to Mother Goose*) But what if he *finds* her? Won't she be in *danger*?
Mother Goose (*uncertainly*) One never knows. It all depends.
　　　　Some giants are evil. Some are friends.

It's best if time we cease to waste
And to her rescue, straight-way haste.

All but Corydon look startled

Wrack   (*aghast*) You mean — you want *us* to go with you?
Ruin   (*horrified*) To a land full of giants? (*Firmly*) Not likely.
King   (*pleading*) I'll give half my *kingdom* to the one who finds her.
Corydon   (*bravely*) Don't worry, Your Majesty. *I'll* go with Mother Goose.
Giggles   And so will I.
Dame   (*aghast*) Oh, no. My only son's going to fight a giant — and he hasn't
even got red trousers.
King   (*startled*) Eh?
Dame   It's in all the history books. Whenever *Napoleon* went into battle, he
wore red trousers so if ever he got hurt, no-one could tell he was bleeding.
Giggles   (*remembering*) She's *right*. He *did*. I'd better nip back to the palace
and get *mine*.
King   I didn't know *you* had a pair of red trousers, Giggles.
Giggles   I haven't. But I've got a pair of *brown* ones.
Mother Goose   (*firmly*) Your farewells make. No more delay.
We really *must* be on our way
If soon you hope to make a stand
'Gainst what may wait in Giant-land.
Corydon   Don't worry, everyone. With Mother Goose to help us, we'll be
back with the Princess before the day is out. For once in my life I know just
where I'm heading.

The Lights begin a slow fade

And as it seems, right now, my great adventure must begin.
If fight a giant I must, I *shall* — and promise you I'll *win*.

Song 8 (*Corydon*)

*A spotlight highlights Corydon while he sings, whilst the rest of the stage is
silhouetted. At the end of the song, the spotlight snaps off to Black-out*

Curtain

ACT II

Scene 1

The Land of the Giants

A Swiss-type village of stylized chalets, their window-boxes a cascade of scarlet and white blooms, before a backdrop depicting a mountainous pine-tree covered region. Partial chalets or flower-draped stone arches conceal entrances and exits L and R

When the Curtain *rises, it is daylight, and Villagers in Slavic-style national costume are singing and dancing*

Song 9 (*Villagers*)

Tapioca, the cobbler, enters UL *and moves* DC. *He is a fussy, grey-haired, little man wearing tiny spectacles, white, balloon-sleeved shirt, dark velvet knee breeches, white cotton tights and buckled shoes. Over his clothing is a cobbler's apron and he carries a small hammer*

Tapioca (*fretting*) Oh, do be *quiet* for a moment. It's all very well *celebrating*, but you've been singing and dancing out here for *hours*. Some of us are still trying to work, you know.

Girl (*contritely*) Sorry, Tapioca. We didn't *mean* to disturb you. It's just that we're all so happy.

Tapioca (*grumpily*) As if I couldn't *tell*. But if I don't get his *present* finished in time, he *could* flood the village again. You know what he's like when things upset him.

Boy (*grimacing*) Don't remind us. It took *weeks* to dry out the *last* time. (*Reassuringly*) But he's sure to stay happy *today*.

All agree with nods and smiles

Tapioca He wasn't too pleased this *morning*. He'd found that battered old shoe he lost the other day, but couldn't get his foot inside because someone had turned it into a *house*.

Everyone looks surprised

Girl (*curiously*) So what did he *do* with it?

Tapioca How should I know? The last time I saw him, he was carrying it towards the castle. (*Firmly*) Now if you *don't* mind, I'd like to get on with what I'm supposed to be *doing*.

Boy (*to the others*) Come on, everybody. We'll leave Tapioca in peace. (*To him*) But we'll see you tonight at the party.

The Villagers exit, smiling

Tapioca (*giving a deep sigh*) Oh, I don't know how they stay so cheerful. The times we've had to rebuild the village. Twice he's flooded us out. Three times he's flattened it into the ground and I can't *remember* how many earthquakes he's caused. (*Wearily*) Who'd have a giant for a neighbour?

Tapioca moves US, *shaking his head, and exits* L. *Corydon enters* DR *carrying a sword, followed by Mother Goose*

Corydon (*to Mother Goose*) Did you *hear* that? What a *monster* this Giant must be. (*Anxiously*) We've just *got* to rescue Marigold.

Mother Goose (*nodding*) I must admit that things look grim,
But don't despair too soon.
There's lots of magic left inside
My trusty wooden spoon. (*She displays it*)

Corydon All the same, we'd better find her before *he* does. (*Glancing round*) But where's Giggles?

Mother Goose Not far behind, I guarantee.
He'll catch us up anon.
But time's too short to wait for him.
We really must press on.

Corydon (*nodding*) And there's only *one* road leading to the castle, so he can't get lost, can he? We'll meet him there later.

Corydon exits UL, *followed by Mother Goose. Giggles enters* DR *looking exhausted*

Giggles (*weakly*) Hallo, everybody.

Audience response

Oooh, I thought I'd never get here. (*Indignantly*) Just wait till we get home again. I'm going to *sue* (*local travel agency*) for giving me wrong information. I rang up just before we set off and asked the manager how

long it would take to get to Giantland. "Just a minute," she said, and put the
phone down. (*Disgustedly*) A minute. It's taken us *hours*. I've got so many
blisters on this foot (*he shows one foot to the audience*) I've had to walk
on the other one. Mind you — we came through some funny little villages.
There was one (*he names a local village*), where we saw something
amazing. I mean — we all know they're a bit *peculiar*, there, don't we? But
you'll never believe *this*. Everybody was up on the church roof watching
a satellite dish get married to next door's television aerial. No, no. I'm not
joking. It wasn't much of a *ceremony*, but the reception was *fantastic*. (*He
chortles*)

*The Dame enters R in another amazing dress. She carries a wicker
shopping basket, covered with a cloth*

Giggles (*surprised*) Diphtheria? What are *you* doing here?
Dame Well — I couldn't stay at *home*, could I? We haven't *got* one any more.
So I've sent all the children to Disneyworld and come after you lot to help
fight the Giant. (*She puts the basket down*)
Giggles (*after a reaction*) Well, I hope you've brought some *food* for us 'cos
we've not had a thing to eat since breakfast.
Dame (*beaming*) As a matter of *fact*, I've brought you a lovely big Kit-e-Kat
casserole. (*To audience, chiding*) No. No. Don't laugh. It was my late
husband's favourite meal. I told Jamie Oliver (*or other famous chef*) about
it, last week, and *he* didn't believe me, either. "You can't feed a feller cat
food," he said, "it'll finish him off". "Give over," I said, "he ate it every day
for *weeks* before he died." "Well, there you are, then," he said, "it was the
cat food that killed him." "No, it wasn't," I said — "he was crossing (*local
road*), sat down to lick his leg and a *bus* ran over him." (*She stoops as
though to pick up the basket*)
Giggles (*uneasily*) I — er — I don't think I'm as hungry as I *thought* I was,
Diphtheria. Perhaps we'd better wait till we get home? We can have a meal
at (*local restaurant*).
Dame (*straightening*) You must be joking. I'm not going in *there*. Didn't you
see the notice on the door? Meals from seven in the morning till midnight.
Giggles (*puzzled*) What's wrong with that?
Dame (*patiently*) If we spent all that time *eating*, there'd be no time for
anything else. (*Remembering*) And anyway, we can't go just *yet*. We've
got to wait for King Cole to get here.
Giggles (*surprised*) You mean — *he's* coming with us as well?
Dame Of course he is. But he was a bit worried about being killed by the
Giant, so he's stopped off for a few minutes to join the Labour Party.
Giggles (*protesting*) He can't have done. He's been a Conservative all his
life. Why would he want to join the Labour Party?

Dame He said he'd sooner one of *them* died than a Conservative. (*Skittishly*) Anyway, there's no point in *us* wasting time, is there? Why don't we make a few wedding plans while we're waiting for him to catch up? (*She simpers at Giggles*)

Giggles (*startled*) Eh?

Dame (*reasonably*) Well — you'll want to get married *sometime*, won't you? So why not marry *me*?

Giggles (*hastily*) Oh, I couldn't do *that*, Diphtheria. You see, when I get married, it'll have to be to somebody *small* and *cute* who loves outdoor life and goes swimming and catching fish every day.

Dame You don't want a woman. You want a *penguin*.

Song 10 (*Giggles and Dame*)

Giggles takes to his heels and dashes off UL. *The Dame snatches up the basket and hastens after him. The Lights dim and Calumnia enters* DL *in a green follow spot*

Calumnia (*balefully*) A thousand curses. Once again
My plan seems set to fail.
That Giant, Mother Goose has found
And brought pursuers on his trail.
But mark my words, I'll beat them yet;
For happiness I *hate*.
And I alone will soon decide
How each shall meet their fate.
(*She cackles*)

Calumnia exits DL

The Lights return to the normal setting

The King enters wearily DR

King Oh dear, oh dear. I'll never catch them up at this rate. Perhaps someone here knows a short cut? I'll knock on one of these doors. (*He knocks; calling*) Hallo? Hallo? Is anyone home?

Tapioca enters

Tapioca Is there *never* any peace in this village? (*Crossly*) It's no use banging on *that* door. There's nobody home.

The King turns to Tapioca

(*Startled*) Lord Chamberlain. I mean — *Your Majesty*. (*He quickly bows*)

King (*recognizing Tapioca*) Tapioca. Where on earth have you *been*? We've been searching for *you* for the past thirty years. Ever since the prince ran away saying he'd only marry the girl of his dreams and no-one but Tapioca, the shoe-maker, would know where he'd gone. (*Firmly*) You've got to tell us where to find him.

Tapioca (*sighing unhappily*) Oh, dear. I just *knew* you'd ask me *that*. It's *exactly* the reason I left Entertainia and came to live here.

King (*alarmed*) Don't say something *happened* to him?

Tapioca (*hastily*) No, no. But he *did* make me promise I'd never tell a soul where he was.

King (*protesting*) But you *must*. He's the *real* King of Entertainia. *I'm* only ruler till they find him.

Tapioca (*firmly*) I'm sorry, Your Majesty, but my lips are sealed.

King (*defeated*) Well at least you can tell me he's *safe*. (*Dejectedly*) Not like *my* poor daughter. Kidnapped by a terrible giant and carried off inside his shoe.

Tapioca (*surprised*) What?

King (*nodding miserably*) He'd lost it in Entertainia and, as Laurence Llewelyn-Bowen was too busy, Mother Goose turned it into the most wonderful house you've ever seen. We were just paying it a visit when suddenly he came back again and took it away — with Marigold still inside it. (*Unhappily*) If we don't stop him, he'll be eating her for supper.

Tapioca (*laughing*) Oh, *no*, Your Majesty. He'd never do a thing like *that*. He's the kindest giant that's ever lived.

King (*surprised*) Is he?

Tapioca Of course he is. He only causes problems when he's *sad* or catches a *cold*. His tears are so huge they wash half the village away and whenever he *sneezes*, we all wave goodbye to our rooftops and chimneys. But he always helps with the re-building. If he'd known the Princess was *inside* his shoe, he'd *never* have taken it away.

King (*relieved*) Then there's no need to worry?

Tapioca (*shaking his head*) She'll be *perfectly* safe. And as today's his two hundredth birthday, she'll be just in time for his party. Everyone in Giantland is going.

King (*excitedly*) Oh, I must tell the others at *once*. How do I get to the Castle?

Tapioca (*indicating* UL) Just follow that road. You'll be there in next to no time.

The King chortles happily and exits UL

(*Remembering*) And *I'd* better finish wrapping the Giant's present.

Tapioca exits UL

The Squire enters R, *followed, reluctantly, by Wrack and Ruin*

Squire (*impatiently*) Hurry up. Hurry up. Hurry up. (*He moves* DC)
Wrack   (*scowling*) Never mind, "Hurry up. Hurry up. Hurry up". We shouldn't even *be* here now.
Ruin No. You gave us the *sack*, you did. (*He glowers*)
Squire (*laughing falsely*) That was just a small *misunderstanding*. How could I do without you two? And to show how much I appreciate your work, I've decided to give you a *huge* pay rise. Two p a week each — less tax and National Insurance.
Wrack Yes, well, you can keep your rotten pay rise. Once we get the Post Office *reward* money, we'll be nearly as rich as *you* are. (*He smirks*)
Squire (*blankly*) *What* Post Office reward money?
Ruin (*smugly*) There was a notice in the window this morning saying if anybody found a plastic carrier bag in (*local street*) filled with fifty pound notes, they'd get a big reward for its return.
Squire (*amazed*) And you two *found* it?
Wrack No. But we found a plastic carrier bag.
Squire (*begrudgingly*) Oh, very well, then — I'll increase your wages by *three p* a week. But you'll have to *share* it.
Wrack ⎱ (*together: happily*) *Now* you're talking.
Ruin ⎰
Squire (*smirking in triumph*) Then here's what I want you to do. We wait till Corydon rescues the Princess, then you grab him, while I escort her back to Entertainia and claim the reward. Is that clear? You're sure you won't forget?
Wrack 'Course not.
Ruin We're not *all* like my mother, are we, Wrack?
Wrack No. She's got a *terrible* memory, his mother has. Can hardly remember anything. She even forgot she was having him.
Squire (*tartly*) Don't be ridiculous.
Ruin It's *true*. I was four years old when I was *born*.
Squire Bah. Enough of this badinage. We must get to the Giant's castle and put my brilliant plan into action. Follow me.

The Squire exits UL

Ruin makes to follow the Squire

Wrack (*hastily*) Hang on a minute. I've got to get my front door from behind those bushes. (*He indicates off,* DR) I can't go without *that*.
Ruin Well hurry up, then. (*Grumbling*) I still don't know why you wanted to bring it *with* you.

Wrack (*patiently*) I've already *told* you. It's 'cos I've lost the key and can't *lock* it. I've had to bring it with me to stop my house being burgled while I'm away.

Ruin (*protesting*) But that's *stupid*. How will you get back in if you lose the *door* as well?

Wrack (*wearily*) I'm not daft, you know. I left one of the *windows* open.

Ruin (*crest-fallen*) I never thought of that.

Wrack (*kindly*) Well — you don't have the brains *I've* got, do you? But there's nothing to *worry* about. As long as we're mates, *I'll* do all our thinking. Just stick with *me*, and I promise you'll never go wrong.

Song 11 (*Wrack and Ruin*)

Black-out

SCENE 2

The Road Through the Forest

A lane scene depicting ancient and huge trees

When the scene begins the lighting is subdued but not frightening. C *is a child dressed as a tall, colourful-looking mushroom or toadstool, surrounded by a cluster of smaller Children as smaller mushrooms. All are perfectly still. Mysterious sounding music begins to play. The central mushroom becomes animated and the smaller ones follow suit, all turning to face the audience. They perform a quaint and lumbering dance*

Dance of the Mushrooms (*Babes*)

At the end of the dance the mushrooms turn US *again and resume their original positions*

Princess Marigold cautiously enters L

Princess Oh, thank goodness the Giant left his shoe outside and I escaped before he noticed me. (*She glances round*) But where am I? (*Helplessly*) I must be hundreds of miles from home and haven't a *notion* of how to get there. If only there was someone I could ask.

Giggles enters R

Giggles (*brightly*) Hallo, everybody.

Audience response

Princess (*in disbelief*) Giggles. (*She hurries to Giggles with open arms*)
Giggles (*delightedly*) Princess. You're safe. (*He hugs the Princess*)
Princess (*breathlessly*) How on earth did you *find* me?
Giggles (*with false modesty*) Nothing to it. I just followed the Giant's footprints. I learnt how to do things like that when I was big game hunting in Africa.
Princess (*surprised*) I didn't know *you'd* been a hunter.
Giggles (*smugly*) Oh, yes. I was world famous in our street. Mind you … I had some very narrow escapes. I came out of my tent one morning and this great big lion came running towards me. All teeth and claws. (*He snarls*)
Princess (*wide-eyed*) What did you *do*?
Giggles Well, just as he jumped — quick as a flash I ducked right down and he went straight over my head. By the time he'd landed and turned round again, I was half-way up a tree.
Princess (*relieved*) What a lucky escape.
Giggles Yes. But he didn't give up. All that week, whenever I came out of my tent, the same thing happened. The lion'd *jump*, I'd *duck*, over my head he'd go and I'd be stuck up a tree all day instead of out hunting. (*Wryly*) I *was* going to stick it out till he got tired, but then I saw something that made me decide to come home and be a jester instead.
Princess What was it?
Giggles Well — the following week, I made a little hole in my tent so I could see if he was anywhere near before I went out. And there he was. Right in front of me. Practising *low* jumps.
Princess (*amused*) Oh, Giggles. I don't believe a *word* of it. (*Seriously*) But you've no idea how glad I am to see you. I was starting to think I'd *never* get back to Entertainia. (*She glances round*) Which is the quickest way?
Giggles Easy. We follow any road that's got great big cabbages growing on both sides of it.
Princess (*puzzled*) Cabbages?
Giggles Yes. It'll be a dual cabbage-way. (*He laughs heartily at his own joke*)
Princess (*after a moment*) Shall we go then?
Giggles (*puzzled*) Go? Aren't we waiting for the others?
Princess (*blankly*) Others?
Giggles Corydon and Mother Goose?
Princess (*surprised*) You mean *they're* here, too?
Giggles Well, of course they are. It was them who helped you escape, wasn't it?
Princess I haven't seen them since the Giant carried me away. (*Horrified*) Oh, *Giggles*. Don't say they've gone to his *castle*? They could be in *terrible* danger. (*Anxiously*) We've got to stop them.

Giggles (*dismayed*) But they'll be there already.
Princess Then we've got to help them. Come on.

The Princess hurries off L

Giggles (*alarmed*) Wait, Princess. Wait.

Giggles hurries off after the Princess

The mushroom music begins again

Dance of the Mushrooms (*Babes*): Reprise

They mushrooms reprise part of their dance before making their exit L

The Dame's voice is heard off R

Dame (*calling; off*) Coo-ee? Are you there, Giggles?

The Dame enters in another bizarre outfit

(*To the audience*) Do you like the frock, girls? I got it in (*local dress shop*).
It's called "The Indian Rope Trick Dress". (*Archly*) No visible means of
support. (*She hoists her bosom and chortles*) Well — I had to buy
something to cheer myself up. I can't tell you how depressed I was when
the Giant walked off with me shoe-house. They all came to see it, you
know. Arnold Saucy-beggar. Leonardo di Cappuccino. Vera Duckworth.
(*Confidentially*) Mind you, *she* didn't want to look round. She just wanted
to know if I could recommend a plastic surgeon. "Plastic surgeon?" I said.
"You're not thinking of having a *face-lift*, are you?" "Course not," she said
"I want to know if he can put a new handle on my polythene bucket."
(*Brightening*) Still — we'll be all right when Corydon rescues the Princess
and gets that reward money. We can buy a brand new house and still have
plenty to live on. (*She chortles with delight*)

The King enters R

King (*delightedly*) Dame Dallymore. Dame Dallymore. I've just had some
wonderful news.
Dame (*pleased*) Oh, I say.
King It's about the Giant. Apparently he's a *friendly* one. Wouldn't hurt a
fly. So that means Marigold's *safe* and we haven't a *thing* to worry about.
(*Pleased*) By this time tomorrow, we'll be back in Entertainia with
everything just as it was. (*He beams*)

Dame (*anxiously*) And what about the reward money?

King (*brushing it aside*) Oh, there'll be no need for *that*. If she isn't in any danger, she doesn't need *rescuing*, does she? (*Happily*) This has saved me thousands.

Dame (*aghast*) But the *orphanage*? We've nowhere to live and I've dozens of mouths to feed.

King (*kindly*) Don't worry, Dame Dallymore. Sir Hugo's *bound* to help you. There isn't a house in Tumbledown that doesn't belong to *him*.

Dame (*unhappily*) I'd sooner live in a *palace*. (*Hopefully*) Are you *sure* you don't want to get married again? I'd make a wonderful Queen.

King (*surprised*) Would you?

Dame Oh, yes. I'd do exactly the same as that Queen Elizabeth in England.

King (*puzzled*) And what's *that*?

Dame (*confidentially*) Well — I read about it in the paper. She waits in her bedroom till visitors arrive, then puts a frock on and sweeps down the Royal staircase.

King (*curiously*) And what does she do after *that*?

Dame Same as me, I suppose. Vacuums the carpets and dusts all the furniture.

King (*after a reaction*) Well, it's kind of you to think of me, Dame Dallymore, but I don't think I'll be marrying again. Though there's nothing to stop *you*.

Dame (*disappointedly*) Fat chance of that. I thought I might find a husband at (*local club*) last night when they advertised a Seafood Disco-Rave, but the only thing *I* pulled was a *mussel*. (*Sadly*) And to think only last Valentine's Day I got two hundred cards.

King (*startled*) Good heavens.

Dame And I could have had *twice* as many if I hadn't given meself cramp writing out my address.

King (*kindly*) Well, I'm sure you'll meet somebody *some* day.

Dame (*despondently*) Yes. But will he fancy me if I'm old and ugly?

King (*chuckling*) You may grow *older*, Dame Dallymore, but I'm sure you'll never get *uglier*. (*He moves* L) Now come along. We must find the Giant's castle at once and introduce ourselves.

The King exits and, after a reaction, the Dame follows

The Lights rapidly fade to Black-out

Scene 3

The Courtyard of the Giant's Castle

The backdrop depicts an interior wall of the castle's courtyard, with glimpses of distant, snow-capped mountains and thick pine forest. The L side of the stage is dominated by a partial view of the castle itself. The base of a vast round tower, constructed from house-sized blocks of granite, conceals entrances and exits UL, and a huge, ancient, tree conceals the lower entrance. On the opposite side of the courtyard, a rugged stone archway housing a raised portcullis leads off DL whilst part of another gigantic building disguises the upper entrance

When the scene begins, the courtyard is crowded with residents of the surrounding towns and villages, each carrying brightly wrapped gifts for the Giant. A team of gypsies in colourful traditional costumes perform a spirited dance as the others sing

Song 12 and Gypsy Dance (*Villagers*)

Everyone cheerfully exits UL. Mother Goose and Corydon enter cautiously through the arch DR

Corydon (*bewildered*) I can't understand it. They're not the least bit worried about the Giant. I've never *seen* such happy faces.

Mother Goose (*thoughtfully*) That's very true. (*Brightening*) Which indicates
There's not a thing to fear.
This Giant must be the *friendly* kind
And Marigold is safe and near.

Corydon (*still worried*) Then where *is* she? There's not a sign of her out *here*.

Mother Goose (*cheerily*) That's something you can leave to *me*.
Forget all false alarms.
In half a trice, I'll seek her out
And bring her to your waiting arms.
Then back to Entertainia we'll speed without delay
To put things right for once and all — and celebrate your wedding day.
(*She gives a flourish of her spoon*)

Mother Goose exits UL

Corydon (*dreamily*) Our wedding day. (*Sighing*) Ohhhh, I can hardly believe it. What will it be like, living in the Royal palace? Especially with the girl of my dreams.

The Lights dim

Calumnia enters DL *in a green spotlight. Corydon steps back, startled*

Calumnia A thing, I vow, you'll never know.
　　Your hopes I'm sworn to dash.
　　Each castle-in-the-air you build,
　　Shall fall to earth with mighty crash.
　　(*Spitefully*) Despite what Mother Goose foretold,
　　You'll *never* marry Marigold. (*She cackles*)
Corydon (*bewildered*) Who are *you*? And what do you mean?
Calumnia (*sneering*) Don't play the innocent with *me*.
　　Your pleasant thoughts I'll spoil.
　　You shall not find success or fame
　　No matter how you toil.
　　To happiness, you foolish youth,
　　"Goodbye" it's time to wave.
　　I guarantee your Princess bride,
　　You'll never, ever, save.
　　(*She cackles with laughter*)

Calumnia exits L

The green light is extinguished and the Lights return to normal

Corydon (*puzzled*) Who was *that*? And what on earth did she *mean*? I'd better find Mother Goose and tell her what's happened. (*He moves towards the* UL *exit*)

The Princess hurries on DR

Princess Corydon. Wait. (*She runs to Corydon*)
Corydon (*embracing the Princess; delightedly*) Marigold. (*Puzzled*) But how did you escape?
Princess (*breaking free*) There's no time now. I'll tell you later. If the Giant finds out we're *here*, who *knows* what'll happen?

The Princess attempts to pull Corydon to the exit R

Corydon (*reassuringly*) Don't worry. With Mother Goose to help us, he won't dare raise a finger.

Princess I wish I could believe that.

Corydon But it's *true*. And even if it *weren't*, he'd definitely think twice before facing this sword of mine. (*He touches his sword*) Now cheer up. By this time tomorrow, we'll be safely home and asking for permission to marry.

Princess (*relaxing*) Oh, Corydon. I can't *wait* to be back in Entertainia. And once I get there, I'll never want to leave it again.

Corydon Then if I have *my* way, I promise you never will.

Song 13 (*Corydon and Princess*)

The King and the Dame enter DR. *The Dame is wearing another amazing costume*

King (*delightedly*) Marigold. (*He hurries to the Princess*)

Princess Daddy. (*She embraces the King*)

Corydon (*to the Dame, in amazement*) Mother. What are *you* doing here?

Dame (*indignantly*) What do you *think* we're doing? We've come to help *you*. Oooh, and what a time we've had *getting* here. We'd just turned left after passing (*local fish and chip shop*) when poor old Hieronymus broke out in spots from head to toe and we had to go looking for a doctor.

Princess (*to King in concern*) Oh, *no*. And what did he *say*?

King He said it looked like *measles* and I'd to go to bed for a week and *do* nothing. (*Annoyed*) Have you ever heard anything so ridiculous? I can't do *that*, I told him. I'd be bored stiff.

Princess So did he change his mind?

Dame No. He gave him a ball-point pen and told him to join up all the dots.

Corydon Well, now Marigold's safe, I'll find Mother Goose and we can get back to Entertainia before the Giant even knows that we've been here.

King (*beaming*) Oh, there's no need to worry about *him*. According to *my* information he's the friendliest Giant that's ever lived. He wouldn't hurt a *fly*.

Corydon (*to the King*) You mean — she wasn't in danger at all?

King Not for a *moment*.

Princess (*laughing with relief*) And I was *so* frightened.

Everyone joins in the laughter

Mother Goose enters UL, *beaming*

Mother Goose So *there* you are, young Marigold.
        You've led us quite a chase.
        But as you've heard, there's naught to fear.

A *kindly* giant owns this place.
With smiling face, he greets us all
And begs us to partake
Of old-world hospitality,
Champagne and birthday cake.

All look delighted

Then afterwards, he'll do his best
To quickly make amends
And take you back to whence you came,
To home, your families and friends.
Dame (*anxiously*) And what about the shoe-house?
Mother Goose (*smiling*) That too shall be restored to you,
And furthermore, I'm told
As recompense for your distress,
He'll fill that shoe with bags of gold.
Dame (*overwhelmed*) Oh, I say …

Everyone reacts delightedly

Mother Goose So come. It's time to meet your host
And raise a glass in birthday toast.
(*She gestures towards the castle with her wooden spoon*)

The happy group exits UL, *followed by Mother Goose. The Squire enters furtively,* DR

Squire (*annoyed*) Toothache and tommyrot. Not only's that stupid Giant *not* kidnapped the Princess, he's giving the shoe-house back to Dame Dallymore and sending her home with a mountain of gold. (*Grimly*) But I'm not beaten *yet*. If anyone's going to be rich, it's going to be *me*. I'll follow them into the castle and see if I can upset their apple-cart. (*Proudly*) No-one gets the better of Hugo Hepatitis.

The Squire chuckles nastily and exits UL *into the castle. Giggles enters* DR

Giggles Hallo, everybody.

Audience response

Oooh, it isn't half a funny place, this Giantland. I was chasing after the Princess when I tripped head first over a tortoise in the middle of the road.

"Watch where you're going, you great clumsy thing," it said. "You nearly kicked me in the face." "Hang on a minute," I said, "it's not my fault I fell over you. What were you doing in the middle of the road?" "Half a mile an hour," he said.

Wrack enters DR, *holding his stomach*

Wrack   (*groaning*) Quick, quick. Give me some food. I'm starving.

Giggles   (*surprised*) What are *you* doing here?

Wrack   We're supposed to be helping the Squire cheat Corydon out of the reward money, but we're so hungry we can't think.

Giggles   (*shocked*) Oooh, you nasty old thing. Well, I haven't any food *on* me (*he winks at the audience*) but I *do* know how to *get* some. Do you like *honey*?

Wrack   (*excitedly*) Oooh, I *love* honey. It's my favourite food. Lead me to it.

Giggles   Oh, you don't have to *go* to it. If you say a nice little rhyme, the bees'll *bring* it to you.

Wrack   (*scornfully*) Give over. I'm not daft, you know. (*Interested*) What rhyme's that?

Giggles   (*innocently*) "Busy bee, busy bee, what have you got in your hive for me?"

Wrack   (*in disbelief*) You're pulling my leg.

Giggles   (*protesting*) No, no, I mean it. Look. I'll tell you what we'll do. I'll pretend to be a busy little bee and buzz around the Giant's garden collecting honey — and when I get back, you say the rhyme and I'll give it to you.

Wrack   (*after thinking it over*) All right, then. I'll give it a go.

Giggles flaps his arms like wings and makes buzzing noises; he circles the stage, then vanishes into the wings R

Wrack remains C, *repeating the rhyme to give himself confidence*

Giggles enters with a mouthful of water, still flapping his arms. He circles Wrack once, then halts L *beside him and gives him a nod to proceed*

(*With deliberation*) "Busy bee, busy bee, what have you got in your hive for me?"

Giggles blows sharply and soaks Wrack's face with the mouthful of water. Wrack reacts

Giggles laughs and exits L

(*Disgustedly*) Oooh, the rotten thing. I'm soaking. Just look at me.

Ruin enters R

Ruin Oh, there you are. I've been looking … (*He notices how wet Wrack is and looks skywards*) Has it been raining?

Wrack (*annoyed*) No, it *hasn't* been raining. I've just been — (*pulling himself together*) been — been — washing all the honey off my face.

Ruin (*startled*) Honey? You've been eating *honey*? And you didn't save any for *me*? (*Disgustedly*) Some friend *you* are. I *love* honey, I do.

Wrack I didn't know that. Honest. But you don't have to worry. You can get all the honey you want round here and it doesn't cost you a penny. All you have to do is say a little rhyme and the bees'll *bring* it to you.

Ruin (*eyeing him suspiciously*) Have you gone crackers again?

Wrack No, no. It's true. All you have to say is "Busy bee, busy bee, what have you got in your hive for me?" and the bees'll get you some.

Ruin You've got the brains of an idiot.

Wrack (*hastily*) I'll give 'em back to you. Listen. Listen. I'll show you how it works. *I'll* pretend to be a busy bee, buzzing round all the flowers, and when I come back to you, *you* say the rhyme and I'll give you the honey. (*Flapping his arms and buzzing*) Zzzzz Zzzzz.

Ruin (*tiredly*) All right. All right. You be a busy bee and I'll say the rhyme.

Wrack beams, then, repeating Giggles's action, exits R

(*To the audience*) You've got to excuse him. He's not been well.

Wrack enters with a mouthful of water, circles Ruin, then comes to a halt on his L *and nods for him to speak*

(*Uninterestedly*) "Busy bee, busy bee, what have you got in your hive for me?"

Wrack squirts the water at Ruin. Ruin reacts

Wrack chortles merrily and exits L

(*Dismayed*) Oooh, it's gone right through to me Calvin Kleins. (*He mops himself down*) Just wait till I get hold of him.

Giggles enters UL

Giggles Hallo, everybody.

Audience response

Ruin looks at Giggles and smirks at the audience

I've just popped out for an apple from the Giant's orchard. He's got —
Ruin (*moving to him*) Apple? Apple? Did you say an apple? (*Grinning*) You don't want an apple, Giggles. Not if you want something *sweet*. What *you* want is some nice fresh *honey*.

Giggles looks at the audience and smiles

Giggles (*to Ruin, innocently*) Honey?
Ruin Yes. Lovely thick honey. All sweet and sticky. You *do* like honey, don't you?
Giggles Oh, yes. I *love* honey. But I can't afford it, you see. I haven't got —
Ruin (*interrupting*) Oh, you don't have to *buy* it. Not *here*. All you have to do is say a teensy little rhyme and the bees'll bring all the honey you want. For nothing.
Giggles (*in mock amazement*) Give over.
Ruin (*eagerly*) It's *true*. And just to prove it, I'll tell you what we'll do. *I'll* pretend to be a busy little bee, buzzing around and collecting honey, and when I come back, *you* say "Busy bee, busy bee, what have you got in your hive for me?" and I'll give you the honey. (*He beams at Giggles*)
Giggles (*delightedly*) Oooh. (*To the audience*) Did you hear that, everybody? I'm going to get some free honey. (*He winks at the audience then turns back to Ruin*) And you're quite sure I'll get it?
Ruin (*smirking*) Oh, yes. You'll get it all right. (*He grins at the audience*)
Giggles (*excitedly*) Ooh, I can't wait. Well, don't keep me in suspenders. Go and collect some honey. (*He ushers Ruin away*)

Ruin flaps his arms, makes buzzing noises and circles the stage before exiting R

Giggles grins at the audience

Ruin enters with a mouthful of water, arms still flapping, circles Giggles then halts beside him

Giggles looks Ruin up and down but makes no attempt to speak. Ruin urges him to speak with nods and gestures

(*"Remembering"*) Oh, yes. I've got to say something, haven't I?

Ruin nods vigorously

Now what was it? (*He thinks*) Er — er … (*he "remembers"*) oh, yes. (*Reciting*) Busy bee, it's half-past three, I think I'll have an egg for tea. (*He beams happily*)

Frustrated, Ruin swallows the water

Ruin (*annoyed*) No, no, *no*. It's "Busy bee, busy bee, what have you got in your hive for me?"
Giggles (*brightening*) Oh, yes. I remember now. (*Firmly*) "Busy bee, busy bee, what have you got in your hive for me?" (*Beaming*) Right. I've *said* it. (*He holds his hand out for the honey*)
Ruin (*slapping Giggles's hand away*) Yes. But you said it at the *wrong time*, didn't you? I've not got the wat… I mean — I've not got the *honey* yet, have I? I've got to *collect* it. From all the little *flowers*.
Giggles Oh, yes. (*To the audience*) He's got to collect it. From all the little flowers.
Ruin (*heavily*) So we'll give it *another* try, shall we? And don't forget it this time. (*With deliberation*) "Busy bee, busy bee ——"
Giggles (*finishing the line*) "— what have you got in your hive for me?
Ruin Right. (*He begins to move away*) Now wait here while I go and get the honey.

Ruin "buzzes" off again R *for another mouthful of water then hurries back on to Giggles's side and nods for him to say the line*

Giggles (*reciting*) Ha ha ha, he he he. One and one and one make three.
Ruin (*swallowing the water and pushing Giggles angrily*) You've done it *again*, haven't you? You've said the wrong *rhyme*. It's "Busy bee, busy bee, what have you got in your hive for *me*?"
Giggles (*chagrined*) Oh, yes. I got mixed up, didn't I? (*Apologetically*) "Busy bee, busy bee ——"
Ruin (*snarling*) What have you got in your hive for me? (*Glowering*) Can you *remember* that? Is it too *difficult*? Do you want me to *write it down* for you? (*Enunciating clearly*) "Busy bee, busy bee, what have you got in your hive for me?"
Giggles (*contritely*) We'll do it again, eh?

Ruin gives him a baleful look then "buzzes" off for more water. He returns as before

(*Reciting*) Busy bee, I've hurt my knee …

Ruin (*yelling*) What have you got … (*The water pours out of his mouth*)

Ruin rushes off again, gets a mouthful of water, rushes back on again, trips and loses it in a spectacular manner. He rushes off again, re-fills his mouth and rushes on again still holding the glass or bottle before realizing it is still in his hand. At once he does a frantic about-turn and rushes off again to get rid of it

Giggles dashes off R, gets a mouthful of water, then hurries back to his original position, cheeks bulging

Ruin staggers back on with his mouthful of water and moves to Giggles's side

They look at each other. Ruin nods for Giggles to speak. Giggles looks blank. Ruin attempts to prompt him

(*Cheeks bulging*) Mhi-I-mee, mhi-I-mee.
Giggles (*pretending to misunderstand*) Mmm?

Ruin engages in frantic urgings to communicate with Giggles, who shows no sign of understanding. Finally Giggles prods Ruin's cheek gently with his finger, causing some of the water to dribble out. This may be repeated at will. Eventually Ruin swallows what is left of the water and grabs Giggles by his tunic front

Ruin (*yelling furiously*) What's the matter with you? Are you stupid? (*Loudly and firmly*) "Busy bee, busy bee, what have you got in your hive for me?"

Giggles squirts his mouthful of water directly into Ruin's face who gives an outraged yell

Giggles exits UL, laughing. Ruin gives angry chase

The Lights rapidly fade to Black-out

SCENE 4

The Giant's Wine Cellar

A lane scene depicting a vast wine cellar beneath the Giant's castle

Gloomy lighting. The Squire enters R, furtively

Squire (*delightedly*) Black cats and horseshoes. Not a soul in sight. (*He chortles*) With everyone upstairs in the ballroom, there's not a chance of being spotted whilst I help myself to a few bags of gold from that stupid giant's treasure house. By this time tomorrow I'll be the richest man in Entertainia. (*He sings and dances*) Soon I'll be a rich man — diddle, diddle, daddle, diddle, daddle, diddle, daddle, dee ... (*He stops singing and glances off* L *in dismay*) Someone's coming. I must hide.

The Squire dashes off R

The Dame enters L *wearing another extraordinary dress*

Dame (*to the audience, excitedly*) Oooh, I say — talk about having a *ball*. Everybody's upstairs eating and drinking and playing silly games. (*She chuckles*) We've spent the last two hours playing "Jockey's Knock". Have you played it, "Jockey's Knock"?

Audience response

No? Oh, you've *got* to. It was invented for Channel 4. It's a bit like "*Postman's* Knock", but there's a lot more *horseplay*. (*She chortles*) Oooh, and you should see the Giant's *presents*. One feller's given him a music stool that once belonged to Android Lloyd Webber. Can you imagine it? Android Lloyd Webber's very own music stool. (*Confidentially*) Mind you — I think it's a *fake*, myself. I sat on it for nearly an hour this afternoon and it never played a *note*. (*Remembering*) Still — I mustn't stand here gossiping. I'm supposed to be looking for more champagne. (*Glancing around uneasily*) I wish I'd brought a candle, though. I didn't expectorate it being *this* gloomy.

King enters L, *nervously*

King (*hopefully*) Is that *you*, Diphtheria? (*Relieved*) Oh, thank goodness I've found you. (*He hurries to the Dame*)
Dame (*alarmed*) Why? What's wrong?
King (*hastily*) Nothing. Nothing at all. It's just that it's so *dark* down here, I didn't like to think of a beautiful woman like *you* struggling to carry those heavy bottles.
Dame (*to the audience, delightedly*) Did you hear that, girls? He thinks I'm beautiful.
King (*nodding*) I have to admit it, Diphtheria. Drink makes you look quite *ravishing*.
Dame (*flattered*) Oooh, you old saucepot. (*Puzzled*) Hang on a minute, I haven't *been* drinking.

King No. But *I* have.

Dame (*disgusted*) Oh, shurrup and help me find the champagne. (*Glancing around*) It must be here *somewhere*. That nice Mr Giant said it was all in bottles with big red corks. (*Glancing* R) Oh, look. I can see one over there. (*She crosses* R *and reaches into the wings*)

Squire (*off*) Owwww.

The Dame recoils back C, *pulling the Squire on by his nose*

King (*surprised*) Sir Hugo.

Dame Nobody told me there were *rats* down here. (*She releases him*)

Squire (*furiously*) How *dare* you pinch my proboscis, you pop-eyed poltroon?

Dame (*grimly*) Never mind the *flattery*. Who invited *you*?

Squire (*haughtily*) If you *must* know, I'm delivering a special birthday present for my oldest and dearest friend, the Giant.

King But what are you doing in his wine cellar?

Squire (*caught out*) Well … I … Er … (*Thinking quickly*) I was just looking to see which wine he should *drink* with his present. It's a *fish*, you see. A very *expensive* kind of fish. (*Improvising*) In fact, it's the only fish in the world whose name begins with a K and ends with a K. (*He smirks*)

Dame (*puzzled*) No fish has a name that starts with a K and ends with a K.

Squire Yes they have. (*Smugly*) *Kilmarnock*.

King That's not the name of a *fish*.

Squire Yes it is. It's a pla(i)ce in Scotland. (*He preens*)

Dame (*glowering*) I don't know about *plaice*, but I *do* know he's not telling the truth — (*to the audience*) is he, boys and girls?

Audience response

I think we should take him upstairs and see what the *Giant* has to say.

King Good idea. (*Glancing around*) But which way do we go? It's so dark down here I can hardly see a thing.

Dame (*uneasily*) Me neither. But I know I turned a lot of corners.

King (*worried*) Oh, dear. Then it looks like we're lost.

Dame (*airily*) Well — there's no need to worry. As soon as they know we're missing, they'll come looking for us, won't they?

King But if they *don't*, we could be down here for ever. (*Nervously*) And who *knows* what's lurking in the shadows? There could even be *ghosts*.

Squire (*grandly*) Tommyrot and tarradiddle. There's no such thing as ghosts.

Dame (*firmly*) Oh, yes there *is*. You ask the manager of (*local café*). There's always ghosts trying to get in there. He/she's had to put a notice on the door. (*Declaiming*) "No spirits served in *this* café."

King And there's definitely a ghost in (*local public house*). It goes round all the bedrooms, moaning and groaning, with a ticket punch in its hand.

Dame (*remembering*) Oh, yes. I've heard about *that* one. It's an *inn* spectre. (*She looks scared*)

King The landlord asked me what I'd do if it came through *my* bedroom door. "Well," I said, "there's only one thing I could do. I'd run through the connecting door into the *next* room." "Oh, you can't do *that*," he said. "*Your* room hasn't got a connecting door into the next room."

Dame So what did you do?

King I asked him to mark the wall where he *wanted* one.

The Dame and the King chortle with glee

Squire (*unamused*) Bah. It's nonsense and tarradiddle. Even if ghosts *did* exist, it's easy enough to get rid of them. (*Smugly*) As every Internet user knows, ghosts hate singing. Just a few little notes and off they go, screaming in agony.

King Sounds like the listeners to (*local radio*).

Dame Well, in that case, while we're stood standing here waiting to be rescued, we'd better sing a song.

King Good idea. And while we're doing it, the boys and girls out there could tell us if they see anything *funny*. (*He grimaces*)

Squire (*balefully*) If they see anything funny on *this* stage, they'd better tell *tomorrow* night's audience.

Dame (*glowering at him then turning to the audience*) Will you do that for us? Give us a shout if you see something horrible hanging around?

Audience response

Right, then. All we've got to do now is decide what song to sing.

King How about "Daisy, Daisy"? It's my favourite song and everybody *here* knows it.

Dame (*enthusiastically*) Oh, yes. I like that one as well. Is everybody ready, then?

They sing

The Ghost enters L, *glides behind them and exits* R

The audience shout a warning; the singers falter and come to a halt

What are you shouting for? You've not *seen* something, have you?

Squire (*snootily*) Of course they haven't. There was nothing there to see.

King (*uncertainly*) I don't know about that. (*Indicating*) The little girl down there says *she* saw a ghost.

Dame (*shocked*) Oh, I say. (*To the audience*) Did anybody else see it?

Audience response. The Dame and the King look concerned

Squire (*sneering*) Well *I* didn't see one, so I'm just going to ignore them.
King (*to the Dame*) They could have made a *mistake*, couldn't they? Perhaps we should sing a little bit *more*?
Dame And perhaps a bit *louder*?

They sing again

   The Ghost enters R, *flits behind them and exits* L

The audience shouts. The singers fall silent again and glance nervously about

King (*to the Dame*) They've seen it again. They're going crackers.
Squire (*scornfully*) They were crackers to start with. Ignore the horrible little brats and they'll soon stop trying to frighten us.
Dame (*indignantly*) Less of the nasturtiums, you. They're all my friends, they are, and if they say there's a ghost, then I believe them.
King (*firmly*) And so do I. Perhaps we'd better look round?
Dame Good idea. (*She indicates* L) We'll go this way. Follow me.

To the accompaniment of creepy music, the trio tiptoe around in a wide circle, glancing around nervously

   As the Squire passes the entrance L, *the Ghost appears and tags on the end of the line. As the singing trio return to their original places, the Ghost slips off into the wings* R

(*Baffled*) Well I didn't see anything. (*To the others*) Did you?
King Not a thing.
Squire (*smugly*) What did I tell you? A complete waste of time.
Dame (*to the audience*) Are you sure you saw a ghost?

Audience response

King Perhaps we should look the other way? (*He indicates* R)
Squire (*annoyed*) Oh, very well, then. Follow me.

   They repeat their previous actions, the Ghost entering R *and tagging on behind the Dame and exiting* L *as the others resume their original positions*

(*To the Dame and the King*) You see? You see? Not a ghost in sight. (*To the audience*) Wash your mouths out for telling fibs, you disgusting little squirts. (*To the Dame and the King*) Now just ignore them and let's get on with our song.

They sing again

> *The Ghost enters* L, *and moves to stand behind the Squire. He taps the Squire on the shoulder. The Squire looks round and sees the Ghost, screams, and exits* L, *followed by the Ghost*

The Dame and the King stop singing

King (*startled*) What happened? (*Looking around*) Where's the Squire?
Dame (*baffled*) Must have gone for the last bus. (*Brightening*) Still — we don't need *him*, do we? If *his* voice was trained, they must have done it with a *whip*. We can do the song on our own. We'll be a cruet instead of a triplet.

They sing again, this time waving their arms from left to right, ending each movement with an upward flick of the fingers. After a few lines, the King "accidentally" hits the Dame on her cheek

> Owwww. (*She stops singing and touches her cheek*) You hit my cheek.
King (*aghast*) I'm *terribly* sorry. (*Anxiously*) Let me kiss it better.

The Dame's eyes sparkle as she inclines her face for him to kiss her cheek. After the kiss she turns away, simpering; the King hastily wipes his lips. They sing again as before and this time he "hits" her hand

Dame Owwww. You hit my hand. (*She holds her painful hand*)
King (*sincerely*) I *do* apologize. Let me kiss it better.

Simpering, the Dame extends her hand and the King kisses it. Again, the Dame turns away and the King wipes his lips. They sing again, but this time as the King continues with his arm movements, Dame turns her back to perform a few dance steps and he strikes her bottom

Dame Owwww. You hit my bottom. (*She rubs her painful bottom*)
King How dreadfully *clumsy* of me. Let me ——

The Dame coyly turns her bottom to the King

> —— move a bit further away. (*He does so*)

Dame (*to the audience, shrugging*) It was worth a try.

They sing again

> *The Ghost enters* L *and moves to the King, tapping him on the shoulder. The King turns, sees the Ghost, screams and runs off behind the Dame and exits* R, *followed by the Ghost. The Dame stops singing*

> (*Nervously*) Hieronymus? (*She looks round*) Ooo-er. He's gone as well. (*To the audience*) What's happened to him?

Audience response

> Oooo, I don't like it down here. All by meself in the dark. I'll have to sing on me own, now. (*Brightening*) Still — it's quality that counts, not quantity. I did all the solos in the church choir till I had to give it up. Well — I had a sore throat one week and couldn't sing a note — and the choirmaster thought they'd had the organ repaired. (*She sings again*)

> *The Ghost enters* R *and taps the Dame on the shoulder. The Dame turns to see the Ghost. The Ghost screams in terror and rushes off* R

The Dame looks at the audience in bewilderment

The Lights fade

SCENE 5

The Giant's Banqueting Hall

A vast, stone-built hall in medieval style. It is decorated with celebratory banners and brightly coloured balloons, etc.

When the scene begins, the lighting is warm and full. The Chorus are on stage in fancy dress and the party is in full swing

Song 14 (*Guests at the party*)

> *Giggles enters* R *and moves* C

Giggles (*calling*) Hallo, everybody.

Audience response. Giggles moves DS *to talk to the audience. The others fall into small groups and chat silently with animation and smiles*

(*Happily*) Oooh. What a party *this* is. I've just drunk eight bottles of Pepsi Cola and burped 7up. (*He chortles*) Mind you. I feel sorry for the Giant. He's hardly eaten a thing all day. His doctor's put him on a diet to make him lose weight. (*He grimaces*) "Oh," I said "I'd take no notice if I were you. They're *dangerous*, diets are." "Dangerous?" he said. "What are you talking about?" "Well," I said. "Didn't you hear what happened to (*well known fat man*) when *he* was told to lose weight? He went on one of those *crash* diets and ended up in *hospital*. (*He nods*) Crashed six cars, two lorries, and an ice-cream van." (*He chuckles*)

Corydon and the Princess enter UR

Corydon   Giggles. (*He moves to Giggles*) You've not seen Mother, have you?
Princess   (*following Corydon*) We can't find her *anywhere*.
Giggles   (*dismayed*) Oh, don't tell me *she's* gone peculiar as well.
Corydon   (*taken aback*) Peculiar?
Giggles   (*nodding*) Well … She was telling me about her *brother* this afternoon. When *he* got to her age, he went all strange and started thinking he was a *moth*. She was worried sick when he vanished one afternoon, but eleven o'clock that night she found him in (*local shop*).
Princess   What was he doing *there*?
Giggles   Somebody'd left a *light* on. (*He chortles*)
Corydon   (*patiently*) Well if you *do* happen to see her, try to make sure she's here when the Giant gets back.
Giggles   (*surprised*) Gets back??? I didn't know he'd *gone* anywhere.
Princess   He left the castle half an hour ago. He was so sorry about the trouble he'd caused, he wanted the children from the orphanage to come to his party too.
Corydon   Which is why he's set out for Tumbledown. To collect them all. They'll be here in the next few minutes.
Giggles   Oh. (*Thinking*) Well the last time *I* saw her she was playing cards in the kitchen. With the Giant's sausage-dog.
Princess   (*in disbelief*) It must be a very *clever* sausage-dog.
Giggles   I wouldn't say that. It's only beaten her *twice*. (*Brightly*) But don't worry. If we all look for her, we'll find her in no time. (*To the others*) Come on, everybody. Search the castle.

Giggles and the guests exit UR *and* UL

Princess   And *we'd* better find *Father*. We still haven't told him we want to get married.
Corydon   (*looking off* R) Here he comes now.

The King enters DR

King Ah, *there* you are, Marigold. It's getting late so I've e-mailed the Royal Coach to collect us. We must say goodbye to the Giant before it arrives. (*He heads for the exit* L) Come along, dear.

Princess (*surprised*) But we can't go *yet*, Father. We haven't told you the news. (*Happily*) We're going to be married.

Corydon (*quickly*) With your permission, of course.

King (*startled*) But ... But ... You *can't*. I mean ... It's out of the question. Absolutely impossible.

Princess (*dismayed*) Why not?

King (*unhappily*) Because of the missing *Prince*. They only made *me* King until they managed to find *him*. And to make sure there'd be a *real* king on the throne *some* day, I had to promise you'd marry no-one but a prince or king if they *didn't*. They wouldn't possibly let you marry a *commoner*.

Corydon and the Princess look dismayed

The Squire enters DL, *followed by Wrack and Ruin*

Squire (*firmly*) And quite right, too. We don't want peasants like *him* running the country.

Wrack No. You should let her marry *me*.

Squire (*surprised*) What? (*He glares at Wrack*)

Wrack Well, *I'm* a prince, aren't I?

Ruin How do you work that out?

Wrack Me *dad* told me. (*Proudly*) "If *you've* got a brain in that thick skull of yours," he said, "then *I'm* the King of England."

Ruin reacts, snatches off his hat and slaps Wrack with it

Squire (*to the King*) If you take *my* advice, Your Majesty, you'll banish this ragamuffin and his mother from Entertainia and send their snivelling little orphans with them. (*He smirks*)

Corydon and the Princess look shocked

Princess (*anxiously*) Don't *listen* to him, Father. They've done nothing *wrong*. (*Firmly*) And if they won't let me marry Corydon, then I'll *never* get married.

King (*despairingly*) Oh, Marigold. If I wasn't King, you could marry him *tomorrow*.

Corydon (*to the Princess*) This must be what that strange old woman meant. What are we going to *do*?

Squire (*smirking*) You can pack your bags and leave the country at once. (*He indicates that Corydon should leave* R)

The Dame and Giggles enter DR

Dame (*grimly*) Not so fast, tricky-knickers. You can keep your marching orders to yourself. If *I* marry the King, that'll *make* my Corydon a prince. (*To the King*) Take me. I'm yours. (*She flings herself at him*)

The Squire looks dismayed. Corydon and the Princess look hopeful

King (*releasing himself*) But I *can't* marry you, Diphtheria. The same rule applies to *me*. I can only marry a member of a royal family.

The Squire brightens and the others react appropriately

Giggles (*to the Dame*) Oh, Diphtheria … If only you were an old queen.
Dame (*to an audience member*) One word out of *you* and there'll be *trouble*.

Tapioca enters DR, *in a fluster*

Tapioca So sorry I'm late. It took me *ages* to wrap the Giant's present and — (*he stands open-mouthed*) Diphtheria.
Dame (*staring at Tapioca*) Tapioca?
Squire (*glaring at Tapioca*) Who's this?
Dame Me late husband's best friend, and the feller that made me shoes for the wedding.
Tapioca (*surprised*) *Late* husband? You mean — he's no longer with us?
Dame (*shaking her head; sadly*) Buried these last eighteen years and never even *saw* his little boy. (*She indicates Corydon*) Oooh, I can't tell you how much I *miss* him. He was just like a little wood fire. (*She blinks back tears*)
Tapioca (*understandingly*) All warm and comforting?
Dame No. If I didn't keep an *eye* on him, he went out.
King (*excitedly*) Never mind all that. I've just *thought* of something. If Tapioca tells us where the missing prince is, perhaps we can persuade him to come back to Entertainia and take over the kingdom. That way, *I* can go back to being Lord Chamberlain, and Marigold can marry Corydon.

Corydon and the Princess look hopeful

Princess (*to Tapioca*) Oh, please, *please* tell us, Tapioca.
Tapioca (*giving in*) Well … There's no point in keeping it a secret any longer. When he ran away from the palace, he changed his name and went to live in a little village called Tumbledown. *That's* where he stayed for the rest of his life, and *that's* where he married Diphtheria.

Everyone reacts

Dame (*dazed*) Me? You mean *my* little Marmaduke was the King of
Entertainia?
Corydon (*in disbelief*) And you were the *Queen*?
King (*delightedly*) Not *were*. As Marmaduke's widow, *she still is*.
Giggles (*nodding*) And not only *that*. It means Corydon's a *prince* and next
in line for the royal throne.

Everyone reacts in character

   Mother Goose enters R

Mother Goose (*beaming*) Now *here's* a turn-up for the books.
     The table's turned upon these crooks, (*she indicates the Squire, Wrack
     and Ruin*)
     In you they've met their match, and now
     The Royal Crown shall grace *your* brow.

The King hastily takes off his crown and extends it to the Dame

     In palace great, of golden hue,
     You'll reign. Not in a giant's *shoe*,
     But where each day is filled with laughter
     And all live happily ever after.
Dame (*embarrassed*) Oooh, I don't know. If I have to sit on the throne all
day, I'll not be able to look after my children, will I? (*Hopefully*) Can't I
just keep my lovely shoe-house and let *Corydon* do all the ruling?

The King at once offers the crown to Corydon

Mother Goose (*smiling*) If that solution you prefer,
     With you, I'll *cheerfully* concur.
     (*To Corydon*) So take the crown with princely pride
     And kiss your future blushing bride.

Corydon takes the crown

   Calumnia enters DL *in a green follow spot*

All but Mother Goose react

Giggles Blimey. It's (*well-known and unpopular female*).
Calumnia (*snarling*) Enough. It's time to play my ace,
     Bring gloom and doom upon your race.
     Turn ev'ry friend into a foe
     And fill your lives with grief and woe.

Dame Too late, love. Tony Blair (*or other unpopular politician*)'s been
    doing that for years.
Calumnia (*furiously*) Silence, foul-faced, ancient hag,
    Before your mouth I firmly gag.
Dame (*indignantly*) I beg your puddin'. Who are *you* calling foul-faced? I
    was the prettiest girl in Tumbledown, I was. My parents had me kidnapped
    twice a year just to get my picture in the (*local newspaper*).

Calumnia takes a sudden step towards the Dame and she hastily retreats

Calumnia (*snarling*) Now bid farewell to carefree hours
    And feel the force of witch's powers. (*She cackles in triumph and raises
    her arms to cast a spell*)

The mortals cower

Mother Goose (*chuckling*) No need to quake and shake with fear.
    Had you forgotten? *I'm* still here.
    Such foolish threats I've *often* heard.
    And take my word, they're *quite* absurd.
    I'll teach you all a little trick
    To deal with witches, double-quick.
    Just point your finger at them, so …
    (*She points her finger at Calumnia*)
    Then laugh out loud and watch them go.
Calumnia (*dismayed*) They wouldn't *dare*. (*Looking wildly around*) It's all
    a lie.
Dame (*firmly*) We'll soon find out. It's worth a *try*.

*Everyone points at Calumnia and begins to laugh. Calumnia shrieks and
staggers, covering her ears*

Giggles (*to the audience*) Come on, everybody. Give us a hand.

The audience join in. The chorus enters and adds to the laughter

Calumnia finally staggers off L

The follow spot goes off

Everyone congratulates each other

Mother Goose (*beaming*) With danger well and truly passed,
    The new King claims his throne at last,
    And wedding bells, if I'm not wrong,
    Will sound across his land ere long.
    So *home* let's shortly make our way

To greet the joyful Wedding Day.
(*She gaily waves her wooden spoon*)

Song 15 (*Full company*)

There is general celebration

Swift Black-out

SCENE 6

Back home in Entertainia

A lane scene

When the scene begins the stage is fully lit

Giggles enters

Giggles (*calling*) Hallo, everybody.

Audience response

Oooh, I did enjoy myself at the Giant's party, but I'm glad I'm back home
again. Well — there's a lot to do, isn't there? What with everybody getting
ready for the wedding. Now she's got her shoe-house back and the Giant's
given her all that gold, Queen Diphtheria's buying new clothes for the
orphans, King Cole — sorry — *Lord Chamberlain* Cole is teaching the
Fiddlers Three how to play the wedding march, and even the Squire's
turned over a new leaf. Not that it's done him much good. He went out
shopping for a wedding present and the police arrested him for doing it too
early. It was twenty past two in the morning and the shop was shut. Oooh,
and you'll never guess what. I've just had a word with the vicar and he's
told me why bells ring when somebody gets married. (*To someone in the
audience*) I bet *you* don't know, do you? (*He grins*) It's because they have
bell ringers pulling the ropes. But I mustn't waste time. The reason I've
come out here's to invite you all to the wedding. Would you like that?
Would you? The only thing is — half the church choir are poorly. They've
all got *Alice*. You know? The same thing Christopher Robin went down
with. But anyway — I thought that seeing as *you're* all going to be there,
you could help with the singing. (*To an audience member*) It's no use
looking for the way out. We've got the doors locked. (*Brightly*) Now what
we're going to do is: *I'm* going to sing a little song, and after I've finished,

I want to see if you can sing it back to me at the top of your voices — 'cos
it's a very big church and we want to make sure everybody can hear you.
So are you ready?

Audience response

If you're not, you'll be here all night.

Song sheet routine

Song 16 (*Giggles*)

*As the final verse is being sung by the audience, Giggles waves goodbye
and exits, leaving them to finish*

At the end of the song, there is a Black-out

SCENE 7

The Royal Palace of Entertainia

A glittering ballroom scene with an ornate central staircase

*When the scene begins, the stage is fully lit. Palace guards are dancing to a
lively tune*

When the dance ends, the troupe divides, half exiting L, *half* R

The finale walkdown commences to another lively tune, in this order:

Babes
Juniors
Palace guards
Bo-Peep and Boy Blue
Tapioca
Mother Goose and Calumnia
Squire
Wrack and Ruin
King Cole (as Chamberlain)
Giggles
The Dame (as Queen)
Corydon and Marigold

Princess Our pantomime is over. It's time to say good-night.
Corydon And as in all *good* fairy tales, each wrong's been put to right.
Giggles So till we meet again next year, there's nothing left to do ——
Dame But hope you've all enjoyed the tale
All Of the Woman who Lived in a Shoe.

There is a reprise of a "celebration" song previously used in the show

CURTAIN

FURNITURE AND PROPERTY LIST

ACT I

PROLOGUE

On stage: Crystal ball for **Calumnia**

Personal: **Mother Goose**: wooden spoon (carried throughout)

SCENE 1

Off stage: Large envelope affixed with wax seal (**Squire**)
Bundle of twigs (**Corydon**)
Shopping basket containing battered book (**Dame**)
Hopsack bag (**Giggles**)

SCENE 2

Personal: Purse containing pound coin (**Dame**)
Five pound note (**Squire**)

SCENE 3

On stage: Easel. *On it*: blackboard with piece of white chalk and duster
Teacher's desk or lectern. *Hanging from it*: slapstick
Two or three benches
Shorter bench with only two supports

Off stage: Crumpled paper balls, paper aeroplanes, etc. (**Children**)
Large hand-bell (**Dame**)
Large sugar lollipop (**Wrack**)
Large catapult (**Ruin**)

SCENE 4

No additional props

SCENE 5

On stage: Large water-butt

Off stage: Piece of paper with writing on it (**Wrack**)

ACT II

S<small>CENE</small> 1

Off stage: Small hammer (**Tapioca**)
                 Sword (**Corydon**)
                 Wicker shopping basket covered with cloth (**Dame**)

Personal: **Tapioca**: tiny spectacles

S<small>CENE</small> 2

No additional props

S<small>CENE</small> 3

On stage: Brightly wrapped gifts (**Chorus**)

Off stage: Glass or bottle of water (**Ruin**)

S<small>CENE</small> 4

No additional props

S<small>CENE</small> 5

No additional props

S<small>CENE</small> 6

Off stage: Song sheet (**Stage Management**)

LIGHTING PLOT

Practical fittings required: nil
Various interior and exterior settings

PROLOGUE

To open: Green, blue and red light

Cue 1	**Mother Goose** enters *White follow spot on* **Mother Goose**	(Page 1)
Cue 2	**Mother Goose** exits *Black-out*	(Page 2)

ACT I, SCENE 1

To open: General exterior lighting; bright, sunny morning effect

Cue 3	**Corydon** and the **Dame** exit *Dim lights*	(Page 8)
Cue 4	**Calumnia** enters *Green follow spot on* **Calumnia**	(Page 8)
Cue 5	**Calumnia** exits *Cut follow spot and brighten lights to opening setting*	(Page 9)
Cue 6	Muffled thud from bass drum *Dim lights during following action*	(Page 13)
Cue 7	Unmuffled thud *Dim lights further*	(Page 14)
Cue 8	Everyone cries out in panic *Black-out*	(Page 14)
Cue 9	The shoe replaces the orphanage *Return to opening setting*	(Page 14)
Cue 10	**Song 3** ends *Black-out*	(Page 15)

ACT I, Scene 2

To open: Darkness

Cue 11   When ready   (Page 15)
            Green follow spot UL *on* **Calumnia**

Cue 12   **Calumnia** exits L   (Page 15)
            Cut follow spot; bring up general exterior lighting

Cue 13   The **Princess** and **Corydon** exit R   (Page 21)
            Fade lights to black-out

ACT I, Scene 3

To open: General interior lighting

Cue 14   The **Squire** is tipped to the ground   (Page 31)
            Rapid fade to black-out

ACT I, Scene 4

To open: General exterior lighting

Cue 15   **Calumnia** enters   (Page 32)
            Green follow spot L *on* **Calumnia**

Cue 16   **Calumnia** exits   (Page 32)
            Cut follow spot

Cue 17   **Corydon** and the **Princess** exit   (Page 33)
            Rapid fade to black-out

ACT I, Scene 5

To open: General exterior lighting

Cue 18   The **Squire**: " … of turning the tables."   (Page 35)
            Green follow spot L *on Calumnia*

Cue 19   **Calumnia** exits L   (Page 35)
            Cut follow spot

Cue 20   Heavy drum-thud   (Page 37)
            Fade lights during following action

ACT II, SCENE 1

To open: General exterior lighting; daylight

ACT II, SCENE 2

To open: General exterior lighting, subdued but not frightening

ACT II, SCENE 3

To open: General exterior lighting

ACT II, Scene 4

To open: Gloomy interior lighting

Cue 33	The **Ghost** exits; the **Dame** looks at the audience *Fade to black-out*	(Page 64)

ACT II, Scene 5

To open: General interior lighting; warm and full

Cue 34	**Corydon** takes the crown *Green follow-spot on* **Calumnia** DL	(Page 68)
Cue 35	**Calumnia** staggers off L *Snap off follow spot*	(Page 69)
Cue 36	**Song 15** ends. General celebration *Swift black-out*	(Page 70)

ACT II, Scene 6

To open: General exterior lighting

Cue 37	**Song 16** ends *Black-out*	(Page 71)

ACT II, Scene 7

To open: General interior lighting

No cues

EFFECTS PLOT

ACT I

Cue 1   The stage plunges into total darkness   (Page 14)
          Great crash

ACT II

No cues

Consumer behaviour in China

Consumer Research and Policy Series
Edited by Gordon Foxall

Consumer behaviour in China

Customer satisfaction and cultural values

Oliver H. M. Yau

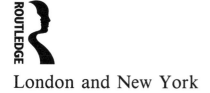

London and New York

First published 1994
by Routledge
11 New Fetter Lane, London EC4P 4EE

Simultaneously published in the USA and Canada
by Routledge
29 West 35th Street, New York, NY 10001

Typeset in Times by
Mathematical Composition Setters Ltd, Salisbury, Wiltshire
Printed in Great Britain by
T.J. Press (Padstow) Ltd, Padstow Cornwall

British Library Cataloguing in Publication Data
A catalogue reference for this book is available from the British Library.

ISBN 0-415-00436-5

Library of Congress Cataloging in Publication Data
Yau, Oliver H. M., 1946-
    Consumer behaviour in China : customer satisfaction and cultural
values / Oliver H. M. Yau.
        p. cm. – (Consumer research and policy series)
    Includes bibliographical references and index.
    ISBN 0-415-00436-5
    1. Consumer behavior – China. 2. Consumer satisfaction – China.
I. Title. II. Series.
HF5415.33.C6Y38   1992
658.8′342′0951 – dc20   92-33019
                                                              CIP

Contents

List of figures

List of tables

Preface

Most things when not at peace will sound. Plants and trees have no voice, but rustled by the wind they sound. Water has no voice, but ruffled by the wind it sounds, splashing, when struck, gathering speed when obstructed, and seething when heated. Metal and stone have no voice, but when beaten they sound. And human utterances are the same: men speak out when forced to it. If they long for something, they sing; if they are sad, they weep. Sound passes their lips whenever they are not at peace. . . .
Translated from *A Farewell of Meng Chiao* which was originally written in classical Chinese by Han Yu in the Tang Dynasty.

Comparatively speaking, consumer behaviour is a new discipline, but Chinese consumers are not new at all. China has a history of several thousand years and its civilization is regarded as one of the oldest in the world. Since Fu Hsi (2852 BC), the inventor of Chinese writing, the behaviour of Chinese has been prolifically recorded in books such as the *Five Classics*, the *Four Books*, and the *Three Words*. However, it is only since the early 1980s that Chinese consumer behaviour has begun to receive greater attention and has been studied systematically as a sub-discipline of Chinese psychology in the four huge Chinese communities: the People's Republic of China, Hong Kong, Taiwan and Singapore. The emergence of this endeavour is a result of the re-opening of the enormous China market since 1978, together with China's recently fast economic growth. However, in developing Chinese consumer behaviour as a marketing-related discipline, we have faced stumbling blocks that refrain us from moving forward at a quicker pace than we intend. First, we have found, not to our surprise, that information about Chinese consumer behaviour in Chinese classics is very much fragmented. Thus, much work is needed to collate, to classify and to analyse. Second, most information on Chinese consumer behaviour is not empirical in nature and therefore generalisation drawn from this information would be difficult. With drastic political changes in China during the past two centuries, some cast doubt as to whether traditional Chinese values described in the classics still prevail in Chinese societies. However, this doubt has urged us to examine seriously our approach to the study of Chinese consumer behaviour. Professor K. S. Yang of the National Taiwan University has advocated the 'localisation' of the study of social science (Yang and Hwang 1991). On several occasions, I have also pledged academics who are interested in Chinese marketing to conceptualise consumer behaviour in the Chinese culture context. In so doing, we can achieve three objectives. First, when we try to explain or predict Chinese consumer behaviour it can help in disentangling ourselves from blindly applying models and theories of consumer behaviour developed in the West (especially North America). Second, from a positive viewpoint, to contextualise Chinese consumer behaviour, we can benefit ourselves from better understanding the Chinese and how they behave as consumers. Therefore, we can effectively explain and predict the behaviour of Chinese consumers. Third, it can help us discover the real differences and similarities between Chinese and Western consumers so that we can identify human commonalities and cultural values that cause the differences.

This book is one of the attempts to achieve the above objectives. It focuses on Chinese cultural values and their impact on consumer satisfaction and other related variables. We are at the infancy stage of contextualising Chinese consumer behaviour as we need at least two or three decades to have our collective effort begin to bear fruits. As the Chinese proverb says, 'Casting a brick to draw in a jade piece', I would like the readers to treat this book as a 'brick' (something worthless) and therefore I expect to draw in many 'jade pieces' (valuable comments) from the readers in the future. I also hope that this book will serve as a catalyst to stimulate more research projects and publications in Chinese marketing studies.

Many persons are deserving of mention for their association with this book. I am grateful to Professor Kenneth Simmonds of the London Business School for his valuable comments on an earlier model of the study, to Professor Graham Hooley of Aston Business School and Professor Gordon Foxall of Birmingham University for their continuing interest in the research, and for their valuable suggestions and criticisms.

I am also very grateful to Ms Suk-ching Ho and Mr Leo Sin, my good friends at the Chinese University of Hong Kong for their continuing encouragement.

Sincere appreciation is extended to Mr Archie Man, the Managing Director of Marketing Decision Research Ltd and his colleagues for their professional assistance in the fieldwork and to the Institute of Hong Kong Studies, the Chinese University of Hong Kong, for the financial support to purchase the ball-pens and the mini-cassette players used in the research.

Thanks are due to Mr Ray Offord and Ms Rebecca Garland, copy editor and desk editor respectively of Routledge, for their patience and professional assistance with the manuscript and to Ms Meredith Lawley and Ms Jannelle McPhail for reading the manuscript. I, however, take full responsibility for any errors found in the book.

Lastly, I would like to express my deepest gratitude and love to my wife, Julie. Marrying a bookish and absent-minded academic is an ordeal that many women would find hard to endure. Not only has she turned this ordeal into a satisfying undertaking through her patience and affection, but enlightened her husband with unceasing encouragements, and the required perseverance to complete this book. She has shown all virtues of a Chinese woman. To express my appreciation and respect for her, I would like to dedicate this book to Julie and my two little daughters, Joanna and Rosena, with deep affection and devoted love.

Oliver Hon Ming Yau
Professor of Marketing
Faculty of Business
University of Southern Queensland
January 1993

1 Introduction

This book describes a study which considers the effects of Chinese cultural values, use situations and other determinants on consumer satisfaction/dissatisfaction. In this introductory chapter five main areas of interest are considered. First, the significance of consumer satisfaction and dissatisfaction for research is outlined. Second, the reason why the study was conducted in one cultural context is explained. Third, the objectives of the study are discussed. Fourth, consideration is given to the limitations of the study. Finally, the organization of the remaining chapters is presented.

THE SIGNIFICANCE OF CONSUMER SATISFACTION AND DISSATISFACTION

Most modern marketers agree that the primary goal of the firm is to satisfy customers' needs and wants at a profit. Yet today consumer discontent appears to be of particular interest. Evidence has been found that there is a high level of dissatisfaction with some products, such as automobiles, electrical appliances and photographic equipment (Hong Kong Consumer Council 1977, 1979; Day and Bodur 1977). At the same time, there seems to exist a loss of consumer confidence in both the marketplace and the marketer (Greyser and Diamond 1974). There are different viewpoints which try to explain why consumers are discontented. Some writers point out that consumers' expectations of product quality in general have been steadily rising, owing to the increasing income and sociological forces which prompted high expectations of a better life style (e.g. Jones and Gardner 1976). This can result in a discrepancy between expectation and perceived product performance and lead to consumer dissatisfaction. From a different angle, Jones (1975) attributed the causes of consumer discontent to the negligent attitude of business and government. She stated:

> Problems of consumer dissatisfaction are not with the economic system itself, nor with its essential capability to respond to the needs and desires of individuals in our society. They lie rather with the failures of both business and government to perceive that needs and desires of consumers have changed drastically over the past decades, partly because of many technological and service developments and partly because of the impact of these technological developments on the livability of our cities, on the survival of our environment and on our overall ability to enjoy the quality of life that our material abundance was designed to produce.
>
> (Jones 1975: 127)

There is evidence that the level of consumer dissatisfaction seems to be rising. Consumer complaint has been regarded as an objective measure of consumer dissatisfaction (McNeal 1969; Cavusgil and Kaynak 1982). In many places of the world, there has been a record of an increase in the volume of consumer complaints in recent years. According to the Hong Kong Consumer Council (1977, 1979), which receives consumer correspondence and complaints, the number of complaints recorded per thousand population was 0.97 in 1977 and 1.3 in 1979 (Smith, 1982: 205). This implies an increase of almost 34 per cent over two years. In the United Kingdom, the number recorded was 10.58 per thousand population in 1977 and 11.34 in 1979 (Smith 1982: 205). While the rate of increase in the number of complaints in the United Kingdom was smaller, the total number of complaints per thousand population is about nine times that of Hong Kong. There are two possible explanations for the increase in consumer complaints. The first explanation is that consumers are now more sensitive to irritating business practices. They have learned how to protest their rights and are therefore more prone to complain than they were before. The second explanation is that there has been a higher level of consumer dissatisfaction as reflected by consumer complaints. In the case of Hong Kong, the Consumer Council has been criticized as a dummy organization because of its lack of judicial power (*Hong Kong News Digest* 1984). In a study concerning consumerism in Hong Kong (Hung and Leung 1977), the majority of respondents failed to identify the functions of the Consumer Council. Furthermore, about one-third of the respondents had no knowledge of the Council. Hence, it seems that the second explanation would be highly likely to provide the potential answer to the increase in consumer complaints.

The consequences of consumer satisfaction/dissatisfaction are salient to business, government and consumers. At the business level, satisfaction is seen as a dimension of market performance (Czepiel and Rosenberg 1977b). Increasing consumer satisfaction may mean a growth of long-term as well as short-term sales, and of market share as a result of repeat purchasing.

The trends towards a high level of consumer dissatisfaction indicate a rather difficult future for business. Business faces an increased threat through four sources: consumerist actions, government interventions, competitors' reactions and substitutes of new entries into the market. Consumer dissatisfaction can help business identify weak spots of products which have fallen below consumer and government standards. Hence, modifications can be made to improve the products to prevent future interventions. In this age of discontinuity and turbulence, consumer satisfaction can show the direction which business firms should follow if they want to survive. Furthermore, consumer satisfaction can help business strengthen the competitive position of products through segmentation.

At the government level, the concept of consumer satisfaction can help identify and isolate those products and industries where government action is desirable to enhance consumer welfare. Furthermore, the concept can also be of great value for government consumer protection agencies when planning consumer education and information programmes. Government consumer protection agencies have different motivations from those of business towards consumer satisfaction. The goal of government in studying consumer satisfaction is to improve social welfare. For example, in the United States, some of the earliest studies in consumer satisfaction were conducted by research consultants of the Department of Agriculture to develop an index of consumer satisfaction on products as a supplement to the consumer price index (Pratt 1972; Pfaff *et al.* 1972, 1975).

Finally, consumers are interested in the notion of consumer satisfaction to obtain better information about how satisfied or dissatisfied others have been with products. Usually laws are founded on the ground of 'buyer beware' (Fulop 1979; Greyser and Diamond 1974). This means that consumers are at their own risk and therefore must be very careful in choosing products/services. With more information, consumers could improve their life by avoiding hazardous experiences and by making wise decisions about products under consideration.

Although the issue of consumer satisfaction and dissatisfaction has been of interest to all three parties in the marketplace, academic interest in the topic seems to be just starting to gain momentum. The concept of consumer satisfaction is not new. However, the emergence of consumer satisfaction as an operational concept has only been a matter of the mid-1970s. It is not surprising therefore to see conflicting points of view, and different interpretations of observed results can be found in the literature on consumer satisfaction/ dissatisfaction. At present, there are several aspects on which marketing academics may contribute to knowledge of consumer satisfaction/dissatisfaction.

Conceptualization. Academics have to bring about an interpretation of ideas and approaches to form a theoretical framework of consumer satisfaction/dissatisfaction. They can also help increase the understanding of what are the determinants of consumer satisfaction and what results are caused by it.

Measurement. Academics can help disentangle the typically action-oriented surrogates of satisfaction such as sales, market share, brand loyalty and complaint letters, etc., from a more direct and objective measure of consumer satisfaction. For example, this is specially true given the Chinese tendency to a very low propensity to complain, and therefore the number of complaints about a certain product may not be a good measure of consumer dissatisfaction. Furthermore, more valid and reliable measures have to be identified and tested from the existing work, or have to be developed according to a well-defined concept of satisfaction. It is not surprising that some recent studies have approached the direct measurement of consumer satisfaction from the perspective of psychology, economics and utility theory (Sirgy 1982; Valle and Wallendorf 1977; Maddox 1981; Braden 1979; Pfaff *et al.* 1972; Huppertz 1979).

Applications. Based on consumer satisfaction, academics can develop effective policies and strategies for the products and the market segments concerned. Attempts have been made in some specific areas, such as markets for the elderly, retail stores, supermarkets, product warranties, and pricing, to secure more pragmatic information for business decision making (Ash *et al.* 1980; Mason and Bearden 1979; Hughes 1977b; Hager and Handy 1979; Aiello and Czepiel 1979). Furthermore, academics are in a better position to objectively conduct research and analyse the approaches used by government and business because they are in a more independent position and therefore tend not to be influenced by institutional goals and pressures.

IMPORTANCE OF CONDUCTING A STUDY IN A SPECIFIC SETTING

In the last decade, international business research has changed more drastically than ever before. The focus of attention has been shifting from North America to Western Europe and the Asia–Pacific region. This can be seen from an increasing number of journals and articles published during the past ten years.

The literature on consumer satisfaction has its roots in American culture. The literature largely tends to disregard fundamental cross-cultural variations which would probably make the process of consumer satisfaction different in other cultures. In order to achieve a perspective on consumer satisfaction/dissatisfaction, there is an urgent need to conduct research in specific cultural settings so that similarities or differences among cultures can be found and compared.

Recently, there have been several incidences in the literature on consumer behaviour which strongly support this point of view. Most important of all, Engel (1985a) confessed in an international conference that his model has not worked well.[1] Engel (1985b) perceived that models and perspectives developed in North America suffer to a great extent from lack of cross-cultural validity. Any generalization from them can be a fatal trap. He also warned that direct transplantation of these models and perspectives to other cultures without considering their relevance is extremely dangerous, because people in different cultures have different world views and individual choices are affected by very complex social influences or situations. Hence, there is a genuine need to return to basic premises and to contextualize consumer behaviour. Contextualization is the process by which marketing strategies are designed to be culturally relevant and meaningful, taking account of differences in consumer motivation and behaviour. To contextualize, it is advisable not to accept completely the standardized approach by consumer researchers in constructing models. Other approaches may yield more appropriate results. Further, researchers should go back to the philosophical and religious premises of life. In each culture, there is a rich literature on values which reflect these premises of life. Such values have received little consideration in consumer research, and might have been uncovered by research done culturally and cross-culturally. Unless these values are first investigated, consumer research will be hard pressed to explain why people of different cultures behave the way they do.

On the same occasion, Sheth (1985a) agreed with what Engel said. He suggested that it is crucial to focus on comparative consumer behaviour so as to pinpoint the relative perceptions and behaviour of the market rather than absolute perceptions and behaviour (1985b). Therefore, to expect 'global consumer behaviour' research and theory to emerge, it is necessary first to understand consumer behaviour in each individual culture, so that comparisons may be made.

Two decades ago, similar suggestions were made by Triandis (1974), who suggested a start by conducting cross-cultural research in a particular cultural group so as not to miss out any variables particularly relevant to that culture. This is exactly what Engel (1985b) has proposed when constructing consumer behaviour models.

Conducting consumer research in a specific setting can contribute greatly to our knowledge of 'global consumer behaviour'. It is, in fact, a basic but mandatory step if generalization is to be made later when cross-cultural comparisons become feasible. Realizing the importance of returning to basic premises and of contextualizing consumer behaviour, this study attempts to build the first consumer satisfaction model which incorporates the values of a particular culture, use situations in a highly Chinese context, and other determinants of consumer satisfaction.

OBJECTIVES OF THE STUDY

This study has two objectives. The first objective is to draw together the various directions of theory and research in the study of determinants of consumer satisfaction/dissatisfaction by (1) developing a comprehensive model which conceptually ties all these determinants together and (2) testing the hypothesized causal links between determinants in the model. Previous research on consumer satisfaction has not attempted to construct a comprehensive model which includes cultural values, situations, and experiences, etc., as potential determinants of consumer satisfaction. This study attempts to make a contribution to the literature of consumer satisfaction/dissatisfaction by providing a better understanding of the concept, giving directions for future research, and offering recommendations for international marketing managers in making consumer policy decisions. Whereas other research has focused on building models to identify determinants of consumer satisfaction, few have employed scientific sampling procedures necessary for meaningful results. In their attempt to test relationships between determinants of consumer satisfaction both Churchill and Surprenant (1982) and Wilton and Tse (1983) employed convenience sampling methods to recruit respondents. In addition, in the latter's case, a small sample size which was not sufficient to satisfy the assumption of normality for the analytical techniques adopted was used. In these cases where less defined procedures were used the results of these efforts and the subsequent interpretation may be spurious. To improve the credibility of the findings, in this study, a probability sample provided by the Census and Statistics Department of Hong Kong is employed.

The second objective is to construct a valid and reliable scale to measure Chinese cultural values, which is regarded as a component of the model. Other instruments have been adopted to identify Chinese cultural values. However, none of these instruments was specifically designed for Chinese culture or Eastern culture, nor have they followed sound methodological procedures necessary for meaningful results. For example, Bond (1985) has attempted to measure Chinese cultural values by judgmental procedures and the use of student samples, in deference to methodological procedures for the development of his instrument. With knowledge of the shortcomings of previous research in the area of consumer satisfaction, this research concerns itself with the methodological consideration established by precedents in scale development in other disciplines. Furthermore, an attempt is also made to investigate the underlying dimensions of Chinese cultural values and their linkages with consumer expectations and satisfaction.

LIMITATIONS OF THE STUDY

A first attempt to build a comprehensive model of consumer satisfaction which incorporates Chinese cultural values, situations, product categories, experiences and other determinants of consumer satisfaction is inevitably subject to certain limitations, although efforts have been made to make the research as rigorous as possible.

The first limitation concerns the place where the Chinese cultural value scale is developed. In the study, the scale is tested and found to be valid and reliable for the Chinese population of Hong Kong. Since cultural values are a sort of terminal value which change little over time, the scale should still be valid and reliable when applied to Chinese in mainland China. However, in recent years, China has undergone a drastic change towards modernization which will probably lead to changes in cultural values. Hence, it is necessary to further test the scale if generalizations are to be made.

Another limitation deals with the identification of the dimensions of the Chinese cultural values. In the conceptualization of Chinese cultural values, there are still cultural values that authors in the past and at present have divergent opinions on. Since there is no previous empirical evidence as a guide, the generation of items for the scale using common sayings could be, therefore, an overspecification or underspecification of the actual domain of the Chinese cultural values.

The third limitation deals with the choice of products. In the study, only consumer durable and non-durable products are involved. No consideration was given to industrial products and services. However, the researcher has been aware of this limitation and therefore no implications are adduced with respect to industrial products or services.

A further limitation is related to the experiment used in the research, which has tried to simulate a pre-purchase/consumption and post-purchase/consumption experience for respondents in the study. In fact, respondents did not actually purchase and use the products. The elapse time between the expectation manipulations and the collection of the dependent measures was limited. Respondents tried the products and evaluated them on the assumption that the products had been purchased and used for some time. Therefore, the experiment may not necessarily portray a real purchase situation in which respondents might have the necessary learning whereby satisfaction with the use of the products could be experienced. Hence, satisfaction measures may be confounded with attitudinal measures (Churchill and Surprenant 1982). Given these limitations, this study has taken consideration of their presence. These limitations have prompted the study to proceed so as to minimize or avoid possible errors.

STRUCTURE OF THE BOOK

In Chapter 2 the nature of consumer satisfaction/dissatisfaction is first explored. The literature dealing with the conceptualization of consumer satisfaction/dissatisfaction is surveyed, followed by a discussion of research investigating factors influencing consumer satisfaction/dissatisfaction. The chapter is concluded with a discussion of how a model can be built on previous research.

Based on the survey of the literature on consumer satisfaction/dissatisfaction, a structural model of consumer satisfaction and Chinese cultural values is proposed. Chapter 3 contains the main theoretical part of the work. With respect to each theoretical dimension of Chinese cultural values, potential marketing implications are presented. Each component of the model as well as related hypotheses are presented and discussed.

In Chapter 4, the methods of collecting empirical data for testing the model and hypotheses are discussed in parallel with the problems related to measurement instruments. Results of the pilot survey are also presented and discussed.

Chapter 5 contains the analyses used in constructing the Chinese cultural value scale and testing the model and hypotheses. The chapter can be divided into five parts. The first part looks into the measure reliability of multi-item measures. The second part is the construction of the Chinese cultural value scale and the investigation of underlying dimensions of Chinese cultural values by means of factor analysis. The third part examines the two-way relationships between variables. Further, an attempt to evaluate product manipulation and situation effects is described. Finally, the whole model and the hypothesized links between determinants of consumer satisfaction/dissatisfaction are tested by the analysis of covariance structure.

The concluding chapter serves to summarize the research, and draw conclusions based on the results against the hypotheses and objectives of the study. It also offers implications and recommendations for further research.

NOTE

[1] This statement has not been confirmed by James Engel. However, the author and his colleagues have a record of the statement 'has not worked well' on the same occasion.

2 Consumer satisfaction and dissatisfaction

In this chapter, three main areas of interest are discussed. First, the conceptualization of consumer satisfaction/dissatisfaction. Second, a review of the literature associated with consumer satisfaction/dissatisfaction and its influencing variables is presented. Third, details are given of how this book builds on previous research in the area of consumer satisfaction/dissatisfaction. Therefore, this chapter consists of three parts which aim to answer the following questions:

1 What is consumer satisfaction/dissatisfaction?
2 What are the variables in the literature which have been shown to affect consumer satisfaction/dissatisfaction?
3 How can previous research be built upon?

WHAT IS CONSUMER SATISFACTION?

Before discussing the conceptualization of consumer satisfaction/dissatisfaction, it is useful to consider what is 'satisfaction' and how 'satisfaction' differs from 'attitude'. This section first considers this issue, followed by a discussion of the terms 'consumer satisfaction' and 'consumer dissatisfaction', and concludes with the definition that is used in this book.

Consumer satisfaction and consumer attitude

In order to reach a satisfactory definition of consumer satisfaction, it is necessary to distinguish between consumer satisfaction and attitude. There are quite a number of definitions of the term 'consumer satisfaction'; amongst the earliest, Howard and Sheth (1969) define consumer satisfaction as 'the buyer's cognitive state of being adequately or inadequately rewarded in a buying situation for the sacrifice he has undergone'. According to Miller (1977), consumer satisfaction results from the interaction of levels of expectation about anticipated performance and evaluations of perceived performance. From the marketing aspect, Andreasen (1977) stated:

> Business, government, and other nonprofit organizations need measures of how well products and services (performance) are meeting client needs and wants so that they can enhance their own and/or society's well-being. The extent to which these needs and wants are met has come to be called consumer satisfaction/ dissatisfaction. . . .

Though being different, these definitions implicitly contain four common elements (Day 1975):

1 The performance of the product or service as perceived by the consumer.
2 The expectations of performance which the consumer has.
3 The perceived costs or 'sacrifices' involved in making the purchase and using the product/service.
4 The time at which the satisfaction with the product/service is assessed.

It is not difficult to find definitions which consist of elements other than those listed above, because researchers usually define consumer satisfaction according to the theory which it explains. Fortunately, more recent theoretical and empirical work in consumer satisfaction (Andreasen 1977; Day 1977; Oliver 1977) generally agree that satisfaction results from a subjective comparison of expected and perceived product attribute levels, as originally proposed by Howard and Sheth (1969), and Engel *et al.* (1968). Even so, the implicit meaning of satisfaction still remains in dispute. Different interpretations in the conceptualization of consumer satisfaction will be the subject of the next section.

Triandis (1971), summarizing central ideas used by other attitude theorists, defined attitude as 'an idea charged with emotion which predisposes a class of actions to a particular class of social situations'. His definition suggests the three principal components of attitudes:

1 The cognitive component is the IDEA which a person, as an evaluator, perceives in a given context.
2 The affective component is the EMOTION which charges the idea so that a person has positive affect (like) or negative affect (dislike) toward an object.

3 The behavioural (or conative) component is the PREDISPOSI-
   TION TO ACTION, such as shopping at a department store,
   buying a shirt or hiring a car.

These components are equivalent to the concepts of perception,
preference and behavioural intention respectively which were mentioned by Fishbein and Ajzen (1975) and other psychologists.

Many researchers (Miller 1977; Pfaff 1977; Oliver 1977, 1981;
Czepiel and Rosenberg 1977a) agree that satisfaction, to a great
extent, is analogous to attitude. Especially, Pfaff (1977) suggested that
consumer satisfaction can be denoted, in part, by all components of
attitudes. The cognitive component indicates the confirmation or disconfirmation of expectation and performance of the product; the
affective component indicates whether the consumer is satisfied or dissatisfied with the product; and the conative component, whether to
stop or arouse future purchases in post-purchase situations. Therefore, satisfaction is not only an attitude, it is a richer concept than attitude. The following paragraphs discuss the differences between
satisfaction and attitude.

First, consumer satisfaction is more experience-specific than attitude. It is difficult to report the change in attitude before and after the
purchase/experience. Satisfaction is more sensitive to such changes, as
consumers are cognitively ready to reflect their satisfaction with
products/services in every purchase or use experience. This response
is natural, and a possible explanation is that the consumers are cognitively rehearsing their expectation as a comparison standard which is
more readily available for comparison than attitude. Hence, after the
experience, performance is immediately evaluated for comparison.

Furthermore, satisfaction may change by itself independently of
any additional stimulus which motivates a change. Results of the
experiments in dissonance theory, equity theory and contrast theory
conducted by Anderson (1973), Austin and Walster (1974) and
Olshavsky and Miller (1972) respectively all show that this characteristic of satisfaction exists.

Second, consumer satisfaction involves post-experience. According
to Czepiel and Rosenberg (1977b), consumer satisfaction is an attitude
in the sense that it is an evaluative orientation which can be measured.
Furthermore, they claimed that it is a special kind of attitude because
by definition it cannot exist prior to the purchase or consumption of
the attitude object. This view was opposed by Olander (1977a), who
pointed out that satisfaction or dissatisfaction could exist prior to
purchase/consumption; for example, dissatisfaction with out-of-town

supermarkets which caused a consumer's local store to shut down; and dissatisfaction with advertisements for products a consumer would never have a use for. However, Hunt (1977) argued that the Czepiel and Rosenberg position is still possible. It is because the consumer must have had experience of the local store that he finds himself dissatisfied with the out-of-town supermarkets, or of the advertisement so that he can be angry with it.

From a different angle, Ortinau (1979, 1982) has attempted to define expected satisfaction as the satisfaction with a product prior to consumption/use. However, it was found that models which predict actual satisfaction are more accurate than the expected satisfaction (Ortinau 1982). Hence, in the context of consumer behaviour, it seems that post-purchase experience or behaviour is more relevant. This particular nature of consumer satisfaction/dissatisfaction makes it more applicable for studying consumer post-purchase experience or behaviour.

Third, satisfaction gives additional insights into attitude. Czepiel and Rosenberg (1977a) have specified that consumer satisfaction as an attitude is incomplete because it is an attitude that has meaning as a feedback concept for society, managers and consumers. They regarded consumer satisfaction as an indicator of product performance. From a different angle, Tse (1980) suggested that satisfaction adds additional dimensions to the explanation of a consumer's information receptivity, choice behaviour and brand loyalty. Taking brand loyalty as an example, he presented the interaction of attitude and satisfaction in a contingency table as in Figure 2.1.

Cell 1 represents the situation where the consumer likes the product or service and is satisfied with it. In this situation, the consumer has stable loyalty and will continue using the product/service. Cell 2 represents the situation where the consumer likes the product/service but is dissatisfied with it. This situation may be caused by a sudden decline in the performance of the product/service or too high an expectation of the consumer toward the product/service. Lacking confidence in the product/service, the consumer has unstable loyalty and will continue purchasing the product/service only when there is a guarantee of performance or quality. Cell 3 represents the situation where the consumer does not like the product, but is still satisfied with it only because it meets certain basic demands, for example low price. In this situation, the consumer has equitable loyalty, no alternative available and is receptive towards advertisements and sales promotions.

Satisfaction

	Satisfied	Dissatisfied
Positive	1 Stable loyalty	2 Unstable loyalty
Negative	3 Equitable loyalty	4 Captive loyalty

Attitude

Figure 2.1 Loyalty in different situations of satisfaction and attitude
Source: Tse (1980)

Cell 4 represents the situation where the consumer neither likes the product/service nor is satisfied with it. This situation is probably caused by market imperfections such as lack of competition, and time pressure. In this situation, the consumer has to continue using the product until market imperfections are relaxed. Therefore, by studying attitude alone, we cannot account for more detailed differences in the consumer's loyalty towards brands.

Conceptualization of consumer satisfaction/dissatisfaction

Since 1976, the term 'consumer satisfaction/dissatisfaction' has frequently appeared in the marketing literature. However, as mentioned in the last section, no consensus on a definition of it has been reached. Hunt (1977) attributed this situation to one simple reason: many researchers plunged ahead with measurement problems in consumer satisfaction/dissatisfaction when they had not understood the basic conceptual problems. These pioneering researchers, who were involved in public-policy affairs inside and outside government in the United States, could afford only a minimal effort to conceptualize consumer satisfaction/dissatisfaction before getting started on the measurement problems. Up to now, consumer satisfaction/dissatisfaction has been interpreted in the following ways (see Figure 2.2):

Psychological interpretation

A large amount of research has been done by consumer psychologists and marketing researchers, applying a variety of psychological theories to explain product evaluation, and to assess satisfaction in the consumer decision-making context. Theories which have received a considerable amount of attention in consumer satisfaction literature are:

1 Cognitive dissonance.
2 Contrast.
3 Contrast and assimilation.
4 Opponent-process.
5 Adaptation-level.
6 Equity.

These theories provide explanations of how the consumer behaves in different ways when his perceptions of the performance of a product are at variance with the perceived expectations of the product (Anderson 1973). Each theory is discussed below.

Theory of cognitive dissonance Proposed by Festinger (1957), the cognitive dissonance theory begins with a consideration of two cognitive elements. If one element does not follow from the other, the two elements are said to be in dissonance. If the two cognitive elements are in dissonance, psychological discomfort will motivate the person to reduce dissonance and achieve consonance in several ways:

1 By changing one of the two elements.
2 By lowering the importance of the cognitive elements.
3 By adding new cognitive elements which will be consonant with the element in question.
4 By making relevant elements irrelevant.

The terminology used in describing cognitive dissonance theory may be translated into connotations in consumer satisfaction. The two cognitive elements may be viewed as the perceived expectation towards the product before use or consumption, and the performance of the product. Dissonance is the discrepancy between expectation and the performance of the product. The consumer's expectations will be

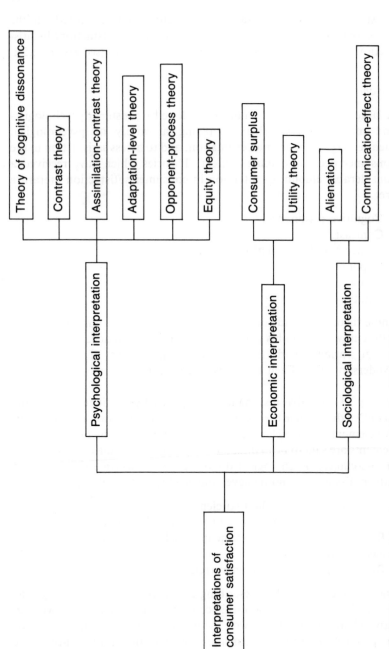

Figure 2.2 Interpretations of consumer satisfaction/dissatisfaction

negatively disconfirmed if the product performs worse than expected, positively disconfirmed if the product performs better than expected, and confirmed if the product performs as expected. The disconfirmation, if it occurs, will be reduced (assimilated) by the consumer, who adjusts his perception of the product to be more consistent with his expectations.

In the marketing literature, Olson and Dover (1976) tried to support this theory by conducting an experiment in the judgment of coffee bitterness. They created expectations about the bitterness of a new brand of coffee by exposure of three advertisement-like messages which were then disconfirmed through actual product trial. Subjects were exposed to the three messages, which stressed that the sample coffee had no bitterness. Two groups of subjects were asked to taste the coffee and rate four measures of bitterness of the sample coffee. However, the results were not statistically significant. Only one of the four measures of bitterness showed a significant difference between the experimental group and the control group.

Contrast theory   The contrast theory of consumer satisfaction predicts consumer reaction in just the opposite way. Instead of reducing dissonance, the consumer will magnify the difference between expectation and the performance of the product/service. If the product's performance exceeds expectations, he will be highly satisfied, but if the product's performance falls below expectation, he will be highly dissatisfied (Day 1977). This implies that the consumer is very sensitive to unmatched expectations and may react in an exaggerated way.

Several studies in the marketing literature have offered some support for this theory. Cardozo's (1965) experiment provided the foundation for the later experimental research in consumer satisfaction. In his experiment, subjects were asked to evaluate the desirability and quality of ball-point pens. Subjects were involved in a simulated shopping task to seek information about descriptions and prices of ball pens from catalogues at different effect levels. Expectation was induced by variation in the prices of the product in the catalogues. The results of his experiment showed that when expectations were negatively disconfirmed, subjects rated both product and shopping experience unfavourably (Cardozo 1965).

Swan and Combs (1976), in their experiment measuring satisfaction with clothing purchases, found that consumers who were dissatisfied were more likely to have had their expectations negatively disconfirmed than were consumers who were satisfied with their purchases. This result supports the contrast theory.

Assimilation–contrast theory This theory was introduced by Anderson (1973) in the context of post-exposure product perform-ance, based on Sherif and Hovland's (1961) discussion of assimilation and contrast effect, in studies of communication effects on attitude change. It has been used to explain consumer satisfaction by applying one or both of the two theories discussed above. In the case of a moderate level of disconfirmation of expectation and performance, the consumer will behave according to the theory of cognitive dissonance. That is, the consumer will try to reduce the discrepancy by adjusting his perception. In the case of a high level of disconfirma-tion which is beyond some 'latitude of acceptance', the consumer will behave in accordance with the contrast theory, that is, will magnify the difference between expectation and performance of the product (Day 1975.)

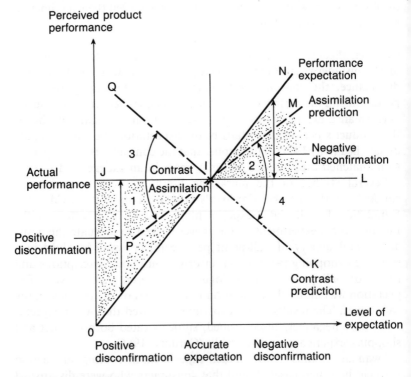

Figure 2.3 Assimilation–contrast theory
Source: Adapted from Anderson (1973, p. 39)

This theory can be best described by the diagram reproduced as Figure 2.3 (Anderson 1973). In the figure, the vertical axis is the perceived product performance and the horizontal axis the level of expectation. The line ON emanating from the origin is the iso-curve of performance and expectation which is formed when the consumer's expectations alone determine perceived performance. The horizontal line JL is the actual performance of the product under consideration. The interaction of the lines ON and JL at I represents the condition of accurate expectation or confirmation. Therefore, the shaded area OJI where expectation is lower than the actual performance defines a region of positive disconfirmation. Similarly, the shaded area NLI where expectation is higher than the actual performance defines a region of negative disconfirmation.

Therefore, according to Sherif and Hovland (1961), the assimilation interpretation predicts that when the actual performance of the product is at variance with the consumer's expectation, he will 'assimilate' the expectation in the direction shown by arrows 1 and 2 in Figure 2.3. Thus perceived performance falls on the sloped dotted line PM in the shaded regions. Similarly, the contrast interpretation predicts that the consumer will overreact in the direction shown by arrows 3 and 4 in Figure 2.3. Thus the perceived performance will fall on the negatively sloped dotted line QK.

Adaptation-level theory Adaptation-level theory is another theory which is consistent with expectation and disconfirmation effects on satisfaction. This theory was originated by Helsen (1964) and applied to consumer satisfaction by Oliver (1980b, 1981). Helsen (1964) simply put his theory as follows:

> it posits that one perceives stimuli only in relation to an adapted standard. The standard is a function of perceptions of the stimulus itself, the context, and psychological and physiological characteristics of the organism. Once created, the 'adaptation level' serves to sustain subsequent evaluations in that positive and negative deviations will remain in the general vicinity of one's original position. Only large impacts on the adaptation level will change the final tone of the subject's evaluation.

Adaptation-level phenomena in satisfaction processes can be described in more familiar concepts such as expectation, performance and disconfirmation, etc., which are explained earlier in this chapter. Oliver (1980a, 1981) suggested that a consumer's expectation serves as a standard against which the performance of the product is judged.

This standard serves as what Helsen described as the adaptation level. Moreover, disconfirmation serves as a principal force causing 'positive or negative deviation' from the level. The net effect, which is the revised adaptation level in Helsen's model, is equivalent to satisfaction. This basic paradigm is depicted in Figure 2.4 (Oliver 1981).

This theory is gaining acceptance, as it is able to explain some counter-intuitive predictions made by assimilation–contrast theorists (Oliver 1977).

Opponent-process theory   This was originally a theory of motivation reformulated by Solomon and Corbit (1974) which has been adapted from the basic physiological phenomena known as homeostasis (Fletcher 1942). Homeostasis assumes that many hedonic, affective or emotional states, being away from neutrality and exceeding a threshold level of hedonic feelings, are automatically opposed by central nervous system mechanisms which reduce the intensity of the feelings, both pleasant and aversive, to some constant level (Solomon and Corbit 1974).

Oliver (1981) further explained that the onset of the opponent process is totally dependent on the effect of the primary process, in which an emotional state is initiated by a known stimulus. If the initial stimulus is eliminated to reduce completely or partially the primary process effect, the opponent process will continue to operate at a decaying rate determined by inertia factors. In the absence of the

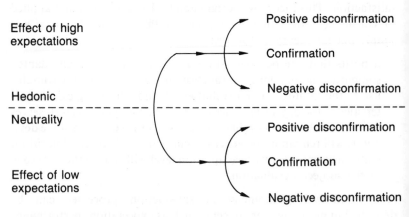

Figure 2.4 Expectation and disconfirmation effects on satisfaction consistent with adaptation-level theory.
Source: Oliver (1981, p. 28).

primary process effect, the decaying opponent process will cause the body to experience a negative after-effect in a direction opposite to the initial response.

The terminology used in describing opponent-process theory can be translated into the familiar concepts used in the theories previously discussed. The neutral state (or neutrality) can be viewed as expectations of a product/service. The primary process can be interpreted as the positive or negative disconfirmation which provokes a state of satisfaction or dissatisfaction. Finally the opponent process is purely an internal drive which causes satisfaction/dissatisfaction to decay to a new or original level. Therefore, the degree to which satisfaction is achieved depends upon the magnitude of disconfirmation as well as upon the strength of the opponent process. The opponent process in a satisfaction context is shown in Figure 2.5.

Equity theory An early recognition of this theory first came out of research by Stouffer and his colleagues (1949) in military administration. They referred to 'relative deprivation' (equity) as the reaction to an imbalance or disparity between what an individual perceives to be the actuality and what he believes should be the case, especially where his own situation is concerned. This imbalance or disparity will induce an attitude of satisfaction or dissatisfaction in him. This led to Homans's concept of 'distributive justice', which refers to a condition where an individual's investments are balanced by his rewards.

Among other psychologists (Spector 1956; Patchen 1961) who worked along similar lines, Adams (1963) was the first to adopt the

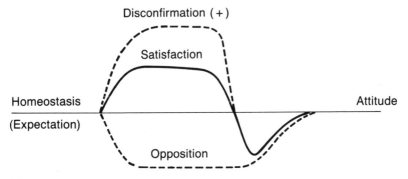

Figure 2.5 Operation of opponent-process phenomena as applied to consumer satisfaction and its determinants
Source: Oliver (1981, p. 31)

term 'equity' to explain his work on the amount of effort expended by production workers. He stated that 'equity exists for a person whenever his perceived job inputs and/or outcomes stand psychologically in an obverse relation to what he perceives are the inputs and/or outcomes of others'. In other words, the perceived inputs (investments or costs) to the job must be in equilibrium with the perceived benefits (rewards) or the individual will be in a state of imbalance, and will attempt to reduce the resulting tension. Adams's definition differs from his antecedents' in stressing the concepts of costs and rewards. It must be realized that another person's perceptions of his own investments, costs and rewards do not always coincide with a person's own perceptions of them. With two people in any interaction, it is not the actuality nor is it the other person's perception that matters most. It is the individual's own perception of his situation which continues to have overriding significance in determining his response pattern. This theory can be treated as a special case of cognitive dissonance.

In explaining consumer satisfaction, a consumer makes his judgment in a buying decision-making process, by weighing the costs (inputs) and benefits (outcomes) of the product selected, relative to those rejected. If the outcomes of this comparison are constant, then the consumer will be satisfied. Otherwise, the consumer will attempt to achieve equilibrium by adjusting the perceived costs and benefits of the product selected (Adler and Robinson 1980). Hence, the costs and benefits of the product selected can be viewed as performance, while those of the product rejected as expectation. The outcome of the comparison can be treated as the confirmation or disconfirmation between expectation and performance.

Huppertz (1979), studying satisfaction associated with shopping, developed different measures of the inputs and outcomes of consumer and seller from shopping events. He first gave some examples of the events which measure outcomes and inputs. Consumer input could be the price paid, or the distance to the store. Consumer outcome could be the time span that the product lasts, or the amount of help given by advertising. The seller input could be the amount spent on advertising or the availability of salespersons to serve the consumer; and the seller outcome could be the profit made, or the compliments from shoppers. These ratios were then compared to give a measure of equity or inequity which represents consumer satisfaction/dissatisfaction. In such a way Huppertz successfully discriminated between satisfied and dissatisfied consumers. He used the ratios to make the concept of equity or inequity (satisfaction or dissatisfaction) more operationalized. This was indeed a contribution to the application of equity theory to both the conceptualization and the measurement of consumer satisfaction; however, what is needed is the development of better measures of inputs and outcomes for specific situations.

Economic theory interpretations

Consumer satisfaction/dissatisfaction can also be conceptualized in terms of economic theory. Two branches of economic theory are discussed here.

Consumer surplus In economic theory, a rational consumer will allocate his scarce resources in such a way that the ratio of marginal utilities to the prices of the products will be equal. Hence, the total utility which he derives from all products is at its maximum. If there are any changes in the prices of the products, his resources have to be reallocated in order to reach a new equilibrium. Furthermore, in a given market under perfect competition, the market price is determined by the interaction of consumers and firms in such a way that, when at equilibrium, the price required by the firm is exactly the price the consumer wishes to pay for a given quantity. Therefore, all consumers in a given market are assumed to be prepared to pay the same market price. However, there is a gap between total utility and the total amount of money the consumer pays to obtain the products. This gap is in the nature of a surplus to the consumer. The reason why this consumer surplus occurs is simply the fact that market price is determined by marginal rather than total utility. Each unit of a product is bought at the same price as the last unit. But according to the law of diminishing marginal utility, the earlier units are worth more to the consumer than the last. Thus the consumer enjoys a surplus on each of the earlier units.

Samuelson (1980) showed how consumers reap the surplus by a diagram which is reproduced in Figure 2.6. In Figure 2.6, when consumers buy OQ_1 units of a product at the price of OP_1 for each, the total amount of money they pay is OQ_1 times OP_1, represented by the shaded area OQ_1EP_1. However, the total utility of OQ_1 units of the product in monetary terms is the whole area under the demand curve dd bounded by both the quantity and the price axes. Therefore for all those consumers who expect to pay a price at a level higher than OP_1, there exists a consumer surplus which is equal to the difference between the two areas, i.e. the area of the triangle P_1ER (Samuelson 1980).

24   *Consumer behaviour in China*

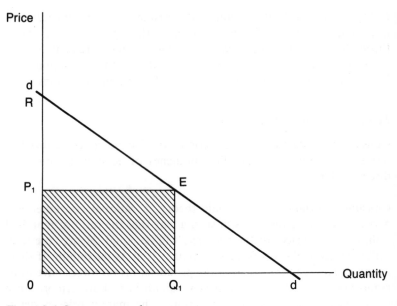

Figure 2.6 Consumer surplus
Source: Samuelson (1980, 10th ed. p. 413)

Consumers reap a surplus from their purchase at the expense of the producers or sellers. Surplus reaping by consumers implies a loss of the same amount to the producer. Similarly, surplus lost by consumers implies surplus gained by the producers. Wonnacott and Wonnacott (1978) explained this phenomenon when they defined the term 'producer surplus'. If the market price changes, there will be an increase or decrease in consumer surplus. Figure 2.7 shows that the supply curve shifts from S_1 to S_2 when other things are equal. The new market price is now P_2. To the consumers, the consumer surplus which they reaped at the market price P_1 was represented by the sum of the areas 1, 2 and 3. At the new equilibrium, the consumers' situation is worse. The consumer surplus which they can now enjoy has diminished by the sum of the areas 2 and 3. It means that their total consumer surplus is now represented only by area 1. The surplus originally reaped by the consumers and represented by areas 2 and 3 has been lost to the producers. This is called the producer surplus (Wonnacott and Wonnacott 1978).

From the view point of the producers, at the initial equilibrium R in Figure 2.8, the producers have a total revenue of the area OP_1RQ_1 (area 1) at the initial price OP_1. Now if the price rises the new

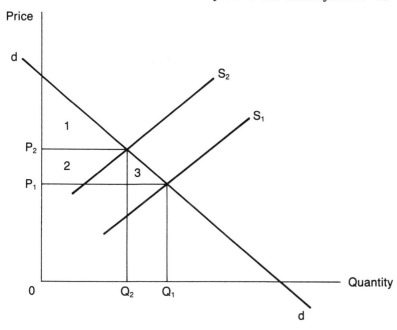

Figure 2.7 Producer surplus and consumer surplus

equilibrium moves from point R to T. At the new equilibrium, OQ_2 units are sold for a total revenue of OP_2TQ_2 (i.e. area $1 + 2 + 3$) at the new price OP_2. Thus, total revenue increases by areas 2 and 3. However, area 2 represents the increased cost. For those producers who expect to sell at the initial price OP_1 reap a surplus of the area 3 in total.

It is obvious that the larger the surplus, the more satisfied the consumers will be with the product. However, there are three points worth noting. First, consumers' surplus is measured at an aggregated level rather than an individual level. Since the price of the product is determined by the market and not by an individual consumer himself, the measurement of consumer surplus is difficult. Second, the assumption that the market is in perfect competition is not always true. Third, the satisfaction derived from consumer surplus does not represent the consumers' total experience in purchasing/consumption of the product/service (Pfaff 1977). It is a result of a consumer's reaction to the price and quantity of a product. It ignores many aspects of the product such as quality, packaging, convenience, taste, etc. Furthermore, according to the concept of consumer surplus, it seems impossible to arrive at a definition for satisfaction as the discrepancy between

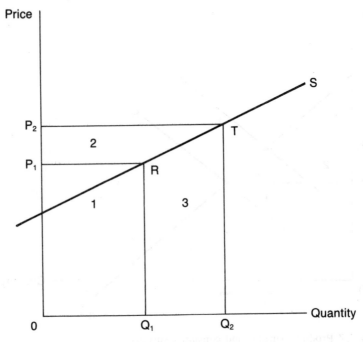

Figure 2.8 Producer surplus

the market price and the consumer's hypothetical price. Using this definition, it would be very difficult to conclude which consumer is more satisfied with the product, when consumers have the same hypothetical price, and those who do not buy are dissatisfied with the product.

Utility theory   A variety of theories of utility have been developed primarily in different disciplines, such as economics, psychology, statistics and management science. Since economics is the father of utility theory (Fishburn 1968: 340), this section is deliberately placed under the umbrella of the economic theory interpretation of consumer satisfaction. This section of the book will only give an account of some of the basic notions in utility theory in order to explain how utility of products/services can reflect consumer satisfaction.

On the practical level, utility theory is concerned with how the consumer chooses and makes his decisions according to his preferences and judgments of value (Fishburn 1968). The basic ingredient of utility theory is an individual's preference/indifference relations applied to a set of alternatives under a set of internally consistent assumptions. There are three fundamental assumptions of utility theory:

1 *Connectivity*. All the alternatives in the set are connected. This implies that alternatives should be related to each other by the preference/indifference relations.
2 *Consistency*. The preference relation between two alternatives cannot be reversed at some point in time. This implies that if the consumer prefers A to B, he cannot prefer B to A or be indifferent between A and B.
3 *Transitivity*. If there are three alternatives, A, B and C, in the set, and if the consumer prefers A to B and B to C, then he must prefer A to C.

With these three assumptions, it is then possible to arrange the set of alternatives in a ranking order according to the consumer's preference. This implies that if these three assumptions are held, an ordinal scale of utility can be generated for the consumer with respect to the alternatives. One of the major developments in utility theory is to derive ratio or interval utility scales for alternatives in the set, so as to make interpersonal comparisons possible. As a result of this development, marketing researchers have been able to derive metric utility scales and to assign individuals (consumers or stimuli) as points on common metric scales or to multidimensional metric spaces.

On a utility scale, a number is assigned to each of the preference objects (alternatives) so that the preference relations among the objects remain unchanged. If a scale is developed for several brands of a product, the point on the scale which represents the best of all possible brands as judged by a consumer is called the ideal point (or brand). (This ideal point might or might not be any of the brands being compared.) The concept of the ideal point provides the basis for assigning individuals as well as objects preference on a utility scale or a multidimensional space.

The concept of the ideal point is very useful in interpreting consumer satisfaction in terms of the individual's utility scale or space. For an individual, the ideal point serves as the highest expectation of the product he has bought. If he expects that performance of the product will be as good as the ideal point and after purchase/consumption perceives its performance as providing a lower level of utility than the ideal point, he will be dissatisfied with it (see Figure 2.9). If he expects that the performance of the product will be far lower than the ideal point and after purchase/consumption perceives its performance as providing a level of utility between that of the ideal

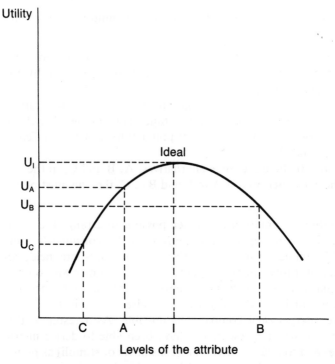

Figure 2.9 Hypothetical utility curve

point and that of his expectation, he will be highly satisfied with it (see Figure 2.9). Hence, distances are interpreted as reflections of satisfaction. The closer the actual product is to the ideal point, the higher the satisfaction. The same is true when the actual product is located in a multidimensional space.

During the past decade, multidimensional scaling methods have been used to assign stimuli and consumer ideal points in multidimensional spaces so that satisfaction, which is a function of the distance between the ideal point and the product, can be measured (Green and Rao 1975). Recently, conjoint measurement has been popularly used to estimate attribute utilities of a product (Green and Tull 1972; Green and Wind 1975). Day (1977) suggested that it could be very promising in the study of consumer satisfaction. However, these methods are not without problems when dealing with ideal points. Huber (1976) envisioned four problems related to the representation of individual preference as an ideal point in a multidimensional space:

1 Lack of symmetry of preference about the ideal.

2 Multiple ideal points for an individual in a given space.
3 Existence of preference due to subject-specific attributes such as habit or past behaviour rather than product-specific attributes such as sportiness or masculinity of image.
4 Presence of situations where some or all of the attributes are monotone with respect to preference.

He called the first two technical problems and argued that they could be solved by first specifying the kind of solution needed and then by applying techniques such as PREFMAP which were modified to weigh inputs to the quadratic regression in terms of their preference. However, he pinpointed that the last two problems could hardly be solved because they are conceptual in nature.

In the marketing literature, Pfaff (1972) and Lingoes and Pfaff (1972) were amongst the first to approach consumer satisfaction/ dissatisfaction from the perspective of economics utility theory. They adopted conjoint measurement in developing an 'index of consumer satisfaction' which could be used to measure consumer satisfaction at an aggregated level. Along the same lines, Bechtel (1977) also succeeded in developing an index of consumer satisfaction by LOGIT analysis. Differing from Pfaff, he constructed his index at a disaggregated level to facilitate the formulation of marketing strategies for each commodity. Braden (1979) made the first attempt to investigate consumer dissatisfaction using utility as a reflection of satisfaction, with a luxury car paint surface condition using conjoint measurement. His survey was not very satisfactory, owing to a high attrition rate. Over 75 per cent of the subjects made illogical choices in the scenario rankings.

In summary, it seems possible for utility theory to provide a simpler way to conceptualize satisfaction than the confirmation of expectations approach. However, from a theoretical point of view, utility theory provides a useful but highly abstract model when use is made of 'utility' (or distance) and 'ideal point' to reflect the level of satisfaction, and an explicit criterion such as expectation is not provided. (The ideal point is only an implicit criterion.) Utility theory is not without problems. As mentioned above the multidimensional scaling method and the conjoint measurement method both encounter problems concerning ideal point and high attrition rates respectively.

Sociological interpretations

Satisfaction/dissatisfaction is not only a term in the marketing literature, it also exists in the sociological literature under the heading of alienation and communication effect theory. These two concepts have been extensively used in the marketing literature to interpret consumer satisfaction/dissatisfaction.

Alienation The concept of alienation has a long history in sociological literature. It has been the main theme in studies of authoritarian personality (Adorno *et al*. 1950), political apathy (Rosenberg 1951; Dean 1960), maladjustment at work (Powell 1958), the behaviour of some student intellectuals (Hajda 1961) and other forms of anti-social behaviour. Hence, it is not surprising that it can be used to interpret consumer dissatisfaction.

Alienation is a psychological state of an individual (Clark 1959). There are a variety of definitions of alienation in the sociological literature (Clark 1959; Nettler 1957; Seemen 1959; Dean 1961), but the concept of alienation can be identified in four commonly accepted forms: powerlessness, meaninglessness, normlessness and isolation. These four forms, as Clark (1959) argued, all pertain to a man's feeling of lacking in means to eliminate the discrepancy between his definition of the role he is playing and the one he feels he should be playing in a specific situation.

Powerlessness. Seemen (1959) defined this form of alienation as 'the expectancy or probability held by the individual that his or her own behaviour cannot determine the occurrence of the outcomes'. From a consumer point of view, powerlessness is the feeling of not being able to influence business behaviour in order to protect one's interests as a consumer. Allison (1977) gave the following examples of powerlessness: 'Most companies are (not) responsive to the demands of the consumers,' and 'People are unable to help determine what products will be sold in the store.' In some cases, a consumer will feel powerless when a firm does not respond to his/her requests for corrective action due to the failure of a product/service to meet his/her reasonable expectation.

Meaninglessness. Seemen (1959) defined meaninglessness as 'a low expectancy that satisfactory predictions about future outcomes of behaviour can be made'. From the consumer standpoint, meaninglessness occurs when a consumer finds himself/herself not able to make wise decisions on purchases because of lack of self-confidence, insufficient information about alternative products, or intelligence. According to Lambert (1976), it is generally unintelligible product claims that contribute to meaninglessness. Hence if consumers are able to consider an appropriate amount of easily understood and objective information about product characteristics, meaninglessness will be greatly reduced.

Normlessness. According to Dean (1961), there are two types of normlessness: purposelessness and conflict-of-norms. Purposelessness can be described as the absence of values that might give purpose or direction to life, and the loss of intrinsic and socialized values (MacIver 1950). Conflict of norms can be defined as the difficulties of a person who incorporates conflicting norms in his/her personality. In the consumer context, purposelessness is usually used. Hence, normlessness may be described as the belief that generally businesspeople are engaged in unethical and unjust marketing practices. Evidence has shown that feelings of normlessness exist among consumers. Most consumers believe that they have been deceived or cheated by businesspeople (Lambert and Kiffin 1975). The belief that manufacturers purposely produce new styles of cars to phase out the old ones is another manifestation. Normlessness will result in scepticism, distrust of businessmen, and even loss of confidence in the marketplace.

Isolation. According to Clark (1959), isolation is a feeling of separation from the group or from group standards. It has been shown that isolation can result in many behaviours such as low social participation, spatial mobility, lower percentage of voting, greater unemployment, and a higher rate of job turnover (Jaco 1954). In the consumer context, the feeling of isolation occurs when consumers are not able to understand the real meaning of advertisements, to identify with business practices or to experience pleasant shopping conditions. Reich (1970) attributed the cause of this feeling to the grossly commercial nature of American culture. Consumers have repudiated society's primary values and beliefs, and the marketplace is in fact one of the outlets for venting the consumers' resentment and frustration. Hence, Lambert (1976) concluded that isolation is probably the most difficult form of alienation for businesspeople to cope with.

In the marketing literature, the concept of alienation has served to explain consumer dissatisfaction from the macro aspect. It shows why the ineffectiveness of the marketplace has brought about consumer discontent (dissatisfaction) (Allison 1977; Lambert 1976). Lundstrom (1974) and Lundstrom and Lamont (1976) conducted a comprehensive study to develop a scale to measure consumer discontent. In a more recent study, they also found that consumer discontent is positively correlated with different forms of alienation (Lundstrom and Kerin 1976).

Recent work has reported that consumer alienation fails to discriminate between complainers and non-complainers (Clabaugh 1978;

Clabaugh *et al.* 1979). This implies that consumer alienation, though being able to explain consumer discontent, is ineffective as an indicator of complaint behaviour. This might be due to the fact that it has acted as a more remote and indirect variable than consumer discontent.

Communication effect theory   This theory is completely different from the theories mentioned above, in that it does not emphasize disconfirmation of expectation and performance of a product/service. It states that consumer satisfaction/dissatisfaction is a result of the consumer's responses to changes in communication but not his cognitive or affective evaluation of a product/service (Pfaff 1977). Communications are only received in interpersonal, intergroup, or mass-communication situations.

Communication effect theory makes no attempt to explain how satisfaction would be changed by the effect of interactions and communications within which the consumer is placed. This is because the effects of a message are always entangled with the predisposition of the consumer towards the product/service, which makes it difficult to explain why consumer satisfaction/dissatisfaction changes (Pfaff 1977).

Classifications of consumer satisfaction

For the purposes of marketing management, consumer satisfaction/ dissatisfaction may be classified in several ways. Some taxonomies which have been suggested are outlined below.

Pfaff (1972), in developing an index of consumer satisfaction, initially classified satisfaction into two basic types:

1 *Product satisfaction*, which is a result of consumers' evaluation of the attributes of the product, such as size, or some special features.
2 *Marketing satisfaction*, which is a result of consumers' evaluation of the price, availability and image of the product.

Pfaff's classification was very rough. The two types of satisfaction he suggested were in fact not mutually exclusive. In 1973, Renoux tried to distinguish between micro-marketing satisfaction and macro-marketing satisfaction. He advocated the following three levels of consumer dissatisfaction in the micro-marketing system:

1 *Shopping-system dissatisfaction* is a result of the unavailability of products or services, or retail outlets.

2 *Buying-system dissatisfaction* results from problems rising from the selection of products/services from retail outlets.
3 *Consuming-system dissatisfaction* results from problems in using or consuming products or services.

Along the similar lines, Czepiel *et al.* (1975) have suggested three different levels of consumer satisfaction:

1 *System satisfaction*, which is defined as consumers' subjective evaluation of all the benefits they have obtained from the operations of the marketing system.
2 *Enterprise satisfaction*, which is defined as the benefits or gains the consumers have received in their dealing with the enterprises.
3 *Product/service satisfaction*, which is the consumers' subjective evaluation of the benefits from the consumption of a specific product/service.

Fornell (1976) proposed the division of dissatisfaction into two general categories:

1 Dissatisfaction resulting from shopping, buying and decision-making.
2 Dissatisfaction resulting from post-purchase evaluation of the purchased object when it has been fully or partially consumed.

He advocated further splitting the latter into first-purchase and re-purchase dissatisfaction. He emphasized that loyalty towards brands would probably make consumers susceptible to brand faithfulness and resistant to change. Hence dissatisfaction in repurchase situations needs special attention.

Westbrook (1978), concentrating more on the buying process, has classified consumer satisfaction into:

1 Pre-purchase satisfaction.
2 During-purchase satisfaction.
3 After-purchase (or post-purchase) satisfaction.

The dimension of after-purchase satisfaction implies the causal attribution of dissatisfaction with product/service as well as the complaining behaviour. Hence it is a typology with broader scope than the previous ones.

Based on Westbrook's and Czepiel *et al.*'s classifications, and looking at it from the viewpoint of the sellers, Wikstrom (1981) grouped satisfaction into:

1 *Before-sales*. This refers to consumer satisfaction with the infor-mation searching process, the shopping process and the availability of alternative products in the marketplace.

2 *Product and price.* This refers to satisfaction derived from the product being purchased with special emphasis on price concern.
3 *After-sales.* This refers to satisfaction with the after-sales service of the seller as well as consumers' experience in using the product.
4 *Marketplace structure/performance.* This refers to consumer satisfaction with the marketing system and its performance, such as advertisements, marketing practices, packaging and labelling, etc.

Marketplace structure/performance may be interpreted as the macro-marketing satisfaction and the rest as the micro-marketing satisfaction. Although in different terminology, this classification seems more exhaustive.

From a different angle, Withey (1977) further categorized consumer satisfaction by identifying different 'domains of life', which include marriage, children, conditions at work, pay, housing, neighbourhood, and local government. He suggested that these semi-independent domains would put consumers in different situations which facilitated or restricted the extent to which they could have satisfaction. Hence, this unusual classification implies that satisfaction can be regarded as a generic concept.

Summary

Following a discussion of the distinction between satisfaction and attitude, this section has presented varying conceptualizations and classifications of 'consumer satisfaction/dissatisfaction'. Consumer satisfaction/dissatisfaction is a complex concept. Throughout this book, it is defined as: *a measurable evaluative attitude which is derived from the disconfirmation of expectations and perceived performance of the product consumed or experienced by the consumer. The level of the expectations and perceived performance are determined by every aspect of the purchase–consumption process.* The next section examines the existing evidence relating to the factors which affect the level of consumer satisfaction/dissatisfaction.

DISCUSSION OF RELATED RESEARCH

Research investigating factors influencing consumer satisfaction/dissatisfaction can be classified into three groups (see Figure 2.10):

1 Product-specific factors.
2 Consumer-specific factors.
3 Situation-specific factors.

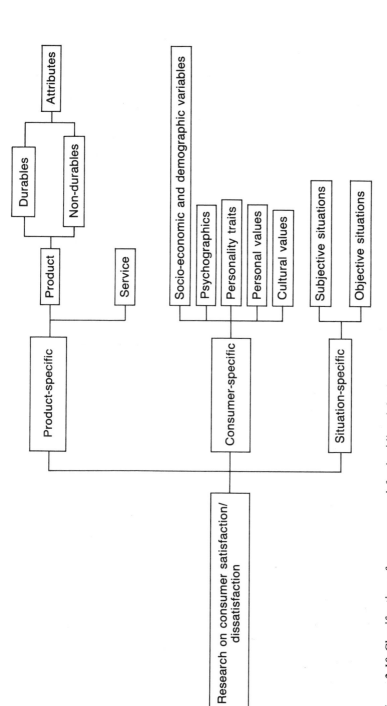

Figure 2.10 Classification of consumer satisfaction/dissatisfaction research

Research into product-specific factors is a study of how products and their attributes affect consumer satisfaction/dissatisfaction. The product factors are typically the consumer's satisfaction/dissatisfaction with different kinds of products such as durable and non-durable products and services. The attribute factors are the specific attributes which affect consumer satisfaction, such as functional and aesthetic attributes, and post-sales service. Functional attributes are all attributes which affect the fitness of the product/service to the task and for the consumer, for example, price and quality. Aesthetic attributes are often included with functional attributes, but they belong to a different motivational set, and therefore should be treated separately. These attributes are usually associated with product categories such as furniture, clothing and artwork (Levy and Czepiel 1974; Czepiel and Rosenberg 1977a). Post-sales services are equally important, and may often account for a great part of satisfaction/dissatisfaction, especially with durable products such as electrical and electronic appliances and automobiles. These three kinds of attributes are most commonly studied and are apparently mandatory in any study concerned with consumer satisfaction/dissatisfaction.

Consumer-specific factors are the personal characteristics of the consumer which affect satisfaction. These characteristics may contribute to explain why, and not how, satisfaction or dissatisfaction is derived. Very often when functional attributes fail to show any relationship with satisfaction, these characteristics come into effect (Baumgarten *et al.* 1972). This research involves five kinds of variables. They are socio-economic variables, pyschographical variables, personality traits, personal values and cultural values.

Situation-specific factors are the ways in which purchase, consumption, communication and response situations affect satisfaction. This kind of research is growing in importance in the consumer satisfaction literature.

The studies most relevant to this research according to the above classification will now be discussed.

Product-specific research

Product-specific research is usually exploratory in nature. It has been found that consumers may have different levels of satisfaction/dissatisfaction across different product categories. Day and Bodour

(1979) conducted a mail survey of 125 households from a two-stage probability sample.They were concerned with the satisfaction/ dissatisfaction of the households with each of seventy-three categories of services. Among the categories, repairs and general services and rental services were found to be the two on which dissatisfaction was highest. Ash and Quelch (1980) also found a similar result. In a comprehensive survey from a national probability sample of 1,052 households, they focused on data covering twenty-three categories of services. The results showed a widespread variation in the proportions of dissatisfied users over the twenty-three categories. However, the results tended to be parallel with those reported by Day and Bodour (1979). Rentals, public transport and utilities, and repairs were also found to be the two most serious problems.

In a more recent article, Ash *et al.* (1982), using the same data, tried to compare the levels of satisfaction and dissatisfaction reported by older as opposed to younger consumers in relation to twenty categories of repairs and general services. The results showed statistically significant differences between the old and young consumers across the following service categories:

1 Repairs and general services.
2 Professional and personal services.
3 Financial services.
4 Rentals, public transport and utilities.

Nevertheless, repairs, general services, rentals, public transport and utilities still remained the two most dissatisfied service categories reported by both the old and the young consumers.

Focusing on dissatisfaction with durable products, Day and Ash (1978) classified durable products into four categories:

1 Housing and home furnishings.
2 Home appliance and personal care products.
3 Entertainment, recreation and education durables.
4 Cars and other transport durables.

It was reported that the most unsatisfactory products in the first category were swimming pools and baby furniture; exercise machines in the second; pool tables and card tables in the third; and new car, used car and used truck purchases in the fourth. However, the findings also showed that the proportion of dissatisfied users varied between items in all categories of durable products. This may suggest that complaint statistics based on simple counts will fail to reveal even exceptionally high rates of dissatisfaction with products which are in fact less widely used.

Along similar lines, Leigh and Day (1979) focused on satisfaction/ dissatisfaction with non-durable products. They conducted a survey using a convenience sample of 291 respondents. Non-durable products were also classified into four categories:

1 Food products.
2 Clothing, shoes and accessories.
3 Household and family supplies.
4 Personal and health care products.

Under the food products category, it was found that meat products, convenience food products and restaurant-prepared products caused most dissatisfaction. Insect products, magazines and newspapers were ranked most dissatisfying amongst the household and family supplies. Deodorants, anti-perspirants and disinfectant products caused most dissatisfaction in the category of personal and health care products. However, dissatisfaction with products under the clothing, shoes and accessories category was quite evenly distributed.

Zinkhan and Wallendorf (1982), analysing data from a national survey similar to that of Day and Quelch (1977), were concerned whether similar perceptions in product categories led to similar patterns of satisfaction/dissatisfaction. They formed four service categories – utilities and government services, upscale travel, downscale travel, and housing and furnishings – and four social activities – cultural and upscale activities, sports involvement, new experience, and religious participation – using factor analysis. Then, for each service category, they performed multiple regression analysis to explain why particular service categories emerged. The four social activities and some other demographic variables were used as independent variables.

In this study, two important results are worth noting. First, factor analysis succeeded in forming product (service) categories. Second, the results of the multiple regression analysis showed that consumer satisfaction/dissatisfaction was partly a consumer-based phenomenon. Stimulus variation might have effects on the recognition and experience of dissatisfaction across products (services) in the product categories.

Not much effort has been put into investigating the relationships between satisfaction and product attributes. In the literature, ratings on product attributes have been used to measure the consumer satisfaction/dissatisfaction score. A US national survey of 1,831 households was undertaken to measure consumer satisfaction/ dissatisfaction with food products, food stores, and various sources of products by Handy (1977). He reported that regression analysis showed the food attribute 'taste' as the most important factor in consumer satisfaction in almost 70 per cent of the food products; the second most important food attribute was freshness.

Using factor analysis, Rodgers and Sweeney (1981) have identified five categories of attributes of store type with respect to consumer satisfaction/dissatisfaction:

1 Trustworthiness.
2 Product assortment.
3 Price/value.
4 Personal service.
5 In-store convenience.

With regard to the four store types they investigated, they produced the following findings:

1 Neither general merchandise chains nor conventional department stores showed any unique strength or weakness. Consumers were less satisfied with general merchandise chain stores' personal service and in-store convenience, and with department stores' price/value and personal service.
2 Discount stores were especially strong in price/value, weak in personal service and in-store convenience.
3 Specialist stores had a clear and unique strength in the personal service category. However, consumers were most dissatisfied with the price/value attribute.

In summary, most consumers were quite satisfied with retailers' performance in most of the attribute categories. However, consumers were somewhat dissatisfied with their ability to shop effectively and efficiently when they were in the store.

Hughes (1977b) was particularly interested in consumer satisfaction/ dissatisfaction related to the price paid. He selected three major appliances, colour televisions, refrigerators and vacuum cleaners, for investigation. He found that the price paid did not emerge as a predictor of satisfaction/dissatisfaction. Unexpectedly, service calls after purchase turned out to be the most powerful predictor of consumer satisfaction. Along the same lines, Hager and Handy (1979) found that it was the taste factor which appeared as an important variable in explaining satisfaction with beef. This result was in line with those of Handy (1977).

There are other studies which have shown that difficulties for consumers in obtaining post-purchase service have a positive effect on consumer dissatisfaction. Ash *et al.* (1980) examined consumers' satisfaction and warranty-related experiences with a comprehensive set of products and services, including twelve categories of automobiles and major home appliances. They reported that a substantial minority of consumers were dissatisfied with new car and truck warranties.

Bernacchi *et al.* (1980b) focussed on new car warranty service. They conducted a survey with a stratified cluster sample of 2,330 respondents with at least one warranty repair made in the year before the survey was undertaken. The results were as follows:

1 At least a quarter of the respondents were dissatisfied with the warranty service offered by the manufacturers, because of repeat visits for the same problem.
2 Eighty-five per cent of the respondents were dissatisfied with the service, which they had expected to be better.

Consumer-specific research

Socio-economic and demographic variables

Evidence on the characteristics of satisfied and dissatisfied consumers is limited. Consumer satisfaction field studies have mainly stressed the socio-economic and demographic characteristics of consumers. Barksdale and Darden (1972) found that dissatisfied consumers were younger and more liberal than satisfied consumers. Hustad and Pessemier (1973) described consumers with anti-business attitudes as relatively young, educated, affluent and with high occupational status. Kinnear *et al.* (1974) reported that consumers who were dissatisfied with environmental pollution tended to have higher income than those who were satisfied. Miller (1970) hypothesized that consumers who had higher than average expectations would be younger, more mobile and have a better educated spouse. This hypothesis was the first to use an intervening variable to help understand the relationship between socio-economic variables and consumer discontent. The findings of Miller's research supported his hypothesis. Hughes (1977a) in his survey of jeans buyers found that age was the most important factor in consumer satisfaction. Wall *et al.* (1978) showed that young consumers displayed more dissatisfaction than older consumers with clothing performance.

Bearden and Mason (1977) collected data concerning consumer satisfaction with utilities by means of structured personal interviews with 754 randomly selected respondents. It was found that dissatisfied consumers tended to be younger, better educated, wealthier, responsible for more pre-school children, and more likely to own their own home than satisfied consumers. In a more recent study, Mason *et al.* (1982) found that the elderly tended to show less worry about marketplace problems than general consumers.

In studies concerned with complaining behaviour, similar results were found. Thompson (1972) in his survey of household products revealed that people who made complaints tended to be of a higher income and education level. Mason and Himes (1973) found that complaints were positively related to the age of households, family size and income. Liefeld *et al.* (1975: 73) pictured the average consumer complainer as a 'middle-aged, well-educated, affluent, managerial–professional man or woman'. Best and Andreasen (1976) found that complainers were of a higher social status. In constructing a model of consumer complaining behaviour, Bearden *et al.* (1980) showed that sex and race turned out to be significant variables influencing complaining behaviour.

Warland *et al.* (1977) conducted a telephone survey of 1,215 adults in 1972. They separated the respondents into three groups: 'upset', 'upset-but-no-action', and 'not-upset' consumers. Three discriminating analyses were performed among three groups with demographic characteristics, consumer actions and some other variables. The results showed that groups differed the most on age and education. The 'not-upset' group was much more satisfied with the business system and less interested in consumerism than the two upset groups.

However, conflicting relationships have also been reported with regard to socio-economic variables. Lundstrom *et al.* (1979) found some inconsistent results. In their study of 240 rural consumers, they discovered that older people were more discontented than younger ones. Day and Bodur (1977), Ash (1977) and Day and Ash (1978) in their analysis of the relationships between demographic variables and satisfaction score revealed generally weak results across different services. Ash and Quelch (1980) also discovered that demographic variables had a weak relationship with satisfaction. Pfaff (1972) found no relationship at all between socio-economic variables. Gronhaug (1977) reported both positive and negative relationships depending on product, but all of them were generally weak. Kraft (1977) also found that there was no significance in the education and income of consumers in distinguishing between complainers and non-complainers.

Similarly, Handy (1977) failed to significantly separate dissatisfied consumers from satisfied consumers by their education.

In summary, there has been a considerable divergence of findings. The only consistent relationship to emerge is the effects of age on satisfaction with products. Relationships of varying strength and direction have been reported with respect to education, income, sex and social class.

Psychographics

The relationship of psychographics and satisfaction has seldom been explored in the literature. Anderson (1973) has suggested that life style characteristics may relate to consumer satisfaction and expectations for product performance. Plumer (1977), amongst the earliest, adopting George Kelley's theory of personal construct, tried to position consumer satisfaction into a broader framework. He utilized a longitudinal approach to examine secondary data from different sources. He found that the economic, social and life style trends had changed the nature of consumers' expectations and perceptions of product quality, the motivations of marketers, and the value of relevant information. He also stressed that 'these trends not only underline the need to examine consumer satisfaction in a broad framework and how the ground rules have become more demanding from the consumer's perspective, but they suggest that a new strategy for dealing with satisfaction is in order' (Plumer 1977).

Wall *et al.* (1977) examined several correlations of satisfaction and dissatisfaction with clothing performance. A sample of 891 respondents for their survey was successfully drawn from a telephone directory, utilizing a computer to generate random numbers for page, line and column combinations. Respondents were asked to rate the clothing performance satisfaction and life styles statements. Each of the two categories of statements were first reduced to a manageable size by factor analysis. Using a stepwise regression procedure, taking the clothing performance satisfaction factors as dependent variables, and the life style factors as independent variables, they found that the following variables were good predictors of clothing performance satisfaction:

1 Problem-proneness.
2 Information seeker.
3 Courtesy.
4 Commanding.

5 Self-controlled/easy-going.

Hawes and Arndt (1979), in a national survey of the United States using a consumer mail panel, tried to determine consumer satisfaction through benefit profiling. They developed a satisfaction scale consisting of thirty-two satisfaction statements covering the active–passive, individual group, and indoor–outdoor spectra. Factor analysis was used to cluster statements across all activities into the most popular category for females and males. A five-dimension profile of satisfaction which in fact indicated the life styles of respondents was found for both females and males. These dimensions were labelled as:

1 Newness relating to people.
2 Mental versus physical activity.
3 Competence-seeking.
4 Overcoming challenges.
5 Introspection.

Personality traits

The role of personality in differentiating between satisfied and dissatisfied consumers has been neglected. Kassarjian (1971) has warned that studying personality effects upon consumer behaviour without a prior conceptualization of expected relationships is dangerous. However, Day (1977) has suggested that evaluative reactions to consumption experiences might be based partially on personality factors, even though he observed that Pfaff had failed to find significant relationships between personality traits and consumer satisfaction (Pfaff 1972). His suggestion raised again the possibility that basic psychological variables might serve to influence consumer satisfaction and dissatisfaction. Further suggestions of this possibility came from Hughes's (1977a) results in his survey of consumer satisfaction with jeans and slacks. He found that the reported incidence of other product was a predictor of dissatisfaction with women's jeans. The reported incidence may well reflect a generalized tendency of a consumer to feel positively or negatively about all aspects of his experiences. He may basically have an optimistic or a pessimistic outlook which is in turn a product of some personality trait such as ego strength (Barron 1953) and internal control (Rotter 1966). Hence, expressions of consumer satisfaction/dissatisfaction might be attributable as much to the individual consumers themselves as to the shortcomings of the marketplace and its offering of products and services.

Faircy and Magiz (1975) examined the proposition that a set of personality variables was needed to understand the multidimensional nature of consumer satisfaction. Three instruments were administered to ninety-one subjects in a survey:

1 Rotter's Internal–External Control Scale.
2 Troldahl and Powell's Dogmatism Scale.
3 A six-point satisfaction scale.

Four dissatisfaction dimensions were identified by factor analysis. Then a canonical analysis was performed, using the four dissatisfaction dimensions as the criterion set and the personality variables as the predictor set. It was found that the locus of control was highly correlated with the blamed resolution and individual action, and dogmatism was highly correlated with governmental role and tendency to complain.

Swan (1977) has tried to extend the Howard and Sheth model to buyer behaviour concerning satisfaction and patronage of a retail department store. He dealt with the relationships between intention, confidence and pre-shopping attitudes and satisfaction. The results showed that satisfaction was high when confidence was high and vice versa. Furthermore, by employing the analysis of variance, both confidence and fulfilment were significant as main effects, but the interaction between confidence and fulfilment was not significant. Though the relationship between confidence and satisfaction was established, he found that confidence as a predictor of satisfaction was difficult to interpret, because the literature of consumer satisfaction provided little guidance on this relationship.

Zaichkowsky and Liefeld (1977) attempted to understand the personality profile of consumer complaint letter writers. A hundred complainers and 100 non-complainers were recruited to participate in the study. To measure the personality profiles of the two groups, the Cattell's sixteen personality factors (16PF) questionnaire was used. Principal component analysis on the 16PF was first performed to yield the personality dimensions of the complainers. A stepwise discriminant analysis was then employed to sort out significant and discriminating personality dimensions between the two groups. It was concluded that consumer complaint letter writers could be not distinguished by personality type.

Westbrook (1980c) in his survey of 232 owners of a major household appliance tried to find the relationship between satisfaction and personal competence/efficacy. He measured personal competence/ efficacy with a three-item forced choice scale developed originally by previous researchers. Multiple regression was employed while holding constant the effect of sex, age and education of consumers. It was found that satisfaction varied directly with personal competence/ efficacy. The relationship was significant although the portion of variance which the variable explained was modest.

Personal values

In the consumer satisfaction literature, there are only a limited number of studies devoted to personal values to date. From the psychological point of view, a personal value is defined as 'a centrally held, enduring belief which guides actions and judgments across specific situations and beyond immediate goals to more ultimate end-states of existence' (Rokeach 1968). Both Kluckhohn (1951) and Rokeach (1968, 1973) have suggested that personal values have influences on human behaviour. Research in consumer behaviour has shown the application of personal values to the explanation of both attitudes toward brands and the purchase of products (Lessig 1973, 1975; Munson and McIntyre 1978; Gutman and Vinson 1979; Stein and Stampfl 1981; Vinson, Scott and Lamont 1977; Pitts and Woodside 1983). Most of these studies were heavily influenced by Rokeach's work and his thirty-six-item values inventory. According to Rokeach, personal values are divided into two categories: terminal and instrumental values. Instrumental values relate to modes of conduct and terminal values have to do with preferred end-states of existence. The eighteen terminal and eighteen instrumental values had test–retest reliabilities of approximately 0.70. From these two kinds of value, Howard (1977) constructed a model of two levels of choice. The two levels of choice are brand choice and product-class choice. He hypothesized that terminal values were the source of choice criteria for product classes whilst instrumental values were the source of choice criteria for brands. Boote (1975) examined Howard's model in a survey using 124 housewives who were considering the purchase of one or more of nine household appliances (cf. Pitts and Woodside 1983). The results supported Howard's two hypotheses.

In relating personal values to consumer research, Scott and Lamont (1973a) suggested that changes in personal values affected the expectations that consumers held regarding the conduct of business institutions, and the criteria they used to evaluate the products and services available in the marketplace.

Based on the studies of Vinson, Munson and Nakanishi (1977) and Vinson and Nakanishi (1976), which further asserted that personal value systems influenced the extent of consumer discontent, Vinson and Gutman (1978) conducted a survey to examine the relationship between personal values and consumer discontent. The data were collected from a random sample of ninety-nine residents by the mail questionnaire method. Two sets of personal values were selected for investigation. The first set were global values which represented the thirty-six terminal and instrumental values originally developed by Rokeach. The second set of values were referred to as consumption-specific values. These values pertained to specific qualities of products/ services and evaluations of manufacturers' marketing behaviour. Examples of these values are reasonable prices, quiet-running products, prompt service, being deceptive in advertisements. Vinson and Gutman adopted Lundstrom's Consumer Discontent Scale to measure consumer discontent. In analysing the data, factor analysis was first employed to group the terminal values into six factors:

1 Personal gratification.
2 Social harmony.
3 Love and affection.
4 Personal contentedness.
5 Tranquillity.
6 Friendship.

and the instrumental values into five factors:

1 Social benevolence.
2 Performance.
3 Competence.
4 Integrity.
5 Self-control.

The same was done to values relating to qualities of products and marketing behaviour. The following eight factors were found:

1 Price utility.
2 Fashion.
3 Tranquillity.
4 Health-promoting.
5 Maintenance.
6 Honesty.
7 Responsibility.
8 Helpfulness.

These results were consistent with those of Vinson and Nakanishi (1976) and Vinson, Munson and Nakanishi (1977).

Using stepwise regression analysis, they found that responsibility, social benevolence, personal gratification, true friendship and helpfulness were significant predictors of consumer discontent. It was concluded that value analysis might be a productive method of assessing the nature and extent of consumer dissatisfaction.

Vinson and Gutman's research suffers from a number of problems generally encountered by exploratory research. First, they put terminal and instrumental values at the same level to predict consumer discontent, when these two kinds of values seem to be in a structural hierarchy. Haines (personal correspondence, 1979) has also criticized the fact that further explanation was required of why both the terminal and instrumental values were linked directly and simultaneously to consumer discontent. Second, they failed to find whether personal values affected expectations directly, as Scott and Lamont (1973a) indicated.

Using the same methodology, except that expectation statements were added, Vinson and Yang (1979) found that consumer discontent with product performance, marketing activities and the business system in general did not necessarily originate from the discrepancy between expectations and product performance. This result solves the second problem posed by Vinson and Gutman's study.

Along the same lines, Vinson (1977) tried to explore personal values which discriminated between discontented and contented consumers. The level of consumer discontent for each respondent was assessed by the individual's total score on Lundstrom's consumer discontent inventory. Respondents were clustered into two groups – discontented and contented consumers – according to the score. Stepwise discriminant analysis was then employed to discriminate these two groups using terminal-value, instrumental-value, marketing-activity and quality-of-products factors as predictors. The result of the analysis was interesting. Only two values relating to marketing activities were found able to discriminate between the two groups.

Cultural values

Among the three highly acclaimed models of consumer behaviour – the Nicosia Traditional Model (Nicosia 1966), the Howard–Sheth model of buyer behaviour (1969) and the Engel *et al.* model (1968, 1983), only Engel *et al.*'s model incorporates culture as an environmental variable which yields impact on the problem recognition of a consumer. Until recently culture has not gained attention from academics in the area of consumer behaviour. Nevertheless, the relation between culture and consumer behaviour seems debatable. Kassarjian and Robertson (1978) attributed the lack of recognition of culture as an important variable in consumer behaviour in the past to the fact that the influences are indirect and difficult to delineate empirically.

However, many experts have expressed their confidence and consensus in the specific link between culture and consumer behaviour. Markin (1974) strongly proposed that:

> knowledge of a culture makes it possible to predict a good many of the actions of the persons who share that culture. Because behavior is somewhat orderly, one familiar with the culture of a group can, to a certain extent, predict its future behavior.
>
> (Markin 1974: 469)

Along the same lines, Sheth and Sethi also suggested that:

> an understanding of the process and conditions by which different cultures move on the continuum can help in understanding and predicting the circumstances under which a given product or idea tends to be accepted in a society.
>
> (1977: 374)

Culture and cultural values   There are many definitions of culture. Markin (1974) catalogued definitions into three types. Each was represented by a typical definition which reflects a different orientation to culture. The first type was represented by Linton's definition:

> [culture is] 'the configuration of learned behaviour and results of behaviour whose component elements are shared and transmitted by the members of a particular society'.
>
> (Linton 1945: 32)

This definition emphasizes that culture is dynamic and transmissive. Its characteristics are shared by members of a given society.

The second type emphasizes problem-solving and decision-making. It defines culture as:

> a system of solutions to unlearned problems as well as learned problems and their solutions, all of which are acquired by members of a recognizable group and shared by them.
>
> (Ullman 1965: 181)

The third type defined culture as the:

> transmitted and created content and patterns of values, ideas, and other symbolic-meaningful systems as factors in the shaping of human behaviour and the artifacts produced through behaviour.
>
> (Kroeber and Parsons 1958: 583)

This definition stresses the patterned system of values which are objects and orientations of actions for members of a given society. It explicitly shows that culture consists of values which serve as norms of behaviour. In fact, this definition is well in line with that of Kroeber and Kluckhohn, who summarized several hundred definitions of culture as follows:

> the essential core of culture consists of traditional ... ideas and especially their attached values ...
>
> (1952: 181)

In this book, the third type of definition is adopted because it is well oriented to the purpose of the book – cultural values.

At this point, it is necessary to define the term 'cultural values' in order to distinguish it from personal values as discussed in the previous section. In a human society, there are values which are traditionally retained as part of an explicit culture. At the individual level many of these values become incorporated as enduring beliefs which affirm what is desirable by other members of the culture and have some impact on activities (Nicosia and Mayer 1976: 67). These values are called cultural values. Cultural values differ from personal values in several ways.

First, personal values are referred to as the beliefs of individuals in a culture, while cultural values refer to *normative beliefs* which individuals have about how they are *expected* to behave by their culture. Hence, a cultural value is not necessarily a personal value. For example, Chinese believe that harmony with other people and nature is not a personal value but a cultural value. Though sometimes it is difficult to draw a clear dividing line between between personal values and culture values (Hofstede 1980), these two types of values have different meanings for consumer behaviour and therefore should be treated differently. Second, since cultural values are shared beliefs, they are small in number. Thus an individual may have hundreds of personal values but only a dozen cultural values.

Dimensions of cultural values   What are the cultural values which constitute a culture? This is a difficult question which anthropologists, social psychologists and sociologists have long been trying to answer. It seems that there are two levels of dimensions of culture or profile of cultural values. On the micro-level, different cultures may have their own unique or specific values. In a culture, individual differences can and do occur as a result of variations of these cultural values (Hollander 1967). On the macro-level, Kluckhohn (1951) argued that there should be universal categories of culture so that cultures can be meaningfully ordered. The choice of the universal or specific dimensions of culture, or profile of cultural values, depends on the research strategy available. Specific dimensions or values of different cultures should first be carefully investigated before any attempt is made to generalize and examine universal dimensions or values of culture.

Hofstede (1980) has given a detailed review of literature on the dimensions of cultures. However, in this book, only relevant literature on cultural values, which is related to Chinese culture as well as consumer behaviour, is drawn on.

Parsons and Shils (1951) offered a multidimensional classification of culture in the development of a 'General Theory of Action'. They claimed that all human action was determined by the following five cultural values:

1 Affectivity versus Affective neutrality.
2 Self-orientation versus Collectivity orientation.
3 Universalism versus Particularism.
4 Ascription versus Achievement.
5 Specificity versus Diffuseness.

Based on a field study of five small communities in the United States, Kluckhohn and Strodtbeck (1961) suggested another multidimensional classification of culture. They found that the following five value orientations were able to discriminate among five subcultures in America:

1 Man−nature orientation.
2 Man−himself orientation.
3 Relational orientation.
4 Time orientation.
5 Activity orientation.

For each value orientation, there is a three-point span of alternatives. For example, the three-point span of alternatives for the Time orientation is: past, present, future. Respondents are asked to choose one value alternative from each of the five value orientations.

The essential advantage of Kluckhohn and Strodtbeck's value

orientations is their exhaustiveness. They differ from Parsons and Shils's classification in that they were formulated around basic human problems, especially of interpersonal relations, which lead to different solutions and actions. Parsons and Shils's was only constructed around dominant modes of actions. Hence, Parsons and Shils's classification could be regarded as a special case of Kluckhohn and Strodtbeck's.

Henry (1976) was among the first to examine the relation between culture and consumer behaviour. Adopting Kluckhohn and Strodtbeck's five value orientations, he obtained 498 usable family responses in the form of a self-administered questionnaire using random sampling. He treated value dimensions as predictors of ownership within five generic categories of automobiles: full-size, intermediate, compact, subcompact and sports. Analysis of data by multiple classification analysis showed the following results:

1 Heavy ownership of intermediate and subcompact category automobiles seem to be favoured by families with collateral orientation; opposite results were observed with the category of compact automobiles.
2 Ownership of compact and subcompact automobiles by one and two-automobile families tended to be correlated with becoming orientation. The same observation was found with ownership for three or more automobile families.
3 Young and large multi-auto, multi-driver families tended to have value orientations toward tradition, harmony with the environment and a strong self-fulfilment perspective.

To some extent, the results of Henry's research indicated that individual value dimensions were correlated with particular automobile categories.

After an extensive review of the literature on national character and modal personality, Inkeles and Levinson (1954) summarized three cultural values which they labelled 'standard analytic issues':

1 Relation to authority.
2 Self conception.
3 Primary conflicts and the ways of dealing with them.

They set forth two criteria for comparative (cross-cultural) analysis:

1 Universality, which means that the cultural value under evaluation should be common to man and to all human societies.

2 Significance, which means that the cultural values under evaluation should have functional significance for the individual personality as well as for the social system.

(Inkeles and Levinson 1954)

They found that the two standard analytic issues met the two criteria.

Hofstede (1980) in studying international differences in work-related values suggested the following four dimensions:

1 Power distance.
2 Uncertainty avoidance.
3 Individualism.
4 Masculinity.

These dimensions are quite similar to those of Inkeles and Levinson. 'Power distance' corresponds to the first, 'Individualism' and 'Masculinity' to the second, and 'Uncertainty avoidance' to the third of Inkeles and Levinson's standard analytic issues (Hofstede, 1980).

Morris (1956) used another typology which he assumed to be valid for cultural level. In his study of 'ways to live', he designed an instrument consisting of thirteen alternative conceptions which included values advocated and defended in the several ethical and religious systems of human societies. Morris had put this instrument to the test in three countries: the United States, China and India. Each 'way to live' was described in a paragraph of about seven to eight statements. Respondents were asked to rank the thirteen 'ways to live' according to their preference after reading the paragraphs, so that a cultural value system for each country could be found. The thirteen 'ways to live' were summarized by Morris as follows:

1 Preserve the best that man has attained.
2 Cultivate independence of persons and things.
3 Show sympathetic concern for others.
4 Experience festivity and solitude in alternation.
5 Act and enjoy life through group participation.
6 Constantly master changing conditions.
7 Integrate action, enjoyment and contemplation.
8 Live with wholesome, carefree enjoyment.
9 Wait in quiet receptivity.
10 Control the self stoically.
11 Meditate on the inner life.
12 Chance adventuresome deeds.
13 Obey the cosmic purposes.

The instrument suffered from a number of problems. First, respondents found it difficult to rank the thirteen ways to live properly, because the description for each 'way to live' is so long that respondents tended to be unable to remember all the 'ways to live' when ranking. Further, respondents tended to agree only with some of the statements in the paragraph for each way to live, not all. This further aggravated the problem of ranking when respondents tried to make comparisons between pairs of 'ways to live'. Second, the instrument is too specialized around the 'ways to live', ignoring other cultural values.

As noted in the last section, Rokeach's personal values have been treated as cultural values in the literature of consumer behaviour. It seems necessary at this point to give an account of Rokeach's personal values inventory, which is shown in Table 2.1. Rokeach's inventory has eighteen terminal and eighteen instrumental values. Each type of personal value is denoted by eighteen words. In using the inventory, respondents are asked to rank both the eighteen terminal values and the eighteen instrumental values according to their preferences. Munson and McIntyre (1978) have pointed out the disadvantages of using a ranking method for the two types of personal values. They suggested that both types of values could be rated by means of a

Table 2.1 The inventory of Rokeach's personal values

Terminal Values	Instrumental Values
A Comfortable Life	Ambitious
An Exciting Life	Broadminded
A Sense of Accomplishment	Capable
A World at Peace	Cheerful
A World of Beauty	Clean
Equality	Courageous
Family Security	Forgiving
Freedom	Helpful
Happiness	Honest
Inner Harmony	Imaginative
Mature Love	Independent
National Security	Intellectual
Pleasure	Logical
Salvation	Loving
Self-respect	Obedient
Social Recognition	Polite
True Friendship	Responsible
Wisdom	Self-controlled

Source: Rokeach, 1973: 28.

Likert-type scale, as they found that there were no significant differences between ranking and rating methods with respect to the reliability and validity of the inventory.

Clawson and Vinson (1978) have claimed that this inventory has made Rokeach one of the most influential modern contributors to the psychological theory of personal values. However, Zensen and Hammer (1978) were surprised to find that Rokeach's inventory was so influential, and strongly criticized the inventory as a rather crude instrument for portraying the actual ways in which people make value judgments. They also cast doubt on the theoretical foundation which led to the development of Rokeach's value system.

Further, it should be noted that Rokeach's inventory suffers from a drawback when it is treated as an inventory for cultural values. The words used to describe (personal) values will have different meanings to respondents of different cultures. Rokeach tried to solve the problem by attaching a gummed label to each value. This would not serve the purpose, but only make respondents feel puzzled upon seeing the label bearing a meaning or interpretation different from the corresponding value. For example, a comfortable life means a prosperous life to Americans, as indicated by Rokeach, but a peaceful life to the Chinese. Family security means taking care of loved ones to Americans but keeping harmony and performing filial duties to the Chinese. For Chinese, sincerity means to follow the appropriate social norms regardless of one's private views; for Westerners, it normally means consistency between one's private self and public self (Kindle, 1982).

Hence, Rokeach's personal values can be treated as cultural values for Americans. If any attempt is made to adopt Rokeach's inventory, the thirty-six words which denote the terminal and instrumental values must be replaced by another thirty-six statements serving the same purpose. However, this would reduce the simplicity of the inventory.

Summary   An account of cultural values was made. Marketing theorists have accepted that culture, as well as cultural values, is one of the underlying determinants of consumer behaviour. However, it is disappointing that little empirical work has been conducted to date in the field of consumer behaviour, not to mention consumer satisfaction, concerning cultural values.

Situation-specific research

Growing concern about the inability of personal consumer characteristics to explain variation in consumer behaviour has prompted the
need to examine situational influences on behaviour. It has been
indicated that works such as those by Howard and Sheth (1969) and
Engel *et al.* (1968) might have misdirected consumer behaviour
research by implicitly overemphasizing deterministic models of behaviour (cf. Bearden and Woodside, 1976a). Mattson (1982) urged that
factors exogenous to the individual must be considered. Hence, Ward
and Robertson (1973) asserted that situational factors might account
for more variance than consumer characteristics in explaining consumer behaviour. Engel *et al.* (1968) suggested that both individual
characteristics and situational factors had to be considered in order to
explain consumer choices. In a clearer picture, Bowers (1973), in
analysing articles concerned with personal and situational influences
on behaviour, concluded that subject variance was as important as
situational variance but the contribution of either was relatively small
when compared with the amount of variance due to their interaction.
Lutz and Kakkar (1974) were also in agreement with Bowers's viewpoint when trying to build up a taxonomy of consumption situations.

No matter how well consumer characteristics may explain consumer
behaviour, situational analysis remains a seldom explored but important area. Most situational research to date has been focused on the
explanation of attitude–behaviour consistencies, taking situation as
an extraneous variable (Bearden and Woodside 1976b; Gronhaug
1972), or through individual–situation interactions, and the influences
on consumer preferences (Bearden and Woodside 1976b; Berkowitz *et
al.* 1977; Lutz and Kakkar 1974; Mattson 1982). Another line of
development was the conceptualization of situations. Allen (1965)
classified situational characteristics into two dimensions: (1) social
dimension (for example, public or private situations) and (2) task
dimension (for example, difficulty and importance). Kasmar (1970)
developed a scale to describe thirteen aspects of situations: size,
volume, scale, mood, colour, texture, function, illumination,
aesthetic, quality, climate, acoustic quality, and miscellaneous.
Mehrabian and Russell (1974) argued that situations should be subject-
ively defined and hence proposed three comprehensive situational
descriptors: pleasure, arousal and dominance.

Belk (1974), on the other hand, suggested that situations should be
defined objectively without considering intrapersonal factors and
should be adequate in depicting the array of possible situational

dimensions. He suggested the following five groups of situational characteristics:

1 *Physical surroundings*, which include geographical and institutional location, decor, sounds, weather and other material surrounding a consumer.
2 *Social surroundings* is a dimension of situations in which there are interpersonal interactions occurring.
3 *Temporal perspective* provides a time description of a situation.
4 *Task definition* features of a situation include an intent or requirement to select, shop for, or obtain information about a general or specific purchase.
5 *Antecedent states*, which are momentary moods or momentary conditions stipulated to be immediately antecedent to the current situation.

Thus he defined the (objective) situation as 'objective descriptions which may include the existence of external facts and events borne upon current behaviour even though they are not themselves physically a part of that situation'.

However, researchers such as Bearden and Woodside (1976b) and Lutz and Kakkar (1974) did not agree with Belk's definition. Instead, Lutz and Kakkar (1974) supported Mehrabian and Russell's idea of subjective situation and defined situation as follows:

an individual's internal response to, or interpretation of, all factors particular to a time and place of observation which are not stable intra-individual characteristics or stable environmental characteristics, and which have a demonstrable and systematic effect on the individual's psychological process and/or his overt behavior.

This definition helped researchers to understand how situational factors influence consumer behaviour, while Belk's definition is good for managers to understand situations and develop marketing strategies accordingly, and for researchers to manipulate situations for experimental purposes. In fact, these two definitions are complementary rather than competitive with each other.

In the consumer satisfaction literature, Day (1977) asserted in several incidents that situations might trigger the evaluative process of a consumer and thus affect consumer satisfaction/dissatisfaction. Ortinau (1979) in constructing a conceptual model of consumers' post-purchase satisfaction/dissatisfaction decision process stressed that external environmental, and new situational factors affect discrepancies, expectations and the performance of products. In a more recent study, Sirgy (1982) again in developing a psychological model of consumer satisfaction asserted that stimulus factors, which included situations perceived, determined a consumer's perception process, which would in turn affect the degree of discrepancy between the perceived and normative outcomes.

Unfortunately, no empirical studies have been carried out to date to examine the relationship between situations and consumer satisfaction.

Summary

It was revealed that consumer satisfaction varied across product categories. On the one hand, consumers of cars and car repairs have been found to be the most dissatisfied category. Price paid failed to turn up as an important predictor of satisfaction. Furthermore, warranty service also appeared to be a serious source of dissatisfaction in the post-services category. On the other hand, taste and freshness in the food category, and service calls after purchase, were regarded as the most important attributes influencing satisfaction.

Literature about the characteristics of satisfied and dissatisfied consumers is limited. Most works have focused on socio-economic characteristics. However, there has been a considerable divergence of findings with respect to these characteristics. The only consistent relationship to emerge is the effects of age on satisfaction with products. Relationships of varying strength and direction have been reported with respect to education, income, sex, social class, etc.

Work on personality traits of satisfied and dissatisfied consumers was very fragmented, with different results. Personal values were also found to be an important factor influencing consumer satisfaction, according to the work of Vinson and his colleagues who pioneered the examination of the relationship of personal values and satisfaction.

With regard to situation-specific research, researchers have conceptually felt the importance of situations in influencing behaviour. Several conceptual models have been developed but no empirical work has been reported to date.

HOW CAN PREVIOUS RESEARCH BE BUILT ON?

The decision to carry out research in the area of consumer satisfaction/dissatisfaction was first motivated by the increasing importance of consumer satisfaction for individual, company and government decisions, and, second, by the lack of understanding of how satisfaction is affected by factors, especially Chinese culture values in a Chinese-dominated community. Such knowledge would be valuable, especially in guiding an international firm's decision-making in selling products or offering services to Chinese communities.

It was revealed that the terms 'consumer satisfaction' and 'consumer dissatisfaction' are ambiguous, as there have been several conceptualizations and classifications in the literature. It was noted that consumer satisfaction/dissatisfaction is best viewed in terms of expectations, performance and disconfirmation, and it was decided to adopt the psychological conceptualization of consumer satisfaction as the basis of the structural model which is to be introduced in the next chapter.

However, the review of the consumer satisfaction literature clearly shows that it is difficult for psychological interpretations alone to explain fully the phenomenon of consumer satisfaction. Opportunities and directions have been envisaged from the literature of consumer satisfaction.

First, our present theories do not account for the complex relationships of different types of people, settings and behaviour. Too much emphasis has been placed on the relationships between expectations, perceived performance, disconfirmation and satisfaction within a person. Harre and Secord (1972) have tried to unravel the 'models of generation of social behaviour' within a person. However, no matter how consistent the findings about factors influencing consumer satisfaction/dissatisfaction external to a person have been shown, most of these findings were obtained from 'one shot' research and therefore are unstable and unreliable. Furthermore, it is always difficult to integrate these piecemeal findings with those in the psychological interpretation to form a new paradigm. Hence, there is an urgent need to build a broader model by incorporating more extraneous variables such as values, situations and experiences, or by linking with other behavioural constructs.

Second, there is a trend towards building models of consumer satisfaction based on sound theoretical foundations. In the literature, variables such as situations and personal values were directly correlated with consumer satisfaction scores without a theoretical basis. The links between these variables, expectations and performance must be considered. Sources of theoretical cross-fertilization are available in other applied contexts. Though they differ in contexts with consumer satisfaction/dissatisfaction, cross-fertilization on the conceptual level and measurement is possible and may be fruitful. Adler and

Robinson's (1980) consumer satisfaction model based on job satisfaction theory is a good example.

Third, consumer satisfaction is not an isolated area of consumer behaviour. The recognition of the links between other behavioural constructs such as buying intention, brand loyalty and complaining behaviour is very important to marketing managers for decision-making. Furthermore, without establishing these links, it is difficult to contribute to, and integrate findings with, existing knowledge of consumer behaviour.

Fourth, since consumer satisfaction can be a process in itself, initiated by the purchase or use of the product/service, longitudinal research can serve best to help understand the effect of prolonged experience with a product (Oliver 1979). With the exceptions of the studies of Swan (1977) and Oliver (1979), no study to date in the literature on consumer satisfaction/dissatisfaction has involved a real purchase situation whereby consumers make an actual investment in the product and evaluate their expectations of the product before, and satisfaction with the product after, the purchase. In most studies, subjects were exposed to the product for a very short period of time. As a result, dissonance-reducing effects which might influence the impact of expectation against disconfirmation remained untested. Longitudinal studies with long-range use intervals will certainly uncover the influence of dissonance-reducing effects.

Finally, there is the emergence of the inherent need for cross-cultural or cross-national research. Present theories in consumer satisfaction were mostly developed and tested in the United States, where consumers in many aspects behave differently from those in the East. Direct transplantation of theories to other cultures could mean a disaster to people who make marketing decisions or frame public policies, as satisfaction may be constrained by cultural values or norms. The use of consumer discontent scales such as Allison's (1977) might not be suitable, mainly because they were developed according to problems which were faced by the consumers in the States. Many facets of consumer discontent derived from these scales would be either redundant or inadequate.

The search for similarities in behaviour across culture was regarded as an easier way to determine generalization and universality than the search for differences (Triandis 1974). However, the latter is in line with another difficulty with cross-cultural research, which is the necessity to take into account those variables which are relevant to a particular cultural group (Triandis 1974). When searching for differences, researchers should first look into specific variables of the cultural groups. Furthermore, differences between cultures can better serve as reminders for differential marketing strategies or policies for international companies, because international marketers tend to act according to their own self-reference criteria.

The purpose of this research is to develop a structural model indicating causal relationships among Chinese cultural values, consumption situational factors, affective experiences, consumer expectations, perceived performance, disconfirmation and satisfaction. The primary objective of the research is descriptive, but the ultimate objective must be normative: to enable marketing managers to design marketing programmes which more closely satisfy consumers' needs in a Chinese cultural setting.

CONCLUSION

This chapter has revealed a need for empirical research which integrates cultural values and consumption situations with expectations, perceived performance, disconfirmation and satisfaction. It is also necessary to develop a theoretical framework to indicate the hypothesized links between these variables. The model is presented in the following chapter.

3 A structural model of Chinese cultural values and consumer satisfaction/dissatisfaction

A review of the literature pertaining to consumer satisfaction/dissatisfaction was presented in Chapter 2. It was concluded that no study had investigated the full set of interrelationships among cultural values, situational factors, experiences, expectations, performance, disconfirmation and satisfaction. This book is therefore an attempt to fill this gap in the literature. More specifically, the primary objective of the book is to investigate whether, and if so how, cultural values in a specific setting influence consumer satisfaction. To achieve this objective, a theoretical structural model has been developed, to explain consumer satisfaction under the conditions of Chinese values, and some other determinants. The model is presented in this chapter, and the paradigm of it is presented in Figure 3.1.

This section describes in detail each component or variable in the model. The operationalization of the components will be discussed in the next chapter. The model encompasses the following components:

1 Chinese cultural values.
2 Consumption experiences.
3 Affective experiences.
4 Consumption or use situations.
5 Product expectations.
6 Perceived performance.
7 Disconfirmation.
8 Consumer satisfaction/dissatisfaction.
9 Behavioural intention.

The first five components are independent variables of the model while the last four components are dependent variables. The core components of the model are the Chinese culture values and consumer satisfaction. The Chinese culture values component is treated as an independent variable. The major dependent variable is consumer

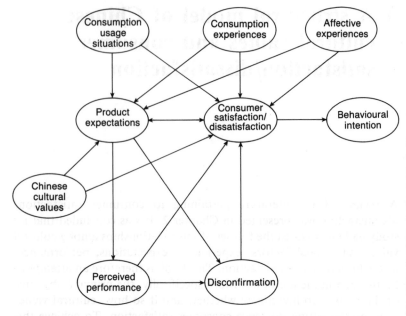

Figure 3.1 The structural model of Chinese cultural values and consumer satisfaction/dissatisfaction

satisfaction, which in turn is related both directly and as a mediating variable to behavioural intentions. Causality between components in the model is indicated by arrows which show the direction of postulated influence. The model assumes that there is a one-way flow of causation. The solid lines together with the arrows show hierarchically how determinants cause or influence other determinants. Although comprehensive, the model is still lacking in attitudinal and/or behavioural variables which will have an impact on consumption, affective experiences and cultural values. Hence, there is no feedback flow in the model.

The model hypotheses that will be presented reflect only a small number of the potential links that could be made. Obviously, the empirical study, which will be discussed in the next chapter, cannot deal with all the variables and possible combinations of relationships contained in the model. Only those relationships which will be formally tested in this book are presented as hypotheses. The formulation of this specific model was mostly determined by prior research and by the basic objective of the book. The various components of the models will be discussed in the following subsections and the analytical method which is chosen to test the relationships between variables in the next chapter.

CHINESE CULTURAL VALUES

With a fifth of the world's population, China has the greatest number of consumers in the world. Since the death of Z. T. Mao, the bamboo curtain has been torn down. China has now opened again the door to trade with the outside world and been pursuing the four modernizations under the leadership of Z. P. Deng. Vast foreign investments in different forms across different industries have been reported. A prosperous consumer market awaits exploration by those who have the will to serve it.

Businessmen may not be interested in the investment or marketing opportunities in the People's Republic of China (PRC) solely because of its political instability. Yet the Chinese are everywhere; businessmen in international trade will often find themselves dealing with Chinese consumers. Waldie (1980) has warned international managers in Hong Kong to examine the cultural differences between Chinese and Western people in general, when making management decisions. An English term can have a different meaning in the Chinese situation. For example, in Western culture, maturity means 'to be able to express one's genuine self, to be free from the constraints of what other people think, to confront others because of the consequence of being individualised or different' (Waldie 1980). But for the Chinese, maturity means a movement towards a harmonious integration into the social fabric of the family as well as the institution in which one is working. Thus, it is crucial and beneficial for international managers to understand the Chinese way of life and value systems.

Researchers in the study of Chinese culture values may find it surprising to learn that Chinese values form a clear and consistent system throughout generations (Kindle 1982; Hsu 1970). Of course, this is not to imply that the values and the system have not changed. In fact, Chinese cultural values have recently undergone rapid change. For example, during the Cultural Revolution in the PRC, the orthodox doctrine of Confucianism, which is the foundation of the Chinese value system, had been severely criticized and deeds according to the doctrine strictly forbidden. Thus, the classical Chinese value system was disrupted and efforts have now been made to rebuild it. Other Chinese-dominated societies such as Taipei, Hong Kong and Singapore have also shown inevitable changes in value systems in the process of rapid social and economic change (Shively and Shively 1972).

Some studies have revealed that Chinese cultural values have indeed changed. In a cross-cultural comparison of human values, Morris (1956) found that there was no noticeable difference in the value systems among subsamples of university students from four large cities in China. Table 3.1 shows the Chinese value systems of the Chinese sample, which he found 'To be in harmony with the universe' and 'To be dominant over the ever changing environment' were the two most important cultural values, while 'To have a contemplative life' and 'To be receptive' were the two least important ones. These results, to a great extent, were well in line with the doctrines of Confucianism and Taoism.

Yang (1972) replicated Morris's study and found that there was a change in the hierarchy of the value systems of college students. He

Table 3.1 The Chinese cultural value system

Original Sequential Item No.	Way	Rank Order by Means (N = 523) (on a 7-point Scale)
1	To preserve the best that man has attained	4.89
2	To avoid dependence upon persons and things	2.95
3	To be sympathetic to other persons	5.10
4	To have solitude and sociality together in life	3.17
5	To realize and enjoy one's life through participation in social activities	5.14
6	To be dominant over the ever changing environment	5.31
7	To integrate enjoyment, action and contemplation	4.72
8	To live in carefree and healthy surroundings	3.98
9	To be receptive	2.57
10	To have self-control	3.69
11	To have a contemplative life	2.58
12	To have a life with daring and adventurous deeds	4.52
13	To be in harmony with the universe	5.47

Source: Adapted from Morris (1956), p. 41.

conducted a survey in Taiwan with a sample of 787 college students from five universities or colleges. Respondents were asked to rank the thirteen values with respect to two criteria: (1) that the values were traditional and (2) that the values were preferred. The results are shown in Table 3.2.

Among these thirteen values, the only value that the college students felt likely to be eradicated as a traditional Chinese value was 'To have solitude and sociality together in life'. They also regarded 'To have a contemplative life' and 'To be in harmony with the universe' as traditional Chinese values; yet they had a tendency to prefer not to hold them. This implies that Chinese college students had forgone the humble way of being contemplative in life and harmonious with the universe. However, they regarded the following as their preferable traditional Chinese values:

1 To preserve the best that man has attained.

Table 3.2   The cultural value system of Chinese college students

		Rank Order by Means (On a 7-point Scale)	
	Way	*Traditional*	*Actual*
1	To preserve the best that man has attained	5.16 (2)	5.39 (1)
2	To avoid dependence upon persons and things	4.80 (4.5)	4.46 (5)
3	To be sympathetic to other persons	5.25 (1)	5.15 (2)
4	To have solitude and sociality together in life	2.53 (13)	3.15 (13)
5	To realize and enjoy one's life through participation in social activities	3.63 (12)	4.27 (7.5)
6	To be dominant over the environment	3.77 (11)	4.14 (9)
7	To integrate enjoyment, action and contemplation	3.82 (10)	4.71 (3)
8	To live in carefree and healthy surroundings	4.48 (7)	4.27 (7.5)
9	To be receptive	4.46 (8)	4.13 (10)
10	To have self-control	4.89 (3)	4.65 (4)
11	To have a contemplative life	4.80 (4.5)	3.98 (11)
12	To have a life with daring and adventurous deeds	4.20 (9)	4.37 (6)
13	To be in harmony with the universe	4.60 (6)	3.89 (12)

Source: Adapted from Yang (1972), pp. 283 and 286.

2 To be sympathetic to others.
3 To have self-control.

This implies that some of the traditional Chinese values are still held by young Chinese nowadays.

When comparing Yang's results with those of Morris, it is obvious that the value system of the college students had undergone a change. For example, the most preferred value 'to be in harmony with the universe' in the 1950s had become almost the least preferable one. To demean or degrade oneself so as to live in harmony with the universe has been one of the traditional Chinese cultural values. This change was probably a result of the influence of Western culture during the past few decades.

However, there are two points which should be noted in Yang's study. The first is that the average ranking of the value 'to be in harmony with the universe' by the Chinese college students is still higher than that of their counterparts in other countries. To some extent, according to Hsu (1970), this indicates that the Chinese are less prone to change than the people of Western countries. The second is that the value systems found by both Morris and Yang did not represent the typical Chinese cultural value system. According to Shively and Shively (1972), college students and professional people were deviant. It is dangerous, therefore, at this point of time to draw any conclusions from their results.

Adopting the methodology from Kluckhohn and Strodtbeck (1961), Lin (1966) tried to uncover the value orientations of school pupils and their parents in Hong Kong. He found, within the limits of variations, that the younger generation showed a considerable change from their parents with regard to the time, man–nature and relational orientations. The school children under study came from three kinds of schools: Anglican, local, and refugee schools. They did vary in their value orientations. However, in general, the sample of students showed that:

1 They were oriented towards the future and optimistic.
2 They tended to be individualistic and preferred dominant value orientations.
3 They still believed in fatalism.

The first two results showed a shift away from the traditional Chinese values. It would be a mistake, however, to conclude that these findings indicate that the traditional Chinese value orientations in Hong Kong will be completely eradicated in the transition to modernization. First, mastery of traditional Chinese learning is regarded as an important prerequisite for achieving status among intellectuals in Chinese society (Lin 1966). Second, strong vestiges of the Chinese heritage are rooted in the family and kinship relations, and not in the educational institutions (Hsu 1947, 1963, 1972). La Barre (1946) has clearly indicated this:

> The Chinese family is one root of Chinese ethnocentrism. . . . most or all of the emotional and cultural values of the individual person are derived from those of his family exclusively, and conditioned largely within the solidarity of one family setting only (p. 375).

As for an individual Chinese, the family is a source which constantly diffuses cultural influences on him throughout his whole life. Even though he might deviate from the traditional value orientations at some point in his life, he would be assimilated again by his culture and enjoy his authority and his social status as he became old. Some researchers have argued that education will introduce new values which will gradually replace the old ones to shape an industrialized society in which family and kinship relations could not survive (Shively and Shively 1972). This may not be true. Traditional values are not necessarily a stumbling block to industrialization or economic development. The success of the Japanese, who have a similar culture to the Chinese, is a typical example. Hong Kong is another good example of how cultural values have served to make the economy unique. It has been shown during the past twenty years that the prosperity of Hong Kong is due not only to the acumen of the Chinese businessmen, but also to the consideration and perseverance of the labour force, who try always to be in harmony with their employers.

The effect of modernization on culture values should not be ignored. It will be considered in the next chapter when culture values are operationalized. Now, an account of Chinese cultural values will be presented.

Chinese cultural values are largely formed and created from interpersonal relationships and social orientations. This can be revealed by the work of Confucius, whose doctrine is still a basic pillar of Chinese life today. To describe Chinese culture, it is therefore more suitable to adopt the value orientation model of Kluckhohn and Strodtbeck (1961), which has the same emphasis. The following is a description of each of the Chinese cultural values according to Kluckhohn and

Strodtbeck's classification, with possible marketing implications discussed for each orientation (see Figure 3.2):

1 Man–nature orientation.
2 Man–himself orientation.
3 Relational orientation.
4 Time orientation.
5 Personal-activity orientation.

However, no attempt is made to use the three-point scales of alternatives for each value dimension developed by them.

Man–nature orientation

Locus of control The theory of locus of control can serve to explain

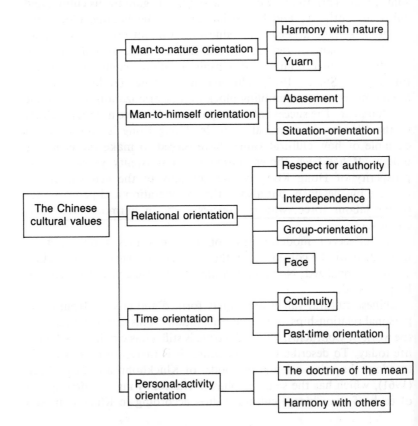

Figure 3.2 Classification of Chinese cultural values

this orientation. The concept of locus of control was first initiated by Julian Rotter (1966) when he developed a test designed to measure internal–external locus of control. Internal locus of control refers to whether people see themselves to have control over their lives while external locus of control refers to whether they see themselves to be governed by forces beyond their control (Sampson 1980). In Western societies, people tend to feel that they have the competence to assert some control over their own lives under the influence of the Protestant ethic's individualism (Rotter 1966). In Chinese societies, this seems not to be the case. Emphasis is put on external locus of control. The Chinese regard man as a part of nature, and believe that man should not try to overcome or master nature but has to learn how to adapt to it so as to reach a harmony. This is because they believe that nature has the Way (Tao, 道) by which all things become what they are (Chan 1963). The Chinese have also taken from Lao Tsu's doctrine of non-being (無為). 'All things in the world come from being. And being comes from non-being' (Chan 1963). It was said that the Way cannot be told.

> There are existence and destruction, life and death, and flourish and decline . . . What is eternal has neither change nor any definite, particular principle itself. Since it [the Way] has no definite principle itself, it is not bound in any particular locality.

Therefore, it is not wise to hold on to what one has got or lost too tightly. There is no such thing as fate or misfortune in life, as they are entangled with each other as well as causes of each other (Wei 1980).

Apart from the doctrine of the Way, Yuarn (Karma, 緣) is another important belief which has been rooted into the hearts of most Chinese. This belief prevailed well before the time of Confucius (557–479 B.C.), who once said, 'Life and death are fated; wealth and honour hinge on the will of providence' (Legge 1960). It resembles the important doctrine, Karma, in Buddhism which was spread to China from India in the Han or Tang Dynasty about two thousand years ago. Hence, to a certain extent, it still has the Buddhist meaning of Karma. However, after two thousand years of assimilation, its meaning has deviated away from its origin. Yuarn can be referred to as predetermined relations with other things or individuals, which are far beyond one's control. The existence or absence of interrelations with the universe is predetermined or governed by a powerful external force. This force could be a supernatural force, or a social law which is too sophisticated to be understood by human beings. Chinese believe that friendships or even marriages are predetermined. When

Yuarn exists, it leads to the chance that two men, living thousands of miles apart, could meet each other and become friends. It also leads a consumer to find products which he would be very much satisfied with. Further, Yuarn will come to an end. When Yuarn ends, couples have to divorce, and friends to separate from each other.

Despite its tragic sense, Yuarn also has its positive side. The concept of Yuarn leads to self-reliance. People cease to complain of their circumstances and try to save themselves from the natural consequences of their own acts before they accept their fate. For example, an individual could beg for Yuarn by giving alms and doing charitable deeds in secret so that the interrelations of himself or his family with the universe could be established. Furthermore, though events are predetermined, he has to try positively to seek for interrelations with others (or things) in order to find out whether he has Yuarn or not. According to the concept of Yuarn, interrelations among people are always passive. But it is only those who actively search for, and try to establish, such interrelations who can successfully have Yuarn.

In social psychological terms, the concept of Yuarn is a particular case of the theory of attribution, in which people attribute their failures to external forces. The concept of Yuarn is consistent with and complementary to the theory of external locus of control previously discussed.

Possible marketing implications of man-to-nature orientation   The man-to-nature orientation has some implications in marketing. According to these two doctrines, it is possible to deduce that a Chinese consumer who holds to this value would generally have low expectations of the product he is going to purchase or consume. Or when the performance of the product does not meet his expectations, he will feel less dissatisfied when he thinks he has to conform to Yuarn.

Chinese have a great tendency to attribute failure of products/ services to fate rather than to the outlet where the product was purchased or even the manufacturer. Hence, they are reluctant to complain about products which do not meet their expectations. Thorelli (1982) includes this evidence in his study of Chinese consumers. Therefore, an objective measurement of dissatisfaction such as frequency of complaints does not adequately reflect the affective attitude of the consumer towards products, and thus is not a good measure of marketing effectiveness, as shown by McNeal (1969) and Cavusgil and Kaynak (1982). Other means of measurement of consumer satisfaction or dissatisfaction are needed.

Man-to-himself orientation

Abasement By studying the child-rearing practices of Chinese families, one can observe dramatic differences compared with Western cultures. From an early age, a child in a Chinese family is brought up to understand the legitimate role of himself in relation to others. The Chinese believe in modesty and self-effacement, which are two important virtues that a child, as well as a subordinate, uses to cultivate his mind. In the past, a Chinese individual would call himself 'the worthless' before his teacher, and 'the unfilial son' before his parents. This sort of behaviour is still very common in today's Chinese society. For example, Western people tend to say, 'Thank you' when praised by others, but Chinese people are prone to say, 'No, I am not worthy,' in the same situation. Furthermore, the Chinese try to avoid saying 'No' when asked to express an opinion. They believe that saying 'No' will embarrass or offend others. Thus, to reply in an indirect or sarcastic way is the best way to express disagreement.

Situation orientation The Chinese today are frequently regarded as situation-oriented and pragmatic (Hsu 1963), owing to child-rearing practices in which a child is taught by parents, uncles and aunts, and other adults in the (extended or joint) family. This child is therefore exposed to many points of view. Consequently, Chinese children learn that circumstances have an important bearing upon what is right or wrong, and compromise in most cases is inevitable. In contrast Western children are usually brought up with the guidance of their parents only, are rarely exposed to other points of view, are kept in a more closed relationship with life's events, and grow up with concepts of one right way to do things (Kindle 1982). Comparatively, the Chinese are less dogmatic and tend to be more flexible in following a learned principle. The root of this Chinese culture value is in Lao Tsu's doctrine of the Way, which clearly states:

> A man must follow his instinct, . . . for there is no principle that is right in all circumstance, or any action that is wrong in all circumstances.
>
> (cf. Shively and Shively 1972)

Possible marketing implications for man-to-himself orientation In marketing, the value of abasement may have implications for sales force management. It can serve as a supplement to other sales force selection techniques, such as objective testing, personal interview and background investigation. If an effective salesman has to be aggressive and positive-minded by American standards, the Chinese tend to be bad salesmen. However, in Chinese society, an aggressive salesman might frighten customers, who would feel humiliated in public. For example, Chinese buyers like to shop in a free environment without interference. If a salesman in a retail store is too eager to help and approaches a customer who has not decided what to buy, the customer will feel uneasy and go away. The proper way is to keep at a distance from the customer but at the same time to let the customer know that he is always ready to help.

The value of situation orientation has particular implications for service marketing. Because of this orientation, Chinese tend to enjoy available things. In the United States or some other Western countries, it is common for consumers to queue up to buy tickets for a movie or to cash a cheque. Customers are requested to go to or are assigned to a counter to be served. The Chinese prefer a short queue even though the waiting time is the same. Moreover, Chinese are anxious to choose a person with whom they are familiar to serve them. Therefore, unless there is no alternative, Chinese tend to feel more dissatisfied with the serving system and are more likely not to repurchase than their counterparts in the USA. In Hong Kong, and even in Taiwan, the multi-queue waiting system is usually adopted, except for some American banks.

Relational orientation

Respect for authority   The Chinese have a strong respect for authority. They are prone to trust totally without questioning. In a classroom, Chinese students expect their teachers to 'teach' them, and not only to guide them. A student will feel himself learning nothing if he is asked to express his opinions or to solve a problem by himself. It is the same in psychological therapy: Chinese patients usually request the psychologist to teach them what to do, and do not believe that finding the solution themselves after consulting the psychologist would be a better way to cure their illness. This may reveal a Chinese dependence on authority.

The early root of Chinese respect for authority is in Confucius's five cardinal relations, which include the relations between sovereign and minister, father and son, husband and wife, old and young, and between friends (Hchu and Yang 1972). These relations have served effectively to control social behaviour in society. Chinese have to observe and act according to the norms prescribed for each instance of interpersonal relations. Thus, the king must be kingly, the minister ministerly, the husband husbandly, the wife wifely, brothers brotherly and friends friendly. It is not surprising to see that Chinese today still prefer to address someone in more structural or hierarchical terms than Westerners. For example, people in the PRC are accustomed to speak of Z. T. Mao as Chairman Mao in order to show respect for his authority. A child is not allowed to call his father's friends by their names. And a venerable man with seniority in an organization is addressed by adding the term 'elder brother' before his surname.

This value has particular implications for advertising. Since the Chinese have great respect for authority that directs them to what is right or wrong, advertisements will tend to be more effective when opinion leaders stand out in the commercials, recommending products/services to their target consumers. Opinion leaders for Chinese consumers include older people, political leaders, family elders and authoritarian types. Kindle (1985) agrees that the Chinese are much more likely to be influenced in their purchasing by opinion leaders than consumers in the USA.

Interdependence   The flexibility of the Chinese in dealing with interpersonal relations comes from the principle of 'doing favours' (人情), which literally signifies one's honour to another. Favours done for others are often considered what may be termed 'social investments' for which handsome returns are expected. The following Chinese proverbs clearly reveal this: 'If you honour me a [linear] foot, I should in return honour you ten feet.' 'A horse received must be returned for an ox; a case of presents received is to be acknowledged by a case of presents in return.' Almost every Chinese person is brought up to be highly conscious of its existence and to practise it heartily . The Chinese believe that reciprocity of favours between two people should be as certain as a cause-and-effect relationship. It should be continuous so that affinity for each other is well established.

The application of the principle of 'doing favours' has a tremendous influence on social as well as business behaviour; it maintains relations amongst Chinese people by the practice of presenting gifts which are regarded as a form of Li-propriety. Chinese small businessmen often believe that to follow the principle of 'doing favours' is of the utmost importance in making the business go smoothly, and in earning more money. They exchange favours by supplying goods or credit without signing legal documents, and believe that the signing of any legal document will terminate the reciprocity of doing favours.

Face   Face is a concept of central importance because of its pervasive influence in interpersonal relations among Chinese. Hu (1944) examined 200 Chinese proverbs and classified face into two types, *lien* (臉) and *mien-tsu* (面子). *Lien* 'represents the confidence of society in the integrity of ego's moral character, the loss of which makes it impossible for him to function properly within the community' (Hu 1944). *Mien-tsu*, on the other hand, 'stands for the kind of prestige that is emphasised ... a reputation achieved through getting on in life, through success and ostentation' (Hu 1944). *Mien-tsu* can be characterized in both quantitative and qualitative terms (Ho 1972). The amount of *mien-tsu* a person has is a function of his social status. It varies according to the the group with which he is interacting. A manager may have more *mien-tsu* before his subordinates, but not in a group of intellectuals.

  Mien-tsu may be claimed on a variety of grounds. It may be obtained either through personal qualities or derived from non-personal characteristics such as wealth, social connections, and authority through personal efforts (Ho 1972). *Mien-tsu* can be lost or gained when there are changes which constitute a departure from the quality or quantity of one's claim. Mien-tsu can normally be gained by obtaining favourable comments from the interacting group or community through exemplary behaviour, superior performance or knowledge, or enhancement of status, as through formal promotion to higher office, etc. *Mien-tsu* may be lost when conduct or performance falls below the minimum acceptable standard, or when some essential requirements corresponding to one's social position are not satisfactorily met. Since the standard and the requirements are social expectations of the group with which one is interacting, the possibility of losing *mien-tsu* may come not only from one's own actions or behaviour, but from how one is expected to behave or be treated by other members in the group. The Chinese are always under a strong constraint to meet the expectations of others, to maintain their *mien-tsu*, and to reciprocate a due regard for the *mien-tsu* of others. The concern for *mien-tsu* exerts a mutually restrictive, even coercive, power upon each member of the social network. To cause others to lose *mien-tsu* is regarded as an aggressive act by those whose face has been discredited, hence the Chinese try to protect others from losing *mien-tsu*, which is regarded as an act of consideration. This is revealed by the following common Chinese sayings: 'At different times and in different places, we will meet again' and 'He who causes others to lose face will eventually lose face in front of others.' These two common sayings in fact bear the same meaning literally. The Chinese observe the importance of assisting one another, because they feel that in later life, in another place, they may be vulnerable to loss of face.

Lien differs from *mien-tsu* in that *lien* is something that everyone is entitled to by virtue of his membership of society, and it can only be lost through misconduct. Thus, it is meaningful to speak only of losing *lien*, not of gaining *lien*. The loss of *lien* is more serious than that of *mien-tsu*, which can be more easily regained; when *lien* is lost, an individual's integrity of character is cast in doubt, or even destroyed. For example, prostitutes and thieves are alike people who renounce their concern for *lien*. Disregard for *lien* can therefore lead to a total transformation of one's social identity.

The significance of *lien* can not be fully appreciated without realizing its close relationship with the concept of *ch'ih* in the Chinese context, which has literally the same meaning as the word 'shame' in English. King and Myers (1977) suggested that, in Chinese culture, *lien* (face) is an incomplete concept. They demonstrated a dichotomy between the Chinese face–shame complex and the Western sin–guilt complex. *Lien* implies the presence of *ch'ih*, which is one of the fundamental requirements of being human. Thus, Mencius declared that 'a man without a sense of *ch'ih* [shame] is not a man' (see *The Works of Mencius*, Legge, 1970, pp. 451–2, vol. II, i, 6–7). Losing *lien* is experienced as *wu ch'ih* ('without a sense of *ch'ih*'). In cases of complete loss of *lien*, committing suicide may be a final resort to show the presence of *ch'ih*. Even in today's Chinese society, women often commit suicide to demonstrate their innocence when the misfortune of being raped falls upon them.

Group orientation The concept of face is in conflict with individualism, which assumes the individual's well-being or interest. Hofstede (1980) has indicated in his monumental work that Chinese as well as Asian people are collectivistic. And the collectivistic nature of China is reflected in the Chinese family and kinship system (Hsu 1968). Hsu (1968) argued that 'the primary concern of the majority of Chinese was how to protect and enhance their private kinship interests'. He indicated that the Chinese regard the kinship system as a basis for relating to others. Among Chinese, the kinship system means continuous and long-lasting human ties which do not have clearly defined boundaries. For example, the American parent–child relationship legally comes to an end when children reach the age of 18 or 21, after which parents lose their say about the marriages of their children. Husband and wife in the United States also maintain individual privacy which cannot be intruded upon except by invitation. Efforts at disciplining children by grandparents and other adults in the family are regarded as interference. Thus, there exist in the family system dividing lines which make the boundaries clearly defined, and the human ties supersede each other rather than being additive (Hsu 1968).

The Chinese tend to behave in the opposite way. When getting married, children still regard seeking approval from parents as mandatory and necessary (Salaff 1981). Sometimes, parents have the final say. Sons and daughters after marriage are still liable to support the family (in terms of their parents or parents-in-law) even though they may live apart. Further, they spend leisure time to preserve a viable relationship with parents and parents-in-law by a variety of activities such as taking tea in restaurants, and meals at home on Saturday or Sunday evenings. Normally, parents live with one of their children (usually with the eldest son) even after his or her marriage. Therefore, in contrast to Americans, marriage for any Chinese person means an increase in psycho-social involvement with parents or parents-in-law. Marriage is not only an occasion for the bride and the bridegroom, but for the family to reciprocate affection to friends and other members in the kinship system (Salaff 1981).

The Chinese may have to make sacrifices to gain the benefits that largely accrue to a particular social unit, or even to society as a whole. In a poor Chinese family, daughters and the eldest son may have to forgo their education opportunities to secure the financial well-being of the whole family by going out to work (Salaff 1981). When making decisions, a Chinese individual should always take into account other members in the family, in contrast to husband–wife joint decisions in the United States. He is more motivated towards achieving the goal of the (extended) family or the group that he is affiliated with rather than with individualized self-fulfilment. Wilson and Pusey (1982) have confirmed this in the investigation of achievement motivation and small-business relationship patterns in Chinese society. They found that group orientation correlated more significantly with achievement motivation in the Chinese sample than in the American sample.

However, there is one point worth mentioning. The Chinese are only group-oriented towards the social units with which interactions have been found. They follow the appropriate social norms regardless of their own private views, but they appear to be quite suspicious and cold towards strangers with whom relationships have not been established.

According to the above discussion, it is expected that satisfaction with a product may be derived not solely from one's expectations towards or disconfirmation with the product, but from most members of the family. This is especially true in an extended family.

Possible marketing implications of relational orientation   The values of interdependence and face are particularly meaningful in the study of gift-giving behaviour. To the Chinese, gift-giving is one way to build up relationships with friends. There are festivals in the Chinese lunar calendar such as the Chinese New Year, Mid-autumn Festival and Dragon Boat Festival when gifts are presented to respected friends or superiors. In contrast to Western societies, there are some norms that Chinese are constrained by when giving gifts. For example, gifts presented should be expensive enough to match the income of the givers so that they are giving face to those who receive their gifts, and so that they gain face at the same time because they are thought of as being sincere. For friends, a gift of comparable or even higher value should be returned as soon as possible. In marketing products which can be regarded as gifts in Chinese society, the packaging is extremely important. The products should be packed prestigiously and beautifully in red, which means happiness and good luck, and priced at a level to match their packages. When the products are launched by well-known firms or manufacturers, the prices can be even higher than other competitive products, as the Chinese believe in established brands and companies.

From a different angle, the concept of interdependence is important to Western executives working in Chinese society. They should be reminded that off-duty personal behaviour through which the relationship with the community is built up is highly important to the firm's image and its effectiveness.

Several aspects of the value of group orientation are noteworthy in marketing, too. First, that Chinese are strongly collective may imply that the informal channel of communication is important in Chinese society. In comparison with their counterparts in the USA, Chinese consumers tend to rely more on word-of-mouth communication. Because of the high contact rate among group members, communication of a given product idea is quick to circulate within the informal channels. Furthermore, given that the informal channel of communication carries both facts and rumours, Chinese consumers are much more likely to rely on and make use of the hearsay element in the informal channel, rather than on what is actually stated in the message, so as to increase the speed of communication (Kindle 1985).

Second, Chinese consumers tend to have higher brand loyalty than their counterparts in the USA. Chinese consumers often endeavour to conform to group norms and therefore have a high tendency to purchase the brand or product which members of the group recommend. In other words, if a reference group has established a product as the normative standard, Chinese consumers are not likely to deviate from the accepted product on their own.

Third, since the Chinese are group-oriented only towards social units with which close interactions have been established, they tend to confine their activities within a small social circle. Hence, they are members of a small number of reference groups. This may be one of the reasons why mass advertising through formal channels (e.g. television) is of limited potential for attracting attention when using reference groups which are often small in size. In Hong Kong, Winston, an American cigarette brand, has suffered a continuous decline in sales because of the use of an inappropriate reference group in its advertisements.

Fourth, the concept of the extended family is important to advertisements of family products. In contrast to Western societies, the Chinese concept of a family is of an extended family which includes even distant relatives. Therefore, if an advertisement for a family product includes only husband, wife and children, it does not really form a picture of a family at all. Other members of the extended family such as grandfather and grandmother should be included as well to make the advertisement more persuasive.

Time

Past-time orientation   Kluckhohn and Strodtbeck (1961) have noted that Chinese have a strong preference for past-time orientation:

> Historical China was a society which gave first-order preference to the past-time orientation. Ancestor worship and a strong family tradition were both expressions of this preference. So also was the Chinese attitude that nothing new ever happened in the Present or would happen in the Future; it had all happened before in the far distant Past (p. 14).

Van Oort (1970) even believed that Chinese people were very history-minded. He said,

> A second culture value is the principle of respect for the past, or almost veneration of history. If there is one people in the world that is history-minded, it is certainly the Chinese people.

Van Oort did not attempt to explain his theory. It was Burkhardt (1955) who clearly stated:

> China has always been a conservative country ... which held to the belief that what was good for their forefathers, and had been tested by countless generations, was sacrilege to tamper with.

The Chinese have a strong admiration of their culture, which has a history of several thousand years. The following proverb clearly depicts the feeling of most Chinese: 'Among the three unfilial duties, to have no heir is the greatest.' There are three reasons why having no heir is unfilial. First, it is necessary to have an heir to extend the biological line of the parents and ancestors. To carry out this duty is not difficult, but it is fundamental. Second, it is necessary to live, to pass on to the next generation the Chinese culture. To do so, parents have to provide the best education they can for their children. To do this they should themselves have a deep understanding of Chinese culture. Third, it is necessary to fulfil the hopes that parents or the ancestors have not yet accomplished (Yang 1979).

The salient ethnological fact about Chinese culture is that it is and always has been based fundamentally and predominantly on agriculture. Agriculture provided the economic margin of security for the people. In contrast to pastoral people, the Chinese were averse to taking risks and were less innovative since, to secure a stable food supply, it was safer to follow the traditional proven method which had been workable for thousands of years.

Continuity The Chinese believe that interrelations with objects and others are continuous. Once a relation is established, it can hardly be broken. Hence, the Chinese proverb says, 'If you have been my teacher for a day, I will treat you like my father for ever.'

Possible marketing implications of time orientation The values of past-time orientation and continuity may again imply that Chinese tend to have great brand loyalty. Unless the product or brand performs very unsatisfactorily they are not likely to switch to other brands or products. Crow (1937) also pointed out that the Chinese are 'the world's most loyal customers', with a high degree of brand consciousness. Furthermore, Chinese consumers, especially those who are married, are likely to consider the opinions, values and influences of deceased relatives and respected figures in their current consumption choice. Attention should be paid from time to time to these opinions and values when producing advertising copy for the Chinese market.

Personal activity orientation

The evidence for the activity orientation of the Chinese is conflicting. As mentioned earlier in this chapter, the Chinese have been greatly influenced by the doctrine of the Way, which emphasized the 'being' orientation. However, the Chinese have found themselves conforming to Li-propriety, which denotes a system of semi-formal norms of behaviour. Jarvie and Agassi (1969) gave a description of the predominance of this value orientation:

> The highest value in China is to live properly, which particularly concerns being polite and obeying the rules;and this makes even the social aspect of personal transactions of supreme importance. In other words, in traditional China being considerate to others is equated with ... strict observance of the accepted code. To observe the code is to be human; to forget it is to become barbarian.

However, Jarvie and Agassi did not mention the doctrine of the mean which has been the most important Chinese cultural value (Chu 1973).

The concept of the mean   The mean, according to Confucius, was 'without inclination to either side' (*The Doctrine of the Mean*, I, Legge 1960). Confucius did not believe in suppressing passions and impulses, but in regulating them so as to achieve internal harmony. He said,

> While there are no stirrings of pleasure, anger, sorrow, or joy,the mind may be said to be in the state of equilibrium. When those feelings have been stirred, and they act in their due degree, there ensues what may be called the state of Harmony. This equilibrium is the great root from which grow all the human actions in the world, and this harmony is the universal path which they all should pursue.

(*The Doctrine of the Mean*, I, Legge 1960: 384)

Therefore, the Chinese are taught not to let primitive passions and impulses be completely repressed or unrestrictedly satisfied. To explain what is meant by the mean, Confucius declared,

> The gentleman does what is proper to the station in which he is; he does not desire to go beyond this. In a position of wealth and honour, he does what is proper to a position of wealth and honour. In a poor and low position, he does what is proper to a poor and low position. ... In a low situation, he does not court the favour of his superiors. He rectifies himself, and seeks for nothing from others so that he has no dissatisfactions. He does not murmur against Heaven, nor grumble against men.
>
> (*The Doctrine of the Mean*, XV, Legge 1960: 395)

Thus, a concern for the mean leads to a high degree of moral self-control or self-regulation, at least publicly, for the individual Chinese person. His family members or intimate friends are the only channel to express his inner feelings. Hchu and Yang (1972) also supported this point of view after a study into the individual modernity and psychogenic needs of Chinese college students. It was found that the more socially oriented Chinese students tended to blame or punish themselves after reacting with frustration. In similar vein, Yang (1981) also found that the traditional Chinese were more cautious and more conforming when composing their responses. China has never been an aggressive country in world history; traditionally the Chinese were depicted as a non-military and self-contented people (La Barre 1946; Russell 1966). This can be taken to explain why today it is only on rare occasions that one sees a Chinese person lose control and become angry, insulting or threatening in public (Kindle 1982).

Possible marketing implications of activity orientation One of the possible marketing implications of the value of activity orientation is complaining behaviour. As previously mentioned, the Chinese tend not to take public action, such as complaining to manufacturers, companies or to the Consumer Council when they are dissatisfied with products or services. One of the explanations is that Chinese regard public action as something very serious. Careful consideration has to be given to whether public action is the proper way to solve the problem concerned. Legal action, which is regarded as extreme behaviour, is normally not considered at all. Marketing managers who wish to obtain data on satisfaction/dissatisfaction of Chinese consumers should play a more active and initiative role rather than waiting for consumer feedback.

The doctrine of the 'Mean' might have an influence on Chinese consumers' attitude in adopting new products. Chinese consumers are slow to accept new fashion or technology, and resist marketing innovations involving complicated features. The reason may be that the Chinese are more averse to taking risks, or that they regard adopting, or using, a new product as extreme behaviour which is not proper in their position.

Summary

The Chinese cultural values in terms of Kluckholn and Strodtbeck's classification were discussed in detail in the last five subsections. Possible marketing implications and their relationships with product expectations were also presented. In recent years, Western thought and ideology have played an important part in the cultural changes in many Chinese societies, especially in Taiwan, Hong Kong and Singapore. It seems that it is time to investigate the expected relationships between Chinese cultural values, expectations and satisfaction. Hence, the following hypotheses emerge:

Hypothesis 1. There is a positive relationship between traditional Chinese cultural values as a whole and product expectations.

Hypothesis 1A. There are positive relationships between value dimensions and product expectations.

Hypothesis 2. There is a positive relationship between traditional Chinese cultural values as a whole and consumer satisfaction. That is, the more Chinese a consumer is, the more satisfied he is.

Hypothesis 2A. There are positive relationships between value dimensions and consumer satisfaction. That is, the higher the score for a value dimension, the higher the level of satisfaction.

Since this study only deals with consumer satisfaction, no hypothesis about Chinese cultural values and complaining behaviour will be developed and tested.

CONSUMPTION EXPERIENCES

It is important to consider the role of experience in influencing expectations and consumer satisfaction. Experience is defined as the totality of a person's perceptions, thoughts and encounters

(*The Shorter Oxford Dictionary* 1978). It can be gained and accumulated

> through the exercise or use of various sensorimotor or symbolic organisations of the mind, and through adaptive modifications of these inner organisations in the course of assimilating newly encountered impressions and information and in the course of making adaptive modifications in those organisations
>
> (Hunt 1980)

to cope with the demands of various consumption and use circumstances. As noted in Chapter 2, no research on the causal relations between experiences, expectations and consumer satisfaction has yet been undertaken. However, speculations upon the relations have been reported.

There are several types of consumption or use experience, which are discussed below:

1 Experience with other products.
2 Experience with similar products.
3 Experience with new products.

Experience with other products can have either a direct or an indirect influence on consumer satisfaction. As previously stated in Chapter 2, a consumer judging a product (or service) might compare the perceived benefits of the product with those of other products of which he has experience. If the outcome of this comparison results in a constant state, satisfaction will occur, otherwise dissatisfaction will occur. That is, if the consumer has had a better experience with other products, he will be more dissatisfied with the present product, or if he had poor experiences with other products, he will be more satisfied. Hence, in this book, according to the equity theory, the following hypothesis is proposed.

Hypothesis 3. There is a negative relationship between consumption experiences with products and consumer satisfaction. That is, the more dissatisfaction the consumer experiences, the higher the level of consumer satisfaction.

All three types of experience will also have an impact on the level of expectations. Andreasen (1977) stated that bad consumption or buying experiences lowered one's expectations of other (or similar) products and vice versa. Bad experiences lead to negative feelings, and good experiences lead to positive feelings. Thus, the more bad experiences a consumer encounters, the lower the expectations of similar or other products will be. This view was also supported by Deshpande and Zaltman (1979) in a study of the impact of elderly consumer dissatisfaction and buying experience on information search. They found that the greater the number of bad buying experiences, the greater the number of information sources used in making a purchase decision. The need for greater information is due to the lowering of expectations as a result of dissatisfaction with the previous products or services.

Hypothesis 4. There is a positive relationship between satisfactory consumption experiences with products and product expectations. That is, the more positive the consumption experiences, the higher the level of expectation.

AFFECTIVE EXPERIENCES

Attributions and complaining behaviour might affect a consumer's expectations for the future (Valle and Wallendorf 1977). By attributing satisfaction to himself, a consumer could somehow take pride in his choice, and hence increase his confidence (Weiner *et al.* 1978). This means that the attribution process serves as a reinforcement of existing expectations, making it very difficult to lower expectations. Conversely, dissatisfied consumers might attribute unexpected performance to external forces such as fate or ill luck, to confirm their internal respect. These external forces fail to create a sense of importance when determining expectations in future. Thus, the attribution process serves to lower expectations of the product in the future.

Hypothesis 5. There is a positive relationship between affective experiences and consumer satisfaction. That is, the more the negative affective experience, the lower the level of consumer satisfaction, and vice versa.

Hypothesis 6. There is a positive relationship between affective experiences and expectations. That is, the more the negative affective experiences, the lower the level of expectations, and vice versa.

CONSUMPTION OR USAGE SITUATIONS

Consumption or use situation is a seldomly explored variable in the literature on consumer satisfaction, despite its recent steady growth in interest in the consumer behaviour literature. In this book, it is hypothesized that consumption or use situations will have a significant impact on both anticipated performance and satisfaction, i.e. anticipated performance and satisfaction may vary significantly in different consumption or use situations.

As previously indicated in Chapter 2, the definitions of situation by Belk (1974) and Kakkar and Lutz (1975) were complementary. Belk's definition includes the existence of external facts and events influencing current behaviour even though they are not themselves physically a part of that situation. The advantage of Belk's definition is its ease in manipulating situations for experimental purposes. Kakkar and Lutz's emphasis is on the three psychological descriptors: pleasure, arousal and dominance. Their psychological definition is helpful in translating objective reality into psychological terms, to explain why situations lead to satisfaction or dissatisfaction. Both approaches will be adopted in this book, and the operationalization of situations will be discussed in the next chapter.

The conformity experiments of Asch (1956) provided some evidence for the hypothesized relationship between situation and expectations (cf. Lutz and Kakkar 1976). Asch found that group pressure can cause individuals to perceive stimuli differently when the same stimuli are viewed in private. This implies that group pressure tends to influence individuals' expectations towards stimuli. Further, it was also found that induced changes in an individual's moods lead to changes in perceptions of products as being associated with those moods (cf. Lutz and Kakkar 1976). According to the psychological definition of situation, it seems plausible that a consumer would have different expectations towards a product under different situations. Magnusson (1981) also agreed that situations will steer an individual's expectations towards specific stimuli and events. Hence, in a consumer context for example, a consumer would see shopping at department store A as very convenient when he had a car but view department store A as inconvenient when he had not.

Hypothesis 7. There is a significant relationship between use situation and product expectations. That is, the situation in which the product is encountered will induce higher or lower expectations of the product.

Evidence has shown that situations may exert influence directly on behavioural intentions and behaviour (Sheth 1972; Triandis *et al.* 1972; Bandura 1977; Bearden and Woodside 1976a,b). However, it can be seen that a relationship between situation and satisfaction might well be established. A situation may put restrictions upon a consumer who would emotionally respond according to his interpretation of the situation (Lutz and Kakkar 1974; Belk 1975). He would feel pleasure if he felt that the consumption of a product was appropriate in the situation, but displeasure when it brought him psychological loss or risk. The pleasure of consuming or using of the product would probably lead to satisfaction with the product; and displeasure would probably lead to dissatisfaction as well as causal attributions.

Hypothesis 8. There is a significant relationship between use situation and consumer satisfaction. That is, a use situation will induce higher or lower expectations of the product in that situation.

Magnusson (1981) suggested that situation perception could serve as an intervening variable between personality and behaviour. Allport and Vernon (1931) were in fact amongst the earliest to suggest the relationship between personal traits and situations, when attempting to give an idiographic view of the nature of individual differences. They pinpointed that 'individuals differ not only in the ways in which traits are related to one another in each person but that they differ also in terms of which traits are even relevant' (Bem and Allen 1974). In the same vein, Stokols (1981) also emphasized that those 'functioning in an environment that is to some extent homogeneous in essential physical, biological, social and/or cultural respects will, to some degree, share common world conception and have some common situation perception variances'. This point of view was confirmed by Magnusson and Stattin (1978), who demonstrated empirically that results on anxiety reactions showed striking cultural differences for the following specific situations:

1 In the woods at night.
2 Alone at home.
3 Alone in the woods.

Thus, in the same culture, consumers are likely to have a similar or common response pattern with respect to a situation. The following hypothesis therefore emerged:

Hypothesis 9. There is a significant relationship between each Chinese cultural value and situational factors.

PRODUCT EXPECTATIONS

Expectation has been found to be an important human factor in explaining a variety of phenomena, including students' achievement behaviour (Parsons 1983), interpersonal interactions, external social influences and work motivation (Olson and Dover 1979a). In the literature on consumer satisfaction, numerous studies have also demonstrated, explicitly or implicitly, the importance of consumer expectations in explaining satisfaction and dissatisfaction (Cardozo 1965). However, there is no precise conceptual and operational definition of expectation. The definition usually varies according to the theories in which expectation is involved. Stogdill (1969) defined expectation as readiness for reinforcement. He further explained that expectation is a 'function of drive, the estimated probability of a possible outcome, and the estimated desirability of the outcome' (Stogdill 1969). Churchill and Surprenant (1982) simply defined it as the anticipated performance. In an explicit way, Day defined it as the consumer's estimate at the time of purchase, or prior to use, of how well or poorly the product will supply the benefits of interest to the consumer (1975). Olson and Dover (1979b) in their study of disconfirmation of consumer expectations through product trial defined expectation as pre-trial beliefs about a product. They argued that the definition was acceptable for three reasons. First, belief was a generally accepted concept, relateable to a product and an attribute. Second, beliefs could be operationalized for measurement. Third, to define expectations as beliefs enabled researchers to trace the process by which beliefs were formed and changed. In this book, Olson and Dover's definition is adopted in order to examine the relationships between expectations and other variables.

Typologies of expectations

The consumer satisfaction literature also suggests that there are different types of expectations when forming opinions about pre-trial belief about a product. Miller (1977) identified the following four types of expectation:

1 The Ideal, which is the 'wished for' level of expectation that the consumer feels towards the product.
2 The Expected, which reflects what the consumer feels the performance of the product 'will be'.
3 The Minimum Tolerable, is the lowest level of performance of the product that will be accepted by the consumer.

4 The Deserved, which reflects what the consumer feels the performance of the product 'should be' in the light of his investment in the product.

Summer and Granbois (1977) suggested the need for differentiating consumer expectations into normative expectations and predictive expectations. They defined the former as how the consumer perceives the way that a product should perform, or a marketer should practise his business; and the latter as what a consumer realistically expects from a product or a marketer. In fact, the former is identical with 'the deserved' in Miller's classification and the latter with 'the expected'.

Swan and Trawick (1980) found it necessary to add one more class to Summer and Granbois's classification. They defined desired expectations as the consumer's pre-use specification of the level of product performance that would be necessary in order to satisfy or please the consumer, which is the same as Miller's definition. From a broader perspective, Day (1977) classified expectations into three categories: expectations about the nature of the product or service, expectations about the costs and efforts involved in obtaining benefits, and expectations of social benefits or costs. In this study, all three categories of expectations are taken into consideration. It is assumed that consumers will have taken them all into consideration when expectations about a product are formed.

Links with other components

Inconsistent findings, however, have been reported in studies examining the effect of expectations on consumer satisfaction. Summer and Granbois (1977) failed to find a positive relationship between normative expectations and consumer discontent. Wotruba and Duncan (1975) found that dissatisfaction was actually caused by predictive expectations, while Vinson and Yang (1979) came up with the result that consumer discontent was associated with normative expectation rather than predictive expectation. Predictive expectations are expectations dealing with beliefs in the likelihood of the performance level. Normative expectations are the ideal standards of how a product should perform, and are identical to the 'ideal' classified by Miller. Since no attempt is to be made to distinguish between normative expectations and predictive expectations, the predictive expectations which are generally used in consumer satisfaction research are adopted. Hence, the following hypothesis of expectation about a product and consumer satisfaction emerges:

Hypothesis 10. There is a positive relationship between product expectations and consumer satisfaction. That is, the higher the product expectations, the higher the level of satisfaction.

Inconsistent results have also been found in studies examining the link between expectations and disconfirmation. Some researchers have found that dissatisfaction has no relationship with disconfirmation between expectations and product performance (Wotruba and Duncan 1975; Oliver 1977, 1979, 1980b). They argued that dissatisfaction was actually caused by expectations. However, Vinson and Yang (1979), Swan and Trawick (1980) and Churchill and Surprenant (1982) reported the opposite result.

The following hypotheses are proposed to explain the expected relationships between expectations and perceived performance and disconfirmation:

Hypothesis 11. There is a positive relationship between expectations of a product or service and perceived performance. That is, the higher the expectations, the higher the perceived performance of the product.

Hypothesis 12. There is a positive relationship between expectations of a product and positive disconfirmation. That is, the higher the expectations, the higher the positive disconfirmation.

PERCEIVED PERFORMANCE

In the literature on consumer satisfaction, performance has a different definition from that of other disciplines. Performance is defined as the perceived benefits of the product or service during consumption or use. In other disciplines, such as psychology and education, performance is usually referred to as the outcome of an action in which the subject has been involved.

Performance is one of the primary standards of comparison by which satisfaction is assessed. Swan and Trawick (1980) found that perceived performance has relationships with both disconfirmation and satisfaction. However, the effect of performance via disconfirmation on satisfaction had not been tested. Churchill and Surprenant (1982) constructed a structural model to test the effect by experimental procedures, using two products; a video disc player and plants. Inconsistent results were found with the two products. In the plant experiment, expectations, disconfirmation and performance all affected satisfaction (directly or indirectly). However, in the video disc player experiment, only performance had a dominant impact on satisfaction, contributing 88 per cent of the total variance.

Hypothesis 13. There is a positive relationship between perceived performance and disconfirmation (between expectations and perceived performance of a product or service). That is, the better the perceived performance, the greater the level of positive disconfirmation.

Hypothesis 14. There is a positive relationship between perceived performance and consumer satisfaction with a product or service. That is, the better the perceived performance of the product, the higher the level of consumer satisfaction with the product.

DISCONFIRMATION

In the consumer satisfaction literature, disconfirmation has played an important role as an intervening variable. Disconfirmation is defined as the discrepancy between expectations and perceived actual performance. Positive disconfirmation arises when the actual performance is more desirable than the anticipated performance; negative disconfirmation arises when actual performance is less desirable than the anticipated performance.

Engel *et al.* (1968) and Howard and Sheth (1969) were among the first to propose that disconfirmation led to consumer satisfaction. Olander (1977a), La Tour and Peat (1979) and Oliver (1977) have re-emphasized the importance of disconfirmation as distinct from expectations. Oliver (1977, 1980a, 1980b) further suggested that expectation and disconfirmation might have an additive effect on satisfaction. He added to the work of Weaver and Brickman (1974), who argued that an individual implicitly makes summary comparative judgments as an input to his feelings of satisfaction, confirmed his proposition and found by linear path analysis that disconfirmation measures appeared to produce the greatest impact on satisfaction (Oliver 1980b).

Churchill and Surprenant (1982) found a contingent result that disconfirmation might or might not affect satisfaction. Using one product, it was found that disconfirmation had a strong and positive effect on satisfaction, as in the case of Oliver (1980b). Using another product, satisfaction was determined only by the performance of the product, and not by either expectation or disconfirmation. This implies that the link between disconfirmation and satisfaction might be dependent on the type of product used. Replication research using different types of products seems necessary to warrant this link.

Hypothesis 15. There is a positive relationship between disconfirmation (between expectations and perceived performance) and consumer satisfaction. The greater the positive disconfirmation between expectations and perceived performance, the greater the level of consumer satisfaction.

CONSUMER SATISFACTION/DISSATISFACTION

The significance and definition of consumer satisfaction have been discussed in Chapters 1 and 2. The following is a discussion of the link between satisfaction and behavioural intention.

In a study of leisure time, Winter and Morris (1979) indicated that satisfaction could be used as an intervening variable between disconfirmation and propensity to change. The coefficient of multiple determination (R^2) of the reduced regression analysis was found to be significant and fairly substantial. However, the percentage of propensity to change appeared small.

In building a conceptual model, both Richins (1979) and Ortinau (1979) proposed the incorporation of behavioural intention to find the predictive effect on satisfaction. In more recent research, Oliver (1980b) showed empirically that satisfaction was significantly related to both the consumers' post-exposure and to their pre-exposure intentions. Further, he pointed out that his model of satisfaction, which incorporated behavioural intention, dovetailed well with attitude models suggested by Fishbein (Oliver 1980b).

The consequences of satisfaction decisions are important to marketing managers as well as public policy-makers. It is necessary to find out how satisfaction with a product will lead consumers to further purchase actions. Behavioural intention can serve well to help establish the predictive validity of the model.

BEHAVIOURAL INTENTION

The last component in the model is behavioural intention. Behavioural intention is defined as the subjective probability that an individual will perform the behaviour in question (Fishbein and Ajzen 1975). Intentions have usually been classed with the concept of attitude, and viewed as the conative component of attitude. Fishbein and Ajzen (1975) have sought to disentangle intention from attitude.

They showed by empirical evidence that intention to perform a behaviour is determined by attitude towards the behaviour and the subjective norm concerning that behaviour. As was noted in Chapter 2, the conceptualization of consumer satisfaction leads to the assumption of a strong relationship between satisfaction and intentions. The previous section also showed some evidence in support of the relationship.

Fishbein and Ajzen (1975) found that intentions encompass four elements:

1 The behaviour which is intended to perform, e.g. to have a meeting.
2 The target object at which the behaviour is directed, e.g. Mr Wong of the Consumer Council.
3 The situation in which the behaviour is to be performed, e.g. at Connaught Centre.
4 The time at which the behaviour is to be performed, e.g. at 9.30 on 20 October 1983.

When the above four elements are particularly specified for a given behaviour, an intention is classified as specific. However, since a person's intentions can be gregarious, co-operative or cautious, it may be difficult to determine an intention as specific when most of the elements are not specified. This type of intention is thus classified as a general intention.

In the consumer satisfaction literature, general behavioural intentions are mostly used. In a recent study, Bearden and Teel (1983) incorporated behaviour intentions into a model of consumer satisfaction and complaint reports. They adopted two seven-point scaled statements to measure general behavioural intentions. The relationships between the post-purchase attitude and the behavioural intentions were found highly significant ($r = 0.99$). Churchill and Surprenant (1982) have tried to regard intention as a measure of consumer satisfaction but failed. Hence, behavioural intention is treated as a variable and not a measure of consumer satisfaction in the study.

In this book, the following hypothesis will be tested:

Hypothesis 16. There is a positive relationship between satisfaction and behavioural intention. That is, the greater the satisfaction, the greater the intention to purchase.

CONCLUSION

This chapter has presented a model of Chinese cultural values and consumer satisfaction/dissatisfaction. Each component or variable in the model has been outlined in conjunction with a brief discussion of the relevant literature, and sixteen hypotheses have been proposed.

Finally, considering the structural relationships of all components or variables in the model which has just been described, the following composite hypothesis emerges:

Hypothesis 17. There is no significant difference between the causal model and the data. That is, the model fits the data significantly.

In the next chapter, the research design involves a pilot test of the scale for Chinese cultural values as well as a statistical test for each of the seventeen hypotheses which leads to an answer to the central question posed in Chapter 2. The research design is discussed in detail in the following chapter.

4 Research design and methodology

The last chapter presented an outline of the theoretical model designed to explain the satisfaction/dissatisfaction of consumers. The discussion was organized through the constituent variables of the theory. This chapter discusses the research design and methodology, showing how the model can be tested. The discussion begins with a description of the research design used. Four basic stages in the research design are outlined, followed by a description of the structural equation model and parameter estimation procedures.

The research design included a series of steps. According to the model described in Chapter 3, the selection of the data collection method is discussed first. This is followed by a presentation of how measurement techniques were chosen. A full account of the selection of the sample for the study is then given. Finally, the data collection procedures are explained.

SELECTION OF DATA COLLECTION METHOD

There are three basic methods of collecting data. They are observation, survey and experimentation (Mun and Yau 1979). It is believed that three criteria should be considered in the choice of data collection method:

1 Effectiveness in demonstrating causality.
2 Avoidance of bias.
3 The achievement of acceptable levels of response and/or coverage of the population at a reasonable cost.

Effectiveness in demonstrating causality is the ability of the method to establish and measure causal relationships among the variables under consideration. Avoidance of bias is the ability to provide data which are free from potential bias resulting from the use of a particular method. The third criterion is the ability of the method to obtain a satisfactory response rate at a cost affordable by the researcher and at the same time to reach the designated units in the sampling plan effectively so that the target population's interest in the research does not vary.

Of the three methods, it seemed that the observation method was unable to meet the criterion of acceptable levels of response. Furthermore, since this study deals mostly with psychological measurement, the observation method was again not possible.

In this study, both the survey and the experimentation methods were adopted. The survey method was chosen as it was believed that, with careful questionnaire construction and administration, the above-mentioned criteria could be fulfilled. Experimentation was adopted mainly because it was the most effective way of demonstrating causality. Since this study deals with the measurement of product expectations before purchase, the evaluation of product performance, and satisfaction after purchase, the use of the experimentation as opposed to the survey method was considered most practical and suitable.

Once the survey method was selected, it remained to choose one or more of the possible data collection techniques; personal interview, telephone interview, and mail questionnaire. There are several criteria which are adopted to evaluate which type of survey to use in a particular situation. These criteria are:

1 Speed.
2 Amount of information obtained.
3 Cost.
4 Desired accuracy.
5 Acceptable level of non-response.
6 Representativeness of the sample.

(Tull and Hawkins 1980; Mun and Yau 1979).

With respect to the first criterion speed, a personal interview survey takes less time than a mail survey. However, the use of a telephone survey still remains a possibility. A personal interview survey has some advantages over the other survey techniques, especially when a large amount of information is to be obtained, as in this study, and a more representative sample is needed. It is also possible for mail surveys to use long questionnaires to secure a large amount of information. But long questionnaires lead to lower response rates. In Hong Kong, the return rate of mail surveys for households is about 20 per cent (Sin and Yau 1984). A long questionnaire would surely aggravate the return rate to an unacceptable level. Hence, it was not advisable to choose a mail questionnaire in this study.

Telephone interviews usually generate a response rate as high as personal interviews. However, they have the disadvantage of being unable to handle complex and long questionnaires.Furthermore, telephone interviews do not allow the use of visual presentation, which is a part of the experimentation in this study. Hence, telephone interviews were only used as a method of validating returned questionnaires.

SELECTION OF MEASUREMENT TECHNIQUES

The above discussion justified the choice of a personal interview survey with the incorporation of experimentation as the data collection method. In the following paragraphs the design of the research instrument is described. Two questionnaires were used, one for the ball-pen sample and one for the mini-cassette sample. The questionnaires were similar in nature except for the names of the experimental instrument. A questionnaire is in itself a measurement instrument that utilizes various types of more specific measuring devices or scales.The questionnaire design involves two basic stages: the overall questionnaire structure and the operationalization of variables. These two stages are explained in the following sections.

Questionnaire structure

There are three considerations which govern the basic structure of a questionnaire. They are the specific objectives of the questionnaire, the intended respondent of the questionnaire, and the method of administering the questionnaire (Tull and Hawkins 1980). In this study, the specific objectives of the questionnaire were to provide information on the following:

1 Respondents' perception of their culture values.
2 Respondents' overall expectation about two ball-pens/mini-cassettes under different situations.
3 The evaluation of the performance of two ball-pens/mini-cassettes under different situations.
4 The confirmation between expectation and performance of the products under different situations.
5 Respondents' satisfaction/dissatisfaction with the products under different situations.
6 The respondents' behavioural intention.

7 The affective experience of the respondent with similar products.
8 The experience of the respondent with other products.
9 Attribution of the respondents when they are dissatisfied with products.

The intended respondents of the questionnaire were those adults who had experience of purchasing either mini-cassette(s) or ball-pen(s). Detailed description of these respondents is presented on p. 132.

As was mentioned in the last section, the method used to administer the questionnaire was personal interview, which was found to be the most suitable method to deal with sophisticated measurement scales and experimentation. The general approach to the interview and treatment of the respondent also influenced the design of the questionnaire. For example, sponsorship as well as the purposes of the survey were explained at the beginning of the interview. Respondents were also reminded that a prior notification letter had been sent to them by the researcher. The questionnaire was also designed to remind the interviewer to show to the respondent the appropriate instrument (rating card, situation card, mini-cassette or ball-pen) for specific purposes.

The model of consumer satisfaction/dissatisfaction described in Chapter 3 suggests a concise way of organizing the questionnaire. It was possible to divide the questionnaire into sections according to the model. Table 4.1 shows how the questionnaire was organized, and the English version of the two original questionnaires (one for ball-pens and one for mini-cassette players) administered in Chinese can be found in Appendix A. An attempt was made to fulfil the requirement of Tull and Hawkins (1980) that the overall questionnaire should move from one topic to another in a logical manner, with all the questions on one topic being completed before moving on to the next. Hence, the initial section contained questions which were used to help the interviewer screen and select the right respondent. This was then succeeded by Section 1 which contained forty-five Chinese cultural values in the form of common sayings. In Section 2, the respondent was asked to evaluate his expectations, the actual performance of the products in four different situations, disconfirmation between expectations and performance of the products, his satisfaction/dissatisfaction with the products, and the behavioural intention of the respondent. Section 3 dealt with the experiences of the respondent and his attribution when he was dissatisfied with some products. Finally the respondent was asked to give some personal information.

Table 4.1   Questionnaire structure

Section	Content	Question No.
0	Screening	1a
	The recently purchased instrument (mini-cassette player/ball-pen)	1b
1	The Chinese cultural values statements	2.1–45
2	Suitability of the products in four simple situations	3a, 3b
	Overall expectation of the products in different situations	4a, 4b
	Expectation of attributes of the products in different situations	5a, 5b
	Ask what information does the respondent want	6
	Performance of the products in different situations	6a, 6b
	Performance of the attributes of the products	6c, 6d
	Confirmation of expectation and performance of the products in different situations	7a, 7b
	Confirmation of expectation and performance of the attributes of the products in different situations	7c, 7d
	Satisfaction/dissatisfaction with the instrument in different situations	8a, 8b
	Satisfaction/dissatisfaction with the attributes of the products in different situations	8c, 8d
	Behavioural intention of the instrument in different situations	9a, 9b
3	Frequency of purchase of the ball-pen/mini-cassette	10
	Experience of dissatisfaction with ball-pen/mini-cassette	10a
	Experience of dissatisfaction with other products	11
	Experience of dissatisfaction with other related products	12
	Attribution	13a–d
4	Personal data	14–20

Operationalization of variables

It is well acknowledged that the function of a questionnaire is to achieve the research objectives through the measurement of variables of interest (Oppenheim 1966: 24). In this study, the variables of the model were described in Chapter 3. The discussion of the measurement of operationalization of the variables will proceed in three steps. First, general comments regarding question construction are made, illustrated with examples from the questionnaire. Second, considerations on question phrasing are discussed. Third, detailed explanations of the operationalization of the variables are provided.

Question construction

Question construction is the translation of planned contents into interviewable form. This stage of questionnaire design, therefore, deals with decisions about question content, the response format and question phrasing.

Question content

Tull and Hawkins (1980) suggest that there are five major issues involved with question content:

1 The need for the relevant data.
2 The ability of the question to produce the data.
3 The ability of the respondent to answer accurately.
4 The willingness of the respondent to answer accurately.
5 The potential for external events to bias the answer.

The need for the relevant data may arise from the specific objectives of the questionnaire. Each question was constructed to ensure that the results of the analysis provided sufficient information for testing the model described in Chapter 3. In the questionnaire, there are two questions, 1b and 6, which are not part of the planned analysis. Tull and Hawkins (1980) suggested two reasons for the inclusion of this kind of question: to obtain respondent involvement and rapport prior to asking more sensitive questions, and to help disguise the purpose of a study. Neither of their reasons applied. In fact, the purpose of including question 1b, which asked respondents to give the brand name of products purchased, was to check whether the respondent had really purchased the products. If he could not answer it, the interview would stop. Question 6 asked whether the respondent would like to know more information about the products which he had just inspected and tried. If yes, the interviewer would provide him with appropriate answers. Hence, the purpose of this question was to make sure that the respondent knew exactly what he had tried.

In the questionnaire, most questions asked the respondent to express how strongly or intensely he held certain views. In order to ensure that these questions would have the ability to generate the needed information, they provided all the choices or preferences to the respondent. Furthermore, during the interview, an interview card on which all the choices or preferences were written was presented to the respondent to enable him to give the answer.

The inability of the respondent to answer accurately may arise from three major sources: (1) never having been exposed to the answer, (2) having been exposed to the answer but forgetting it and (3) the inability of the respondent to verbalize the answer. It was assumed that the respondent, as a consumer, would be familiar with ball-pens or mini-cassette players. If he was not, he would not be selected as a respondent. Attempts were made to verify this, for example, see questions 1a and 1b. For the questions in section 3, the choice 'never tried' was given.

The unwillingness of the respondent to answer accurately may be attributable to one of the following reasons:

1 The questionnaire is so long that the respondent is too tired to answer accurately.
2 The information request may be considered by the respondent as none of the interviewer's business.
3 The questions are embarrassing or sensitive.

To tackle these problems, the length of the questionnaire had been reduced after the pilot survey so that an interview would normally end within forty-five minutes. Information dealing with personal data was put at the end of the questionnaire (questions 14–20). In addition, explanation of why the information was required was provided at the beginning of the section for personal data. Embarrassing questions were deleted, for example, the common saying 'You will make mistakes if you talk too much,' which was originally placed in Section 1. In the pilot survey, it was found that many respondents refused to continue the interview after reading this common saying. Prestige-oriented questions such as education and personal income were handled with care. These questions (see numbers 15–18) were designed as closed questions instead of open questions. Furthermore, interview cards were used and respondents were only requested to read out the number which corresponded to their choice.

Response format

There are basically two types of response format: open-ended questions and closed questions. The decision as to which response format to use depends on the objective of the particular question.

Open-ended questions have a number of advantages. First, they allow elicitation of a wide variety of responses. Second, they also allow the respondent to express any pertinent feelings on the topic and make him accustomed to the topics and the process of answering questions. Third, open-ended questions help reduce potential frustration of the respondent, especially in mail surveys. Finally, they can provide the researcher with a basis for judging the actual values and views of the respondent, which are often difficult to capture with structured techniques.

However, open-ended questions are subject to a number of problems. First, they cannot be pre-coded or pre-categorized. Cost of coding and categorizing may contribute to a large portion of the total cost of the research. Second, interviewer effects exist in the process of collecting data. Interviewers will vary in their ability to record the respondents' answers, in their intensity of probing and in their objectivity. Third, open-ended questions may not measure the real issue, but how articulate the respondent was (Dohrenwend 1965). A respondent might not be willing to express himself, whilst another might talk for several minutes without clearly answering a question.

These disadvantages have caused several authors (Payne 1965; Tull and Hawkins 1980; Dohrenwend 1965) to disagree with the use of open-ended questions. Despite the difficulty in developing closed questions, it was recommended that open-ended questions be used for preliminary research and for categorical question development. Hence, considering the length of the questionnaire as well as the nature of the research, closed questions were widely used in this study.

Closed questions can be divided into three types: multiple-choice questions, dichotomous questions and scales. In the questionnaire, all of them were used. Multiple-choice questions were used in Section 4 to secure personal information. The Likert scale was used in Section 1 to measure the Chinese cultural values and the semantic differential (remote) scale was used in Sections 2 and 3. Dichotomous questions were only used on three occasions in the questionnaire.

Question phrasing

The above section showed how question content and response format were defined. The remaining task was to decide on question phrasing. According to Tull and Hawkins (1980), question phrasing is the translation of the desired question content into words and phrases that can be understood easily and clearly by the respondents. The pilot survey was of great value in checking the questionnaire's general intelligibility and respondents' ability to deal with certain measurement techniques.

In general, questions in the questionnaire were phrased as simply and straightforwardly as possible. There was no difficulty in achieving this as the whole questionnaire basically consists of attitude statements which each respondent was requested to rate according to measurement scales. For example, the Chinese cultural values in Section 1 of the questionnaire were rated on a six-point Likert scale; and the expectations and performance of the products, etc., were rated on six-point semantic differential scales.

Special care was taken to avoid the pitfall of leading questions when requesting respondents to do the rating, with the help of interview cards on which measurement scales were drawn. One issue of concern is whether words or phrases are understandable to respondents, especially those in Section 1, where there are forty-five common Chinese sayings. In the pilot survey, some old common sayings which had many non-responses were deleted. Since the questionnaire consisted mostly of attitude statements, the issue of whether all alternatives were included in the questions did not arise.

Finally, since the respondents were Chinese who spoke Cantonese, the most frequently spoken Chinese dialect in Hong Kong, the questionnaire was *written* in Cantonese, instead of in the formal Chinese language. By doing this, it was easier for the respondent to understand the questions in the questionnaire.

Variables

The variables chosen and described in Chapter 3 as the components of the model of Chinese cultural values and consumer satisfaction/ dissatisfaction are:

1 Chinese cultural values.
2 Consumption or usage situations.
3 Consumption experiences.
4 Affective experiences.

5 Product expectations.
6 Perceived performance.
7 Disconfirmation.
8 Consumer satisfaction/dissatisfaction.
9 Behavioural intention.

The Chinese cultural values

An inventory of sixty-six common Chinese sayings was collected to present the Chinese cultural values previously discussed in Chapter 3. There are two steps by which these sixty-six common Chinese sayings were selected. The first step is to conduct a survey of literature on Chinese cultural values to identify possible cultural dimensions. The results of the survey were previously presented in Chapter 3. In the second step, 100 common sayings were selected from sources where common Chinese sayings could be found, based on the cultural dimensions (Chen 1973; Lai 1970; Wei 1980). Three colleagues from the Chinese University of Hong Kong were invited as judges to screen common sayings that they thought matched the cultural dimensions. Common sayings were selected on the criterion that at least two judges agreed that the common sayings were acceptable to be included in the scale. Finally, sixty-six common sayings were selected.

Consumption or usage situations

In general, there are two broad ways to envisage a situation. The first is to view it as a bundle of physical characteristics that are in some way coercive, facilitative, or constraining on the respondent, or some other physical events related to the respondent. The second, which was the one used in the study, is to model the situation through the psychology of the respondent.

Belk (1975) gives five groups of situational characteristics which represent the general features from which a situation can be defined. He also listed situational inventories for seven different products, showing that modelling a situation was heavily dependent on the products to be consumed or used. In this study, because of the particular interest in Chinese cultural values, and the selection of ball-pens and mini-cassettes as the experimental instruments, the social dimensions which had been found to affect conformity were used to model the situations in the study (Allen 1965). The social dimensions used were public/private and interdependence of participants. Belk (1975) also agreed that these dimensions were potentially relevant to describe a situation. The dimension of public/private was operational-ized as 'when the subject (respondent) is with other people'/'when the subject is alone', while the dimension of interdependence of participants was operationalized as 'the experimental instrument was bought as a gift'/'used by the subject himself'. As a result, by using a 2×2 factorial design (see Figure 4.1), the following four situations were modelled:

1 The product is to be used when the respondent is alone.
2 The product is to be bought as a gift and used when alone.
3 The product is to be used when the respondent is with other people.
4 The product is to be bought as a gift and to be used when with other people.

Consumption experiences

According to the discussion described in Chapter 3, the measurement of consumption experiences can be divided into three parts:

Dimension 1

Private/Public

		Private	Public
	Bought as a gift	Bought as a gift and to be used when alone	Bought as a gift and to be used when with other people
Dimension 2 Interdependence	Used by oneself	Used by oneself when alone	Used by oneself when with other people

Figure 4.1 Factorial design of situations using two social dimensions

1 Experiences with other products.
2 Experiences with similar products.
3 Experiences with new products.

The commonly used measure of experience with a product is the frequency of purchase. No other attempt is made to develop sophisticated indices of experiences. However, it seems impossible for the respondent to have accurate recall of the frequency of dissatisfied purchases across a wide range of products. In this study, therefore, not only the frequency of purchase of the experimental instrument was asked. Moreover, a scale which attempted to measure experience of dissatisfied purchases with each type of aforementioned products was constructed.

Respondents were asked to show how often they encountered purchases of:

1 Ball-pens (or mini-cassette players).
2 Other products.
3 Writing instruments (or audio equipment).

which they were dissatisfied with, on a six-point semantic differential scale ranging from 'never' to 'very often'. On the scale, 1 indicates that the respondent has no experience at all while 6 indicates that the respondent *very often* encounters products which he is not dissatisfied with.

Affective experiences

Trying to propose an attribution model of information processing, Mizerski (1982) found that past attribution could have a significant effect on individual attitude toward products. In the study, affective experiences, therefore, refer to the experiences of causal attribution which the respondent had made before the personal interview.

Most of the research relating attribution to consumer behaviour has been loosely based on the theory developed by Harold Kelley (1967). The operationalization of the causal attribution was based on the two-dimensional schema developed by Weiner *et al.* (1972), that is, internal/external and stable/unstable. A success or failure can be attributed either to something about the actor (internal) or to something about the environment or situation (external). In addition, the performance can be attributed to something which does not vary over time (stable) or to something which varies over time (unstable). However, as complaining actions were being studied, a modified schema by Day (1977) and by Day and Landon (1977), actions taken and internal/external, was adopted.

The dimension 'actions taken' refers to the degree with which the individual reacts when he encounters unsatisfactory products. Three possible actions might be taken: no action at all, complaining to friends, etc., and legal action. The two dimensions can fit into the two-dimensional schema (see Figure 4.2). In Figure 4.2 cells 2 and 3 are empty, since there will be no public action taken for internal blame. Hence, four scales were used to represent affective experiences.

Product expectations

Miller (1977) identified four types of expectations: ideal, expected, minimum tolerable, and desirable. Day (1977) also distinguished between expectations about the nature of the product or service; the costs and effort of obtaining benefits; and social benefits or costs. But in this study, expectations previously defined as anticipated or perceived expectations according to Churchill and Surprenant (1982) were indicated through a single-item global scale and a multi-item, attribute-specific scale. The answers were rated on a six-point bipolar

Actions taken

	None	Complaining to friends, etc.	Legal actions
Internal blame	Self (1)	— (2)	— (3)
External blame	Fate (4)	Complaining to friends etc. (5)	Legal actions (6)

Figure 4.2 The schema for causal attribution in the study

scale with 'not very good' at one end of the scale and 'excellent' at the other.

Perceived performance

Perceived performance was also measured by two scales. Respondents were asked to evaluate the performance of the ball-pens/mini-cassettes after the trials on a single-item global scale and a multi-item, attribute-specific scale. The answers were rated on a six-point rating bipolar scale ranging from 'not very good' to 'excellent'.

Disconfirmation

In consumer satisfaction literature, disconfirmation is measured by two approaches. The traditional approach defines disconfirmation as a discrepancy between expectation and performance, and thus it is measured as the difference between the two variables. That is, disconfirmation is determined jointly by the combination of the expectation and the performance of the product, which Swan (1977) called inferred disconfirmation. Therefore it is difficult to manipulate disconfirmation independently.

The second approach, as suggested by Oliver (1977), stresses the importance of measuring disconfirmation apart from expectation and performance. Hence, perceived disconfirmation, as Oliver (1979) labelled it, is to be maintained as the construct which has independent additive effects on satisfaction.

Even though Trawick and Swan (1980) found that there was a close relationship between inferred and perceived disconfirmation, in the study, the latter approach was adopted. As in the previous two constructs, disconfirmation was measured through a single-item global scale and a multi-item attribute-specific scale. Respondents were asked to evaluate whether the performance of the ball-pen/mini-cassette player lived up to their expectations. The answers were rated on a five-point scale ranging from 'it performs worse than I expected' to 'it performs better than I expected', with the middle point being 'it performs exactly the same as I expected'.

Consumer satisfaction/dissatisfaction

The literature on consumer satisfaction reflects controversy about whether satisfaction and dissatisfaction are on the same continuum. Aiello *et al.* (1977) found that satisfaction and dissatisfaction seemed to be on the same scale while others (Leavitt 1977; Swan and Combs 1976; Maddox 1981) regarded them as two factors. In the study, a single satisfaction/dissatisfaction continuum was used. It was believed that the use of separate satisfaction/dissatisfaction scales was not worth while, partly because it would increase the already lengthy questionnaire and partly because the evidence on whether satisfaction and dissatisfaction were on the same scale was still uncertain. Satisfaction with each product was assessed by using single global and multi-item attribute-specific measures in accord with Churchill and Surprenant (1982). The answers were rated on six-point scales ranging from 'completely satisfied' to 'completely dissatisfied'.

Behavioural intention

This construct was operationalized in accord with Sheth's (1971) definition, which regards behavioural intention as a verbal expression of intent to buy a product (or brand)/service. In the study, respondents were asked whether they would purchase each product if it was available on the market. The answers were rated on a six-point bipolar scale with 'definitely would not buy' at one end and 'definitely would buy' at the other.

Other operationalizations

In addition to the above variables which comprise the primary data for investigation, a number of other variables were measured. Data on background characteristics were recorded for each respondent. The data included sex, age, level of education, marital status, personal income and other related variables such as the geographical area and the type of housing where the interview took place.

THE SELECTION OF THE SAMPLE

This section deals with the specification of the respondents required to participate in the personal interview survey. First, the choice of products for the study and, second, the population and the sampling frame are discussed. Third, a presentation of the determination of sample size is given, followed by a description of how respondents in the survey were identified.

The choice of products

Two products were chosen for inclusion in the study, a ball pen and a mini-cassette player, because of financial and time resources. There were several considerations in making the choice of products. First, two roller-ball pens and two mini-cassette players were used in the experiment during the interviews. One in each product category was a new product on the market. It was believed that consumers would not have preconceived ideas of what a new product would deliver. Furthermore, it was assumed that consumers would have some familiarity with new products which belonged to large classes of products.

Second, it was expected that the choice would enable a respondent to evaluate the products under four different situations:

1 To be used when the respondent is alone.
2 To be bought as a gift and used when alone.
3 To be used when the respondent is with other people.
4 To be bought as a gift and to be used when with other people.

Third, the performance of these products could be evaluated by the respondent after a short trial. A ball-pen had been used as an experimental instrument in a consumer satisfaction experiment (Cardozo 1964), whilst the mini-cassette player was used for the first time. However, similar products such as video cassettes have been used by Churchill and Surprenant (1982) in an experiment to investigate the determinants of customer satisfaction.

Fourth, the effects of using different brands of the products were considered. It was believed that the respondent might have biased evaluation toward more prestigious brands. That is to say, even though the performance of two different brands of a product was the same, the respondents would tend to give higher rating to the brand which had a better prestige over the other. Taking this effect into consideration, it was decided that two designs would be used for the two sub-samples. Hence, for the mini-cassette sub-sample, two different models of the same brand, Sony, were used for the experiment in the personal interview; the low-profile Model WM20 and the prestigious Model FM15. In order to make a comparison, for the ball-pen sub-sample, two different brands were used: Parker and Artline. The prestigious model, Parker Silver 45, was chosen to manipulate higher expectations of the product while the popular and basic model, Artline 200, was chosen to manipulate lower expectations of the product.

Fifth, one durable product and one non-durable product were chosen. The mini-cassette player basically represents the durable product category while the ball-pen represents the non-durable product category. Unfortunately, one of the ball-pens, Parker Silver 45, fails to fulfil the criterion, as it can be refilled, and therefore cannot be regarded as a fast-selling product.

The population

Once it was decided to examine the model using two types of products (ball-pen and mini-cassette player), the sampling technique had to be considered. However, before the procedure of selecting the sample is described, the population of interest has to be defined. Sudman (1983) suggests that there are at least two basic steps in defining the population under study. The first step is to decide whether the population is of individuals, households, institutions, transactions or some other category. The second step is to decide the units to use. To do this, he suggests the following criteria for consideration:

1 Geography.
2 Age of individuals.
3 Other demographic variables.
4 Individual variables.
5 Household variables.

Following the steps suggested by Sudman, the population under study was defined as all Chinese individuals who fulfil the five criteria:

Geography

The geographical definition of the population is the entire Hong Kong islands, although this limits the ability to generalize the results to other areas such as mainland China, Taiwan and Singapore. In fact, Hong Kong was chosen as it has some particular advantages over these places. First, research of this type, although possible, would be difficult to conduct in China at this time. Though mainland China has opened its doors to the rest of the world, officials have been very cautious in allowing research to be conducted. Special permission has to be obtained from the regional government. Application for permission to conduct research might take half a year to be approved. Furthermore, the lack of detailed street maps may be a stumbling block to a good sampling design (Yau *et al.* 1985).

Second, it would have been very difficult to conduct this study in Taiwan because of the unfamiliarity of the place as well as the lack of financial and time resources. In fact, Taiwan is thought to be the most suitable place to conduct research which is concerned with the Chinese because of the composition of its people, who came from the various provinces of China before 1949 when the Nationalist Government of China lost power. Yang (1972 and 1979) and Yang and Hwang (1991) have indicated that research on Chinese cultural values has been done in Taiwan and Hong Kong.

Third, Hong Kong is a better choice than Singapore even though Singapore is a country quite similar to Hong Kong in terms of size and economic development. Singapore is a multinational country with only 75 per cent of its population being Chinese. Most of these Chinese are descendants of those who came to Singapore before it became independent. Under the present education system, they are hardly able to read and write Chinese. However, in Hong Kong, more than 98 per cent of the population are Chinese. Under the bilingual education system, most people can read, write and speak Chinese.

Age of individuals

Sudman (1983) suggests that the minimum age is usually eighteen for attitude research. Since this study basically deals with psychological measurements, it is logical to follow Sudman's suggestion.

Other demographic variables

Sex, race, marital status and education were other variables used to define population. In this study, the population was confined to Chinese only. No other constraints were adopted as regards other demographic variables.

Individual variables

The population of this study only included those individuals in the housing units, who had experience of either ball-pens or mini-cassette players. In the case of the ball-pen, only those who bought a ball-pen in the past two years were included. However, since mini-cassette players were more expensive, only those who had ever bought a mini-cassette player were included.

Household variables

The population of this study did not include those housing units which were located on outlying islands, or living on boats. The rationale for excluding these housing units was twofold. First, housing units in these areas constitute only a very small portion of the population of Hong Kong. Second, the cost of conducting personal interviews would have been extremely high.

Sampling frame

The sampling frame was obtained from the Census of Hong Kong, 1981, with the help of the Department of Census and Statistics of the Hong Kong government. According to the Department of Census and Statistics, Hong Kong is made up of 210 tertiary planning units (TPUs) covering the whole population. A TPU is in fact a district for government administrative purposes. There are in total 270 TPUs in Hong Kong. Each TPU is broken down into about 100 enumerating blocks. An enumerating block is an area which is bounded by four streets, so that each block demands the same amount of work by a team of enumerators. An enumerating block therefore consists of a certain number of living quarters. The area of an enumerating block may vary, but the time spent by a team to finish all enumerations is usually fixed. Hence, excluding those blocks located on outlying islands and on water, it was found that there were 2,000 enumerating blocks.

After the 1981 census, using a multi-stage random sampling method, for further research purposes, the Department of Census and Statistics drew eight replicates, each of which is about three thousand living quarters. These eight replicates have been continuously updated and each of them is regarded as representing the whole population. In January 1985, two replicates were given by the Department of Census and Statistics for the purpose of conducting this research. For the past four years, two of the eight replicates have been used for the Study of Household Expenditure by the department, and the present two replicates obtained are those updated but unused by the department. These replicates in total consisted of 6,323 living quarters. However, before the procedures of how the samples of living quarters are drawn, the determination of sample size should first be discussed.

The determination of sample size

Usually there are two ways to determine sample size. The first is to set an arbitrary size within the constraint of the research budget, and to measure the precision of the sample at the analysis stage if probability sampling is used. The second is to calculate the optimal sample size, given a desired level of precision and cost, according to the standard error formula. Given the limited research budget, time and manpower, the arbitrary method was used. Sudman (1983) has indicated that the most common sample sizes used for regional attitude research range from 400 to 1,000, with 700 being the optimum. He also mentions that typical sample sizes in which few or no segments (groups) are to be analysed vary from 200 to 500. These sample sizes assume that optimal stratified sampling procedures are used. Furthermore, Bearden *et al.* (1982) have indicated that a researcher who wants to reduce the risk of drawing erroneous conclusions should not use samples of less than 200 when using the analysis of covariance structure for analysis or LISREL, which is the methodology used for testing the model in this book. They also emphasize that the general rule of thumb that LISREL is appropriate in cases where sample size minus degree of freedom exceeds 50 does not hold. Hence, it is obvious that the sample size for this study should exceed 200 if accurate conclusions are to be drawn.

Tull and Hawkins (1984: 410–14) have suggested several ways to determine the sample size. One of them is to calculate the sample size in estimation problems involving means. The optimal sample size can be determined if the relative allowable error, the coefficient of variation and the standard error are available. In this study, the standard error is set to be equal to 2.58, which is required to give a 99.5 per cent level of confidence, and the relative allowable error is 0.05 of the mean. In order to find out the coefficient of variation, a pilot survey was conducted. (The sampling procedures and the results of the pilot survey are discussed at p. 117–19.) Table 4.2 shows the mean satisfaction scores for ball-pens and mini-cassettes under four different situations. Since the values of Z and R are fixed, the coefficient of variation is the variable left to determine the sample size. The greater the coefficient of variation, the larger the sample size will be. For the ball-pen sub-sample, a conservative choice of 0.348 for the greatest coefficient of variation was selected. Therefore, the sample size for the ball-pen sub-sample was computed to be 320. Similarly, the sample size for the mini-cassette player sub-sample is 318. (The

Table 4.2   Satisfaction scores in the pilot survey

Statistics	Situation			
	1	*2*	*3*	*4*
Ball-pen 1				
Mean	3.830	3.430	3.320	3.050
Std. Dev.	1.060	1.030	1.080	1.150
Coef. of Var.	0.276	0.300	0.325	0.348
Ball-pen 2				
Mean	4.620	4.620	4.670	4.700
Std. Dev.	0.980	0.880	0.960	0.990
Coef. of Var.	0.212	0.190	0.205	0.211
Mini-cassette 1				
Mean	3.500	3.280	3.400	3.140
Std. Dev.	0.970	1.030	0.990	1.100
Coef. of Var.	0.277	0.314	0.291	0.348
Mini-cassette 2				
Mean	4.750	4.700	4.730	4.780
Std. Dev.	0.840	0.720	0.880	0.900
Coef. of Var.	0.176	0.153	0.186	0.188

formula and all calculations of the sample size for the two samples can be found in Appendix C.)

According to the results of the pilot survey, it was found that there was a refusal rate of 40 per cent, that is to say, there were only six successful contacts out of ten. Furthermore, 82 per cent of the household units had bought a ball-pen within two years; and only 51.5 per cent had ever bought mini-cassette players. Hence, to be conservative in allowing provision for non-responses, it was assumed that 80 per cent of the household units had bought a ball-pen within two years and that 50 per cent had ever bought a mini-cassette player. Therefore, 664 living quarters were drawn from the sampling frame as the ball-pen sub-sample and 1,060 as the mini-cassette player sub-sample for the main survey.

Specification of the sampling plan

In this study, a random sampling procedure was adopted for the selection of living quarters in the replicates. The first step was to assign a number to each of the living quarters in the listing of the replicates. The second step was to draw random numbers by means of the random number table. These two steps resulted in a listing of 1,063 living quarters for the mini-cassette player sub-sample, and 664 for the ball-pen sub-sample. The sampling plan involved the specification that each of the decisions made so far is to be implemented. Although living quarters were the sampling unit, it was assumed that each living quarter was a housing unit. Hence, the identity of the household (individual informant) must be explained. At this point of time, it is necessary to define the term 'household'. In this study, the definition of 'household' by Sudman (1983) was adopted:

> ... a household as everyone ... who eats and lives with other persons in a housing unit to which there is (a) either direct access from the outside of the building or through a common hall and (b) complete kitchen facilities for the use of the occupants (p. 151).

Identity of respondent

The last section only shows how a sample of 1,727 housing units was drawn. It was recognized that households in a housing unit are not homogeneous, but have individual values and characteristics such as income, sex, education, marital status, and purchase experiences, etc. Information sought only from the head of the housing unit would be unrepresentative. Hence a selection table was designed to be used to select the correct respondent for interview from the households (Kish 1965; Deming 1960) when more than one person in the housing unit had bought a mini-cassette player or ball-pen. (A sample of the table can be found at the beginning of the questionnaire in Appendix A.) Names of the members of the households who were eighteen or above and had bought ball-pens or mini-cassettes were written on lines in the second column of the table. These lines are numbered 1–8. The oldest member of the household was to be entered on line 1, the next oldest on line 2, and the next on line 3, and so on. A sequential interview order 1, 2, 3, etc., on a specific day was selected, using the rows of the table. With reference to the interview order, the number on the lowest line was read; this number corresponds to the line number in column 1. Hence, in such a way, a respondent is selected for interview.

DATA COLLECTION PROCEDURES

Data collection procedures will be described in three parts, covering the pilot survey, the reduction of non-response error, and the data collection process.

Pilot survey

A pilot survey is a small-scale version of the main survey. Generally, its purposes are as follows:

1 To uncover possible problem areas.
2 To evaluate findings in terms of how far they achieve overall research objectives.
3 To assess the likely degree of error and the reliability and validity of the expected information.

Prior to the pilot survey, four focus group interviews were conducted to find out the salient attributes of ball-pens and mini-cassettes. Two focus group interviews were arranged for each product. Each group was made up of ten participants from various occupations and income levels. By means of scree-test, seven salient attributes were found for ball-pens and five for mini-cassettes. A list of the attributes of both products is shown in Table 4.3.

After the initial questionnaire had been drafted, a test was carried out to check the validity of the questionnaire. A convenient sample of respondents were invited to assess the basic intelligibility format and comprehensiveness of the questionnaire in the early draft in relation to the research objectives. As a result of this test, the wording of some questions was changed.

Table 4.3 Initial attributes for ball-pens and mini-cassette players

A. Salient Attributes of Ball-pens
   1 Smoothness in writing
   2 Good appearance
   3 Durability
   4 Weight
   5 Prestige
   6 Slimness of the pen
   7 No leaking of ink
B. Salient Attributes of Mini-cassette players
   1 High value
   2 Good appearance
   3 Convenience in carrying
   4 Sufficient functions for the situation concerned
   5 Sound quality

Conducting the pilot survey

In February 1985 a formal pilot survey was conducted. A random sample of 360 was drawn from the two replicates provided by the Department of Census and Statistics in Hong Kong, with the aim of obtaining 120 successfully completed questionnaires, half for the mini-cassette sub-sample and half for the ball-pen sub-sample. The personal interviews were conducted by ten experienced interviewers of the research company. The questionnaire was administered exactly in the same manner as it would be in the main survey. After the personal interview, some pre-test respondents were asked to explain, precisely and in detail, why they answered each question as they did. The purpose of doing this was to uncover possible weaknesses of the questionnaire and problems which the pre-test respondents had encountered.

Finally, 120 successful personal interviews were completed out of 314 household units, sixty for each sub-sample. The refusal rate was found to be about 40 per cent. The rate of ever having purchased a mini-cassette player was 51.5 per cent while the rate of having purchased a ball-pen within the past two years was 82 per cent respectively.

The way that the results of the pilot survey were used in determining the sample size for the main survey was discussed at pp. 247–8. The following describes how modifications were made to the pilot questionnaire.

Modification to the pilot questionnaire

Analysis of the pilot data as well as the information obtained from the discussions with pilot respondents showed that the questionnaire on the whole was a satisfactory instrument for obtaining answers to the research questions. The following describes the slight modifications that were undertaken.

Question content In Section 1 of the questionnaire, five common sayings were added to improve the content validity of the construct of the Chinese cultural values.

In Section 1, the number of common sayings which represent the Chinese cultural values were reduced to forty. These deletions were made either because the reliability of the items was low or because non-responses for the item were high.

Most pilot respondents complained that they were not able to differentiate among the performance of the attributes of the experimental instrument in the four situations. It was said that the performance of the attributes could not be situation-specific. Hence, questions 6c and 6d were changed so that respondents were only asked to rate the performance of each attribute of the experimental products without referring to the four situations as in other questions in the same section.

In the questionnaire for ball-pens, some attributes were found to be unclear and unspecific for the situations concerned, and thus were excluded. The attributes 'smoothness in writing' and 'no leaking of ink' were combined to form a new attribute, 'quality in writing'. Similarly, in the questionnaire for mini-cassettes, the attributes 'prestige' and 'prettiness in appearance' were combined to form a new attribute, 'prestigiously pretty'.

Question phrasing   Pilot respondents found the words 'private' and 'public' on the descriptions of the situations unclear. In order to make the descriptions of the situations more understandable, the word 'private' was changed to 'when you are alone' and the word 'public' was changed to 'when you are with other people'. Thought had been given to changing the word 'public' to 'in business/at work'. However, when considering that respondents were not necessarily working people, this idea was turned down.

Response format   The measurement scale for evaluating disconfirmation between expectations and perceived performance of the experimental products was changed from a six-point scale to a five-point scale. The five-point scale, therefore, allowed the respondent to have a neutral point where the perceived performance of the instrument was exactly the same as his expectations.

Reducing non-response error

In order to increase the response rate and to reduce non-response error, two measures were taken. First, each housing unit was notified beforehand by a letter signed by the researcher (see Appendix B). It was believed that prior notification by letter would produce a lower refusal rate. The letter was written using a local university letter head and mailed in a university envelope. It was believed that a letter with university identification would produce even better results. Second, interviews were conducted by experienced interviewers of the Market Decision Research Company, instead of university students. These interviewers were trained to get access to the housing units and to persuade respondents to be interviewed.

Data collection process

In May 1985, prior to the interview survey, a letter which was addressed to the head of each housing unit in the sample was written in Chinese and signed by the researcher on headed notepaper of the Chinese University of Hong Kong. It notified the households that a survey on consumer satisfaction/dissatisfaction would be conducted and an interviewer of the Market Decision Research Company would come to interview one of their members within one or two weeks' time. It was also stressed that information sought would be kept in strict confidence. A sample notification letter can be found in Appendix B.

The actual interviews were conducted during the first two weeks of June 1985 by interviewers of the Market Decision Research Company, one of the best known research companies in Hong Kong. Twenty experienced interviewers were trained and briefed about the sampling, the sample, the way to select the right respondent, the experiment and each question on the questionnaire. In order to identify himself, each interviewer wore the badge of the research company and carried a copy of the notification letter which had to be presented before he could get access to the housing units for interviews.

During the interview, after the section on the Chinese cultural values had been rated, the subjects (respondents) were shown a message with a picture of the product giving information about the capabilities of the product, its general quality and its price. They were asked to rate their expectations of the product. They were then given a demonstration of the product and its capabilities. During the demonstration, they were given the opportunity to examine the product and to ask questions. Then they were asked to imagine that they had purchased the ball-pens or the mini-cassette players a month ago, and that it was operating exactly like the one they had just seen. They were then asked to assess their level of performance, disconfirmation and satisfaction as described in this chapter. Finally, personal information was obtained.

In order to make sure that every respondent is properly interviewed, careful supervision and validation of each interviewer's work as the survey progresses are needed. There are four common methods of validating interviewers; spot checks, telephone checks, mail checks and questionnaire check (Mun and Yau 1979). In this study, a mail

mail check was not used, because of the time constraint. In order to identify the sequence of interviews and to group the interviews into batches for editing, coding and checking to ensure that each interviewer was maintaining the schedule, a sequence number was assigned to the interviews (Tull and Hawkins 1980). Then 45 per cent of the interviews conducted by each interviewer were validated by telephone. If the telephone number had not been secured during the interview, a spot check was made by an interview supervisor of the research company. Furthermore, the returned questionnaires of each interviewer were checked for irrational interview routeing and illogical answers. Finally, five questionable questionnaires were discarded.

HOW LISREL IS APPLIED TO THE MODEL

In this section, an attempt is made to specify the structure of the model of Consumer Satisfaction and Chinese Cultural Values.

Notations used in LISREL model

Figure 4.3 presents the initial structure of the model of Consumer Satisfaction and Chinese Cultural Values, consistent with the depiction of models in LISREL. All variables, except for two dummy variables, situations and products, are measured using interval scales. In the figure, the observable variables are denoted by small boxes. These variables are also denoted by x_i if they are observable independent variables, and by y_i if they are observable dependent variables. Measure error of the ith observable independent variable is denoted by δ_i, and of the ith observable dependent variable by ε_i.

Unobservable variables are denoted by big circles. The signs ξ and η are used to indicate that they are unobservable independent variables and unobservable dependent variables respectively. In the figure, there are five independent variables. They are (1) the Chinese Cultural Values (ξ_1), (2) Use situation (ξ_2) (3) Products (ξ_3), (4) Consumption Experiences (ξ_4), and (5) Affective Experiences (ξ_5). Each of the independent variables is composed of several observable variables. For example, Chinese Cultural Values is denoted by ξ_1 with twelve observable variables, $x_1 \ldots x_{12}$, in small boxes, and the variable Situations is denoted by ξ_2 with four observable variables, $x_{13} \ldots x_{16}$. Measurement errors in the unobservable dependent variables are denoted by ζ, while the coefficients emanating from each unobservable independent variable to its indicator (observable variable) are represented by the symbol lambda (λ_i). Since there might be correlations between

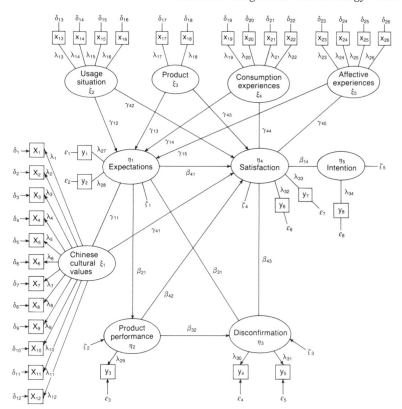

Figure 4.3 Links of variables of the structural model of Chinese cultural values and consumer satisfaction/dissatisfaction

unobservable independent variable, the existence of the relationship can be expressed using the symbol ϕ.

There are five unobservable dependent variables in the model as well. They are (1) expectations (η_1), (2) product performance (η_2), (3) disconfirmation (η_3), (4) satisfaction (η_4), and (5) intention (η_5). Again, each unobservable dependent variable is made up of one to two observable variables. In the model, expectations, disconfirmation, and satisfaction have two observable variables, the global measure and the attribute-specific measure, while perceived performance and intention have only one observable variable. The coefficients emanating from each unobservable dependent variable to its indicators are represented by the symbol λ_i, and the existence of correlation between unobservable dependent variables is denoted by the symbol β_i.

Finally, the links between unobservable dependent variables and unobservable independent variables are represented by γs.

Specification of the model

Now consider the links between variables in the structural model in Figure 4.3. The variable, expectations, is dependent on the following five variables:

1 Chinese cultural values.
2 Usage situations.
3 Product.
4 Consumption experiences.
5 Affective experiences.

This relationship can be expressed by the following equation:

Expectations = f (Chinese cultural values, Usage situations, Products, Consumption Experiences, and Affective experiences) (4.1)

Or, using the notations previously described, the relationship can also be expressed as follows:

$$\eta_1 = \gamma_{11}\xi_1 + \gamma_{12}\xi_2 + \gamma_{13}\xi_3 + \gamma_{14}\xi_4 + \gamma_{15}\xi_5 + \zeta_1 \qquad (4.1a)$$

The variable, product performance, is dependent on expectations. Therefore

Product performance = f (Expectations) (4.2)

or

$$\eta_2 = \beta_{21}\eta_1 + \zeta_2 \qquad (4.2a)$$

With respect to the variable, disconfirmation, it depends on two variables: expectations and product performance. This relationship can also be expressed in the following form:

Disconfirmation = f (Expectations, Product performance) (4.3)

or

$$\eta_3 = \beta_{31}\eta_1 + \beta_{32}\eta_2 + \zeta_3 \qquad (4.3a)$$

Several factors affect consumer satisfaction. Their relationships can be expressed in the following equation:

Satisfaction = f (Chinese cultural values, Usage situation, Product, Consumption experience, Affective experiences, Expectations, Product performance, Disconfirmation) (4.4)

or

$$\eta_4 = \gamma_{41}\xi_1 + \gamma_{42}\xi_2 + \gamma_{43}\xi_3 + \gamma_{44}\xi_4 + \gamma_{45}\xi_5 + \beta_{41}\eta_1 + \beta_{42}\eta_2$$
$$+ \beta_{43}\eta_3 + \zeta_4 \tag{4.4a}$$

However, in the model, satisfaction is the only variable which affects intention. Therefore

Intention = f (Satisfaction) (4.5)
$$\eta_5 = \beta_{54}\eta_4 + \zeta_5 \tag{4.5a}$$

The above equations are recursive and can also be expressed in reduced matrix form as follows:

$$
\begin{bmatrix} \eta_1 \\ \eta_2 \\ \eta_3 \\ \eta_4 \\ \eta_5 \end{bmatrix}
=
\begin{bmatrix}
0 & 0 & 0 & 0 & 0 \\
\beta_{21} & 0 & 0 & 0 & 0 \\
\beta_{31} & \beta_{32} & 0 & 0 & 0 \\
\beta_{41} & \beta_{42} & \beta_{43} & 0 & 0 \\
0 & 0 & 0 & 0 & \beta_{54}
\end{bmatrix}
\begin{bmatrix} \eta_1 \\ \eta_2 \\ \eta_3 \\ \eta_4 \\ \eta_5 \end{bmatrix}
$$

$$
+
\begin{bmatrix}
\gamma_{11} & \gamma_{12} & \gamma_{13} & \gamma_{14} & \gamma_{15} \\
0 & 0 & 0 & 0 & 0 \\
0 & 0 & 0 & 0 & 0 \\
\gamma_{41} & \gamma_{42} & \gamma_{43} & \gamma_{44} & \gamma_{45} \\
0 & 0 & 0 & 0 & 0
\end{bmatrix}
\begin{bmatrix} \xi_1 \\ \xi_2 \\ \xi_3 \\ \xi_4 \\ \xi_5 \end{bmatrix}
+
\begin{bmatrix} \zeta_1 \\ \zeta_2 \\ \zeta_3 \\ \zeta_4 \\ \zeta_5 \end{bmatrix}
\tag{4.6}
$$

Now, the structural equation model has been tentatively specified. However, variables in the model are unobservable. In order to solve the system of equations, it is necessary to express further all unobserved variables in terms of their observed variables respectively, of which measurements have been made.

First, consider the relationships between the unobservable independent variables and their indicators in Figure 4.3. The variable, Chinese cultural values can be expressed in terms of its twelve factors as follows:

$$x_1 = \lambda_1 \ \xi_1 + \delta_1$$
$$\vdots \quad \vdots \quad \vdots \quad \vdots$$
$$x_{12} = \lambda_{12} \ \xi_1 + \delta_{12} \tag{4.7}$$

Similarly, the other four variables can also be expressed in terms of their indicators as follows:

$$x_{13} = \lambda_{13} \ \xi_2 + \delta_{13}$$
$$\vdots \quad \vdots \quad \vdots \quad \vdots$$
$$x_{16} = \lambda_{16} \ \xi_2 + \delta_{16} \tag{4.8}$$

$$x_{17} = \lambda_{17} \ \xi_3 + \delta_{17}$$
$$x_{18} = \lambda_{18} \ \xi_3 + \delta_{18} \tag{4.9}$$

$$x_{19} = \lambda_{19} \ \xi_4 + \delta_{19}$$
$$\vdots \quad \vdots \quad \vdots \quad \vdots$$
$$x_{22} = \lambda_{22} \ \xi_4 + \delta_{22} \tag{4.10}$$

$$x_{23} = \lambda_{23} \ \xi_5 + \delta_{23}$$
$$\vdots \quad \vdots \quad \vdots \quad \vdots$$
$$x_{26} = \lambda_{26} \ \xi_5 + \delta_{26} \tag{4.11}$$

These five equations can be summarized in reduced form as follows:

$$
\begin{bmatrix} x_1 \\ x_2 \\ x_3 \\ x_4 \\ x_5 \\ x_6 \\ x_7 \\ x_8 \\ x_9 \\ x_{10} \\ x_{11} \\ x_{12} \\ x_{13} \\ x_{14} \\ x_{15} \\ x_{16} \\ x_{17} \\ x_{18} \\ x_{19} \\ x_{20} \\ x_{21} \\ x_{22} \\ x_{23} \\ x_{24} \\ x_{25} \\ x_{26} \end{bmatrix}
=
\begin{bmatrix} \lambda_1 & & & & \\ \lambda_2 & & & & \\ \lambda_3 & & & & \\ \lambda_4 & & & & \\ \lambda_5 & & & & \\ \lambda_6 & & & & \\ \lambda_7 & & & & \\ \lambda_8 & & & & \\ \lambda_9 & & & & \\ \lambda_{10} & & & & \\ \lambda_{11} & & & & \\ \lambda_{12} & & & & \\ & \lambda_{13} & & & \\ & \lambda_{14} & & & \\ & \lambda_{15} & & & \\ & \lambda_{16} & & & \\ & & \lambda_{17} & & \\ & & \lambda_{18} & & \\ & & & \lambda_{19} & \\ & & & \lambda_{20} & \\ & & & \lambda_{21} & \\ & & & \lambda_{22} & \\ & & & & \lambda_{23} \\ & & & & \lambda_{24} \\ & & & & \lambda_{25} \\ & & & & \lambda_{26} \end{bmatrix}
\begin{bmatrix} \xi_1 \\ \xi_2 \\ \xi_3 \\ \xi_4 \\ \xi_5 \end{bmatrix}
+
\begin{bmatrix} \delta_1 \\ \delta_2 \\ \delta_3 \\ \delta_4 \\ \delta_5 \\ \delta_6 \\ \delta_7 \\ \delta_8 \\ \delta_9 \\ \delta_{10} \\ \delta_{11} \\ \delta_{12} \\ \delta_{13} \\ \delta_{14} \\ \delta_{15} \\ \delta_{16} \\ \delta_{17} \\ \delta_{18} \\ \delta_{19} \\ \delta_{20} \\ \delta_{21} \\ \delta_{22} \\ \delta_{23} \\ \delta_{24} \\ \delta_{25} \\ \delta_{26} \end{bmatrix}
\tag{4.12}
$$

Similarly, the relationships between unobservable dependent variables and their indicators can be expressed as follows:

$$
\begin{bmatrix} y_1 \\ y_2 \\ y_3 \\ y_4 \\ y_5 \\ y_6 \\ y_7 \\ y_8 \end{bmatrix}
=
\begin{bmatrix} \lambda_{27} & & & & \\ \lambda_{28} & & & & \\ & \lambda_{29} & & & \\ & \lambda_{30} & & & \\ & \lambda_{31} & & & \\ & & \lambda_{32} & & \\ & & \lambda_{33} & & \\ & & & \lambda_{34} & \end{bmatrix}
\begin{bmatrix} \eta_1 \\ \eta_2 \\ \eta_3 \\ \eta_4 \\ \eta_5 \end{bmatrix}
+
\begin{bmatrix} \varepsilon_1 \\ \varepsilon_2 \\ \varepsilon_3 \\ \varepsilon_4 \\ \varepsilon_5 \\ \varepsilon_6 \\ \varepsilon_7 \\ \varepsilon_8 \end{bmatrix}
\tag{4.13}
$$

The above equations 4.12–13 describe the measurement model of LISREL.

Furthermore, it is assumed that there is an interaction effect between the two independent variables: use situation and product. This relationship should also be incorporated in the LISREL model, by setting the matrix of errors of measurement for the independent variables as follow:

$$
\varepsilon =
\begin{bmatrix}
\varepsilon_1 & & & & \bigcirc \\
 & \varepsilon_2 & & & \\
 & & \cdot & & \\
 & & & \cdot & \\
 & & & & \cdot \\
\bigcirc & & & & \varepsilon_{26}
\end{bmatrix}
\quad (4.14)
$$

It is noteworthy that in the initial model it is assumed that all measure errors are uncorrelated. Hence, variance–covariance matrix for measure errors is diagonal in nature.

Estimation and examination of values of the parameters

Together with the specification of the model, the correlation matrix for the thirty-four observable variables is computed as the input into the LISREL VI package. Though the covariance matrix could have as easily been used, LISREL VI accepts either type of data input and there is no difference in output between the two types of input matrix (Dillon and Goldstein 1984). The maximum likelihood estimation procedure is used to estimate the parameters of the model. Since the two samples in the study are fairly large, there may not be any violations of the assumed normality of the observable variables. Furthermore, the size of the two samples in the study justifies the use of the asymptotic properties of the maximum likelihood estimation. However, there are several aspects worth noting. First, there should not be any negative estimates of variance. Second, assurance has to be made to identify the model that t-values can be computed and obtained for each parameter. Third, with such a fairly large sample size in the study, it is very likely that the Chi- square goodness-of-fit test will reject the null hypothesis that a proposed model provides an acceptable fit of the observable data. Other tests must be used to assess the overall fitness of the model. Furthermore, it has been found that weak observable variable relationships increase the probability of obtaining a good fit using the chi-square test (Dillon and Goldstein 1984). Since the main objective of this study is to find out the causal relationships between determinants of consumer satisfaction, significant relationships therefore might still exist even though the model does not provide a good fit to the data.

CONCLUSION

This chapter has described the research methodology of the study. The design was based on the four stages – selection of data collection method, selection of measurement techniques, selection of the sample, and the data collection procedures. The four stages were discussed in detail. The personal interview methods, together with experimentation, were selected to collect data. The structure of the questionnaires, which made wide use of measurement scales, was fully explained. Two samples (one for the ball-pen and one for the mini-cassette player) of 320 and 319 were drawn from two replicates of the 1981 census in Hong Kong. The data collection procedure, with a description of the pilot survey, was discussed. The possible actions taken to reduce anticipated error in the collection procedures were given. The analysis of covariance structure based on Joreskog's LISREL VI was discussed in a non-mathematical manner.

The analysis of the results from the research will be presented in Chapter 5. Chapter 6 offers the conclusions and recommendations.

5 Data analysis and results

In the data analysis phase of this study, the theoretical model of the Chinese cultural values and consumer satisfaction/dissatisfaction will be verified, using the data collected from respondents described in Chapter 4. The first section of the chapter describes the survey responses, which include response analysis and the characteristics of the respondents. This is of critical importance to any survey research because the representativeness of the final sample very largely affects the conclusions that can be drawn from the research. The second section explores the reliability and validity of the multi-item measures used in this study. The final two sections provide the results of the analysis of covariance structure for the two samples respectively.

SURVEY RESPONSES

This section deals with the response analysis, followed by an analysis of background data of respondents. (Mini-cassette player has been shortened to mini-cassette in much of this chapter.)

Response analysis

Table 5.1 gives a breakdown of response to the pilot and main interview surveys. The total number of usable questionnaires from the main survey was 640. Thus the response rate for the main survey, as shown in Table 5.2, was 61.95 per cent, which is higher than 55.27 per cent for the pilot survey. For the ball-pen sample it was 62 per cent and for the mini-cassette player sample, 61.77 per cent. The result was considered satisfactory for an interview survey of this type in which particular respondents who had use/consumption experiences with ball-pens/mini-cassettes had to be called upon. It was higher than TARP's (1977) response rate of 43 per cent in its national study of complaining behaviour involving personal interviews of households.

Table 5.1 Survey responses

Survey	Ball-pen	Mini-cassette player	Total
Pilot Survey			
No. of addresses drawn	130	230	360
No. of addresses unused	13	23	36
Unsuccessful contact (i.e. empty homes, refusal)	45	80	125
Irrelevant respondent contacts (i.e. did not buy ball-pens/mini-cassettes)	12	67	79
Unusable questionnaires	0	0	0
Usable questionnaires	60	60	120
Main Survey			
No. of addresses drawn	664	1,060	1,724
No. of addresses unused	36	64	100
Unsuccessful contact (i.e. empty homes, refusal)	214	340	554
Irrelevant respondent contacts (i.e. did not buy ball-pens/mini-cassettes)	91	334	425
Unusable questionnaires	2	3	5
Usable questionnaires	321	319	640

Table 5.2 Survey response summary (per cent)

Sample	Successful Contact Rate(1)		Use Rate(2)		Total Response Rate(3)	
	Pilot	Main	Pilot	Main	Pilot	Main
Ball-pen	61.53	65.92	83.33	78.02	55.38	62%
Mini-cassette player	61.35	65.86	47.24	49.08	55.21	61.27%
Total	61.42	65.89	60.30	60.28	55.27	61.95%

[1] Successful Contact Rate = No. of successful contacts/No. of addresses used.
[2] Use Rate = percentage of households having members who bought ball-pens/mini-cassette players in successful household contacts.
[3] Total Response Rate = No. of usable questionnaires/No. of addresses used in the survey (Churchill, 1991: 617).

As expected, the level of response in this study was higher than some other studies in the literature on consumer satisfaction, not to mention those studies in which a convenience sample was drawn (Churchill and Surprenant 1982; Tse and Wilton 1985; Cardozo 1964). For example,

Swan and Longman's (1972) study of consumer activism involved a telephone survey of 400 new car owners; it achieved a 31.2 per cent response rate. Similarly, Zaichkowsky and Liefeld (1977) obtained a response rate of 17.3 per cent from complainers of the Better Business Bureau of Canada, after both mail and telephone follow-ups.

In Table 5.2, it can be seen that the response rate for the ball-pen sample was higher than that for the mini-cassette sample. This was simply because the use rate of ball-pens for the ball-pen sample (78 per cent) was higher than that of mini-cassettes for the mini-cassette sample (49 per cent). However, the successful contact rate for both samples was about 65 per cent which was higher than the rate for the pilot survey. According to the Market Strategy Research Company, the successful contact rate is usually about 60 per cent in Hong Kong. The higher successful rates for the two samples might be attributed to the prior notification letter on university notepaper sent to each target household by the researcher before the survey started. Overall, the survey responses shown in both Table 5.1 and Table 5.2 clearly indicate that the response results were quite stable and consistent across the two samples, as well as the pilot survey.

Characteristics of the sample

Of the 34 per cent of unsuccessful contacts, it was found that they fell into three categories:

1 Not at home.
2 Non-existent living quarters.
3 Refusals.

Not-at-homes in the study referred to those living quarters where the occupants had not answered the door for three visits. Refusals referred to those cases when interviewers were not able to get into the building or when householders refused to accept an interview. Non-existent living quarters imply that the addresses provided by the Census and Statistics Department were outdated. Since the listing of the two replicates was received in early January 1985 but the main survey was conducted in June 1985, some houses or buildings might have been pulled down during those six months.

One factor of crucial importance to the adequacy of the data obtained was the degree to which respondents match non-respondents in terms of variables of interest to the study. Non-response bias can be examined, for example, by comparing early respondents with late respondents. However, this method is only suitable in mail surveys.

Unfortunately, there were no lists available that would have given the characteristics of the non-respondents for comparison purposes. Therefore, the representativeness of the final samples has to be assessed indirectly. Certain characteristics of the respondents are described in order to assess the adequacy of the samples. The descriptive summary of the respondents is provided in Table 5.3. For comparison purposes, the statistics of the 1981 census from which the samples were drawn are also presented (Census and Statistics Department, Hong Kong.) However, the statistics have been adjusted by the researcher to include only those who are above seventeen years old. Hence, the statistics reported are approximate percentages, as there were no breakdown statistics for each age category for adjustments.

The distribution of the seven characteristics can be regarded as realistic and typical indicators of consumers in Hong Kong. As regards sex, even though both samples were 'male' biased, given that the results of the census in 1981 indicated that males contributed 52.4 per cent of the population in Hong Kong (Census and Statistics Department 1982), yet the figures were still within tolerable limits.

Judging from the age distribution of the two samples, respondents in the mini-cassette sample appeared to be younger. This is simply because of the short history of the mini-cassette, which was only introduced in Hong Kong at the turn of 1980, as compared to the ball-pen, which was first introduced to Hong Kong in 1960. In today's Hong Kong, the mini-cassette has become a toy of young people as well as of those who are interested in music.

For the same reason, it was found that the distribution of marital status for the mini-cassette sample was skewed to the category 'single'. This implies that the mini-cassette sample had more 'single' respondents than the ball-pen sample, as young respondents tend to be 'single'. However, the distributions for the combined sample and that of the census are extremely similar.

With respect to the personal income of the respondents, the two samples show extremely similar patterns of income distribution, while the distribution for the 1981 census shows that there is a high percentage of low-income households. It seems that there is a great difference between the distributions of the two samples and that of the census. Care should be taken in any direct comparison between personal incomes in 1981 and 1985. Because of economic inflation, which has been about ten per cent for the last few years in Hong Kong, a personal income of HK$2,000 in 1981 could mean HK$3,200 in 1985. Hence, in order to make sound comparisons, it is necessary to shift the distribution of the census one category forward. That is

Table 5.3   Profiles of respondents of the main survey

Characteristics	Ball-pen (N = 321) n (%)	Mini-cassette player (N = 319) n (%)	Total (N = 640) n (%)	1981 Census %
1 Sex				
Male	181 (56.4)	201 (63.0)	382 (59.7)	(52.4)
Female	140 (43.6)	118 (37.0)	258 (40.3)	(47.6)
2 Age				
18–20	60 (18.7)	91 (28.5)	151 (23.6)	(9.8)
21–30	131 (40.8)	132 (41.4)	263 (41.1)	(30.5)
31–40	82 (25.5)	76 (23.9)	158 (24.7)	(18.1)
41–50	30 (9.1)	17 (5.3)	47 (7.3)	(14.6)
51–60	17 (5.3)	9 (2.8)	26 (4.0)	(13.4)
Above 60	1 (0.3)	1 (0.3)	2 (0.3)	(14.6)
3 Level of education				
No education	3 (0.9)	1 (0.3)	4 (0.6)	(2.0)
Some primary	17 (5.3)	14 (4.4)	31 (4.8)	(46.1)
Primary	52 (16.2)	22 (6.9)	74 (11.6)	
Some secondary	77 (23.9)	78 (24.5)	155 (24.2)	(42.3)
Secondary	113 (35.2)	120 (37.6)	233 (36.4)	
Matriculation	32 (10.0)	40 (12.5)	72 (11.2)	(3.4)
University	27 (8.5)	44 (13.8)	71 (11.2)	(6.3)
4 Marital status				
Single	142 (44.2)	210 (65.8)	352 (55.0)	(53.4)
Married	179 (55.8)	108 (33.9)	287 (44.8)	(41.4)
Others	0 (0.0)	1 (0.3)	1 (0.2)	(5.2)
5 Personal income (HK$)				
None	79 (24.6)	72 (22.6)	151 (23.6)	(24.1)
Below 2,000	61 (19.0)	52 (16.3)	113 (17.7)	(50.0)
2,000–3,999	108 (33.6)	107 (33.5)	215 (33.6)	(18.5)
4,000–5,999	43 (13.4)	49 (15.3)	92 (14.4)	(3.0)
6,000–7,999	20 (6.2)	19 (5.8)	39 (6.1)	(3.0)
8,000–9,999	4 (1.3)	3 (0.9)	7 (1.1)	(0.4)
10,000–12,499	1 (0.3)	5 (1.6)	6 (0.9)	(1.0)
12,500–14,999	1 (0.3)	4 (1.3)	5 (0.8)	*
Above 15,000	4 (1.3)	8 (2.5)	12 (1.8)	*
6 Geographical area				
Hong Kong Island	69 (21.5)	69 (21.6)	138 (21.6)	(24.7)
Kowloon	57 (17.8)	54 (16.9)	111 (17.3)	(15.0)
New Kowloon	108 (33.6)	102 (32.0)	210 (32.8)	(34.5)
New Territories	87 (27.1)	94 (29.5)	181 (28.3)	(26.8)
7 Housing type				
Private	148 (46.1)	139 (43.6)	287 (44.8)	(40.6)
Government	169 (52.6)	178 (55.8)	347 (54.2)	(48.9)
Temporary	4 (1.2)	2 (0.6)	6 (1.0)	(10.5)

* Negligible

to say, the category of HK$2,000–HK$3,999 should read HK$4,000–HK$5,999 and so on. When this adjustment has been made, the distributions of the two samples and the census then become quite similar.

As to the other three characteristics of the respondents, the two samples appear to be very similar in distribution. As far as the geographical areas where the respondents lived are concerned, the distributions for both samples are extremely similar. There were about 22 per cent of the respondents living on Hong Kong Island, 50 per

Table 5.4 Profiles of respondents of the pilot survey

Characteristics	Ball-pen (N = 60) n (%)	Mini-cassette player (N = 60) n (%)	Total (N = 120 n (%)
1 Sex			
Male	32 (53.3)	31 (51.7)	63 (52.5)
Female	28 (46.7)	29 (48.3)	57 (47.5)
2 Age			
18–20	3 (5.0)	8 (13.3)	11 (9.2)
21–30	23 (38.3)	34 (56.7)	57 (47.6)
31–40	22 (36.6)	15 (25.0)	37 (30.8)
41–50	5 (8.3)	2 (3.3)	7 (5.8)
50–60	3 (5.0)	1 (1.7)	4 (3.3)
Above 60	4 (6.7)	0 (0.0)	4 (3.3)
3 Level of education			
No education	0 (0.0)	0 (0.0)	0 (0.0)
Some primary	0 (0.0)	0 (0.0)	0 (0.0)
Primary	9 (15.0)	2 (3.3)	11 (9.1)
Some secondary	8 (13.3)	14 (23.3)	22 (18.3)
Secondary	32 (53.3)	31 (51.7)	63 (52.5)
Matriculation	8 (13.3)	8 (13.0)	16 (13.3)
University	3 (5.0)	5 (8.3)	8 (6.6)
4 Marital status			
Single	34 (56.7)	40 (66.7)	74 (61.6)
Married	26 (43.3)	20 (33.3)	46 (38.4)
Others	0 (0.0)	0 (0.0)	0 (0.0)
5 Personal income			
None	1 (1.7)	6 (10.0)	7 (5.9)
Below 2,000	14 (23.3)	11 (18.3)	25 (20.8)
2,000–3,999	20 (33.3)	22 (36.7)	42 (35.0)
4,000–5,999	8 (13.3)	16 (26.7)	24 (20.0)
6,000–7,999	8 (13.3)	4 (6.7)	12 (10.0)
8,000–9,999	4 (6.6)	0 (0.0)	4 (3.3)
10,000–12,499	4 (6.6)	3 (5.0)	7 (5.9)
12,500–14,999	0 (0.0)	2 (3.3)	2 (1.6)
Above 15,000	1 (1.7)	1 (1.7)	2 (1.6)

cent in Kowloon and New Kowloon, and 28 per cent in the New Territories. The spread of geographical areas was quite similar to that of the census and moreover to the recently updated results of the Hong Kong population, reported by the Market Strategy Research Company. According to the report, the distributions of geographical areas were 24.2 per cent on Hong Kong Island, 48 per cent in Kowloon and New Kowloon, and 25.8 per cent in the New Territories (internal report of the Market Strategy Research Company). Obviously, this comparison further strengthens the belief that the two samples were representative by and large.

With regard to housing type, both samples had a percentage of about 55 in government housing. Even though this figure is different from that of the 1981 census, it is consistent with the statistics reported by the Hong Kong government (*A Yearbook of the Commonwealth*, 1981), which estimated that there was 50 per cent of the population living in public (government) housing. People living in temporary housing were negligible in number, contributing about 2.5 per cent of the whole population (internal report of the Market Strategy Research Company). Hence, the distribution of housing type did in fact reflect a true picture of the Hong Kong population.

A further comparison with the profiles of the respondents in the pilot survey is even more encouraging (see Table 5.4). To a great extent, the distributions of most characteristics for the two samples were quite similar. Hence, there is no reason to suspect that the final samples of respondents are not representative of the whole sample of consumers. To summarize, the data concerning the response rate and the characteristics of the respondents for two samples seem to indicate that the two samples provides a good setting for testing the theoretical model concerned.

SCALE RELIABILITY AND VALIDITY

Being an introduction to the concepts of reliability and validity this section is primarily divided into two parts. The first deals with the measurement of the reliability of multi-item measures of constructs in the model. The second seeks to describe the procedure for constructing the Chinese cultural value scale, with emphasis on item selection, and the validity and reliability of the scale.

Reliability

The reliability of a scale is the degree to which the scale produces consistent and stable scores of a subject on a series of repeated tests (Cronbach 1970). Tull and Hawkins (1980) have pointed out that there are five approaches to the estimation of reliability: (1) test–retest reliability, (2) split-sample reliability (3) alternative or parallel forms reliability, (4) internal-comparison reliability, and (5) scorer reliability.

Test–retest reliability estimates are obtained when the same scale was measured under two or more similar situations. The results of two separate administrations are then compared by computing the correlation coefficient on an item-by-item basis. The smaller the differences between corresponding items, the higher the reliability. However, there are a few pitfalls in this approach. First, some items can only be measured once, for example, initial reaction to a new advertisement. Second, in many situations, the initial measurement may alter the characteristic being measured. Thus, a survey, which focuses the respondent's attention on a certain topic, may cause new or different attitudes to be formed about it. Third, there may be some form of a carrying-over effect from the first measure. Fourth, factors extraneous to the measuring process may cause shifts in the characteristic being measured. Thus, for example, switch of brands may occur between the tests.

The above factors may cause changes in the reliability coefficient. In addition to these problems, higher costs and more time will probably be needed as two or more tests are administered. Because of these, the test–retest reliability approach was not used.

Split-sample reliability measures are obtained by dividing the sample into two or more randomly selected sub-samples and comparing results for each item of interest for each sub-sample. This approach is capable of eliminating the four problems described for the test–retest approach. However, there is a basic requirement for this approach. The split sub-samples should be larger than fifty. In the study, this approach was used to compare the scale reliability of multi-item measures and the Chinese cultural scale across two fairly large sub-samples, which were randomly selected from the population.

Parallel-form method is the measurement of the construct on two comparable test forms. This approach requires the construction of two forms which have psychologically equivalent items (statements) and measure the same construct. Hence, the basic logic of this approach is the same as the test–retest approach. However, two primary problems are involved in this approach. The first is the extra time, expense and trouble involved in obtaining two parallel forms. The second is the problem of constructing two truly equivalent forms.

In the study, besides the multi-item measures for expectations, product performance, disconfirmation and satisfaction, a global measure for each of the constructs was also designed. Simple correlation analysis was employed to measure the parallel-form reliability. Furthermore, the reliabilities for the individual global measure and the composite construct in the model were also imputed as estimates by LISREL (see pp. 139–41).

Internal-comparison reliability is estimated by the intercorrelation among the scores of the items on a multi-item index. Split-half reliability is a type of internal comparison. It is obtained by comparing the results of half the items on a multi-item measure with the results from the remaining items. The reliability estimates for the Likert-type items can be computed using Flanagan's formula (Cronbach 1970). The Spearman–Brown formula was also employed as a corrective measure of the split-half reliability (Hull and Nie 1981).

The difficulty with the split-half method is that the correlations between halves will vary, depending on how the items are divided into halves. Therefore, it is more sensible to utilize Cronbach alpha coefficient and item-total correlation than the split-half approach to avoid the presence of a distinct sub-scale. Tull and Hawkins (1980) have also recommended the use of the Cronbach alpha coefficient to measure internal comparison. This measure, in fact, also produces the mean of all possible split-half coefficients resulting from different splittings of the measurement scale. The Cronbach alpha coefficient has the important property of being the lower bound for the reliability of a composite scale (Bagozzi 1978). That is, it gives the smallest reliability for a particular test scale. In the study, the coefficient was widely used to measure the reliability for multi-item measures such as expectations, product performance, disconfirmation and satisfaction.

Sometimes, when judges or scorers are used to classify consumers' responses, the level of scorer reliability needs to be estimated, simply because these judges or scorers may be the source of unreliability rather than the scale instrument itself. The scorer reliability is simply a measure of the correlation between the various judges. It is often used when observation/open-ended questions are used. In the study since only scale instruments, and no judges are involved, the scorer reliability was not used.

Validity

Validity is one of the most important facets involved in evaluating the worth of a scale. Lundstrom (1974) defines it as the degree to which a specific scale measures what it has been constructed to or purports to measure.

Perhaps Cronbach and Meehl (1955) were among the first to classify validity into four separate categories: content or fact validity, construct validity, concurrent validity, and predictive validity. If a scale is judged on the basis of what it contains, and it appears as though the scale looks valid, it is said to have content validity. Content or fact validity is the weakest form of validity. Berg and Collier (1953) have shown experimentally that scale items supposedly measuring a property may not have any apparent relation to the property being measured.

Concurrent validity and predictive validity present a more philosophically sound basis for measurement. These two categories of validity differ basically on the element of time. Concurrent validity is the presence of a criterion measure as well as a scale score, which are related in the same time frame, whereas predictive validity makes use of the scale score as a predictor of the criterion behaviour that will take place in the future (Shaw and Wright, 1967). As suggested by the model described in Chapter 3, the components were expected to be associated with each other in a predictable way. The examination of the predictive validity of the constructs specified lends itself to correlational analysis.

Of the four categories of validity, construct validity is the most crucial but perhaps the most difficult to pursue for scale construction. Construct validity is the statistical relationship of the scale and its underlying theoretical construct (Lundstrom 1974). In constructing a scale of consumer discontent, Lundstrom (1974) suggested three methods of construct validation:

1 Correlation of the scale under construction with other scales purported to measure the same construct.
2 Item-to-total correlation analysis.
3 The 'known groups' approach.

The correlation method with existing scales measuring the same construct is the most popular of the three methods. It is based on the degree to which the scale on the construct under construction correlates with scales of proven validity. A high correlation coefficient indicates the strength of relationship between the scales and thus a measure of validity for the construct. The pitfall of this method is that the comparative scale may not be a valid measure itself.

The item-to-total correlation analysis tries to find out the degree of homogeneity of the scale. Statistically, if an item on a scale is contributing to the measurement of the same concept as the total scale, the product–moment correlation for this item will be a positive and significant correlation with the total scale score.

The known groups approach deals with the supposition that, if a scale is a true assessment of a construct, then the scale should be able to differentiate between groups possessing the characteristic under investigation.

Since there were no known scales claiming to measure Chinese cultural values, the item-to-total correlation approach was adopted to assess the validity of the scale as well as its dimensions. Furthermore, a modification of the known groups approach was used. Instead of finding groups with a 'known' attitude structure, the scale itself as well as its dimensions on the scale of Chinese cultural values were validated across the two samples: mini-cassette player and ball-pen. As discussed, the samples are basically quite similar, except that respondents in the mini-cassette player sample are a little bit younger, and richer. Therefore, according to the supposition of the known group approach, these two groups (samples) will basically share some common dimensions. However, there also exist dimensions that discriminate between these two groups.

In addition to the three methods suggested by Lundstrom (1974), the convergent and discriminant validity of some constructs was also assessed. Kinnear and Taylor (1983) argue that if a construct exists, it should be successfully measured by methods that are different or independent, and should be distinguished from constructs which differ from it. Convergent validity and discriminant validity are therefore the approaches that can be used to evaluate construct validity. Convergent validity involves the demonstration of high correlation among measures which attempt to measure the same construct. Discriminant validity, on the other hand, involves demonstrating a lack of correlation among different constructs. In the study, a multitrait multimethod (MTMM) matrix (Campbell and Fiske 1959) was used to evaluate these two kinds of validity. Since not all constructs were measured by multi-methods, only those relevant were included.

To summarize, the methods that were followed in the measurement of scale reliability for multi-item measures were presented. Internal comparison reliability, and parallel-form reliability, of the measures were used in the study. As far as the validity of the Chinese cultural value scale was concerned, the item-to-total correlation method was used. In addition, comparison of the dimension structure of the two samples, as a means to test the validity of the dimensions as well as the scale was also adopted.

Scale reliability and validity for multi-item measures

In order to assess the internal consistency of the items contained in each multi-item attribute-specific construct, coefficient alphas were computed as shown in Table 5.5.

The scales indicate adequate reliability and undimensionality. As Table 5.5 indicates, the alpha coefficients for each of the scales for each product and situation are high and in general are well above the minimally acceptable levels of 0.05 to 0.6 recommended for early stages of basic research (Nunnally 1967: 226).[1] Even the lowest alpha coefficient, which measures the reliability of the consumption experiences for the mini-cassette player sample, is 0.655, and all other coefficients are ranging from 0.70 to 0.89.

As previously described, the validity of the measures was assessed by the methods suggested by Lundstrom (1974). First, the item-to-total correlations for all measures were computed in order to examine the internal validity of the measures. The total score for each measure variable (item) was correlated with the score of each item making up the measure. Directly related to this computation is the correlation of each item with the total score of all items minus itself.

Table 5.5 Scale reliability for multi-item measures

Multi-item Measure	Ball-pen Sample		Mini-cassette player Sample	
	Pen 1	Pen 2	Cassette 1	Cassette 2
Expectations				
Situation 1	0.7892	0.7930	0.7727	0.7895
Situation 2	0.7840	0.8341	0.8193	0.8230
Situation 3	0.7740	0.8505	0.8250	0.7982
Situation 4	0.7896	0.8865	0.8493	0.8138
Performance	0.7850	0.7830	0.8602	0.8683
Disconfirmation				
Situation 1	0.7041	0.8257	0.8124	0.8315
Situation 2	0.7404	0.8426	0.8166	0.8438
Situation 3	0.7546	0.8406	0.8165	0.8543
Situation 4	0.7374	0.8740	0.8305	0.8573
Satisfaction				
Situation 1	0.7802	0.8491	0.8226	0.8418
Situation 2	0.7788	0.8578	0.8604	0.8519
Situation 3	0.7920	0.8869	0.8566	0.8470
Situation 4	0.7938	0.8907	0.8452	0.8611
Consumption experiences	0.7100		0.6555	

Results of the item-to-total tests of reliability for the five measures are presented in Table 5.6 and Table 5.7. In the ball-pen sample, the correlation of the variables ranged from 0.381 to 0.870 for the ball-pen 1 (Artline 200) and from 0.495 to 0.868 for the ball-pen 2 (Parker 45). In the mini-cassette player sample, the item-to-total correlation of the items ranged from 0.410 to 0.794 for the cassette 1 (Sony WM) and from 0.522 to 0.765 for the cassette 2 (Sony FM 15). Examination of these correlations shows that the items in each measure do not differ considerably from other items of the same measure. However, the measure, consumption experiences, seems to be more heterogeneous with lower values than other constructs.

In general, it can be concluded that the individual items in each scale adequately describe the constructs of expectations, performance, disconfirmation, satisfaction and consumption experiences.

Second, correlation analysis was performed to examine the internal structure of the observed variables to ensure that they relate to the same construct, as well as the predictive validity of the measures.

Table 5.6 Item-to-total correlation: the ball-pen sample

Construct	Pen 1 Situation				Pen 2 Situation			
	1	*2*	*3*	*4*	*1*	*2*	*3*	*4*
Expectations								
Writing quality	0.568	0.493	0.527	0.496	0.495	0.579	0.593	0.685
Appearance	0.685	0.781	0.697	0.761	0.771	0.764	0.829	0.840
Prestige	0.642	0.617	0.610	0.654	0.656	0.751	0.755	0.819
Performance								
Writing quality		0.417				0.469		
Appearance		0.659				0.720		
Prestige		0.586				0.692		
Disconfirmation								
Writing quality	0.408	0.425	0.451	0.381	0.559	0.596	0.559	0.624
Appearance	0.645	0.717	0.741	0.719	0.779	0.816	0.806	0.868
Prestige	0.552	0.593	0.625	0.622	0.735	0.728	0.765	0.795
Satisfaction								
Writing quality	0.490	0.497	0.508	0.672	0.593	0.595	0.661	0.672
Appearance	0.771	0.772	0.762	0.870	0.821	0.812	0.877	0.870
Prestige	0.621	0.605	0.652	0.827	0.764	0.803	0.812	0.827
Consumption experiences								
Frequency of buying unsatisfactory ball-pens								0.489
Frequency of buying unsatisfactory products								0.500
Frequency of buying unsatisfactory writing instruments								0.601

Intercorrelations were calculated between observable variables (multi-items) of the constructs: expectations, product performance, disconfirmation, satisfaction and consumption experiences. Results of the analysis are shown in Appendices D and E. As expected, the

Table 5.7 Item-to-total correlation: the mini-cassette player sample

Construct	Cassette player 1 Situation				Cassette player 2 Situation			
	1	*2*	*3*	*4*	*1*	*2*	*3*	*4*
Expectations								
Sound quality	0.569	0.619	0.637	0.605	0.597	0.619	0.634	0.622
Convenience in carrying	0.526	0.613	0.622	0.670	0.522	0.613	0.553	0.590
Sufficient functions	0.579	0.709	0.660	0.794	0.640	0.709	0.617	0.694
Prestigious appearance	0.636	0.652	0.684	0.766	0.641	0.652	0.651	0.633
Product performance								
Sound quality		0.605				0.665		
Convenience in carrying		0.670				0.724		
Sufficient functions		0.794				0.765		
Prestigious appearance		0.767				0.725		
Disconfirmation								
Sound quality	0.579	0.588	0.630	0.612	0.635	0.637	0.668	0.663
Convenience in carrying	0.614	0.603	0.581	0.630	0.629	0.659	0.669	0.656
Sufficient functions	0.694	0.686	0.665	0.693	0.717	0.720	0.734	0.739
Prestigious appearance	0.658	0.685	0.681	0.708	0.673	0.711	0.721	0.757
Satisfaction								
Sound quality	0.591	0.636	0.643	0.650	0.591	0.614	0.606	0.650
Convenience in carrying	0.576	0.676	0.658	0.700	0.685	0.706	0.716	0.700
Sufficient functions	0.710	0.779	0.767	0.756	0.731	0.717	0.714	0.756
Prestigious appearance	0.712	0.737	0.737	0.729	0.701	0.740	0.709	0.729

Consumption experiences

Frequency of buying unsatisfactory casette players	0.470
Frequency of buying unsatisfactory products	0.410
Frequency of buying unsatisfactory audio equipment	0.523

correlations are positive and highly significant between items of all constructs at the confidence level of 0.01. Together with the item-to-total correlations in Tables 5.6 and 5.7, it can be concluded that all individual items related to the same construct.

An attempt was also made to find out the predictive validity of the constructs by examining whether they behave as expected with regard to other related constructs. To achieve this, correlation analysis was also utilized. However, it is worth noting that the purpose of utilizing correlation analysis was to confirm that the related constructs did have some relationships among each other, rather than to test the causality between the related constructs.

As was expected, the correlations are positive and highly significant between satisfaction, product performance, disconfirmation and intention, but consumption experiences, as expected, are negatively correlated with satisfaction. About half the correlations are significant at the level of 0.1. The four affective experiences are found to be mostly negatively correlated with satisfaction, but the correlations are rarely significant. This may be due to the fact that respondents were often satisfied with the products they had purchased and seldom made attributions. Therefore, affective experiences seem to be lacking in predictive validity.

Third, a multitrait-multimethod matrix was employed to assess the convergent and discriminant validity of the measures. Because of the constraint of the method, only constructs which are measured by two methods were analysed. The MTMM matrix is primarily a correlation matrix between different traits and methods of the constructs. Table 5.8 and Table 5.9 show pairwise correlations among measures for the two samples. Here, G represents the global measure and AS represents the attribute-specific measure. The entries below the diagonal are the relations for the first product (e.g. ball-pen 1) data and those above the diagonal are the correlations for the second product (e.g. ball-pen 2) data. One aspect of these correlations is worth noting. First, most of the measures appear to have good convergent and discriminant validity. The measures basically correlate much higher with other measures assessing the same construct than with measures assessing different constructs. The only exception is the attribute-specific measure of expectations, which seems to correlate higher with the global measure of satisfaction than with its own global measure. With this exception, however, its correlation with its global measure is still found to be higher than its correlations with measures of other constructs. Overall, the pattern of correlations among the measures is

Table 5.8 The multitrait–multimethod matrix for the ball-pen sample

		Expectation		Confirmation		Satisfaction	
		G	*AS*	*G*	*AS*	*G*	*AS*
Situation 1							
Expectation	G		0.45	−0.05	0.06	0.19	0.23
	AS	0.43		−0.06	0.12	0.19	0.49
Confirmation	G	0.09	0.25		0.62	0.50	0.40
	AS	0.09	0.30	0.67		0.42	0.53
Satisfaction	G	0.28	0.36	0.57	0.46		0.61
	AS	0.21	0.46	0.55	0.59	0.72	
Situation 2							
Expectation	G		0.52	0.16	0.09	0.39	0.37
	AS	0.55		0.10	0.15	0.33	0.54
Confirmation	G	0.15	0.22		0.54	0.49	0.44
	AS	0.18	0.23	0.63		0.43	0.48
Satisfaction	G	0.38	0.40	0.46	0.48		0.61
	AS	0.35	0.49	0.45	0.58	0.74	
Situation 3							
Expectation	G		0.47	0.12	0.19	0.39	0.31
	AS	0.47		0.18	0.30	0.30	0.42
Confirmation	G	0.10	0.21		0.58	0.43	0.40
	AS	0.08	0.22	0.61		0.44	0.52
Satisfaction	G	0.21	0.40	0.41	0.49		0.62
	AS	0.26	0.49	0.40	0.54	0.67	
Situation 4							
Expectation	G		0.50	0.17	0.16	0.39	0.40
	AS	0.49		0.34	0.46	0.35	0.49
Confirmation	G	0.13	0.22		0.59	0.36	0.38
	AS	0.10	0.24	0.62		0.42	0.47
Satisfaction	G	0.30	0.40	0.50	0.50		0.65
	AS	0.33	0.45	0.48	0.58	0.72	

The entries below the diagonal are the correlations for the ball-pen 2 data and those above the diagonal are the correlations for the ball-pen 1 data. Key: G = Global measure. AS = Attribute-specific multi-item measure.

impressive for the two samples in terms of size and direction, given the hypothesized model described in Chapter 3.

In summary, following the procedure to identify appropriate attributes in focus group interviews prior to the pilot survey, all multi-item measures were found highly reliable by means of alpha coefficients. Several methods were used to assess the validity of the measure. First, in order to determine how well the items correlate with one another and with the total score, the item-to-total correlations and the internal consistency of the multi-item measures were tested.

Table 5.9   The multitrait–multimethod matrix for the mini-cassette player sample

		Expectation		Confirmation		Satisfaction	
		G	AS	G	AS	G	AS
Situation 1							
Expectation	G		0.48	−0.24	0.03	0.25	0.21
	AS	0.48		0.03	0.17	0.27	0.36
Confirmation	G	0.01	0.08		0.65	0.50	0.45
	AS	0.15	0.14	0.68		0.48	0.62
Satisfaction	G	0.30	0.35	0.45	0.43		0.69
	AS	0.30	0.40	0.42	0.54	0.68	
Situation 2							
Expectation	G		0.49	0.19	0.15	0.38	0.30
	AS	0.37		0.19	0.18	0.38	0.30
Confirmation	G	0.02	0.18		0.68	0.52	0.50
	AS	0.04	0.23	0.64		0.52	0.63
Satisfaction	G	0.22	0.38	0.48	0.45		0.73
	AS	0.23	0.53	0.44	0.45	0.68	
Situation 3							
Expectation	G		0.49	0.03	0.14	0.28	0.30
	AS	0.43		0.03	0.22	0.30	0.42
Confirmation	G	0.02	0.11		0.61	0.37	0.33
	AS	0.14	0.23	0.60		0.43	0.56
Satisfaction	G	0.27	0.33	0.47	0.38		0.59
	AS	0.29	0.49	0.41	0.56	0.59	
Situation 4							
Expectation	G		0.48	0.08	0.11	0.29	0.26
	AS	0.48		0.14	0.19	0.32	0.42
Confirmation	G	0.17	0.19		0.60	0.42	0.44
	AS	0.07	0.29	0.61		0.41	0.53
Satisfaction	G	0.33	0.38	0.47	0.39		0.62
	AS	0.28	0.52	0.36	0.58	0.61	

The entries below the diagonal are the correlations for the cassette 2 data and those above the diagonal are the correlations for the cassette 1 data. Key: G = Global measure. AS = Attribute-specific multi-item measure.

Drawing on the results represented in this section, the majority of individual items were found related to the same construct. Second, correlation analysis was also used to find the internal structure as well as the predictive validity of the measures. As a result, all measures were found to have high internal structure. With regard to predictive validity, with the one exception of affective experiences, all measures had high predictive validity in terms of size and direction. Third, unfortunately, available resources did not allow the use of a multitrait-multimethod matrix test of the convergent and discriminant validity of all the measures. Only three of the measures were tested and found convergent and discriminant. However, as Campbell and Fiske (1959) indicate, if two variables correlate as highly as the average of their reliabilities, then the measures have no discriminant validity. The correlations and respective reliabilities show that in general other measures do not meet this criterion. Therefore, it seems that all measures in the study have good discriminant validity. All in all, the validity of the measures in the study shows the relevance of the constructs which were conceptualized earlier in the study.

Construction of the Chinese cultural value scale

In this section, the purpose of the data analysis was to establish the items, and the reliability and validity, of the construction of the Chinese cultural values scale. Second, the data were further analysed to ascertain the complexity of the dimensions of Chinese cultural values by estimating the number of dimensions which contribute to the concept, with the basic dimensions that were discussed in Chapter 2. The latter analysis was believed beneficial in enhancing the understanding of Chinese cultural values and in providing a guide for future researchers interested in this area of research.

Empirical researchers generally agree that the considerations of item selection, reliability and validity are of primary importance for the construction of the scale and its ultimate applicability in research (Lundstrom 1974). Hence, in this section, the following topics – item selection, estimation of dimensionality, reliability testing and validity testing – are described.

Item selection

In Chapter 4, a discussion of how items of the Chinese cultural values were generated is presented. To deal with the large number of items that are typically represented by empirical scale construction, the first phase in development is to eliminate those items which do not accurately measure the concept under study. The process by which certain items are eliminated and others retained is called item selection. It is suggested that there are generally six methods in item selection (Lundstrom 1974). They are non-response, judgment, t-test, biserial correlation, and point biserial correlation. As the latter two methods deal only with dichotomous responses, they were not adopted in the study. The non-response method is in fact a basic approach for item selection. That items have a high level of non-responses indicates they are unreliable and should be discarded. In the study, this approach was employed. It was suggested that items which had a non-response rate of over 10 per cent in either of the samples were dropped from the scale. As a result, five items – Nos. 3, 7, 25, 28, and 34 – were not included in the scale.

Judgment is also a popular approach to item selection, especially for ratio scale construction. It requires expert judges to select the items that they believe have a high degree of reliability and validity. Hence, a criterion of the extent of agreement among judges should be established before the item is considered to be accepted for scale inclusion (Dean 1961; Crowne and Marlowe 1960). In the study, due to the tedious nature of the task, this method was not used for item selection. The use of a t-test for item selection was advocated by Edwards (1957). This approach starts with sorting respondents' scores of an item. Then the first quartile and the fourth quartile of the respondents are selected for comparison, that is, the group with the highest 25 per cent of scores, and the group with the lowest 25 per cent scores. The underlying assumption is that these two groups provide the criterion for discriminating between individual items. If there is a significant difference between the mean scores on an item, the item will be accepted for inclusion in the scale. If not, the item will be discarded accordingly.

In the study, respondents' total scores were arrayed from highest to lowest for both samples, and then divided into two groups constituting the highest 25 per cent of respondents (n = 80 for the ball-pen sample and n = 79 for the mini-cassette player sample) and the lowest 25 per cent of the respondents. An item-by-item summary statistic for each group was computed, giving the mean and standard deviation for each item for the two groups. These statistics were then used to compute the t-value of each item, which denoted whether the two groups were significantly different at the level of 0.01. As a result, all forty items were found able to differentiate between the high and low groups and all were included in the scale for further testing. Table 5.10 and Table 5.11 show all the items, their mean and standard deviation scores for both the high and the low score groups, and their t-values.

Reliablity

As previously discussed, two methods were used to assess the reliability of the scale: alpha coefficient, and split-half method.

First, the alpha coefficient was calculated for each sample. Table 5.12 indicates that the reliability coefficient is 0.829 for the ball-pen

Table 5.10 T-tests for item selection for the ball-pen sample

Item No.	Mean Low Score Group	Mean High Score Group	Standard Deviation Low Score Group	Standard Deviation High Score Group	t-value
1	4.04	6.00	0.83	0.00	21.12
2	3.63	6.00	0.66	0.00	31.58
4	2.31	5.75	0.83	0.43	32.89
5	3.00	6.00	0.97	0.00	26.73
6	1.46	5.49	0.66	0.69	37.59
8	2.80	5.87	0.52	0.19	48.97
9	1.28	5.47	0.37	0.97	34.94
10	3.05	6.00	1.02	0.00	25.44
11	1.41	5.30	0.54	0.65	40.11
12	1.83	5.55	0.79	0.57	32.77
13	2.86	5.98	0.94	0.16	29.11
14	3.50	6.00	0.77	0.00	28.12
15	2.44	6.00	0.77	0.00	41.27
16	3.65	6.00	0.67	0.00	31.61
17	3.64	6.00	1.06	0.00	19.70
18	3.51	6.00	0.79	0.00	28.16
19	1.98	5.59	1.12	0.41	28.32
20	2.38	5.62	0.81	0.48	30.57
21	1.18	4.71	0.35	0.76	36.82
22	2.34	6.00	0.72	0.00	45.44
23	3.21	6.00	0.89	0.00	28.01
24	2.24	5.43	0.88	0.65	29.27
26	3.96	6.00	0.64	0.00	28.33
27	4.06	6.00	0.76	0.00	22.11
29	4.00	6.00	0.85	0.00	21.01
30	2.24	4.91	0.86	1.00	17.50
31	2.78	5.88	0.67	0.33	37.11
32	3.48	6.00	0.71	0.00	31.45
33	3.81	6.00	0.74	0.00	26.55
35	1.50	5.58	0.64	0.52	44.01
36	3.41	6.00	0.43	0.00	54.27
37	3.84	6.00	0.62	0.00	30.95
38	3.38	6.00	0.82	0.00	28.54
39	2.03	5.74	0.89	0.44	33.09
40	3.76	6.00	0.84	0.00	23.45
41	3.61	6.00	0.60	0.00	34.87
42	3.82	6.00	0.50	0.00	38.99
43	2.80	6.00	0.93	0.00	30.60
44	4.00	6.00	0.62	0.00	28.50
45	1.91	5.51	0.82	0.50	33.39

All t-values are significant at the 0.01 level.

Table 5.11   T-tests for item selection for the mini-cassette player sample

| | Mean | | Standard Deviation | | |
| | Low Score Group | High Score Group | Low Score Group | High Score Group | |
Item No.					t-value
1	4.31	6.00	1.48	0.00	10.10
2	3.39	6.00	0.79	0.00	29.23
4	2.18	5.20	0.72	0.58	29.19
5	3.18	5.96	0.83	0.19	28.71
6	1.63	5.16	0.66	0.75	31.09
8	2.51	5.51	0.67	0.50	31.90
9	1.40	4.82	0.49	0.87	30.51
10	2.68	5.79	0.69	0.41	34.49
11	1.40	4.83	0.49	0.78	32.36
12	2.77	5.49	0.73	0.53	33.48
13	3.21	5.82	0.94	0.39	16.96
14	3.51	6.00	0.74	0.00	29.68
15	2.38	5.91	0.89	0.28	33.43
16	3.41	6.00	0.85	0.00	28.34
17	3.66	6.00	0.76	0.00	27.31
18	3.46	6.00	0.63	0.00	35.93
19	2.16	5.56	0.82	0.50	31.55
20	2.38	5.29	0.54	0.62	31.31
21	1.33	4.83	0.47	0.79	35.59
22	2.41	5.76	0.83	0.43	31.97
23	3.30	6.00	0.69	0.00	34.65
24	2.32	5.32	0.73	0.47	18.41
26	3.75	6.00	0.69	0.00	29.11
27	4.35	6.00	0.77	0.00	19.05
29	3.92	6.00	0.78	0.00	23.78
30	2.04	4.99	0.53	0.79	27.33
31	2.92	5.80	0.79	0.34	29.65
32	2.48	6.00	0.85	0.00	26.19
33	3.52	6.00	0.70	0.00	31.19
35	1.42	5.05	0.43	0.76	36.56
36	3.27	5.81	0.78	0.24	27.70
37	3.71	6.00	0.56	0.00	35.29
38	3.25	6.00	0.92	0.00	26.54
39	2.48	5.61	0.71	0.49	32.29
40	3.62	6.00	0.59	0.00	35.45
41	3.43	6.00	0.85	0.00	26.87
42	3.96	6.00	1.15	0.00	9.07
43	2.61	5.80	0.79	0.40	31.36
44	3.69	6.00	0.63	0.00	32.23

All t-values are significant at the 0.01 level.

Table 5.12 Reliability coefficient for the Chinese cultural values scale

	Ball-pen sample (N = 321)	Mini-cassette player sample (N = 319)
Reliability coefficient (40 items)	0.829	0.847
Split-half reliability (40 items)		
for part 1	0.729	0.770
for part 2	0.727	0.727

sample, and 0.847 for the mini-cassette player sample. These coefficients were regarded as high, indicating that the scale is a highly reliable measure of Chinese cultural values. Second, the reliability procedure of the Statistical Package for Social Sciences (SPSS) was used to compute the split-half reliability of the scale. Table 5.12 also shows the alpha coefficients for the two halves of the scale. For the ball-pen sample, the two coefficients are 0.729 and 0.727 for the first half and the second half respectively, which are more or less equal and well above the minimally acceptable level set by Nunnally (1978). For the mini-cassette player sample, the coefficients are 0.770 and 0.727, which are still acceptable even though they are not as stable as in the ball-pen sample.

Validity

Cronbach and Meehl (1955) suggest that correlation analysis of individual item scores with the overall criterion scale score seeks to establish the homogeneity of the scale in the aggregate level. If a particular scale item is contributing to the measurement of the same concept as the total scale, the product-moment correlation of this item will have a positive relationship with the total scale score and be significant.

The internal validity of the Chinese cultural values scale was assessed by the item-to-total correlation method on the two samples. The item-to-total correlations for all items of the scale are presented in Table 5.13. Of all correlations present in the Table 5.13, no item was found to have a correlation coefficient which was not significant at the 0.01 level.

Table 5.13   Item-to-total correlation: Chinese cultural values

Item No.[a]	Item	Ball-pen sample	Mini-cassette player sample
1	A family will be prosperous if it is in harmony.	0.262	0.410
2	Haughtiness invites ruin; humility receives benefits.	0.338	0.349
4	Children should report everything to their parents.	0.304	0.360
5	Reflect on our faults when we take a rest.	0.386	0.312
6	The new generation is worse than the old.	0.124	0.160
8	Reject an old man's advice and you'll soon pay for it.	0.314	0.373
9	An eye for an eye.	0.306	0.113
10	Live as it is predestined.	0.457	0.299
11	He who submits to Heaven shall live; he who rebels against Heaven shall perish.	0.337	0.233
12	Do all that is humanly possible and leave the rest to the will of providence.	0.372	0.201
13	When in Rome, do as the Romans do.	0.400	0.322
14	Blessings abound in a family that perseveres in good deeds.	0.454	0.382
15	Life and death are fated; wealth and honours hinge on the will of providence.	0.359	0.414
16	A family has its rules as a state has it laws.	0.403	0.322
17	Forgive others whenever you can.	0.475	0.400
18	At different times and in different places, we will meet again.	0.467	0.300
19	To have a son for old age is to stock provision for rainy days.	0.308	0.254
20	Children have to respect the decisions of their parents.	0.264	0.247
22	Fate is predestined.	0.316	0.358
23	Those against the laws should be punished.	0.182	0.350
24	Live with your parents after marriage.	0.197	0.770
25	Endure and you will find everything all right; retreat and you will find yourself happy.	0.182	0.163
26	A man depends on his parents at home, and his friends in society.	0.358	0.423
27	Above great talents, there are greater ones.	0.339	0.381
29	If you honour me a linear foot, I should in return honour you ten feet.	0.344	0.478
30	There must be deceit in excessive courtesy.	0.259	0.179
31	Shameful affairs of the family should not be spoken of outside.	0.272	0.290
32	Unmarried children should make their parents well and strong.	0.245	0.187
33	I won't offend others unless I am offended.	0.417	0.369

Table 5.13 (*Continued*)

Item No.	Item	Ball-pen sample	Mini-cassette player sample
35	Of the three practices of unfilial piety, having no son is the greatest.	0.234	0.281
36	Elderly parents are just like a treasure when living in your house.	0.332	0.303
37	A man who can survive in hardship is the man of men.	0.402	0.447
38	Better bend than break.	0.306	0.350
39	To please someone without good cause is either adulterous or greedy.	0.357	0.258
40	Never forget what others have done for you.	0.361	0.429
41	Face is honoured by others; shame is sought by ourselves.	0.517	0.394
42	No matter what you are doing, don't go too far.	0.441	0.405
43	It is more urgent to pay back favours than debts.	0.351	0.379
44	Help each other whenever in need.	0.281	0.430
45	To return favours and take revenge.	0.196	0.117

a Item no. refers to the sequential number in the questionnaire, p. 229–30.

In addition to the item-to-total correlations, an additional test of item consistency was conducted. A t-test for each item was performed to examine whether the scores for each item of the scale across the two samples were statistically significant. If yes, the scale is said to be unreliable; if not, the scale is said to be reliable. Results of the t-tests are shown in Table 5.14. Only eight out of forty items are found to have a significant difference between the two samples. As described earlier in this chapter, the two samples are different to a certain extent. Respondents in the mini-cassette player sample are a little younger and wealthier than those in the ball-pen sample. It sounds logical, therefore, that even though 20 per cent of the items in the scale are significantly different between the two samples, the scale itself can still be claimed as internally consistent.

Results of the item-to-total correlation and t-test for individual items exhibit the internal consistency of the items to the total scale score. However, some criterion measure might have been missed in the construction of the Chinese cultural value scale, resulting in a lack of external validity. Since there is no other known scale at the present

Table 5.14   T-test for the Chinese cultural values scale: comparison between two samples

Item	t-value
1 A family will be prosperous if it is in harmony.	2.36 a
2 Haughtiness invites ruin; humility receives benefits.	1.34
4 Children should report everything to their parents.	3.04
5 Reflect on our faults when we take a rest.	1.24
6 The new generation is worse than the old.	0.32
8 Reject an old man's advice and you'll soon pay for it.	4.21 b
9 An eye for an eye.	0.68
10 Live as it is predestined.	1.02
11 He who submits to Heaven shall live; he who rebels against Heaven shall perish.	0.96
12 Do all that is humanly possible and leave the rest to the will of providence.	2.18
13 When in Rome, do as the Romans do.	1.23
14 Blessings abound in a family that perseveres in good deeds.	1.74
15 Life and death are fated; wealth and honours hinge on the will of providence.	0.46
16 A family has its rules as a state has it laws.	1.69
17 Forgive others whenever you can.	0.74
18 At different times and in different places, we will meet again.	0.55
19 To have a son for old age is to stock provision for rainy days.	0.14
20 Children have to respect the decisions of their parents.	2.03 b
22 Fate is predestined.	1.31
23 Those against the laws should be punished.	0.94
24 Live with your parents after marriage.	0.05
25 Endure and you will find everything all right; retreat and you will find yourself happy.	4.34 b
26 A man depends on his parents at home, and his friends in society.	1.03
27 Above great talents, there are greater ones.	1.38
29 If you honour me a linear foot, I should in return honour you ten feet.	1.98 a
30 There must be deceit in excessive courtesy.	0.56
31 Shameful affairs of the family should not be spoken of outside.	1.04
32 Unmarried children should make their parents well and strong.	1.24
33 I won't offend others unless being offended.	1.64
35 Of the three practices of unfilial piety, having no son is the greatest.	2.16 a
36 Elderly parents are just like a treasure when living in your house.	1.32
37 A man who can survive in hardship is the man of men.	1.15
38 Better bend than break.	1.06

Table 5.14 *(Continued)*

Item	T-value
39 To please someone without good cause is either adulterous or greedy.	1.77
40 Never forget what others have done for you.	1.05
41 Face is honoured by others; shame is sought by ourselves.	0.63
42 No matter what you are doing, don't go too far.	0.79
43 It is more urgent to pay back favours than debts.	2.24a
44 Help each other whenever in need.	2.40a
45 To return favours and take revenge.	0.79

a Significant at $\alpha = 0.05$.
b Significant at $\alpha = 0.01$.

time, correlation of this scale with one of parallel form was impossible. Hence, the 'known group' method, which is also an acceptable approach to testing the external validity of a scale, was adopted in the study. As previously mentioned, the known groups refer to those persons who possess or do not possess the construct under study. They are requested to have the scale administered to them, the scores of which are then compared to see if there is any significant difference between the groups.

The external validity analysis of the Chinese cultural values scale employed the responses of two different groups of people: Chinese, and non-Chinese. The first known group was made up of twenty Chinese undergraduates and academic staff from the Chinese University of Hong Kong, and the second of ten graduate students from the Management Centre, the University of Bradford. The scale was supposed to differentiate between these two groups. The Chinese group would have a higher total score whereas the English group would have a lower total score. After the data were collected from personal interviews, the responses of these two groups were added together so as to obtain a total score for each individual of the group members. Then, the mean and standard deviation for the two groups were calculated. The mean scores derived from the analysis were 177.2 for the Chinese group and 145.8 for the non-Chinese group. The value of t was found to be 5.91, which is significant at the alpha level of 0.01. Hence, the result shows that there is a significant difference between the two groups, and that the scale has external validity.

Estimation of dimensionality

In order to understand the Chinese cultural values, one of the important components in the hypothesized model described in Chapter 3, the estimation of dimensionality of the Chinese cultural values scale becomes necessary. Furthermore, since there has been a lack of empirical findings concerning Chinese cultural values, the exploration of cultural values dimensions will be sure to contribute greatly to the literature. Hence, the data of this study were further analysed in an effort to explore the dimensions of the Chinese cultural values. To achieve this, two analytical methods, factor analysis and stepwise regression, were adopted. The following two sub-sections describe the results of these methods.

Factor analysis   After the forty items were found reliable and valid, a factor analysis was performed for the two samples, for two simple reasons. First, to investigate the contribution of each item to the underlying concepts of Chinese culture values. Second, to determine the dimensions of the Chinese culture values. Hence, by performing a factor analysis on the scores of all items for each sample, hopefully the structure of Chinese culture values would be extracted.

There are basically three steps in performing a factor analysis (Kinnear and Taylor 1983). The first step is to develop a matrix of correlations between items. The second step is to extract a set of initial factors from the correlation matrix. The third step is to rotate the initial factors to find a final solution.

With respect to the first step of computing a correlation matrix, a distinction should be drawn between R-factor analysis and Q-factor analysis. In the former, correlations are computed between variables, while in the latter, correlations are computed between cases. In this study, since items of the scale were concerned, the R-factor analysis was performed.

To extract initial factors for further rotation, Harmon (1967) has suggested a number of methods. The most extensively used is the principal factors method. Specifically, the non-iteration option of the principal factors method was used in this study (Nie and Hull 1976). Since initial factors are often very difficult to interpret, rotation of the initial solution is necessary. Of the many rotation procedures available, the varimax orthogonal method was selected. The utilization of the method was based on the assumption that the underlying dimensions of Chinese cultural values are unrelated to one another.

Another decision in factor analysis is to determine the number of factors to rotate. In the study, the eigenvalue criterion was used as a cut-off point to determine the number of factors (Mun and Yau 1979). There were thirteen factors whose eigenvalues were equal to or less than 1. However, in order to avoid under or over factor analysing so that a meaningful and interpretable factor structure would be missed out, rotations of twelve, thirteen and fourteen factor solutions were performed. The results of these rotations showed that the best factor structure contains twelve meaningful and interpretable factors for both samples. The items that loaded on each of the twelve factors at +0.40 were included in the interpretation of the factor structure. The twelve factors explained 56.0 per cent and 56.8 per cent of variance for the ball-pen and mini-cassette samples respectively. The variance for each extracted factor is shown in Table 5.15. The extracted factors and their respective item loading for the two samples can be found in Tables 5.17 and 5.18.

Tables 5.17 and 5.18 present the results of the varimax factor solution for the two samples respectively. There are several aspects which are worth noting. First, the two factor analyses have a tendency to describe the dimensionality of Chinese cultural values in terms of discrete factors, which were described in Chapter 3. Second, the two samples of consumers do not appear to have exceptionally different factor structures and concerns about values.

Table 5.15 Eigenvalue and percentage of variance of each factor for the two samples

Factor Item	Ball-pen sample Eigenvalue	% of Variance	Mini-cassette player sample Eigenvalue	% of Variance
1	6.638	15.8	6.128	15.3
2	2.612	6.2	2.420	6.1
3	2.181	5.2	1.945	4.9
4	1.790	4.3	1.718	4.3
5	1.670	4.0	1.598	4.0
6	1.364	3.2	1.521	3.8
7	1.323	3.1	1.395	3.5
8	1.265	3.0	1.324	3.3
9	1.213	2.9	1.254	3.1
10	1.174	2.8	1.170	2.9
11	1.143	2.7	1.134	2.8
12	1.094	2.4	1.104	2.8
Total variance		56.6		56.8

With regard to the first aspect, factors of the two factor solutions were interpreted and labelled as they were conceptualized in Chapter 3. A summary of the dimensions of the factor solutions for the two samples are shown in Table 5.16. From the table, most of the factors have identical labels for the two samples. The only exception is the factor 'respect for experience' for the ball-pen sample, and the factor 'endurance' for the mini-cassette player sample.

As far as the second aspect is concerned, it was found that the factor structures for the two samples were quite similar, by and large. The following dimensions are even contributed by almost the same items:

1 Past-orientation.
2 Pao (reciprocity).
3 Harmony with the universe.
4 Continuity.
5 Interdependence.

The only differences found were the dimension 'respect for experience' in the ball-pen sample, and the dimension 'endurance' in the mini-cassette player sample. The rest of the corresponding dimensions were interpreted as quite similar in nature even if they did not possess the same items. This implies that the ball-pen sample had a concern for respect for experience, which was not present in the mini-cassette player sample. At the same time, the mini-cassette player sample showed an interest in endurance, but this was not present in the ball-pen sample. However, there is no indication whether these two dimensions contribute greatly to the explained variance of the scale score for each sample.

Table 5.16   Dimensions of Chinese cultural values for the two samples

Ball-pen sample	Mini-cassette player sample
1 Adaptiveness	1 Interdependence
2 Sincerity/Suspicion	2 Continuity/Respect for authority
3 Continuity/Respect for authority	3 Conformity to activity
4 Harmony with the universe	4 Abasement
5 Harmony with people	5 Harmony with the universe
6 Interdependence	6 Pao (Reciprocity)
7 Pao (Reciprocity)	7 Harmony with people
8 Group-orientation	8 Sincerity/Suspicion
9 Respect for experience	9 Face
10 Face	10 Endurance
11 Abasement	11 Group-orientation
12 Past-orientation	12 Past-orientation

Table 5.17 Varimax factor analysis of the ball-pen sample

Item	Loading	Factor
		Factor 1: Adaptiveness
18	0.65	At different times and places, we will meet again.
13	0.62	When in Rome, do as the Romans do.
16	0.48	A family has its rules as a state has its laws.
14	0.47	Blessings abound in a family that perseveres in good deeds.
37	0.43	A man who can survive in hardship is the man of men.
40	0.41	Never forget what others have done for you.
		Factor 2: Sincerity
2	0.69	Haughtiness invites ruin; humility receives benefits.
30	0.58	Being too polite is insincere.
39	0.55	He who pleases you without a good cause is either adulterous or greedy.
10	0.54	Live as it is pre-destined.
17	0.46	Forgive others whenever you can.
40	0.42	Never forget what others have done for you.
		Factor 3: Continuity/Respect for authority
20	0.71	Children have to respect the decisions of their parents.
4	0.64	Children should report everything to their parents.
19	0.54	To have a son for old age is to stock provision for rainy days.
35	0.53	Of the three practices of unfilial piety, having no son is the greatest.
36	0.46	Old parents are just like a treasure in your house when living with you.
		Factor 4: Harmony with the universe
12	0.71	Do all that is humanly possible and leave the rest to the will of providence.
11	0.70	He who submits to Heaven shall live; he who rebels against Heaven shall perish.
15	0.45	Life and death are fated; wealth and honours hinge on the will of providence.
		Factor 5: Harmony with people
1	0.72	A family will be prosperous if it is in harmony.
23	0.51	Those against the laws should be punished.
42	0.50	No matter what you are doing, don't go too far.
33	0.45	I won't offend others unless I am offended.
31	0.43	Shameful affairs of the family should not be spoken of outside.
		Factor 6: Interdependence
26	0.73	A man depends on his parents at home, and his friends in society.
27	0.46	Beyond a mountain, yet a higher one.

Table 5.17   (*Continued*)

Item	Loading	Factor
		Factor 7: Pao (Reciprocity)
45	0.78	To return favours and take revenge.
9	0.64	An eye for an eye.
		Factor 8: Group-orientation
32	0.78	Unmarried children should make their parents well and strong.
24	0.51	Live with your parents after marriage.
		Factor 9: Respect for experience
8	0.72	Reject an old man's advice and you'll soon pay for it.
		Factor 10: Face-giving
44	0.62	Help each other whenever in need.
43	0.56	It is more urgent to pay back favours than debts.
		Factor 11: Abasement (self-control)
25	0.80	Endure and you will find everything all right; retreat and you will find yourself happy.
5	0.45	Reflect on our faults when we take a rest.
		Factor 12: Past-orientation
6	0.79	The new generation is worse than the old.

Table 5.18   Varimax factor analysis of the mini-cassette player sample

Item	Loading	Factor
		Factor 1: Interdependence
27	0.66	Beyond the mountain, an even higher one.
26	0.61	A man depends on his parents at home, and his friends in society.
29	0.49	If you honour me a linear foot, I should in return honour you ten feet.
32	0.46	Unmarried children should make their parents well and strong.
13	0.41	When in Rome, do as the Romans do.
		Factor 2: Continuity
35	0.68	Of the three practices of unfilial piety, having no son is the greatest.
8	0.64	Reject an old man's advice and you'll soon pay for it.
20	0.58	Children have to respect the decisions of their parents.
36	0.57	Elderly parents are just like a treasure when living in your house.
19	0.48	To have a son for old age is to stock provision for rainy days.
4	0.40	Children should report everything to their parents.

Table 5.18 (*Continued*)

Item	Loading	Factor
		Factor 3: Conformity to activity
44	0.70	Help each other whenever in need.
23	0.58	Those against the laws should be punished.
14	0.58	Blessings abound in a family that perseveres in good deeds.
37	0.50	A man who can survive in hardship is the man of men.
		Factor 4: Abasement (self-control)
5	0.65	Reflect on our faults when we take a rest.
40	0.57	Never forget what others have done for you.
2	0.54	Haughtiness invites ruin; humility receives benefits.
41	0.48	Face is honoured by others; shame is sought by ourselves.
18	0.40	At different times and in different places, we will meet again.
		Factor 5: Harmony with the universe
15	0.76	Life and death are fated; wealth and honours hinge on the will of providence.
22	0.70	Fate is predestined.
12	0.58	Do all that is humanly possible and leave the rest to the will of providence.
11	0.53	He who submits to Heaven shall live; he who rebels against Heaven shall perish.
		Factor 6: Reciprocity
45	0.76	To return favours and take revenge.
9	0.75	An eye for an eye.
		Factor 7: Harmony with people
19	0.65	To have a son for old age is to stock provision for rainy days.
42	0.58	No matter what you are doing, don't go too far.
17	0.58	Forgive others whenever you can.
		Factor 8: Suspicion
39	0.66	To please someone without good cause is either adulterous or greedy.
30	0.43	There must be deceit in excessive courtesy.
		Factor 9: Group-orientation
31	0.73	Shameful affairs of the family should not be spoken of outside.
		Factor 10: Endurance
25	−0.69	Endure and you will find everything all right; retreat and you will find yourself happy.
		Factor 11: Group-orientation
1	0.63	A family will be prosperous if it is in harmony.
10	0.59	Live as it is predestined.
		Factor 12: Past-orientation
6	0.73	The new generation is worse than the old.

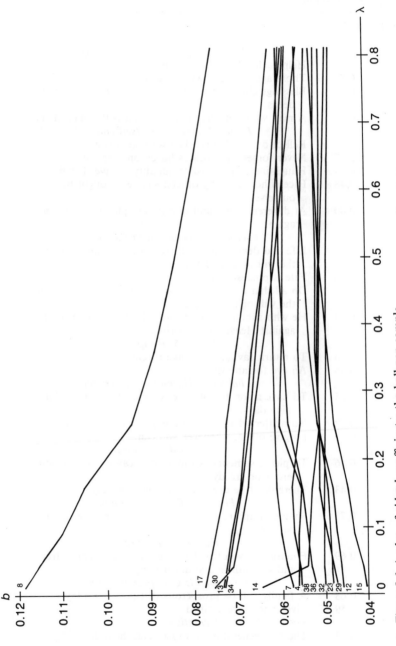

Figure 5.1 A plot of ridged coefficients: the ball-pen sample
(Numbers on the lines are statement numbers.)

From the results of the factor analyses performed for the determination of the dimensionality of Chinese cultural values, it seems that any future efforts at dimensionality estimation would probably lead to the emergence of the dimensions of past-orientation, Pao (reciprocity), harmony with the universe, continuity and interdependence. Essentially, those dimensions extracted make much sense and can be interpreted as expected, and thus provide evidence that the scale is measuring the concept of Chinese cultural values. However, for the two samples in the study, the scale does allow for some small differences in dimension to emerge.

Although the method of factor analysis does provide for an overall structure of Chinese cultural values, it does not explicitly tell which of the items are contributing most to the explanation of the scale score, and hence, the concept. Therefore, it seems necessary to explore which items of the Chinese cultural values scale are paramount contributors to the concept. The procedure by which this exploration was undertaken was through the use of stepwise regression analysis.

Stepwise regression The stepwise regression analysis of the forty items on the Chinese cultural scale for each of the two samples was performed, in the hope of further understanding the scale. It is noteworthy here that the stepwise analysis was only employed as a tool for understanding the contribution of items to the Chinese Cultural Values Scale, and not necessarily as a predictive device as it is normally used. The total scale score was obtained by summing each standardized item score for each respondent in the samples. Then the standardized score of each item was regressed against the total scale score in a stepwise manner. In order to reduce multi-collinearity, ridge stepwise regression analysis was adopted (BMDP 1977: 518). A plot of the ridged coefficients for each lambda is shown in Figures 5.1 and 5.2, which clearly shows that at the lambda value of 0.49, ridged coefficients become stable. Hence, the cut-off of 0.49 was used. The results of the regression analysis for the two samples are presented in Table 5.19, which indicates the amount of variance contributed by, and the beta coefficient of, the items entered into the equation for each sample. Only those items with R squared greater than 0.01 are shown for comparison purposes. It was found that the beta coefficients for all variables included in the equations had a positive sign, since they are an integral part of the scale and, therefore, contribute to the overall scale score.

Keys to item numbers in Table 5.19 are shown in Table 5.20, which indicates the nature of the item entered at each step of the regression

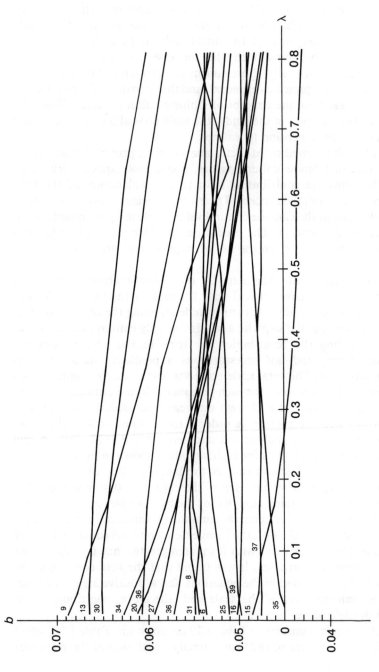

Figure 5.2 A plot of ridged coefficients: the mini-cassette player sample
(Numbers on the lines are statement numbers.)

Table 5.19 Stepwise regression of validated items on total scale score (entry order of items for the Chinese Cultural Values Scale)

Ball-pen sample (N = 321)			Mini-cassette player sample (N = 219)		
Item	b Coef.	R Squared	Item	b Coef.	R Squared
(41)	0.60	0.233	44	0.52	0.1917
(17)	0.508	0.131	29	0.58	0.1402
14	0.54	0.089	(15)	0.64	0.0911
33	0.52	0.063	8	0.56	0.0670
9	0.61	0.050	(41)	0.53	0.0509
43	0.55	0.040	4	0.57	0.0405
(10)	0.84	0.032	42	0.47	0.0371
(26)	0.51	0.029	(35)	0.61	0.0304
(15)	0.64	0.022	40	0.48	0.0259
5	0.59	0.021	(10)	0.53	0.0208
(35)	0.61	0.023	23	0.51	0.0194
37	0.49	0.015	31	0.41	0.0167
19	0.67	0.014	18	0.47	0.0147
16	0.51	0.013	11	0.58	0.0153
(39)	0.64	0.014	36	0.51	0.0139
			(17)	0.44	0.0125
			(39)	0.52	0.0105
Total R Squared		0.7893			0.7985

Number in parentheses indicates that the item appears in both samples.

Table 5.20 Nature of item entered in stepwise regression

Item	Dimension affiliated	Item description
		The ball-pen sample
(41)	Face	Face is honoured by others; shame is sought by ourselves.
(17)	Sincerity	Forgive others whenever you can.
14	Adaptiveness	Blessings abound in a family that perseveres in good deeds.
33	Harmony with People	I won't offend others unless I am offended.
9	Pao (Reciprocity)	An eye for an eye.
43	Face-giving	It is more urgent to pay back favours than debts.
(10)	Harmony with the universe	Live as it is predestined.
(26)	Interdependence	A man depends on his parents at home, and his friends in society.
15	Harmony with the Universe	Life and death are fated; wealth and honours hinge on the will of providence.

Table 5.20   (Continued)

Item	Dimension affiliated	Item description
5	Abasement	Reflect on our faults when we take a rest.
(35)	Continuity/ Having Authority	Of the three practices of unfilial piety, having no son is the greatest.
37	Adaptiveness	A man who can survive in hardship is the man of men.
19	Continuity/ Respect for Authority	To have a son for old age is to stock provision for rainy days.
16	Adaptiveness	A family has its rules as a state has its laws.
(39)	Sincerity	To please someone without good cause is either adulterous or greedy.
		The mini-cassette sample
44	Harmony with people	Help each other whenever in need.
29	Interdependence	If you honour me a linear foot, I should in return honour you ten feet.
(15)	Harmony with the Universe	Life and death are fated; wealth and honours hinge on the will of providence.
8	Continuity	Reject an old man's advice and you'll soon pay for it.
(41)	Abasement	Face is honoured by others; shame is sought by ourselves.
4	Continuity	Children should report everything to their parents.
42	Harmony with People	No matter what you are doing, don't go too far.
(35)	Continuity	Of the three practices of unfilial piety, having no son is the greatest.
40	Abasement	Never forget what others have done for you.
(10)	Group-orientation	Live as it is predestined.
23	Conformity to Activity	Those against the laws should be punished.
31	Face	Shameful affairs of the family should not be spoken of outside.
18	Abasement	At different times and places, we will meet again.
11	Harmony with the Universe	He who submits to Heaven shall live; he who rebels against Heaven shall perish.
36	Continuity	Elderly parents are just like a treasure when living in your house.
(17)	Harmony with People	Forgive others whenever you can.
(39)	Sincerity	To please someone without good cause is either adulterous or greedy.

Note Numbers in parentheses indicate that the item appears in both samples.

for the two samples. In addition, the dimension to which each item belongs is also indicated next to the item to help interpretation. The total variances explained for the items are about 0.80 for both samples. From Tables 5.19 and 5.20, even though there are eight items which are in common, yet differences seem to emerge between the two samples of consumers. But, like the factor analysis of the separate samples, these differences do not appear to be very great. The ball-pen sample appears to be slightly more concerned about adaptiveness, Pao (reciprocity) and sincerity, and the mini-cassette player sample more concerned about abasement and continuity. However, even though the entry order of the variables explaining 80 per cent of the variance differs, the issues of importance to the two samples appear to be quite similar. The two samples indicate that they both consider harmony with people, harmony with the universe, sincerity, face-giving, continuity and abasement as important dimensions. In summary, most of the dimensions involved are similar, and hence the differences do not seem very great.

HYPOTHESES AND RESULTS OF TWO-WAY RELATIONSHIPS

In order that the structural models hold, it is necessary that the individual relationships between variables be statistically significant, in the predicted direction, and of a magnitude warranting further interest. Each hypothesis between variables, which has been discussed in Chapter 3, is re-stated and tested in this section. It should be noted that these hypotheses are for the association among empirical concepts. No causality is intended to be involved. Hence, the most meaningful hypotheses are those among the theoretical constructs and derived concepts. These latter hypotheses are tested through the structural models in the last part of this chapter. The hypotheses are organized through the constituent variables. Each hypothesis is tested by a Pearson correlation coefficient, one of the most commonly used techniques to test association between two variables. Further, the one-tail test is employed for those hypotheses in which the direction of the relationship is known. Otherwise, the two-tail test is used.

The Chinese cultural values

Recall from Chapter 3 that the Chinese cultural values as a whole were posited to be related to product expectations and satisfaction. Each hypothesis is demonstrated below:

Hypothesis 1. There is a positive relationship between traditional Chinese cultural values as a whole and product expectations.

Table 5.21 summarizes the findings of this hypothesis, which, in fact, involves four sub-hypotheses. The correlations in the table were

Table 5.21 Correlations between Chinese cultural values and product expectations for hypothesis 1

	Chinese Cultural Values	
Product Expectations	Ball-pen sample (2,568)	Mini-cassette player sample (2,552)
Global measure	0.0651 a	0.1743
Attribute-specific measure	0.0848	0.1782

a all significant at p < 0.01. Numbers in parentheses indicate sample size.

Table 5.22 Correlations between Chinese cultural value dimensions, product expectations and satisfaction for hypotheses 1 and 2: the ball-pen sample

Factor No.	Value Dimension	Product G	Expectations AS	Satisfaction G	AS
1	Adaptiveness	0.0723 a	0.0546 a	0.0636 a	0.0603 a
2	Sincerity/ Suspicion	− 0.0081	− 0.0004	0.0431 b	0.0346 b
3	Continuity/ Respect for authority	0.0172	0.0228	0.1044 a	0.1011 a
4	Harmony with the universe	0.0031	− 0.0086	− 0.0128	− 0.0175
5	Harmony with people	0.0345 b	0.0699 a	0.0765 a	0.0735 a
6	Interdependence	0.0091	0.0445 b	− 0.0150	0.0113
7	Pao (Reciprocity)	− 0.0101	− 0.0094	0.0606 a	0.0414 b
8	Group- orientation	0.0094	0.0349	0.0197	0.0323 b
9	Respect for experience	0.0497 a	0.0339 b	0.0247	0.0257
10	Face	0.0114	0.0498 a	0.0247	0.0257
11	Abasement	0.0099	0.0017	− 0.0078	− 0.0382 b
12	Past-orientation	0.0410 b	0.0385 b	0.0399 b	0.0160

a significant at p < 0.01. b significant at p < 0.05. Key: G = Global Measure. AS = Attribute-specific Measure.

computed regarding products and situations as treatments which manipulate product expectations and satisfaction. As can be seen from the table, the hypothesis receives strong support. All correlations are in the proper direction and are significant at the level of 0.01. In summary, one may conclude that the more Chinese a consumer appears to be, the higher the level of product expectations.

Hypothesis 1A. There are positive relationships between value dimensions and product expectations.

Recall from previous section in this chapter that twelve dimensions of the Chinese cultural values were found for each sample. Tables 5.22 and 5.23 summarize the findings for hypothesis 1a. In general, the hypothesis receives some support. The hypothesis involves forty-eight sub-hypotheses, twenty-four for each sample. For the mini-cassette sample, most sub-hypotheses are found supported. However, for ten of the twenty-four sub-hypotheses in the ball-pen sample, correlations

Table 5.23 Correlations between Chinese cultural value dimensions, product expectations and satisfaction for hypotheses 1 and 2: the mini-cassette player sample

Factor No.	Value Dimension	Product G	Expectations AS	Satisfaction G	AS
1	Interdependence	0.0975 a	0.0559 a	0.0589 a	0.0468 a
2	Continuity/ Respect for authority	− 0.0227	− 0.0967 a	0.0176	0.0527 a
3	Conformity to activity	0.0510 b	0.0586 b	0.0732 a	0.0863 a
4	Abasement	0.0381 b	0.0696 a	0.0905 a	0.0872
5	Harmony with the universe	0.0461 a	0.0647 a	0.0208	0.0195
6	Pao (Reciprocity)	0.0815 a	0.1146 b	0.0670 a	0.0728 a
7	Harmony with people	0.1361 a	0.0525 a	0.0128	− 0.0144
8	Sincerity/ Suspicion	− 0.0199	− 0.0549 a	0.0517 a	0.0277
9	Face	0.0094	− 0.0090	0.0251	0.0326 b
10	Endurance	− 0.0598 a	− 0.0114	0.0139	0.0207
11	Group-orientation	0.0550 a	0.0523 a	0.0419 b	0.0555 a
12	Past-orientation	− 0.0567 a	− 0.0194	− 0.0309	− 0.0336 b

a significant at p < 0.01. b significant at p < 0.05. Key: G = Global Measure. AS = Attribute-specific Measure.

are significant at the level of 0.05 or better. However, overall, the hypothesis receives some support.

Hypothesis 2. There is a positive relationship between traditional Chinese cultural values as a whole and consumer satisfaction. That is, the more Chinese a consumer is, the more satisfied he is.

Table 5.24 presents the findings for hypothesis 2. All correlations are found significant at the level of 0.01 or better. Thus, the hypothesis receives strong support. Since the scale is a measure of how Chinese the respondents are, one may conclude that the higher the score the higher the level of satisfaction.

Hypothesis 2A. There are positive relationships between Chinese cultural value dimensions and consumer satisfaction. That is, the higher the score for a value dimension, the higher the level of satisfaction.

Table 5.22 and Table 5.23 summarize the findings for this hypothesis. Just as with hypothesis 1a, for twenty-seven of forty-eight sub-hypotheses, the correlations are significant at the level of 0.05 or better. In summary, one may conclude that the higher the score, the higher the level of satisfaction.

Consumption experiences

Recall from Chapter 3 that consumption experiences are hypothesized to be related to consumer satisfaction and product expectations. Further, this construct is treated as multidimensional and measured by three individual scales. Hence, a composite scale is also computed to test its multidimensionality.

Table 5.24 Correlations between Chinese cultural values and satisfaction for hypothesis 2

| | Chinese Cultural Values | |
Satisfaction	Ball-pen sample (2,568)	Mini-cassette player sample (2,552)
Global measure	0.1338 a	0.1304
Attribute-specific measure	0.1229	0.1407

a all significant at p < 0.01. Number in parentheses indicates sample size.

Hypothesis 3. There is a negative relationship between dissatisfied consumption experiences with products and consumer satisfaction. That is, the more dissatisfaction the consumer experiences, the higher the level of consumer satisfaction.

Table 5.25 (*a*) and (*b*) presents the findings for the hypothesis. Overall the hypothesis is not supported. Nearly all correlations appear to be insignificant at the level of 0.05. However, it should be noted that the correlations are in the expected direction.

Hypothesis 4. There is a positive relationship between dissatisfied consumption experiences with products and product expectations.

Table 5.25(a) Correlations between consumption experiences and product expectations for hypothesis 3

| Consumption experiences | Product expectations | | | |
| | Ball-pen sample (321) | | Mini-cassette player sample (319) | |
	G	*AS*	*G*	*AS*
	Ball-pen 1		*Mini-cassette 1*	
Situation 1				
Composite	− 0.0330	− 0.0472	0.0323	0.0279
A	− 0.0049	0.0152	− 0.0319	0.0369
B	− 0.0023	− 0.0670	0.0639	0.0283
C	− 0.0868 c	− 0.0669	0.0399	− 0.0014
Situation 2				
Composite	− 0.0640	− 0.1078 b	0.0041	− 0.0228
A	− 0.0064	− 0.0392	0.0017	− 0.0252
B	− 0.0478	− 0.1010 b	− 0.0153	− 0.0207
C	− 0.1056	− 0.1245 b	0.0111	− 0.1074
Situation 3				
Composite	0.0154	− 0.0965 b	0.0039	− 0.0522
A			− 0.0500	− 0.0742
B	0.0776	0.0227	0.0776	0.0227
C	− 0.0429	− 0.0931 b	− 0.0243	− 0.0739
Situation 4				
Composite	0.0280	− 0.1226 b	0.0090	− 0.0293
A	0.0414	− 0.0695	− 0.0255	− 0.0735
B	− 0.0070	− 0.1099 b	0.0400	0.0236
C	0.0317	− 0.1180 b	0.0038	− 0.0211

a significant at $p < 0.01$. b significant at $p < 0.05$. c significant at $p < 0.1$. Number in parentheses indicates sample size.
Key: A = Dissatisfied experience with same product, e.g. ball-pen.
  B = Dissatisfied experience with other product.
  C = Dissatisfied experience with same category of products, e.g. paper.
  Composite = Composite measure of A, B and C above.
  G = Global measure of construct. AS = Attribute-specific measure of construct.

Table 5.25(b) Correlations between consumption experiences and product expectations for hypothesis 3

Consumption experiences	Ball-pen sample (321)		Mini-cassette player sample (319)	
	G	AS	G	AS
	Ball-pen 2		*Mini-cassette 2*	
Situation 1				
Composite	0.0313	0.0345	− 0.0213	− 0.1461 a
A	0.0642	0.0339	− 0.0568	− 0.1870 a
B	− 0.0319	0.0574	− 0.0164	− 0.0478
C	0.0404	− 0.0105	− 0.0111	− 0.2074 b
Situation 2				
Composite	0.0786	− 0.0125	0.0323	− 0.1113 a
A	0.0055	− 0.0173	0.0490	− 0.0821 c
B	0.0736	0.0222	− 0.0122	− 0.0920 b
C	0.1165 b	− 0.0352	− 0.0403	− 0.0824 c
Situation 3				
Composite	0.0181	− 0.0068	− 0.0508	− 0.1165 b
A	− 0.0091	− 0.0070	0.0016	− 0.0950 b
B	− 0.0128	0.0310	− 0.0222	− 0.0426
C	0.0697	− 0.0417	− 0.0986	− 0.1352 a
Situation 4				
Composite	0.0111	0.0192	0.0012	− 0.1184
A	− 0.0190	0.0196	0.0170	− 0.1038 b
B	0.0303	0.0556	0.0170	− 0.0772 c
C	0.0179	− 0.0313	− 0.0321	− 0.0935 b

Product expectations

a significant at $p < 0.01$. b significant at $p < 0.05$. c significant at $p < 0.1$. Number in parentheses indicates sample size.
Key: A = Dissatisfied experience with same product, e.g. ball-pen.
     B = Dissatisfied experience with other product.
     C = Dissatisfied experience with same category of products, e.g. paper.
     Composite = Composite measure of A, B and C above.
     G = Global measure of construct.
     AS = Attribute-specific measure of construct.

That is, the more dissatisfaction the consumer experiences with products, the lower the level of product expectations.

Tables 5.26(*a*) and (*b*) summarize the findings for the hypothesis. In general, the hypothesis is not supported. Only a few correlations in the mini-cassette sample are significant, although nearly all of them are in the expected direction. Furthermore, there is no consumption experience in particular which is related to product expectations.

Table 5.26(a) Correlations between consumption experiences and satisfaction for hypothesis 4

Consumption experiences	Ball-pen sample (321) G	AS	Mini-cassette player sample (319) G	AS
	Satisfaction			
	Ball-pen 1		*Mini-cassette 1*	
Situation 1				
Composite	− 0.0234	− 0.0027	− 0.0576	− 0.1381 a
A	− 0.0533	− 0.0332	− 0.9646	− 0.1442 a
B	0.0069	0.0401	− 0.0524	− 0.0817 c
C	− 0.0064	− 0.0112	− 0.0152	− 0.0948 b
Situation 2				
Composite	− 0.0096	− 0.0002	− 0.1044 b	− 0.1265 b
A	− 0.0561	− 0.0204	− 0.0739 c	− 0.1219 b
B	0.0363	0.0300	− 0.0784 c	− 0.0768 c
C	0.0010	− 0.0089	− 0.0891 b	− 0.0950 b
Situation 3				
Composite	− 0.0583	− 0.0092	− 0.0406	− 0.0825 c
A	− 0.0448	− 0.0140	0.0048	− 0.0700
B	− 0.0047	0.0262	− 0.0043	− 0.0419
C	− 0.0924	− 0.0348	− 0.0967 b	− 0.0805 c
Situation 4				
Composite	− 0.0914 c	− 0.0435	− 0.0668	− 0.0846
A	− 0.1043 b	− 0.0500	− 0.0003	− 0.0783 c
B	− 0.0353	− 0.0126	− 0.0074	− 0.0478
C	− 0.0776 c	− 0.0408	− 0.1505 a	− 0.0705

a significant at $p < 0.01$. b significant at $p < 0.05$. c significant at $p < 0.1$. Number in parentheses indicates sample size.
Key: A = Dissatisfied experience with same product, e.g. ball-pen.
  B = Dissatisfied experience with other product.
  C = Dissatisfied experience with same category of products, e.g. paper.
  Composite = Composite measure of A, B and C above.
  G = Global measure of construct.
  AS = Attribute-specific measure of construct.

Affective experiences

As discussed in Chapter 3, affective experiences were posited to be related to consumer satisfaction and product expectations. Each hypothesis is treated here.

Hypothesis 5. There is a positive relationship between affective experiences and consumer satisfaction. That is, the more the negative affective experiences, the lower the level of satisfaction.

Table 5.26(b) Correlations   between   consumption   experiences   and satisfaction for hypothesis 4

Consumption experiences	Ball-pen sample (321) G	AS	Mini-cassette player sample (319) G	AS
	Ball-pen 2		*Mini-cassette 2*	
Situation 1				
Composite	0.0069	− 0.0726	− 0.0471	− 0.0526
A	0.0691	− 0.0171	0.0447	− 0.0447
B	− 0.0270	− 0.0541	0.0721	0.0336
C	− 0.0323	− 0.1084 b	− 0.0110	− 0.1164 a
Situation 2				
Composite	− 0.0714	− 0.0615	0.0607	− 0.0669
A	− 0.0007	− 0.0187	0.0332	− 0.0618
B	− 0.0759	− 0.0598	0.0807	0.0344
C	− 0.1011 b	− 0.0726 c	0.0237	− 0.1340
Situation 3				
Composite	0.0566	− 0.0275	0.0325	− 0.0796 c
A	0.0739	0.0140	0.0333	− 0.0429
B	0.0253	− 0.0108	0.0530	0.0125
C	0.0339	− 0.0743	− 0.0136	− 0.1596 a
Situation 4				
Composite	0.0674	− 0.0094	0.0383	− 0.0669
A	0.0437	0.0118	0.0555	− 0.0382
B	0.0748 c	− 0.0032	0.0645	− 0.0039
C	0.0437	− 0.0337	− 0.0344	− 0.1165 b

a significant at $p < 0.01$. b significant at $p < 0.05$. c significant at $p < 0.1$. Number in parentheses indicates sample size.

Key: A = Dissatisfied experience with same product, e.g. ball-pen.
   B = Dissatisfied experience with other product.
   C = Dissatisfied experience with same category of products, e.g. paper.
   Composite = Composite measure of A, B and C above.
   G = Global measure of construct.
   AS = Attribute-specific measure of construct.

Tables 5.27(*a*) and (*b*) summarize the results of this hypothesis. In general, the hypothesis is not supported. Almost all correlations are not significant at the level of 0.05. Recall that the construct of affective experiences is measured by four single-item measures. It is treated as multidimensional. Table 5.27(*b*) indicates that only one measure in situation 4 for the ball-pen sample is significant at the level of 0.05 or better. However, it is noteworthy that, overall, the correlations are in the proper direction. Seventy-four of 128 correlations are negative.

Table 5.27(a) Correlations between affective experiences and satisfaction for hypothesis 5

Affective experiences	Ball-pen sample (321)		Mini-cassette player sample (319)	
	Satisfaction			
	G	*AS*	*G*	*AS*
	Ball-pen 1		*Mini-cassette 1*	
Situation 1				
A	− 0.0449	− 0.0866	− 0.0672	− 0.0305
B	0.0050	− 0.0421	− 0.0216	0.0103
C	0.0244	0.0021	− 0.0395	0.0217
D	0.0526 c	0.0352	− 0.0291	0.0547
Situation 2				
A	− 0.0012	0.0693	− 0.0599	− 0.0115
B	− 0.0329	− 0.0252	− 0.0065	− 0.0057
C	− 0.1214 b	− 0.0762 c	− 0.0155	− 0.0014
D	− 0.1056 b	− 0.1025 b	− 0.0341	− 0.0015
Situation 3				
A	0.0471	0.1517	− 0.0095	0.0037
B	0.0055	0.0431	− 0.0250	− 0.0118
C	− 0.0942	0.0137	0.0490	− 0.0367
D	− 0.0385	− 0.0215	− 0.0302	− 0.0149
Situation 4				
A	0.0112	0.0263	− 0.0081	− 0.0182
B	− 0.0286	− 0.0608	− 0.0008	− 0.0052
C	− 0.0936 b	− 0.0075	0.0427	0.0737
D	− 0.0521	0.0356	− 0.0226	0.0327

a significant at $p < 0.01$. b significant at $p < 0.05$. c significant at $p < 0.1$. Number in parentheses indicates sample size.
Key: A = Take private action. B = Take public action.
C = Blame oneself. D = Attribute to fate.
G = Global measure. AS = Attribute-specific measure.

Hypothesis 6. There is a positive relationship between affective experiences and product expectations. That is, the more the negative affective experiences, the lower the level of product expectations.

Correlations between four measures of affective experiences in different situations for the two samples were computed. The findings are presented in Tables 5.28(a) and (b). In general, the hypothesis is not supported. For twenty of 128 sub-hypotheses, correlations are significant at the level of 0.05. Further, only fifty-two of 128 are in the proper direction.

Table 5.27(b) Correlations between affective experiences and satisfaction for hypothesis 5

Affective experiences	Satisfaction			
	Ball-pen sample (321)		Mini-cassette player sample (319)	
	G	AS	G	AS
	Ball-pen 2		Mini-cassette 2	
Situation 1				
A	− 0.0449	− 0.0866 c	0.0953 b	0.0806 c
B	0.0050	− 0.0421	− 0.0178	− 0.0396
C	0.0244	0.0021	0.0892	0.0337
D	0.0526	0.0352	− 0.0039	0.0288
Situation 2				
A	− 0.0214	− 0.0265	0.0920	0.1020 b
B	0.0333	0.0202	− 0.0242	− 0.0321
C	0.0112	− 0.0260	− 0.0575	0.0137
D	0.0090	0.0299	− 0.0035	− 0.0535
Situation 3				
A	− 0.0945	− 0.0179	0.1103 b	0.1114 b
B	− 0.0501	− 0.0361	− 0.0485	− 0.1119 b
C	− 0.0063	0.0280	0.0410	− 0.0075
D	0.0106	− 0.0313	0.0057	− 0.0034
Situation 4				
A	− 0.0630	0.0263	0.0955 b	− 0.0182
B	0.0037	− 0.0608	− 0.0435	− 0.0052
C	0.0235	− 0.0075	0.0467	− 0.0737 c
D	0.0243	0.0356	0.0157	− 0.0327

a significant at $p < 0.01$. b significant at $p < 0.05$. c significant $p < 0.01$. Number in parentheses indicates sample size.

Key: A = Take private action.   B = Take public action.
    C = Blame oneself.   D = Attribute to fate.
    G = Global measure.   AS = Attribute-specific measure.

Consumption/use situation

Recall from Chapter 3 that consumption/use situations are posited to be related to cultural values, product expectations, and satisfaction. The latter two are treated below, at pp. 192–4, in a section specially devoted to the analysis of experimental effects. The former will be treated here.

Hypothesis 9. There is a positive relationship between Chinese cultural values and situational factors which constitute situations.

Early in the chapter, twelve underlying dimensions of the Chinese cultural values for each sample were found. Also recall from

Table 5.28(a) Correlations between affective experiences and product expectations for hypothesis 6

Affective experiences	Ball-pen sample (321)		Mini-cassette player sample (319)	
	G	AS	G	AS
	Ball-pen 1		Mini-cassette 1	
Situation 1				
A	− 0.0033	− 0.0288	0.1169 b	− 0.0154
B	0.0594	− 0.0239	0.0405	− 0.0857 c
C	0.0225	− 0.0261	0.0276	0.0191
D	− 0.0533	− 0.0642	− 0.0612	0.0917
Situation 2				
A	− 0.0178	− 0.0207	0.0415	0.0059
B	− 0.0104	− 0.0838 c	0.0273	− 0.1135 b
C	− 0.0176	− 0.0057	− 0.0187	0.0741 c
D	− 0.1142 b	− 0.0457	− 0.0589	− 0.0582
Situation 3				
A	0.0149	0.0458	0.0904 c	− 0.0305
B	0.0731	− 0.0468	− 0.0723	− 0.1087 b
C	− 0.0436	0.0574	0.0505	0.0490
D	0.0065	0.0234	0.0344	0.0562
Situation 4				
A	0.0159	0.0039	0.0949	0.0100
B	0.0041	− 0.0631	− 0.0416	− 0.1143 a
C	− 0.0017	0.0527	0.0132	0.0906 b
D	0.0191	0.0159	0.0555	0.0624

a significant at $p < 0.01$. b significant at $p < 0.05$. c significant at $p < 0.1$. Number in parentheses indicates sample size.
Key: A = Take private action. B = Take public action.
  C = Blame oneself. D = Attribute to fate.
  G = Global measure. AS = Attribute-specific measure.

Chapter 3 the following four situational factors which constitute situations in the study:

1 To be used when alone.
2 To be used with other people.
3 To be used by oneself.
4 To be used as a gift for someone else.

Respondents were asked whether and if so to what degree the product concerned was appropriate for each situational factor. Zero-order correlations between the twelve Chinese cultural dimensions and the

Table 5.28(b) Correlations between affective experiences and product expectations for hypothesis 6

Affective experiences	Product Expectations			
	Ball-pen sample (321)		Mini-cassette player sample (319)	
	G	AS	G	AS
	Ball-pen 2		Mini-cassette 2	
Situation 1				
A	0.0987 b	− 0.0086	0.0661	− 0.0956 b
B	0.0225	0.0546	− 0.0332	− 0.0511
C	− 0.0048	0.0317	0.0362	− 0.0377
D	− 0.0062	0.0423	− 0.1393 a	0.0204
Situation 2				
A	0.0919	− 0.0098	0.0812	− 0.0263 b
B	0.0503	0.0272	0.0468	− 0.0191
C	0.0314	0.0065	0.0066	− 0.0011
D	0.0506	− 0.0237	− 0.1005 b	0.0143
Situation 3				
A	0.0284	− 0.0159	0.1323 a	− 0.0495
B	0.0217	− 0.0101	0.0017	− 0.0987
C	0.0158	0.0275	− 0.0894	− 0.0025
D	0.1003 b	− 0.0239	− 0.0606	0.0200
Situation 4				
A	0.0602	− 0.0176	0.0755 b	− 0.0310
B	0.0216	− 0.0102	− 0.0240	− 0.0713
C	0.0183	− 0.0022	− 0.0220	0.0227
D	0.0726 c	− 0.1014 b	− 0.0093	0.0554

a significant at $p < 0.01$. b significant at $p < 0.05$. c significant at $p < 0.1$. Number in parentheses indicates sample size.

Key: A = Take private action   B = Take public action.
     C = Blame oneself.   D = Attribute to fate.
     G = Global measure.   AS = Attribute-specific measure.

situational factors were computed. Table 5.29 and Table 5.30 show the findings for the ball-pen sample and mini-cassette player sample respectively. In general, the hypothesis receives weak support. In both samples, for nine of forty-eight sub-hypotheses, correlations are significant at the level of 0.05 or better. Six of the remaining sub-hypotheses are accepted only at the level of 0.10. Although the hypothesis receives only weak support, it is interesting to find that relationships between the cultural dimensions and situational factors make a lot of sense. Recall from discussion in Chapter 3 that there are several Chinese cultural values which lead to external behaviour such as paying back a favour. These values are interdependence, harmony with people, face, and Pao (reciprocity). Table 5.29 indicates that

Table 5.29 Correlations between Chinese cultural value dimensions and situational factors for hypothesis 7: the ball-pen sample (N = 321)

Factor No.	Value Dimension	Private	Public	Self	Gift
			Situational Factor		
Ball-pen 1					
1	Adaptiveness	0.1045 b	0.0718 c	0.0288	− 0.0138
2	Sincerity/ Suspicion	− 0.0450	− 0.0458	− 0.0151	− 0.0986 b
3	Continuity/ Respect for authority	0.1502 a	0.0775 c	0.0369	0.0251
4	Harmony with the universe	0.0928 b	− 0.0316	0.0232	0.0855 c
5	Harmony with people	0.1326 a	− 0.0285	0.0315	− 0.0526
6	Interdependence	0.0437	− 0.0854 c	0.0636	− 0.1022
7	Pao (Reciprocity)	− 0.0402	− 0.0314	− 0.1030 b	0.0310
8	Group-orientation	0.0289	− 0.0560	0.0363	0.0845 c
9	Respect for experience	0.0373	0.0377	− 0.0037	0.0350
10	Face	0.0477	− 0.0180	0.0729	0.0076
11	Abasement	− 0.0250	− 0.0173	0.0746	− 0.0168
12	Past-orientation	0.1673 a	0.1105 b	0.1619 a	− 0.0604
Ball-pen 2					
1	Adaptiveness	0.1095 b	0.0578	0.0610	0.0252
2	Sincerity/ Suspicion	0.0869 c	0.0647	0.0637	0.1104 b
3	Continuity/ Respect for authority	− 0.0083	0.0367	− 0.1021	0.0425
4	Harmony with the universe	0.0095	0.0057	0.0271	0.0422
5	Harmony with people	0.0061	0.0254	− 0.0089	0.0831
6	Interdependence	− 0.0332	− 0.0284	0.0545	0.0944 b
7	Pao (Reciprocity)	0.0831 c	− 0.0290	0.0690 c	− 0.1045 b
8	Group-orientation	0.0727 c	0.1113 b	0.0714 c	0.0345
9	Respect for experience	0.0465	0.0036	0.0628	0.0010
10	Face	− 0.0361	0.1015 b	0.0140	0.0932 b
11	Abasement	0.0297	− 0.0003	0.0730 c	− 0.0011
12	Past-orientation	0.0116	0.0015	− 0.0237	0.0074

a significant at $p < 0.01$. b significant at $p < 0.05$. c significant at $p < 0.10$.

Table 5.30 Correlations between Chinese cultural value dimensions and situational factors for hypothesis 7: the mini-cassette player sample (N = 319)

Factor No.	Value Dimension	Situational Factor			
		Private	*Public*	*Self*	*Gift*
Cassette player 1					
1	Interdependence	0.1501 a	0.1335 a	0.1184 b	0.0255 a
2	Continuity/ Respect for authority	0.1000	−0.0009	0.0774	−0.0936 b
3	Conformity to activity	0.0468	−0.0845 c	−0.0733 c	−0.0128
4	Abasement	0.0873 c	0.0462	0.0373	0.0735 c
5	Harmony with the universe	−0.0765 c	−0.0085	0.0467	0.0595
6	Pao (Reciprocity)	0.0066	0.0635	−0.0401	−0.0986
7	Harmony with people	0.0699	0.1627 a	0.1559 a	0.1151 b
8	Sincerity/ Suspicion	0.0391	0.0829 b	−0.0351	−0.0305
9	Face	0.0576	0.0147	−0.0502	0.0585
10	Endurance	0.0260	−0.0260	−0.0298	−0.0066
11	Group- orientation	0.0011	0.0157	0.0293	0.0619
12	Past- orientation	−0.0551	−0.0913 b	−0.1048 b	−0.0601
Cassette player 2					
1	Interdependence	0.1295 a	0.0235	0.0964 b	0.1054 b
2	Continuity/ Respect for authority	0.0155	−0.0710	0.0009	−0.0173
3	Conformity to activity	0.0824 c	−0.1042 b	0.0986 b	0.0414
4	Abasement	0.0019	−0.0244	−0.0051	0.1299 a
5	Harmony with the universe	−0.0087	0.0241	0.0027	0.0014
6	Pao (Reciprocity)	−0.0210	0.0670	0.1019 b	−0.0528
7	Harmony with people	0.0492	0.0279	0.0679	−0.0529
8	Sincerity/ Suspicion	0.0420	−0.0180	0.0098	−0.0323
9	Face	−0.0252	−0.0239	0.0497	−0.0721 c
10	Endurance	−0.0598 a	−0.0114	0.0139	0.0207
11	Group- orientation	0.0911 c	−0.0021	0.1239 b	0.0411
12	Past-orientation	0.0011 a	−0.0828 c	0.0127	−0.0680 b

a significant at $p < 0.01$. b significant at $p < 0.05$. c significant at $p < 0.10$.

there are relationships between these value dimensions and the situational factors 'gift' and 'public'. Further, the relationships seem to be stronger for good products than for poor products.

Product expectations

Recall from Chapter 3 that the product expectations were posited to be related to cultural values, situations, consumption experiences,

Table 5.31 Correlations between product expectations and satisfaction for hypothesis 11

Product expectations	Satisfaction			
	Ball-pen sample (321)		Mini-cassette player sample (319)	
	G	AS	G	AS
	Ball-pen 1		*Mini-cassette 1*	
Situation 1				
G	0.1912 a	0.2338	0.2501	0.2100
AS	0.1918	0.4147	0.2656	0.3609
Situation 2				
G	0.3926	0.3731	0.3804	0.2917
AS	0.3316	0.5423	0.3413	0.3837
Situation 3				
G	0.3786	0.3137	0.2817	0.2969
AS	0.3019	0.4188	0.3042	0.4246
Situation 4				
G	0.3908	0.4073	0.2856	0.2581
AS	0.3531	0.4949	0.3175	0.4209
	Ball-pen 2		*Mini-cassette player 2*	
Situation 1				
G	0.2756	0.2056	0.3047	0.3048
AS	0.3641	0.4637	0.3455	0.4989
Situation 2				
G	0.3768	0.3459	0.2242	0.2371
AS	0.3981	0.4908	0.3978	0.5287
Situation 3				
G	0.2128	0.2670	0.2680	0.2903
AS	0.4029	0.4924	0.3340	0.4937
Situation 4				
G	0.3012	0.3251	0.3384	0.2807
AS	0.4011	0.4468	0.3807	0.5240

a all significant at $p < 0.001$. Number in parentheses indicates sample size.
Key: G = Global measure of construct.
    AS = Attribute-specific measure of construct.

affective experiences, product performance, disconfirmation, and satisfaction. The relationships of expectations with cultural values, consumption experiences, and affective experiences have already been tested in hypotheses 1, 4 and 6 above. The relationship with situations is tested in the next section. Treatments here will be reserved for the remaining relationships.

Hypothesis 10. There is a positive relationship between product expectations and consumer satisfaction. That is, the higher the level of expectations, the higher the level of satisfaction.

Table 5.31 depicts this hypothesis. The relationship is supported strongly in all situations for the two samples. For all sub-hypotheses, correlations are significant at the level of 0.01 or better. Furthermore, all correlations are in the proper direction. It is noteworthy that the magnitude of correlations is particularly large at the sample size of about 300. It may be concluded that the higher the product expectations, the higher the level of satisfaction.

Hypothesis 11. There is a positive relationship between product expectations and perceived performance. That is, the higher the expectations, the higher the perceived performance of the product.

Table 5.32 illustrates the findings for this hypothesis. The hypothesis is supported strongly. All correlations are significant at the level of 0.01 or better, and in the proper direction. Further, the magnitude of correlations is considerable showing a very tight relationship between the two constructs. Hence, it may be concluded that the higher the product expectations, the higher the perceived performance of the product.

Hypothesis 12. There is a positive relationship between product expectations and positive disconfirmation. That is, the higher the expectations, the higher the level of positive disconfirmation.

Findings for the hypothesis are presented in Table 5.33. In general, the hypothesis received strong support. For forty-three of sixty-four sub-hypotheses, correlations are significant at the level of 0.05 or better, and are in the proper direction. Three negative correlations are found. However, they are far from being significant, showing that their existence may be due to some random errors. In summary, the conclusion may be drawn that the relationship between product expectations and positive disconfirmation is very strong.

Table 5.32 Correlations between product expectations and perceived performance for hypothesis 11

Product expectations	Perceived Performance	
	Ball-pen sample (321) G	Mini-cassette player sample (319) G
	Ball-pen 1	*Mini-cassette player 1*
Situation 1		
G	0.3355 a	0.2514
AS	0.3304	0.3664
Situation 2		
G	0.2877	0.3797
AS	0.3724	0.4579
Situation 3		
G	0.4337	0.2968
AS	0.3924	0.4085
Situation 4		
G	0.4650	0.3566
AS	0.4750	0.4223
	Ball-pen 2	*Mini-cassette player 2*
Situation 1		
G	0.2877	0.3591
AS	0.3724	0.4442
Situation 2		
G	0.3278	0.3666
AS	0.4458	0.5147
Situation 3		
G	0.3050	0.4034
AS	0.4276	0.4040
Situation 4		
G	0.4082	0.4104
AS	0.4972	0.4637

a all significant at $p < 0.001$. Number in parentheses indicates sample size.
Key: G = Global measure of construct.
   AS = Attribute-specific measure of construct.

Perceived performance

As discussed in Chapter 3, perceived performance was posited to be related to disconfirmation and consumer satisfaction. Both of the relationships are dealt with here.

Hypothesis 13. There is a positive relationship between perceived performance and disconfirmation between expectations and perceived

Table 5.33 Correlations between product expectations and disconfirmation for hypothesis 12

Product expectations	Disconfirmation			
	Ball-pen sample (321)		Mini-cassette player sample (319)	
	G	AS	G	AS
	Ball-pen 1		*Mini-cassette player 1*	
Situation 1				
G	− 0.0496	0.0616	− 0.0241	0.0323
AS	− 0.0596	0.1220 a	0.0271	0.1705 a
Situation 2				
G	0.1628 a	0.0857 c	0.1912 a	0.1462 a
AS	0.1042 a	0.1463 a	0.1876 a	0.1759 a
Situation 3				
G	0.1236 b	0.1916 a	0.0284	0.1404 a
AS	0.1839 a	0.2944 a	0.0355	0.2279 a
Situation 4				
G	0.1728 a	0.1614 a	0.0781 c	0.1055 b
AS	0.2362 a	0.3383 a	0.1370 a	0.1897 a
	Ball-pen 2		*Mini-cassette player 2*	
Situation 1				
G	0.0872 c	0.0938 b	0.0121	0.0152
AS	0.2579 a	0.3020 a	0.0828 c	0.1369 a
Situation 2				
G	0.1509 a	0.1758 a	0.0271	0.0403
AS	0.2176 a	0.2302 a	0.1841 a	0.2394 a
Situation 3				
G	0.0984 b	0.0758 c	0.0293	0.0144
AS	0.2067 a	0.2196 a	0.1104 a	0.2311 a
Situation 4				
G	0.1306	0.0988 b	0.1789 a	0.0714
AS	0.2247 a	0.2387 a	0.1873 a	0.2894 a

a significant at $p < 0.01$. b significant at $p < 0.05$. c significant at $p < 0.1$. Number in parentheses indicates sample size.
Key: G = Global measure of construct.
    AS = Attribute-specific measure of construct.

expectations. That is, the better the perceived performance of a produce or service, the greater the level of positive disconfirmation.

Table 5.34 presents the findings for the hypothesis. In general, the hypothesis is strongly supported. Correlations are found in the range between 0.3 and 0.5 which is extremely high at the sample size of about 300. For each sub-hypothesis, correlations are significant at the

Table 5.34 Correlations between perceived performance and disconfirmation for hypothesis 13

Perceived performance	Disconfirmation			
	Ball-pen sample		Mini-cassette player sample	
	G	AS	G	AS
	Ball-pen 1		Mini-cassette player 1	
Situation 1				
G	0.4349	0.3607	0.5019	0.4732
Situation 2				
G	0.4236	0.3322	0.5105	0.4822
Situation 3				
G	0.4481	0.4206	0.4321	0.4537
Situation 4				
G	0.4624	0.3764	0.4916	0.4879
	Ball-pen 2		Mini-cassette player 2	
Situation 1				
G	0.4662	0.3083	0.4131	0.3739
Situation 2				
G	0.4306	0.3060	0.4349	0.4093
Situation 3				
G	0.3597	0.2949	0.4118	0.3635
Situation 4				
G	0.4350	0.3941	0.4201	0.3740

a all significant at p < 0.01. Number in parentheses indicates sample size.
Key: G = Global measure.
   AS = Attribute-specific measure.

level of 0.001. Further, as the positive signs in all correlations indicate, the relationship between the two constructs is in the proper direction.

Hypothesis 14. There is a positive relationship between perceived performance and satisfaction. That is, the higher the perceived performance, the higher the level of satisfaction.

Findings for the hypothesis are found in Table 5.35. In general, the hypothesis is strongly supported. Table 5.35 indicates that the correlations are also of large magnitude. For each hypothesis, correlations are significant at the level of 0.001 or better. In addition, all correlations are positive, showing that the relationship between perceived performance and satisfaction is in the proper direction.

Table 5.35 Correlations between perceived performance and satisfaction for hypothesis 14

Perceived performance	Satisfaction			
	Ball-pen sample (321)		Mini-cassette player sample (319)	
	G	AS	G	AS
	Ball-pen 1		Mini-cassette player 1	
Situation 1				
G	0.5631	0.5003	0.5950	0.5063
Situation 2				
G	0.5490	0.5644	0.6554	0.5686
Situation 3				
G	0.5534	0.6071	0.5906	0.5382
Situation 4				
G	0.5170	0.5502	0.5813	0.5441
	Ball-pen 2		Mini-cassette player 2	
Situation 1				
G	0.5175	0.4677	0.6420	0.5494
Situation 2				
G	0.5445	0.4961	0.6630	0.6015
Situation 3				
G	0.5276	0.4816	0.5866	0.5967
Situation 4				
G	0.5167	0.5474	0.5847	0.5631

a all significant at $p < 0.01$. Number in parentheses indicates sample size.
Key: G = Global measure.
    AS = Attribute-specific measure.

Disconfirmation

Recall from Chapter 3 that disconfirmation was posited to be related to product expectations, perceived performance and satisfaction. The former two have been treated in hypothesis 9 and hypothesis 12 respectively. The latter proposition is treated here.

Hypothesis 15. There is a positive relationship between disconfirmation (between expectations and perceived performance) and consumer satisfaction. That is, the higher the positive disconfirmation between expectations and perceived performance, the higher the level of consumer satisfaction.

Table 5.36 summarizes the results of this hypothesis. In general, the hypothesis is strongly supported. Correlations in the table are found

Table 5.36 Correlations between disconfirmation and satisfaction for hypothesis 15

	Satisfaction			
	Ball-pen sample (321)		Mini-cassette player sample (319)	
Disconfirmation	G	AS	G	AS
	Ball-pen 1		*Mini-cassette player 1*	
Situation 1				
G	0.4049a	0.5026	0.4049	0.5026
AS	0.5309	0.4189	0.5309	0.4189
Situation 2				
G	0.4499	0.4901	0.4499	0.4901
AS	0.4871	0.4311	0.4871	0.4311
Situation 3				
G	0.3997	0.4395	0.3997	0.4395
AS	0.5241	0.4409	0.5241	0.4409
Situation 4				
G	0.3759	0.3604	0.3759	0.3604
AS	0.4666	0.4242	0.4666	0.4242
	Ball-pen 2		*Mini-cassette player 2*	
Situation 1				
G	0.5441	0.5733	0.5442	0.5733
AS	0.5862	0.4625	0.5862	0.4625
Situation 2				
G	0.4556	0.4676	0.4556	0.4676
AS	0.5870	0.4845	0.5870	0.4845
Situation 3				
G	0.4088	0.4147	0.4088	0.4147
AS	0.5424	0.4911	0.5424	0.4911
Situation 4				
G	0.4865	0.5298	0.4734	0.3964
AS	0.5819	0.5769	0.3931	0.5769

a all significant at $p < 0.001$. Number in parentheses indicates sample size.
Key: G = Global measure.
 AS = Attribute-specific measure.

ranging from 0.35 to 0.53 which is considered to be large at the sample size of about 300. Hence, for each sub-hypothesis, correlations are found to be significant at the level of 0.001. Further, positive signs of correlations indicate that the relationship between disconfirmation and satisfaction is in the proper direction.

Satisfaction

The relationships between satisfaction and Chinese cultural values, consumption experiences, affective experiences, product expectations, perceived performance and disconfirmation have already been examined in hypotheses 2, 3, 5, 7, 13 and 14 respectively. The relationship with situations is treated in the next section. Hence, only the relationship between satisfaction and purchase intention will be investigated here.

Hypothesis 16. There is a positive relationship between satisfaction and behavioural intention. That is, the higher the level of satisfaction, the greater the intention to purchase.

Table 5.37 summarizes the results of this hypothesis. In general, the

Table 5.37 Correlations between satisfaction and purchase intention for hypothesis 16

Purchase Intention	Satisfaction			
	Ball-pen sample (321)		Mini-cassette player sample (319)	
	G	AS	G	AS
	Ball-pen 1		*Mini-cassette player 1*	
Situation 1				
G	0.5694 a	0.5190 a	0.6175 a	0.5689 a
Situation 2				
G	0.3924 a	0.4218 a	0.4654 a	0.4593 a
Situation 3				
G	− 0.0964	0.0316	0.1946 a	0.2639 a
Situation 4				
G	− 0.0993	− 0.0990	0.1913 a	0.1892 a
	Ball-pen 2		*Mini-cassette player 2*	
Situation 1				
G	0.1246 b	0.0272	0.1142 b	0.1622 a
Situation 2				
G	− 0.0043	0.0103	0.2154 a	0.1662 a
Situation 3				
G	0.3719 a	0.3921 a	0.4012 a	0.5052 a
Situation 4				
G	0.5279 a	0.5187 a	0.5248 a	0.4237 a

a significant at $p < 0.01$. b significant at $p < 0.05$. Number in parentheses indicates sample size.
Key: G = Global measure.
   AS = Attribute-specific measure.

hypothesis receives strong support. For twenty-five out of thirty-two sub-hypotheses, correlations are found significant at the level of 0.05 or better. Significant correlations also appear in the proper direction. However, insignificant correlations are found to be negative in direction. In summary, one may conclude that there is a positive relationship between satisfaction and purchase intention.

SPURIOUS RELATIONSHIPS

The hypotheses of the previous section are based on zero-order correlations between variables. These results may be misleading, for two reasons. First, moderating effects have not been taken into consideration. The zero-order correlation between two variables might reflect the presence of various indirect and direct relationships. For example, z may affect y directly and indirectly through a moderating variable, forming a chain of effect as follows:

$$x \longrightarrow z \longrightarrow y$$

The structural models tested in the last part of the chapter deal with these direct and indirect causal relationships. Second, the relationship might be spurious. Spurious relationship means that the observed correlation between two variables, say, x and y, might be the result of some third variable, z, affecting both x and y rather than any relation occurring between the variables.

This part of the chapter deals only with spurious relationships. A number of analyses are undertaken to examine whether certain relationships tested in hypotheses in previous sub-sections are spurious. Spurious relationships are tested using partial correlation techniques.

Relationship between product performance and satisfaction

Consider the first relationship between performance and satisfaction. Hypothesis 14 showed the relationship to be direct and highly significant at the level of 0.001 (with r ranging from 0.5 to 0.6). In order to test the possibility that the relationship is spurious, owing perhaps to disconfirmation and expectations, the following partial correlations were computed for each situation and product: the correlation between product performance and satisfaction, with product expectation and disconfirmation held constant simultaneously. The results are presented in Table 5.38. All partial correlations are found to be significant at the level of 0.001. For example, zero-order correlations between these variables in situation 1 for pen 1 for both measures are

Table 5.38 Partial correlations between perceived performance and satisfaction, controlling disconfirmation and expectations

	Perceived Performance			
	Ball-pen sample (317)		Mini-cassette player sample (315)	
Satisfaction	Pen 1	Pen 2	Cassette player 1	Cassette player 2
Situation 1				
G	0.3884 a	0.3353	0.4054	0.4559
AS	0.2949	0.3443	0.2242	0.2912
Situation 2				
G	0.3353	0.3728	0.4711	0.5366
AS	0.3443	0.2758	0.2771	0.3396
Situation 3				
G	0.4162	0.4186	0.4650	0.4221
AS	0.3358	0.2720	0.2919	0.4191
Situation 4				
G	0.3266	0.3743	0.4184	0.4206
AS	0.3524	0.2745	0.2532	0.3381

a all significant at $p < 0.001$. Number in parentheses indicates sample size.
Key: G = Global measure.
　　AS = Attribute-specific measure.

0.5631 and 0.5003 ($p < 0.001$) respectively. The corresponding partial correlations computed are 0.3884 and 0.2949, both significant at 0.001 (see Table 5.38). Even though there is a decrease in the value of each partial correlation when compared with its corresponding zero-order correlation, each partial correlation remains large enough to be significant at the 0.001 level. A further check with partial correlations between these variables with either disconfirmation or product expectations held constant reveals that they are all significant at the level of 0.001. This analysis indicates that the relation between perceived performance and satisfaction is not a spurious one due to disconfirmation and product expectations.

Relationship between disconfirmation and satisfaction

Consider the relationship between disconfirmation and satisfaction. Hypothesis 15 found that a positive relationship between disconfirmation and consumer satisfaction existed, with correlations ranging from 0.36 to 0.53, all significant at the level of 0.001. In order to examine whether the relationship is spurious, owing to product expectation and perceived performance, the following partial correlations were performed. The relationship between disconfirmation and satisfaction was investigated, controlling for both expectations and performance. The results are presented in Table 5.39. All partial correlations are significant at the level of 0.001. For example, the partial correlation between disconfirmation and satisfaction is 0.3521 ($p < 0.001$) in situation 1 for pen 1 when both product expectation and perceived performance are held constant simultaneously. Further, the results show that the correlation with product expectations held constant is 0.5215 ($p < 0.001$) (not shown in Table 5.39); and the correlation with performance held constant is 0.3425 ($p < 0.001$) (not shown in Table 5.36). This clearly shows that the relation between disconfirmation and satisfaction is not a spurious one.

Relationship between intention and satisfaction

Consider the relationship between satisfaction and intention. Hypothesis 16 found that a positive relationship between consumer satisfaction and purchase intention existed, with correlations ranging

Table 5.39 Partial correlations between disconfirmation and satisfaction, controlling performance and expectations

	Disconfirmation			
	Ball-pen sample (317)		Mini-cassette player sample (315)	
Satisfaction	Pen 1	Pen 2	Cassette player 1	Cassette player 2
Situation 1				
G	0.3521	0.3512	0.3176	0.2798
AS	0.4560	0.4478	0.5122	0.4763
Situation 2				
G	0.3512	0.3959	0.2938	0.2930
AS	0.4478	0.5416	0.5174	0.4477
Situation 3				
G	0.2518	0.2832	0.1762	0.3210
AS	0.3744	0.5064	0.4283	0.4564
Situation 4				
G	0.1703	0.3468	0.1976	0.3122
AS	0.2904	0.5047	0.4231	0.4624

a all significant at $p < 0.001$. Number in parentheses indicates sample size.
Key: G = Global measure.
   AS = Attribute-specific measure.

Table 5.40 Partial correlations between satisfaction and intention, controlling performance, disconfirmation and expectations

	Disconfirmation			
	Ball-pen sample *(317)*		*Mini-cassette player sample* *(315)*	
Satisfaction	*Pen 1*	*Pen 2*	*Cassette player 1*	*Cassette player 2*
Situation 1				
G	0.3535	0.3043	0.4134	0.3519
AS	0.3109	0.1206 a	0.3631	0.2677
Situation 2				
G	0.3715	0.2549	0.4688	0.3224
AS	0.2660	0.1079 a	0.3655	0.2746
Situation 3				
G	0.2480	0.3068	0.4384	0.2589
AS	0.3292	0.1730	0.2630	0.2841
Situation 4				
G	0.3414	0.2741	0.4823	0.3959
AS	0.2968	0.2407	0.3809	0.2674

a significant at $p < 0.05$. For other correlations, significant at $p < 0.001$. Number in parentheses indicates sample size.
Key: G = Global measure.
    AS = Attribute-specific measure.

from 0.36 to 0.53, all significant at the level of 0.001. In order to examine whether the relationship is spurious, owing to product expectation, disconfirmation and perceived performance, which have been found to have a strong relationship with satisfaction, the following partial correlations were performed. The relationship between disconfirmation and satisfaction was investigated, controlling for expectations, performance and disconfirmation simultaneously. The results are presented in Table 5.40. Except two correlations which are significant at 0.05, all other partial correlations are significant at the level of 0.001. For example, the partial correlation between the two variables in situation 1 for pen 1 is 0.3535, which is significant at 0.001. A further check on partial correlations between disconfirmation and satisfaction for all situations and products with product expectation, disconfirmation or perceived performance held constant reveals that they are all significant at 0.001. (The results are not shown in Table 5.40.) This again clearly shows that the relation between disconfirmation and satisfaction is not a spurious one.

RESULTS OF EXPERIMENTS

In this section, results concerning the effects of the experimental treatments as well as the situations underlying the process approach are presented. All effects are tested by the analysis of variance (ANOVA). This section is divided into three sub-sections. In the first sub-section, the effect of the message which respondents were asked to read is tested. In the second sub-section, the results of tests conducted to verify the product manipulation of the experiment are presented. It is followed by a discussion of the results of situation effects on different dependent measures.

Analysis of message effects

In the experiment, subjects (respondents) were given a one-page description of each product with a colour picture and some phrases describing salient characteristics of the corresponding product. When they had finish reading the message, they were asked to provide information on a set of pre-exposure measures, including the global and attribute-specific measures for product expectations.

An analysis of variance was employed to test whether there was any significant effect of the message manipulation on product expectations for each of the four situations. Table 5.41 gives the F-ratios of ANOVA. For the ball-pen sample, it is obvious that the message manipulation has not been effective in establishing different expectations of the product within respondents (intra-personally). Except for situation 4 on the global measure, the F-ratios tend to be rather small.

Table 5.41 ANOVA results of message effects (F-ratio)

Dependent Measure	Situation			
	1	*2*	*3*	*4*
Ball-pen sample				
Expectations				
Global	0.75	0.13	0.73	7.45 a
Attribute-specific	0.13	1.67	1.78	0.28
Mini-cassette player sample				
Expectations				
Global	32.64 a	95.93 a	55.25 a	89.01 a
Attribute-specific	51.58 a	89.22 a	78.42 a	89.07 a

a F-ratio significant at $p < 0.01$.

It seems that it is easier to have significant message manipulation between treatment groups (Wilton and Tse, 1983). However, if situations are disregarded, the measures of product expectation do suggest a strong effect for the message. Table 5.42 shows that the F-ratios are 24.05 and 380.21 on global measure and attribute-specific measure respectively. This implies that even though the message(s) did not have much effect in establishing expectations in each situation, yet the message manipulation did create differences in expectations, regardless of situations. Hence, the message manipulation was successful only at macro-level, and not at situation level.

For the mini-cassette sample, more encouraging results are found. In Table 5.41, the F-ratios of ANOVA on both measures are all found significant at the level of 0.01 for all situations. Results in Table 5.43 are also positive. The F-ratios of ANOVA, which are 83.61 and 256.28 for global and attribute-specific measures respectively, are significant at the level of 0.01. These results clearly show that the measures of product expectations suggest a strong effect for the message at both situation level and macro-level.

Analysis of product effects

After providing information about product expectations, respondents received the instrumental product and were instructed on how to operate it. After the trial, respondents were asked to provide information on a set of post-exposure or post-trial measures including

Table 5.42   ANOVA results of treatment and interaction effects for the ball-pen sample

	F-ratio		
Dependent Measure	*Situation*	*Pen*	*Interaction*
Expectations			
Global	39.70 a	24.05 a	344.75 a
Attribute-specific	1.24	380.21 a	0.39
Perceived performance			
Global	15.24 a	417.87 a	81.89 a
Satisfaction			
Global	19.44 a	327.14 a	62.23 a
Attribute-specific	1.47	1254.98 a	0.25

a F-ratio significant at $p < 0.01$.
b F-ratio significant at $p < 0.05$.

Table 5.43 ANOVA results of treatment and interaction effects for the mini-cassette player sample

	F-ratio		
Dependent Measure	*Situation*	*Cassette*	*Interaction*
Expectations			
Global	35.80 a	83.61 a	3.54 a
Attribute-specific	14.58 a	256.28 a	0.94
Perceived performance			
Global	7.39 a	551.28 a	82.69 a
Satisfaction			
Global	6.01 a	685.29 a	1.88
Attribute-specific	1.47	1254.96 a	0.25

a F-ratio significant at $p < 0.01$.

perceived performance, disconfirmation, satisfaction and purchase intention for each situation. For each sample, two products were employed. The results of the analysis of variance which tests the product effects for the two samples are shown in Tables 5.44 and 5.45.

Table 5.44 shows the ANOVA results of the product effect on dependent variables for each of the four situations for the ball-pen sample. With the exception of purchase intention, it appears that the

Table 5.44 ANOVA results of product effects for the ball-pen sample (F-ratio)

	Situation			
Dependent Measure	*1*	*2*	*3*	*4*
Perceived performance				
Global	8.04 b	13.05 a	0.42	0.51
Disconfirmation				
Global	0.05	0.43	3.48 c	4.42 b
Attribute-specific	3.95 b	1.46	14.55 a	5.66 b
Satisfaction				
Global	0.92	0.12	2.17	0.45
Attribute-specific	7.01 b	2.73 c	1.40	0.16
Intention				
Global	12.40 a	5.90 a	13.01 a	14.44 a

a F-ratio significant at $p < 0.01$.
b F-ratio significant at $p < 0.05$.
c F-ratio significant at $p < 0.10$.

Table 5.45 ANOVA results of product effects for the mini-cassette player sample (F-ratio)

Dependent Measure	Situation			
	1	*2*	*3*	*4*
Perceived performance				
Global	22.32 a	41.44 a	37.21 a	41.54 a
Disconfirmation				
Global	8.67 a	6.47 b	13.97 a	17.45 a
Attribute-specific	0.05	2.49	3.53 c	1.54
Satisfaction				
Global	12.52 a	6.26 b	13.34 a	23.19 a
Attribute-specific	33.74 a	41.05 a	39.23 a	33.07 a
Intention				
Global	14.15 a	24.67 a	7.42 a	28.00 a

a F-ratio significant at $p < 0.01$.
b F-ratio significant at $p < 0.05$.
c F-ratio significant at $p < 0.10$.

dependent measures suggest only a weak effect of the product(s).On perceived performance and satisfaction, significant effects are only found for the first two situations for the attribute-specific measure. On disconfirmation, the results appear better. However, the effects on global measures remain unsatisfactory. These results coincided with those of Churchill (1979) and Nunnally (1978), who indicated that the multi-item measures are typically much better than single-item measures.

As with the results of message manipulation, there seem to be considerable product treatment effects for all dependent measures regardless of situations. Table 5.42 suggests that the product treatments had the intended effects. The overall F-tests are significant in each case. Similarly, multi-items show enormous F-ratios and thus perform better than the global measures.

Again, the ANOVA results of product effects for the mini-cassette sample are found to be very encouraging (see Table 5.45). With the exception of the attribute-specific measure on disconfirmation, all F-ratios are found to be significant beyond the level of 0.01 in each situation. Results in Table 5.44 are also consistent regardless of situations.

As can be seen from the foregoing, the choice of products has successfully manipulated product expectations and satisfaction.

Analysis of situation effects

Table 5.46 and Table 5.47 show the ANOVA results of situation effects for the ball-pen sample and the mini-cassette sample respectively. For the ball-pen sample, the F-ratios are all significant at the level of 0.01, showing that the four situations have been highly successful in establishing significant differences in all measures, including product expectations, perceived performance, and satisfaction for the two pens (see Table 5.46). However, the situation effects for pen 2 are smaller than those for pen 1, as the F-ratios for all measures for pen 2 are far smaller. Furthermore, the same results are observed in Table 5.42 regardless of the two pens.

Table 5.47 shows the ANOVA results of situation effects for the mini-cassette sample. With the exception of the measure of perceived performance, all dependent measures show significant differences across situations for both cassettes, mostly at the level of 0.05. These results are expected. Recall from Chapter 4 that respondents in the pilot survey refused to compare the perceived performance of the instrumental products using the attribute-specific measures, since they could hardly distinguish between perceived product performances in different situations. Hence, it is not surprising to find that situation fails to have an effect on perceived performance for both cassette players.

When a check is made on situation effects regardless of the two cassettes, it is encouraging to find that the same results are obtained

Table 5.46 ANOVA results of situation effects for the ball-pen sample

	F-ratio	
Dependent Measure	*Pen 1*	*Pen 2*
Expectations		
Global	248.56 a	40.84 a
Attribute-specific	120.62 a	14.88 a
Perceived performance		
Global	172.56 a	40.77 a
Satisfaction		
Global	178.86 a	19.12 a
Attribute-specific	116.69 a	7.79 a

a F-ratio significant at $p < 0.01$.
b F-ratio significant at $p < 0.05$.
c F-ratio significant at $p < 0.10$.

Table 5.47　ANOVA results of situation effects for the mini-cassette player sample

	F-ratio	
Dependent Measure	Cassette player 1	Cassette player 2
Expectations		
Global	14.37 a	16.08 a
Attribute-specific	4.40 a	6.10 a
Perceived performance		
Global	190.19 a	1.31
Satisfaction		
Global	20.49 a	2.19 c
Attribute-specific	10.70 a	3.56 b

a F-ratio significant at $p < 0.01$.
b F-ratio significant at $p < 0.05$.
c F-ratio significant at $p < 0.10$.

(see Table 5.43). Therefore, as can be seen from the above analysis, the following hypotheses received strong support.

Hypothesis 7. There is a significant relationship between use situation and product expectations. That is, the situation in which the product is encountered will induce higher or lower expectations of the product.

Hypothesis 8. There is a significant relationship between use situation and satisfaction. That is, a use situation will induce higher or lower product expectations.

Analysis of interaction effects between product and situation

Further, there appears to be some interaction between product and situation treatments. However, the results are not consistent. Table 5.42 indicates that interaction effects are only found on global measures for the ball-pen sample. F-ratios appear to be much smaller for attribute-specific measures than global measures. For the mini-cassette player sample, the interaction effects shown in Table 5.43 are even weaker.The interaction effects are found in both global and attribute-specific measures for satisfaction, and the F-ratios appear to be much smaller when compared with those of the ball-pen sample. This result is especially noteworthy, as it indicates the difficulty of separating the effects of a situation from the effects of experience of use when attribute-specific measures are employed. Overall it is difficult to conclude that the two treatments have joint effects on the pre-trial as well as the post-trial measures for the two samples.

ANALYSIS OF COVARIANCE STRUCTURE

In this final part of the chapter, two structural models are presented for each sample. The discussion begins with a structural model consisting of twelve Chinese cultural value dimensions and other determinants of consumer satisfaction. Next, a model consisting of the Chinese cultural value scale and other determinants of consumer satisfaction is presented. For each model, estimation of parameters using the unweighted least square method is performed, and an overall goodness of fit index is applied.

The ball-pen sample

On the basis of the theory, past research and findings discussed earlier in this chapter and in Chapter 3, two structural submodels may be investigated. Figure 5.3 illustrates the first model 3 which is basically the same as the one depicted by Figure 3.1. In the model, the five independent variables are Chinese cultural values (ξ_1), usage situations (ξ_2), products (ξ_3), consumption experiences (ξ_4) and affective experiences (ξ_5), and the five dependent variables are expectation (η_1), product performance (η_2), disconfirmation (η_3), satisfaction (η_4) and intention (η_5). The only difference is the inclusion of the variable 'product' in the model. As discussed earlier, the unobservable variable 'product' is represented by two dummy variables which are designed to manipulate the level of expectations. The nature of the causal relation is represented through a parameter, γ, which indicates the direction and magnitude of the connection binding ξ to η. The theoretical variables are indicated through two types of unobservable variables: ξ by xs and η by ys. Measures of the degree of correspondence (i.e. construct validity) between the observable variables and unobservable variables are represented through λs. Errors in equations are modelled through ζ and errors in variables are indicated by δs and εs.

Model P1

Consider first Model P1 in which the construct Chinese cultural values as a whole is represented by twelve factors (dimensions). It is assumed that there are no correlations between these dimensions. The correlation matrix of thirty-four observable variables for the measures in the

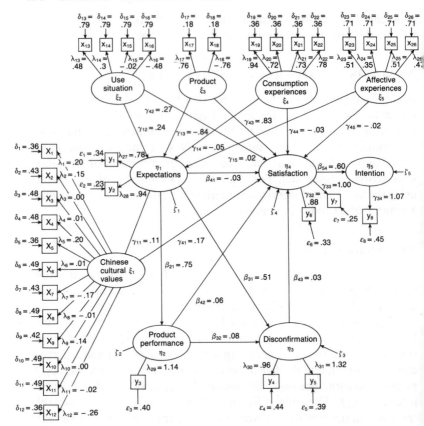

Figure 5.3 Unweighted least square estimates of model P1 for the ball-pen sample

ball-pen sample was computed and treated as input into the SPSSX LISREL VI package. Table 5.48 shows the individual measure and composite construct reliabilities and Table 5.49 and Figure 5.3 summarize the estimated parameters for this model.

The determinant of the matrix was found to be extremely small when compared with the magnitude of the diagonal elements (i.e. 1 in this case). In this case, Joreskog and Sorbom (1985: III.8) advise the adoption of the unweighted least square (ULS) method to estimate the parameters of the model instead of the maximum likelihood (ML) method, though it does not provide a t-value for each parameter, or the chi-square value, which indicates the overall fitness of the model. Further, since chi-square is a valid test statistic only if the analysis is

Table 5.48 Individual measure and composite construct reliability for Model P1 and Model P2 ball-pen samples

Construct/measure	Model P1 Measure	Model P1 Composite	Model P2 Measure	Model P2 Composite
Expectations				
y_1-global	0.665		0.784	
y_2-attribute-specific		0.773		0.852
Performance				
y_3-global	0.601		0.734	
Confirmation				
y_4-global	0.559		0.779	
y_5-attribute-specific		0.607		0.807
Satisfaction				
y_6-global	0.674		0.802	
y_7-attribute-specific		0.749		0.843
Intention				
y_8-global	0.552		0.732	
Chinese Cultural Values Scale				0.962
x_1	0.634			
x_2	0.561			
x_3	0.515			
x_4	0.511			
x_5	0.636			
x_6	0.511			
x_7	0.569			
x_8	0.514			
x_9	0.585			
x_{10}	0.512			
x_{11}	0.513			
x_{12}	0.643			
Consumption experiences				
x_{13}		0.635		0.656
x_{14}	0.635		0.656	
x_{15}	0.635		0.656	
x_{16}	0.635		0.656	
Affective experiences				
x_{17}	0.288		0.463	
x_{18}	0.288		0.463	
x_{19}	0.288		0.463	
x_{20}	0.288		0.463	

based on the sample covariance matrix and not the correlation matrix, the use of the chi-square test is therefore not adopted (Churchill and Surprenant 1982). However, other indicators suggest that the model provides a reasonably good fit with the data. First, the goodness of

Table 5.49   Estimated parameters for the ball-pen sample

	Model P1				Model P2		
Parameter	LISREL Estimate	Parameter	LISREL Estimate	Parameter	LISREL Estimate	Parameter	LISREL Estimate
β_{21}	0.75	λ_{27}	0.78	β_{21}	0.44	Var.(ζ_1)	0.57
β_{31}	0.51	λ_{28}	0.94	β_{31}	0.49	Var.(ζ_2)	0.22
β_{32}	0.08	λ_{29}	1.14	β_{32}	0.08	Var.(ζ_3)	0.62
β_{41}	−0.03	λ_{30}	0.96	β_{41}	0.15	Var.(ζ_4)	0.57
β_{42}	0.06	λ_{31}	1.32	β_{42}	0.11	Var.(ζ_5)	0.21
β_{43}	0.03	λ_{32}	0.88	β_{43}	0.36		
β_{54}	0.62	λ_{33}	1.00	β_{54}	0.32	ε_1	0.22
γ_{11}	0.11	λ_{34}	1.07	γ_{11}	0.10	ε_2	0.15
γ_{41}	0.17	δ_1	0.36	γ_{41}	0.13	ε_3	0.27
γ_{12}	0.24	δ_2	0.43	γ_{12}	0.16	ε_4	0.22
γ_{42}	0.27	δ_3	0.48	γ_{42}	0.16	ε_5	0.19
γ_{13}	−0.84	δ_4	0.48	γ_{13}	−0.75	ε_6	0.19
γ_{43}	−0.83	δ_5	0.36	γ_{43}	−0.61	ε_7	0.16
γ_{14}	−0.05	δ_6	0.49	γ_{14}	−0.04	ε_8	0.27
γ_{44}	−0.03	δ_7	0.43	γ_{44}	−0.02		
γ_{15}	0.02	δ_8	0.49	γ_{15}	0.01	δ_1	0.04
γ_{45}	−0.02	δ_9	0.42	γ_{45}	−0.01	δ_2	0.59
λ_1	0.20	δ_{10}	0.49	λ_1	0.97	δ_3	0.59
λ_2	−0.15	δ_{11}	0.49	λ_2	0.53	δ_4	0.59
λ_3	−0.00	δ_{12}	0.36	λ_3	−0.01	δ_5	0.59
λ_4	−0.01	δ_{13}	0.79	λ_4	−0.16	δ_6	0.01
λ_5	0.20	δ_{14}	0.79	λ_5	−0.42	δ_7	0.01
λ_6	0.01	δ_{15}	0.79	λ_6	0.99	δ_8	0.34
λ_7	−0.17	δ_{16}	0.79	λ_7	-1.00	δ_9	0.34
λ_8	0.02	δ_{17}	0.18	λ_8	0.96	δ_{10}	0.34
λ_9	0.14	δ_{18}	0.18	λ_9	0.72	δ_{11}	0.34
λ_{10}	0.00	δ_{19}	0.36	λ_{10}	0.72	δ_{12}	0.54
λ_{11}	−0.02	δ_{20}	0.36	λ_{11}	0.79	δ_{13}	0.54
λ_{12}	−0.26	δ_{21}	0.36	λ_{12}	0.65	δ_{14}	0.54
λ_{13}	0.47	δ_{22}	0.36	λ_{13}	0.51	δ_{15}	0.54
λ_{14}	0.30	δ_{23}	0.71	λ_{14}	0.44		
λ_{15}	−0.02	δ_{24}	0.71	λ_{15}	0.48		
λ_{16}	−0.48	δ_{25}	0.71	λ_{16}	0.79		
λ_{17}	0.76	δ_{26}	0.71	λ_{17}	0.98		
λ_{18}	−0.76	ε_1	0.34	λ_{18}	0.97		
λ_{19}	0.94	ε_2	0.23	λ_{19}	0.97		
λ_{20}	0.72	ε_3	0.40	λ_{20}	1.11		
λ_{21}	0.73	ε_4	0.44	λ_{21}	0.94		
λ_{22}	0.78	ε_5	0.39	λ_{22}	1.08		
λ_{23}	0.51	ε_6	0.33	λ_{23}	0.96		
λ_{24}	0.35	ε_7	0.25				
λ_{25}	0.51	ε_8	0.45				
λ_{26}	0.47						

Goodness of Fit Index (GFI)	0.92	
Root Mean Square Residual (RMSR)	0.07	
	GFI	0.86
	RMSR	0.16

fit index which is 0.92 shows that the model provides a reasonably good fit. This figure implies that about 92 per cent of the covariation to be explained is accounted for by the proposed structure (Bagozzi 1980). Second, the average residual between the observed correlations and the theoretical correlations given the structural model is only 0.068.

With respect to the estimated parameters of the model, Table 5.49 shows that the structural parameters are fairly large with the exception of those of affective experiences, consumption experiences and use situations. However, the parameters are in the expected directions. Values of all lambda ys are fairly large, indicating that construct validity of all dependent variables exists. As expected, the magnitude of lambda x of the Chinese cultural values varies, ranging from 0.0 to 0.26, indicating that there are several dimensions of Chinese cultural values which have an impact on expectations and satisfaction. Consistently with the results mentioned at pp. 166–7, adaptiveness, sincerity/suspicion, harmony with people, Pao, respect for experience, and past-orientation are found to contribute to the construct validity of the Chinese cultural values. Other independent variables are found to have high construct validity. Table 5.48 reports the reliability values for the individual measures and the composite reliability values for the constructs (Bagozzi 1980). All the reliability values for the individual variables are acceptable except for those of affective experiences, which have reliability coefficients as low as 0.288. The composite reliability values for the constructs are fairly high, the smallest being 0.60 for the disconfirmation measure. This result is consistent with that of Churchill and Surprenant (1982). Further, the total coefficient of determination indicates that the reliability of independent variables is 0.84 while the reliability of dependent variables is 0.99.

With respect to relationships between dependent variables and independent variables, expectations are found to have a positive impact on disconfirmation, with higher product performance leading to respondents rating the products as performing better than expected ($\beta_{31} = 0.511$). Expectations also have a positive impact on the performance of the ball-pens, but have negative impact on satisfaction, although the impact is small ($\beta_{41} = -0.03$). Performance related positively to disconfirmation and satisfaction with a small magnitude ($\beta_{32} = 0.08$ and $\beta_{42} = 0.06$). The relationship between satisfaction and disconfirmation is nominal ($\beta_{54} = 0.03$). The indirect impact of disconfirmation is even smaller. The level of intention to purchase is affected directly by respondents' satisfaction. A further examination of the relationships between dependent variables and independent variables indicates that satisfaction may be affected by Chinese cultural values ($\gamma_{41} = 0.17$), the use situation ($\gamma_{42} = 0.27$) and product ($\gamma_{43} = -0.83$). Since use situation and product are measured by dummy variables, the direction of the links with expectations and satisfaction should be interpreted together with the sign of the corresponding lambda. However, opposite signs indicate that the prestigious ball-pen has a positive impact on satisfaction and that the basic ball-pen has a negative impact on satisfaction. Consumption experiences and affective experiences are also found to have a negative impact on satisfaction, but the impact of each construct is minimal ($\gamma_{44} = -0.03$ and $\gamma_{45} = -0.02$). Similarly, Chinese cultural values, use situation and product also affect product expectations ($\gamma_{11} = 0.11$, $\gamma_{12} = 0.24$, and $\gamma_{13} = -0.84$). The impact of consumption experiences and affective experiences on product expectations are also minimal ($\gamma_{14} = -0.04$ and $\gamma_{15} = 0.02$).

Model P2

Model P2 is basically the same as Model P1 except that, in Model P2, Chinese cultural values are operationalized as a summated scale score. Hence, there is only one observable variable for the independent variable, Chinese cultural values. Since the determinant of the correlation matrix is small when compared with the magnitude of the diagonal elements, the unweighted least square method is again adopted. The goodness of fit index, which is 0.86, indicates that the overall fit of the model is mediocre. The root mean square residual is 0.17, indicating a comparatively high level of residual. The total coefficient of determination for the structural equations is found to be 0.64, which indicates that the independent variables are able to explain about 40 per cent of the variance of the dependent variables. This is not a small amount in consumer research.

Table 5.48 reports the reliability values for the individual measures and the composite reliability values for the constructs. All the reliability values for the individual variables are acceptable except for those of affective experiences, which have reliability coefficients of about 0.46. The composite reliability values for the constructs are fairly high, the smallest being 0.66 for the consumption experiences. Overall reliability for both independent variables and dependent variables is rather high, as is indicated by the total coefficient of determination. As indicated by the squared multiple coefficient of determination, the reliability coefficient for the independent variables is 0.994 while the reliability coefficient for the dependent variables is 1.000.

Findings in Table 5.49 indicate that Chinese cultural values have a high construct validity ($\lambda_1 = 0.97$) as indicated by the squared multiple correlation. The construct validity for consumption experiences is also high, with the smallest being 0.72. Further, it is found that the composite measure for consumption experiences has a higher construct validity than other individual measures, as indicated by lambdas.

Table 5.49 and Figure 5.4 also indicate that expectations have a positive impact on perceived performance, disconfirmation and satisfaction. The impact is less on satisfaction than on performance and

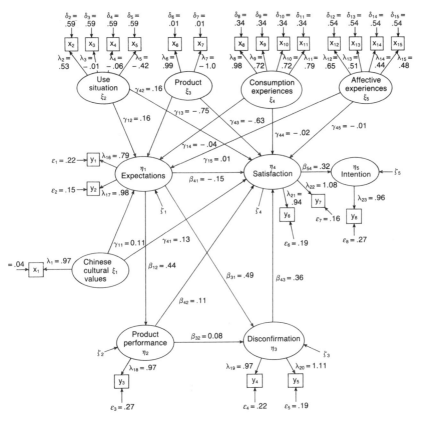

Figure 5.4 Unweighted least square estimates of model P2 for the ball-pen sample

Table 5.50   Individual measure and composite construct reliability for Model C1 and Model C2 of the mini-cassette player sample

Construct/measure	Model C1		Model C2	
	Measure	*Composite*	*Measure*	*Composite*
Expectations				
y_1-global	0.661		0.536	
y_2-attribute-specific		0.713		0.611
Performance				
y_3-global	0.568		0.522	
Confirmation				
y_4-global	0.611		0.523	
y_5-attribute-specific		0.638		0.590
Satisfaction				
y_6-global	0.690		0.640	
y_7-attribute-specific		0.740		0.708
Intention				
y_8-global	0.590		0.531	
Chinese Cultural Values Scale				1.000
x_1	0.688			
x_2	0.556			
x_3	0.554			
x_4	0.602			
x_5	0.554			
x_6	0.737			
x_7	0.554			
x_8	0.648			
x_9	0.567			
x_{10}	0.609			
x_{11}	0.560			
x_{12}	0.554			
Consumption experiences				
x_{13}		0.568		0.579
x_{14}	0.568		0.579	
x_{15}	0.568		0.579	
x_{16}	0.568		0.579	
Affective experiences				
x_{17}	0.226		0.183	
x_{18}	0.226		0.183	
x_{19}	0.226		0.183	
x_{20}	0.226		0.183	

disconfirmation. There is also a positive impact of disconfirmation on satisfaction ($\beta = 0.36$) and of satisfaction on intention ($\beta = 0.32$).

With regard to the relationships between dependent variables and independent variables, it was found that Chinese cultural values, use situation and product have a direct effect on both expectations and satisfaction. As in Model P1, the prestigious ball-pen creates higher expectations than the basic model ball-pen. However, it seems that what is different from Model P1 is that expectations, performance, Chinese cultural values, and use situation contribute equally to affecting consumer satisfaction. Further, expectations and performance thus have a direct impact on satisfaction in addition to their indirect impact through disconfirmation, although the impact of disconfirmation on satisfaction is the largest of the three.

The mini-cassette player sample

Model C1

Model C1 is basically the same as Model P1, discussed in the last section. The correlation matrix of thirty-four observable variables for the mini-cassette player sample was computed from the raw data and was treated as input into the SPSSX LISREL VI package. Table 5.50 shows the individual measure and composite construct reliabilities and Table 5.51 and Figure 5.5 summarize the estimated parameters for this model.

The determinant of the correlation matrix is found to be extremely small when compared with the magnitude of the diagonal elements (i.e. 1 in this case). As in Model P1 and Model P2, the unweighted least square method was used to estimate the parameters of the model. Results of the analysis show that the model provides a reasonably good fit to the data. First, the goodness of fit index, which is 0.89. shows that the model provides a reasonably good fit. This figure implies that about 89 per cent of the covariation to be explained is accounted for by the proposed structure (Bagozzi 1980). Second, the average residual between the observed correlations and the theoretical correlations given the structural model is only 0.09.

With respect to estimated parameters of the model, Table 5.51 shows that the structural parameters are fairly large, with the exception of those of affective experiences, consumption experiences and use situations. However, the parameters are in the expected directions. Values of all lambda λs are fairly large indicating that construct validity of all dependent variables exists. As expected, the magnitude

Table 5.51 Unweighted least square estimates for the mini-cassette player sample

	Model C1				Model C2		
Parameter	LISREL Estimate	Parameter	LISREL Estimate	Parameter	LISREL Estimate	Parameter	LISREL Estimate
β_{21}	0.74	λ_{27}	0.74	β_{21}	0.91	Var.(ζ_1)	0.00
β_{31}	0.77	λ_{28}	0.96	β_{31}	0.84	Var.(ζ_2)	0.00
β_{32}	0.08	λ_{29}	1.10	β_{32}	0.08	Var.(ζ_3)	0.00
β_{41}	−0.06	λ_{30}	0.97	β_{41}	−0.18	Var.(ζ_4)	0.00
β_{42}	0.06	λ_{31}	1.14	β_{42}	0.09	Var.(ζ_5)	0.00
β_{43}	0.17	λ_{32}	0.76	β_{43}	0.17		
β_{54}	0.60	λ_{33}	0.83	β_{54}	0.63	ε_1	0.46
γ_{11}	0.58	λ_{34}	1.00	γ_{11}	0.13	ε_2	0.39
γ_{41}	0.35	δ_1	0.31	γ_{41}	0.19	ε_3	0.48
γ_{12}	0.06	δ_2	0.44	γ_{12}	0.16	ε_4	0.47
γ_{42}	0.07	δ_3	0.45	γ_{42}	0.07	ε_5	0.41
γ_{13}	−0.52	δ_4	0.40	γ_{13}	−0.66	ε_6	0.36
γ_{43}	−0.83	δ_5	0.45	γ_{43}	−0.99	ε_7	0.29
γ_{14}	−0.07	δ_6	0.26	γ_{14}	−0.08	ε_8	0.47
γ_{44}	−0.05	δ_7	0.45	γ_{44}	−0.06		
γ_{15}	0.02	δ_8	0.35	γ_{15}	−0.01	δ_1	0.00
γ_{45}	−0.10	δ_9	0.44	γ_{45}	−0.01	δ_2	1.00
λ_1	0.03	δ_{10}	0.39	λ_1	0.98	δ_3	1.00
λ_2	0.06	δ_{11}	0.44	λ_2	0.11	δ_4	1.00
λ_3	0.07	δ_{12}	0.45	λ_3	−0.08	δ_5	1.00
λ_4	0.06	δ_{13}	0.73	λ_4	0.51	δ_6	0.57
λ_5	0.16	δ_{14}	0.73	λ_5	−0.07	δ_7	0.57
λ_6	0.05	δ_{15}	0.73	λ_6	0.73	δ_8	0.60
λ_7	0.05	δ_{16}	0.73	λ_7	−0.73	δ_9	0.60
λ_8	−0.11	δ_{17}	0.10	λ_8	0.93	δ_{10}	0.60
λ_9	0.01	δ_{18}	0.10	λ_9	0.72	δ_{11}	0.60
λ_{10}	0.02	δ_{19}	0.43	λ_{10}	0.64	δ_{12}	0.13
λ_{11}	0.06	δ_{20}	0.43	λ_{11}	0.75	δ_{13}	0.13
λ_{12}	0.04	δ_{21}	0.43	λ_{12}	0.51	δ_{14}	0.13
λ_{13}	−0.23	δ_{22}	0.43	λ_{13}	0.47	δ_{15}	0.13
λ_{14}	−0.23	δ_{23}	0.74	λ_{14}	0.13		
λ_{15}	−0.23	δ_{24}	0.74	λ_{15}	0.03		
λ_{16}	−0.23	δ_{25}	0.74	λ_{16}	0.68		
λ_{17}	0.88	δ_{26}	0.74	λ_{17}	0.83		
λ_{18}	−0.88	ε_1	0.31	λ_{18}	1.22		
λ_{19}	0.92	ε_2	0.29	λ_{19}	1.02		
λ_{20}	0.92	ε_3	0.41	λ_{20}	1.18		
λ_{21}	0.65	ε_4	0.39	λ_{21}	0.76		
λ_{22}	0.74	ε_5	0.36	λ_{22}	0.84		
λ_{23}	0.69	ε_6	0.31	λ_{23}	1.01		
λ_{24}	0.24	ε_7	0.26				
λ_{25}	0.30	ε_8	0.41				
λ_{26}	0.19						

Goodness of Fit Index (GFI)	0.89	GFI	0.92
Root Mean Square Residual (RMSR)	0.09	RMSR	0.09

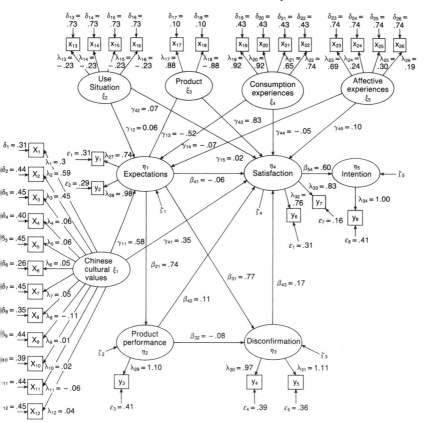

Figure 5.5 Unweighted least square estimates of model C1 for the mini-cassette player sample

of lambda x of the Chinese cultural values varies, ranging from − 0.11 to 0.09, indicating that there are several dimensions of Chinese cultural values which have an impact on expectation and satisfaction. Similarly to the results mentioned at p. 167, Pao, sincerity/suspicion, and group orientation appear to contribute more to the construct validity of Chinese cultural values. Other independent variables are found to have high construct validity. Table 5.50 reports the reliability values for the individual measures and the composite reliability values for the constructs (Bagozzi 1980). All of the reliability values for the individual variables are acceptable except for those of affective experiences which have reliability coefficients as low as 0.23. The composite reliability values for the constructs are fairly high, the smallest being 0.61 for the disconfirmation measure. This result is consistent with that of Churchill and Surprenant (1982). Further, the total coefficient of determination indicates that the reliability of independent variables is 0.698, while the reliability of dependent variables is 0.984.

With regard to relationships between dependent variables and independent variables, there are several aspects of note. First, it was found that Chinese cultural values and product have a direct effect on both expectations and satisfaction ($\gamma_{11} = 0.13$; $\gamma_{41} = 0.19$; $\lambda_{13} = 0.75$; $\lambda_{43} = -0.99$). Second, the impact of use situation, consumption experiences and affective experiences on satisfaction is minimal ($\gamma_{42} = 0.07$; $\gamma_{44} = -0.07$; $\gamma_{45} = -0.01$). As in Model P1, the prestigious cassette creates higher expectations than the basic model cassette. Third, it appears that Chinese cultural values, product and disconfirmation affect consumer satisfaction ($\gamma_{41} = 0.19$; $\gamma_{43} = -0.99$; $\beta_{43} = 0.17$). Among the three, Chinese cultural values have the greatest positive effect on satisfaction. Fourth, expectations have a small and negative impact on satisfaction. Fifth, Chinese cultural values have a direct but very small impact on product expectations.

Model C2

Model C2 is basically the same as Model C1 except that in Model C2 Chinese cultural values is operationalized as a summated scale score (see Table 5.50 and Figure 5.5). Hence there is only one observable variable for the independent variable, Chinese cultural values. Since the determinant of the correlation matrix is small when compared with magnitude of the diagonal elements, the unweighted least-squares method is again adopted. The goodness of fit index, which is 0.92, indicates that the overall fitness of the model is high. The root mean square residual is 0.09, indicating a comparative low level of residual. The total coefficient of determination for the structural equations is found to be 0.93, which indicates that the independent variables are able to explain about 80 per cent of the variance of the dependent variables. This is a very high level in consumer research.

Table 5.50 reports the reliability values for the individual measures and the composite reliability values for the constructs. All the reliability values for the individual variables are acceptable except for those of affective experiences, which have reliability coefficients of about 0.18. The composite reliability values for the constructs are acceptably large, the smallest being 0.56 for the consumption experiences. Overall reliability for both independent variables and dependent variables is quite high, as is indicated by the total coefficient of determination. As indicated by the squared multiple coefficient of determination, the reliability coefficient for independent variables is 0.93 while the reliability coefficient for dependent variables is 0.62.

Each lambda y or lambda x serves to indicate construct validity. The findings in Table 5.51 show that Chinese cultural values have a high construct validity ($\lambda_1 = 0.98$). The construct validity for consumption experiences is also high, the smallest being 0.76. Further, it is found that the composite measure for consumption experiences has a higher construct validity than other individual measures.

Table 5.51 and Figure 5.6 also indicate that expectations have a positive impact on perceived performance, disconfirmation and

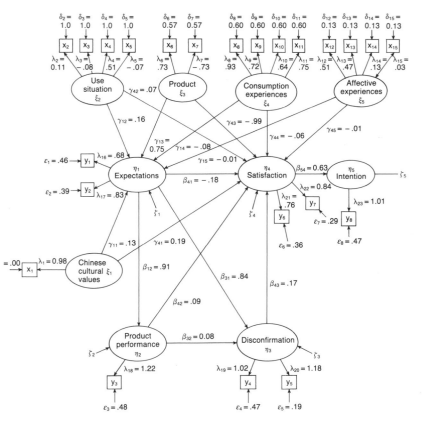

Figure 5.6 Unweighted least square estimates of model C2 for the mini-cassette player sample

satisfaction. Expectations have more or less the same amount of impact on perceived performance as they have on disconfirmation ($\beta_{21} = 0.91$ and $\beta_{31} = 0.84$). However, the impact of expectations on satisfaction is negative in direction ($\beta_{41} = -0.18$). There is also a positive impact of disconfirmation on satisfaction ($\beta_{43} = 0.17$) and of satisfaction on intention ($\beta_{54} = 0.63$).

With regard to the relationships between dependent variables and independent variables, it was found that Chinese cultural values, use situation and product have a direct effect on both expectations and satisfaction. As in Model P1, the prestigious cassette created higher expectations than the basic model. However, it seems that what is different from Model P1 is that expectations, performance, Chinese cultural values and use situation have more or less the same effect on consumer satisfaction. Further, expectations and performance thus have a direct impact on satisfaction in addition to their indirect impact through disconfirmation, although the impact of disconfirmation on satisfaction appears to be large in magnitude when comparing with the other two.

CONCLUSION

In the previous sub-section, data were found to fit the two models for each sample satisfactorily. It can be concluded that hypothesis 17 cannot be rejected. For the four models, most constructs were found valid. However, the reliability of two measures - consumption experiences and affective experiences - was found very low and unacceptable. As to the relationships between dependent variables and independent variables, there is a significant difference between models of the two samples. Usage situation was found to have a significant impact on expectations and satisfaction in the ball-pen sample but not in the mini-cassette sample. Other relationships were found consistent with the results found earlier in this chapter.

NOTE

[1] With respect to the construct 'performance' item-to-total correlations were only measured and calculated without taking the four situations into account. The rationale for doing this was previously mentioned in the section concerning questionnaire construction.

6 Summary and conclusions

This chapter closes the discussion with further thoughts and reflections on the research. It begins by reiterating the objectives and general orientation of the study. Next a brief summary and interpretation of the findings is presented. Third, contributions of the research are outlined. Finally, a number of suggestions for further research are presented.

OBJECTIVES OF THE STUDY

This study primarily concerns the effect of cultural values, situations, experiences and selected other determinants on consumer satisfaction. In recent years, there has been a rising tide of consumer discontent in some parts of the world. On the one hand, some researchers have viewed this phenomenon as a result of increasing income and sociological forces which have prompted higher expectations of a better life style. On the other hand, some have attributed the causes of consumer discontent to the negligent attitude of business and government. However, they all agree that consumer satisfaction is important to business, government agencies and consumers. The study of consumer satisfaction can help businessmen identify weak spots in products/services for future product modification and development, and help in the design of marketing strategies. Government agencies can also benefit by identifying and isolating those products/services where government action is desirable to enhance consumer welfare. To consumers, information about how satisfied or dissatisfied others have been with products helps them make wise buying decisions. To secure relevant information for these three parties, academics, who are independent, are in a better position to objectively conduct research in the area of conceptualization, measurement and application.

The literature on consumer satisfaction has its roots in American culture. It would be dangerous to transplant theories and practices relating to consumer satisfaction to other cultures without looking into the differences and similarities in the process of consumer satisfaction. Evidence has indicated that there is a genuine need to return to basic premises and contextualize consumer behaviour in an individual culture so that generalization can later be made cross-culturally (Engel 1985a, 1985b; Sheth 1985a, 1985b; Triandis 1974). Therefore, this study contextualizes the process of consumer satisfaction by looking into the effect of cultural values and other determinants on consumer satisfaction in a Chinese society.

The study has the following objectives: (1) to draw together the various directions of theory and research in the study of determinants of consumer satisfaction/dissatisfaction by (a) developing a comprehensive model which conceptually ties all these determinants together and (b) testing hypothesized causal links between determinants in the model, and (2) to construct a valid and reliable scale to measure Chinese cultural values, which is regarded as a component of the model.

SUMMARY AND INTERPRETATION OF FINDINGS

This portion of the chapter briefly reviews the findings and places them in perspective. The discussion is organized in the chronological order used in the previous chapter in order to facilitate reference.

Reliability and validity of the multi-item measures

In order to establish a certain degree of faith in the hypotheses and model(s) developed in the study, it is necessary to have reliable measurements. The primary method for measuring the reliability of multi-item measures was the Cronbach alpha coefficient. In general, the reliability coefficients ranged from about 0.7 to 0.89 for the ball-pen sample, and from 0.65 to 0.86 for the mini-cassette player sample. These values compared favourably with those achieved in other studies (Churchill and Surprenant 1982; Bagozzi 1982) and were of high enough levels to warrant confidence in the measures (Nunnally 1978). Furthermore, results of the item-to-total correlation analysis also showed that strong internal consistency of the research instruments was prevalent.

To find out the predictive validity of each construct, correlation techniques were employed to confirm that related constructs did have some relationships. As expected, with the exception of affective experiences, all correlations between constructs were significant at the level of 0.01 and in the expected direction.

The multitrait-multimethod matrix was used to assess the convergent and discriminant validity of three constructs: expectations, disconfirmation and satisfaction. In summary, correlations in the matrix indicated that the constructs possess both convergent and discriminant validity.

It may be concluded that in general the measures used in the study are reliable and valid.

The Chinese cultural value scale

A scale has to be developed on a sound theoretical base which will also meet rigorous reliability and validity standards. This is the Chinese Cultural Value Scale. A review of the literature on Chinese cultural values demonstrated the feasibility of developing a scale for the measurement of Chinese cultural values by employing techniques previously used in the development of other attitude scales. Developing the Chinese Cultural Value Scale involved four independent stages. The first stage was the construction of an item inventory and the selection of items for inclusion in a measure of reliability. This process involved the generation of 100 common Chinese sayings from three famous sources. By judgment of methods, the inventory was reduced to sixty six common sayings. The item inventory was administered to 120 respondents in a pilot study and was reduced to a total of forty five items based on the criterion of non-response. Then the inventory was administered to two samples of respondents in the main survey. As a result, the inventory was further reduced to forty items. T-tests were performed to screen items in the inventory, which did not appear to differentiate statistically between the highest and lowest quartile of scores. As a result, no item was discarded, and all forty items were included in the second stage of reliability testing.

To assess the reliability of the scale, two reliability measures were obtained: (1) alpha reliability coefficient and (2) split-half reliability coefficient. In the third stage of development, the scale was tested for construct validity, using the internal analysis of item-to-total correlations and the external analysis of known groups of Chinese students and non-Chinese students.

The scale analysis indicated that the Chinese Cultural Value Scale is reliable. Meeting rigorous standards of reliability, the measures of construct validity were further provided as evidence for the validity of the scale. The alpha coefficients for both samples were high and above the acceptable level suggested by Nunnally (1978). The split-half reliability coefficients, which ranged from 0.73 to 0.79, were evidence of the scale's reliability.

The scale analysis also indicated that the scale is valid.The results of item-to-total correlation analysis indicated that the scale is highly valid internally. T-tests were applied to see whether scores for each item across the two samples were statistically significant. Results show that only seven out of forty-five were found significant. External validity was assessed by the 'known groups' method. Two known groups – Chinese students in the Chinese University and non-Chinese students in the University of Bradford Management Centre – were used. Results of the t-tests showed that there was significant difference between total scores for the two groups. In conclusion, the scale was found externally valid. In conjunction with the high reliability of the scale, these validity measures demonstrated that the scale consistently measured the concept of Chinese cultural values.

By demonstrating that Chinese cultural values can be measured, this study lends support to the body of research dealing with value systems in Chinese societies. Existing omnibus measures of values such as Rokeach's (1973) and Morris's (1956) do not offer a discrete measure of cultural values in the Chinese context. This research, therefore, offers empirical evidence that individuals can exhibit degrees of Chineseness and that this property can be measured at a micro or individual level.

The findings of this study also contribute to the understanding of Chinese cultural values. It was found that the scale was multi-dimensional. Factor analysis was used to estimate the underlying dimensions of the scale. For the two samples, twelve underlying dimensions were extracted. Among these dimensions, ten were found in common across samples. They were: interdependence, continuity/ respect for authority, harmony with the universe, harmony with people, sincerity/suspicion, Pao (reciprocity), group-orientation, face, abasement, and past-orientation. Specific dimensions are adaptiveness and respect for experience for the ball-pen sample, and conformity to activity and endurance for the mini-cassette player sample. In general, the dimensions extracted were meaningful and well in line with value orientations by other authors (Kluckhohn and Strodtbeck 1961; Morris 1956; Wei 1980).

Further, in order to understand the contribution of items to the scale score for each sample, ridge stepwise regression analysis was performed. It was found that the ball-pen sample seemed to be more concerned with adaptiveness, face, sincerity, interdependence, group-orientation and Pao, while the mini-cassette player sample was more concerned with interdependence, continuity, harmony with the universe, conformity to activity, abasement and face. However, in general, the differences did not seem very great across samples.

In summary, the results indicated that Chinese culture is measurable by means of a reliable and valid scale.

Results of two-way relationships

The third step in the data analysis involved an examination of all the possible two-way relationships between variables in the study. A necessary, but not a sufficient, condition for the model to hold is that the individual relationship between variables should be in the predicted direction. The results are summarized with comments below.

The Chinese cultural values

The Chinese Value Scale score was found to be significantly related in a positive direction to product expectation. The higher the score, the higher the level of product expectation. The relationship was found to hold for both measures across the two samples. No research could be found testing this hypothesis, and therefore no comparison could be made.

The proposition that Chinese Value Scale scores are related to satisfaction also received support. Results showed that, the higher the score, the higher the level of product satisfaction. The relationship was found to hold for both measures across two samples. In conjunction with the results regarding product expectations, the present findings suggest that the Chinese tend to be become satisfied through a theory of cognitive dissonance. Chinese consumers tend to reduce their expectations with the product concerned after purchase in order to be more satisfied.

Consumption experiences

Although consumption experiences were hypothesized to be negatively related to consumer satisfaction, in general, the results showed no significant relationships. However, the non-significant relationship was found in the expected direction.

Finally, consumption experiences were hypothesized to be negatively related to product expectations. The hypothesis was not supported, but the relationship was in the expected direction. No empirical research could be found testing the hypothesis. However, the result was not consistent with what Andreasen (1977) had suggested.

There are three possible explanations of this result. First, consumers have been generally satisfied with products in the market and therefore have had little experience of dissatisfaction. Second, the rather generalized measures of consumption experiences are not able to capture the contingencies of the situations. Third, consumption experiences do not in fact systematically affect satisfaction and product expectations.

Affective experiences

In the literature on consumer satisfaction, several authors have mentioned that affective experiences might well affect consumers' expectations (Valle and Wallendorf 1977; Weiner *et al.* 1978). Although affective experiences were hypothesized to be related to product expectations, in general, the results showed no significant relationship. The relationship was, however, in the expected direction.

It was surprising to find that affective experiences did not have any significant relationship with satisfaction. It was expected that the higher the degree of complaint concerning past products or the causal attribution, the lower the level of satisfaction with future products. However, this hypothesis did not receive support. No empirical research could be found testing the hypothesis.

The reasons why consumption experiences failed to reveal any relation with satisfaction and expectations also apply here.

Product expectations

This study found that there was a positive and significant relationship between product expectations and perceived performance. The results were consistent with those of Anderson (1973) and Churchill and Surprenant (1982).

Second, product expectations were found to relate directly to consumer satisfaction. The results were consistent for the two samples, and the relationship was highly significant. Churchill and Surprenant (1982) also found a direct relationship between satisfaction and expectations, while Oliver (1977, 1979, 1980b) did not find any relationship between these two variables.

Finally, product expectations were hypothesized to relate directly to disconfirmation. This hypothesis received strong support. In the literature on consumer satisfaction there have been conflicting findings about the relationship between these two variables. Oliver (1977, 1979, 1980b) and Wortruba and Duncan (1975) discovered that disconfirmation had no relationship with expectations. However, Vinson and Yang (1979) and Swan and Trawick (1980) reported the opposite result. Churchill and Surprenant (1982) found a significant relationship between these variables, but they failed to confirm the direction of the relationship. In the study, a significant relationship was found in different situations for the two products across the two samples. There is reason to believe that product expectations are directly related to disconfirmation.

Consumption/usage situations

In the literature on consumer research, Henry (1976) provided empirical evidence that culture is an underlying determinant of consumer behaviour. The hypothesis went further to examine situational factors that were related to Chinese cultural values (dimensions). However, it received mixed support. Only some of the cultural values were found to have relationships with situational factors. The higher the values of interdependence, harmony with people, face and Pao (reciprocity), the higher the tendency to present gifts to someone else in daily life and to behave properly in public. This implies that segmentation by cultural values could be possible. These cultural values could be helpful in giving clues in designing advertising copy for products which could be used publicly and purchased as a gift for someone else. Further, the result also indicates that making use of cultural values to design marketing strategies could be effective.

The summary of the impact of situational effects on product expectation and satisfaction is now presented.

Perceived performance

The first relationship tested was that between perceived performance and disconfirmation. A positive and significant relationship was found. The result was consistent with that of Swan and Trawick (1980) and Churchill and Surprenant (1982).

The second relationship tested was that between perceived performance and satisfaction. The findings indicated that the relationship was significant at the 0.01 level and was in a positive direction. Again, this result was well in line with findings by other research (Swan and Trawick 1980; Churchill and Surprenant 1982).

Disconfirmation

The proposition that positive disconfirmation is directly related to satisfaction received strong support. All correlations between these variables were found highly significant and in the expected direction. The result was consistent with Olson and Dover's (1976), and Oliver's (1980b) findings. However, Churchill and Surprenant (1982) found a contingent result that disconfirmation might or might not affect satisfaction. For a product, it was found that disconfirmation had a strong and positive effect on satisfaction, as in the case of Oliver (1980b); for another product, satisfaction was determined only by the performance of the product and not by expectation or disconfirmation. Churchill and Surprenant concluded that the link between disconfirmation and satisfaction might be dependent on the type of product used. In this study, different types of products, durable and non-durable, have been used and it was clear that the link between disconfirmation and satisfaction was warranted across products.

Consumer satisfaction

Consumer satisfaction was positively related to purchase intention. The relationship was found significant at the 0.001 level. The result implies that the higher the level of satisfaction, the higher the propensity to purchase. This result was consistent with the findings in the literature on consumer satisfaction. Winter and Morris (1979), who used the term 'propensity to change' instead of purchase intention found that people who were satisfied with their current dwelling had a negative propensity to change ($r = -0.125$). Bearden and Teel (1983) also found that the relationship between post-purchase attitude and behavioural intentions was extremely high and significant ($r = 0.99$). Oliver (1980a, 1980b) also showed empirically that post-exposure and pre-exposure intention was significantly related to satisfaction.

Spurious relationship

The above hypotheses are based on zero-order correlations between variables. These results may be misleading, since they could reflect interaction effects and spurious correlations. Each of the possible confounds was checked in order to determine the fidelity of the two-way relationship. Spurious relationships were treated by partial correlation techniques. Interaction effects (direct or indirect) were checked in the structural model, and the summary of the results is presented in the following section.

Three spurious relationships were investigated to unearth confounds. All of them were eliminated as possibilities lending support to the observed relationships. They are:

1 The relationship between perceived performance and satisfaction is not a spurious one due to product expectations and disconfirmation.
2 The relationship between disconfirmation and satisfaction is not a spurious one due to perceived performance and product expectations.
3 The relationship between satisfaction and purchase intention is not a spurious one due to perceived performance, product expectations and disconfirmation.

The experiment treatment effects

In this portion of the chapter, a summary concerning the effects of the experimental treatments is presented. All effects were tested by the analysis of variance.

Message effects

The message for each product in the experiment was used to manipulate expectations of the subjects with the product concerned before product trial. It was found that message manipulations had not been effective in establishing different product expectations across situations for the ball-pen sample. However, for the mini-cassette player sample, message manipulations were found very effective.

Regardless of situation, message manipulations were again found effective. Hence it was concluded that the message effects in general were effective.

Product effects

There were two propositions concerning product effects. The first proposition, that products had a significant effect on satisfaction, received weak support for the ball-pen sample and strong support for the mini-cassette player sample. In general, the proposition was accepted. Similarly, the second proposition, that products had a significant effect on satisfaction, was weakly supported for the ball-pen sample, and strongly supported for the mini-cassette player sample. However, when situations were disregarded, product effects on satisfaction and perceived performance appeared to be significant. The results are in line with those of Churchill and Surprenant (1982) and Wilton and Tse (1983). Hence, one may conclude that good products would probably prompt high expectations and satisfaction and vice versa. This result implies that product quality and product package are vitally important to the level of product expectation and satisfaction.

Situation effects

The findings showed that the four situations used in the survey had been highly successful in establishing significant differences in dependent constructs, including product expectations and satisfaction, for the two samples. This implies that the level of consumer satisfaction and product expectations would be dependent on the situation in which products or services are to be consumed or used.

The structural models

In this portion of the chapter, a summary concerning the results of the structural models for the two samples, which were previously discussed in Chapter 3, is presented. Parameters of the models were estimated by the unweighted least squares method, which is one of the estimation methods available in the SPSSX LISREL VI package.

Two models for each sample were fitted to the data. The two models differed in the way the construct of Chinese cultural values was operationalized. In the first model, Chinese cultural values were represented by the twelve factors that were uncovered in Chapter 5. In the second model, Chinese cultural values were measured by the total score of the Chinese Cultural Value Scale developed in Chapter 5. For the ball-pen sample, the goodness of fit index for the first model was found to be high while the index for the second model was found to be low. However, as indicated by the estimated parameters, it was found that both models appear to behave similarly. Most constructs were found valid. Except for consumption experiences and affective experiences, reliabilities of individual and composite measures were found to be acceptable. Chinese cultural values, use situation and product appeared to have an impact on product expectations and satisfaction.

Expectations were found to affect satisfaction negatively. This finding is not consistent with those of Churchill and Surprenant (1982) and Oliver (1977, 1979, 1980b). Churchill and Surprenant (1982) found that expectations have a positive impact on satisfaction for the plant data and no relationship with satisfaction for the video disc data. Oliver also found that expectations do not affect satisfaction at all. Disconfirmation was found to have a direct impact on satisfaction. This result is consistent with those of Olson and Dover (1976) and Churchill and Surprenant (1982). Furthermore, as expected, satisfaction was found to affect purchase intention positively.

For the mini-cassette sample, the data were found to fit the two models satisfactorily. As indicated by the estimated parameters, there is only one significant difference between the models of the two samples. Usage situation was found to have a significant impact on expectations and satisfaction in the ball-pen sample but not in the mini-cassette player sample. This seems to imply that the relationships between usage situation and expectations and satisfaction are dependent on the type of product. One of the possible explanations is that ball-pens are regarded as a type of consumer and non-durable product and therefore tended to be consumed and used in different situations. Another possible explanation is that the mini-cassette player was an innovative, technologically complex, durable product. Respondents might not have the situational experiences that are described in the study. Further, it is also possible that, since mini-cassette players are expensive and the respondents in the study were mostly young people, it is not likely that mini-cassette players would be purchased as a gift for someone else.

CONTRIBUTIONS OF THE RESEARCH

It is felt that the research makes several contributions to marketing theory and practice. Each of these is discussed below.

Marketing theory

The theoretical contribution lies in the proposal and development of an explicit and comprehensive model for explaining consumer satisfaction/dissatisfaction. Very few researchers have proposed theories dealing with the impact of cultural values, usage situations, consumption experiences and affective experiences on consumer satisfaction in addition to expectations, perceived performance and disconfirmation. Even fewer have tested their conjectures. Most of the studies discussed in Chapters 2 and 3 were atheoretical in that explicit psychological or social processes were not hypothesized or tested. Alternatively, these studies tried to apply directly specific theories from related areas of the behavioural sciences in the hope of discovering a good fit.

Most of the latter applications were limited to relatively circumscribed and narrow aspects of behaviour in terms of both explanatory concepts and subjective matter. Rather than view the behaviour and feelings of consumers in a relatively holistic sense, much past research has focused on single or isolated characteristics of consumers such as personal competence, background attributes or attitudes, or on only intrapersonal determinants of satisfaction such as expectations, performance and disconfirmation. Without exception, the research findings have been mediocre at best.

The theory outlined in this study, in contrast, proposes a more comprehensive model that attempts to capture a relatively holistic view of consumer satisfaction. Not only are the theoretical variables defined and operationalized, but much of the theory is grounded in sound social, anthropological and pyschological processes. Further, the research results are, in general, acceptable and better than most previous efforts.

The research makes a contribution to consumer research and social psychology. First, it develops a scale for measuring Chinese cultural values. Unlike those of Rokeach (1968, 1973), Hofstede (1980) and Morris (1956), this scale has been developed for a Chinese culture and is based on the Chinese literature. The scale was tested and found to be both reliable and valid. This scale has succeeded in contributing to the understanding of consumer satisfaction. Furthermore, it also contributes greatly to the knowledge of 'global consumer behaviour' by attempting to develop consumer behaviour theory in the Chinese context. It then enables comparative studies with other cultures to be conducted so that generalizations can be made later.

Second, it hypothesizes a structural theory combining cognitive and affective aspects of behaviour with interpersonal and situational factors. It is one of the few theories explicitly explaining overt and subjective behaviour of consumers as a function of these variables. A portion of the model (i.e. expectations, performance and disconfirmation) operationalizes a sub-set of the Churchill and Surprenant (1982) model of consumer satisfaction. It goes further than Churchill and Surprenant's theory, however, in that it introduces intention as a dependent variable, and interpersonal aspects of behaviour (e.g. use situations, consumption experiences and affective experiences), types of products, and cultural values as independent variables. The research findings indicate that cultural values, types of products and use situations are better determinants of consumer satisfaction than other intra-personal determinants such as expectations, performance and disconfirmation.

Marketing practice

The research makes a number of contributions to marketing practice. The models and findings provide indications for developing marketing strategies. First, cultural values, usage situations and the product itself are determinants of expectations and satisfaction. In addition to the Chinese cultural value scale several Chinese cultural value dimensions have been identified and found to have an impact on satisfaction and expectations. This information may be useful in finding out who are the more satisfied consumers in terms of cultural values. Segmentation based on cultural values will be one of the methods used to achieve this objective.

The prestigious model and the basic model were found to have opposite effects on expectations and satisfaction. In most cases, consumers who have high expectations of a product tend to have a high evaluation of its performance, and vice versa. This indicates that in the Chinese culture managers should put more emphasis on the design of products so as to produce higher levels of satisfaction.

The findings also indicate the importance of usage situation in satisfaction with consumer products, especially non-durables. To date, marketers have neither proposed nor tested the relationships between usage situation, expectations and satisfaction. These findings, therefore, contribute to the theory of consumer satisfaction by establishing such links. The results also provide insights into the development of advertising copy for certain consumer products by advising consumers implicitly or explicitly how to consume or use the products in appropriate situations so that satisfaction can be increased.

Although consumption and affective experiences were found to have no significant impact on expectations and satisfaction, it is worth noting that the findings were in the expected direction. This implies that of past experiences of dissatisfaction with, and complaints about products may lead to dissatisfaction with the same or similar products in future consumption/use. Hence, it is paramount for managers to improve seller and buyer relationships by building up a communication mechanism which provides more and better service during the buying or shopping process, and after purchase. Word-of-mouth is an extremely important and effective way of communication among consumers in the Chinese culture. Managers should make use of it to convey the benefits of products to other consumers, but not grievances and complaints.

In the past, major variables of interest have been expectations, performance and disconfirmation. This bias is perhaps natural for marketers as they help to develop strategies in advertising and product information (Churchill and Surprenant 1982). However, the research indicates that, in general, disconfirmation appears to have greater impact on satisfaction than expectation and performance. It indicates that researchers and managers must direct more attention to the impact of disconfirmation on satisfaction. Furthermore, the findings also indicate that expectations have a negative impact on satisfaction.

This finding suggests that satisfaction could be increased by lowering expectations and increasing performance so as to maximize disconfirmation, which has a greater impact on satisfaction. Hence, even though the direct impact of performance on satisfaction is not great, it is unrealistic for managers to ignore the contribution of performance to the explanation of satisfaction. Managers often have a choice of what level of performance should be delivered to satisfy consumers, and performance must be designed to reach a level that will yield satisfaction through positive disconfirmation.

SUGGESTIONS FOR FUTURE RESEARCH

A number of suggestions can be made both for building upon the present study and for furthering our understanding of the process of consumer satisfaction. In addition to those presented below, suggestions for future research may be found throughout the discussion in Chapters 2 and 3.

The present model can be improved in a number of ways. Since results with respect to consumption experiences and affective experiences failed to appear as expected, it would be useful to find more reliable measures of these constructs. Consumption experiences will be operationalized through an explicit construction of objective measures indicating the absolute frequency of dissatisfied experiences with a variety of related products. In addition, age of consumers might be used as a measure of consumption experiences. There are two directions in which affective experiences could be operationalized. The first is to operationalize them with more specific and exhaustive items rather than using the four somewhat general items in the study. A sample of specific items is presented as follows:

1 To complain to friends.
2 To complain to family members.
3 To complain to the Consumer Council.
4 To complain to the manufacturer.
5 To complain to the store.
6 To return the product for a refund.
7 To take legal action.
8 To recommend others not to purchase.
9 To blame oneself.
10 To attribute the outcome to fate.

Furthermore, since most people are satisfied with the products they purchase or consume (Day and Bodur 1977; Leigh and Day 1979), measures of dissatisfied consumption experiences and affective experiences would probably have weak correlations with satisfaction or product expectations. A better way to cope with this problem would be using a sample of complainers.

Another area for research is the impact that purchase intention has on behaviour or consumer choice. The model in this study was regarded as comprehensive, even without incorporating behaviour or consumer choice in the model. However, it appears that there exists a difficulty in using intention to predict consumer choice. Foxall (1984) has attributed the difficulty to the high probability of expected and unexpected events which will intervene between the expression of an intention and the chance to perform the intended act. He further explains that

> it is inevitable that situational interventions will occur during the ensuing period and that correspondence between intentions and behaviour will be reduced accordingly. The implication is that the context in which buying will occur cannot be accurately predicted.
> (Foxall 1984: 235)

Hence, in order to have high correspondence between intention and consumer choice, situational influences which are considered as intervening variables should be considered and incorporated in the research design of future studies. It also seems that longitudinal research using consumer panels would be a better way to investigate whether consumers choose products they intend to purchase in a specific situation.

Additional insights into the process of consumer satisfaction can be gained by considering the degree of consumption or purchase involvement. Lastovicka and Gardner (1977) classified involvement into four types: physical involvement, financial involvement, social involvement and performance involvement. From a different angle, involvement can also be divided into low and high involvement (Engel 1983). Little research has been proposed using this perspective in studying consumer satisfaction. It is likely that the way that consumers are involved will have an influence on product expectations and their satisfaction with the products. That is, the more the consumer is involved in the buying or consumption process, the higher his expectations will be.

Finally, the question of whether or not the utilization of the scale of cultural values will add to the understanding of Chinese culture can only be answered on the basis of the cumulative evidence accruing from its use in research. With imaginative use, the scale provides an effective tool for selected consumer research for international marketers who wish to understand Chinese consumers. Research efforts could be directed to segmenting consumers, using the cultural values explored in the study. Since consumers with different cultural values would probably have different levels of satisfaction/dissatisfaction, it would be meaningful to understand these segments on the basis of satisfaction level, certain demographic and other personal characteristics, so that better marketing decisions could be made.

Research could also be directed to the determination of change in consumer discontent. As the study has found that some cultural values may have an impact on the level of consumer satisfaction, any findings on changes in these cultural values over time will be significant. Marketers will be interested to know the direction of changes and their long-term effect so as to develop relevant programmes to satisfy their consumers at a profit.

Chinese cultural values would not be expected to change rapidly within a short span of time. However, they could change in greater strides in places where modernization or economic development is moving rapidly e.g. Hong Kong, Singapore and Taiwan. Hence, the scale could also be used to compare consumers, their satisfaction and their behaviour in different Chinese societies or sub-cultures.

CONCLUDING REMARKS

This book ends with several concluding remarks. First, it is felt that the study hopefully contributes to the understanding of the cultural values of Chinese consumers by developing the Chinese Cultural Values Scale. This is the first research of this kind, and hopefully the scale and its underlying dimensions will be very useful to managers who are or will be marketing their products or services in Chinese societies, and to researchers who conduct comparative studies in relation to Chinese or Chinese consumers. Second, this study hopefully contributes to the knowledge of consumer behaviour by successfully constructing a more comprehensive model of consumer satisfaction/dissatisfaction. Some managerial implications which were also derived from relationships between variables (constructs) in the model would be valuable in helping managers develop effective marketing strategies. Finally, this study also contributes by providing a number of suggestions for building upon the present study and breaking new ground for enquiry into the behaviour of consumers.

Appendix A
The interview questionnaires

A translation into English of the original questionnaires administered in Chinese.

QUESTIONNAIRE FOR THE MINI-CASSETTE PLAYER SAMPLE

Recruitment starts here

Good morning/afternoon/evening, I am an interviewer of Marketing Strategy Decisions Company. We are now conducting a survey on consumer satisfaction for the Department of Marketing, the Chinese University of Hong Kong. Here is the sample letter which we sent to you some time ago. I hope that you have received it and were expecting our coming.

Would you please tell me which members of your family, who are over 18, ever buy mini-cassette players? Who is the oldest? Next. *Record the name, sex, and age of the member in the table below. Repeat for all members.*

Name	Sex	Age	1	2	3	4	5	6	7	8
1			1	2	1	3	4	2	6	7
2			1	2	2	1	2	5	5	1
3			1	1	3	2	3	4	7	4
4			1	1	2	4	1	6	4	6
5			1	2	1	1	5	6	2	5
6			1	1	2	4	5	3	1	3
7			1	1	3	3	3	1	7	2
8			1	2	1	2	1	4	3	8

Interviewer: select the right respondent and talk to him/her.

Good morning/afternoon/evening, I am an interviewer of Marketing Strategy Decisions Company, and am now conducting a survey for the Chinese University. Thank you for your interview.

1a Have you ever bought a mini-cassette player/recorder?
    Yes   1 (*Go to 1b*)
    No   2 (*Stop the interview*)

1b What was the brand you bought? _____
1c When did you buy or have it? _____

Section 1 The Chinese cultural values

Here are some common sayings which are in everyday use. I would like you
to think about how much you agree or disagree with them. There is no right
or wrong answer to these common sayings. You will find some of them that
you agree with and some of them that you disagree with. Here is a scale
ranging from 1 to 6. (*Show card no. 1.*) No. 1 stands for completely disagree,
and 6 stands for completely agree. In other words, the greater the number,
the more you agree with the saying.

		Strongly disagree					Strongly agree
1	A family will be prosperous if it is in harmony	1	2	3	4	5	6
2	Haughtiness invites ruin; humility receives benefits	1	2	3	4	5	6
3	The best strategy to deal with changes is not to change at all	1	2	3	4	5	6
4	Children should report everything to their parents	1	2	3	4	5	6
5	Reflect on our faults when we take a rest	1	2	3	4	5	6
6	The new generation is worse than the old	1	2	3	4	5	6
7	I will treat my teacher as my father even though he has bought me for one day	1	2	3	4	5	6
8	Reject an old man's advice and you'll soon pay for it	1	2	3	4	5	6
9	An eye for an eye	1	2	3	4	5	6
10	Live as it is predestined	1	2	3	4	5	6
11	He who submits to Heaven shall live; he who rebels against Heaven shall perish	1	2	3	4	5	6
12	Do all that is humanly possible and leave the rest to the will of providence	1	2	3	4	5	6
13	When in Rome, do as the Romans do	1	2	3	4	5	6
14	Blessings abound in a family that perseveres in good deeds	1	2	3	4	5	6
15	Life and death are fated; wealth and honours hinge on the will of providence	1	2	3	4	5	6
16	A family has its rules as a state has its laws	1	2	3	4	5	6
17	Forgive others whenever you can	1	2	3	4	5	6
18	At a different time and in a different place we will meet again	1	2	3	4	5	6
19	To have a son for old age is to stock provision for a rainy day	1	2	3	4	5	6
20	Children have to respect the decisions of their parents	1	2	3	4	5	6
21	Talk to people in their own language	1	2	3	4	5	6
22	Fate is predestined	1	2	3	4	5	6
23	Those against the laws should be punished	1	2	3	4	5	6
24	Live with your parents after marriage	1	2	3	4	5	6

25 Endure and you will find everything all right; retreat and you will find yourself happy	1	2	3	4	5	6
26 A man depends on his parents at home	1	2	3	4	5	6
27 Beyond a mountain, yet a higher one	1	2	3	4	5	6
28 Man can communicate with Nature and exist in harmony	1	2	3	4	5	6
29 If you honour me a linear foot, I should in return honour you ten feet	1	2	3	4	5	6
30 There is deceit in excessive courtesy	1	2	3	4	5	6
31 Shameful affairs of the family should not be spoken of outside	1	2	3	4	5	6
32 Unmarried children should make their parents well and strong	1	2	3	4	5	6
33 I won't offend others unless offended	1	2	3	4	5	6
34 If we want to criticize others, criticize ourselves first	1	2	3	4	5	6
35 Of the three practices of unfilial piety, having no son is the greatest	1	2	3	4	5	6
36 Old parents are just like a treasure in your house when living with you	1	2	3	4	5	6
37 A man who can survive in hardship is the man of men	1	2	3	4	5	6
38 Better bend than break	1	2	3	4	5	6
39 To please someone without a cause is either adulterous or greedy	1	2	3	4	5	6
40 Never forget what others have done to you	1	2	3	4	5	6
41 Face is honoured by others; shame is sought by ourselves	1	2	3	4	5	6
42 No matter what you are doing, don't go too far	1	2	3	4	5	6
43 It is more urgent to pay back favours than debts	1	2	3	4	5	6
44 Help each other whenever in need	1	2	3	4	5	6
45 I will return flavours and take revenge as well	1	2	3	4	5	6

Section 2. Mini-cassette player

3   Now, we would like you to do a simple experiment. Here are two pictures each showing a mini-cassette player and with a message about it. Please have a look at the pictures. (*Hand the pictures to the respondent. Wait for one or two minutes until he/she has finished reading it.*) Now, I'd like to ask you a few questions about these two cassette players.

3a   First, I would like to know how suitable this cassette (*Show the picture of cassette No. 1*) will be for use in the following situations.

Here is a six-point scale. If you think the cassette is completely appropriate for a situation, give a rating of 1; if you think the cassette player is completely inappropriate for a situation, give a rating of 6. (*Show card No. 2.*)

Now, tell me how appropriate is the cassette player to be used:

	Cassette player 1	*Cassette player 2*
(i) In private		
(ii) In public		
(iii) For yourself		
(iv) As a gift for someone else		

3b I would like you to do the same with this cassette. (*Show the picture of cassette No. 2.*) Tell me how appropriate the cassette is for use in each situation.

4 Now I'd like to know your overall expectations about the cassette in different situations. Here is a scale ranging from 1 to 6. No. 1 means that the cassette is not very good for a situation, and 6 means that the cassette is expected to perform excellently in a situation. (*Show card No. 3*).

4a How would you expect this cassette to perform if it is for use in each situation? (*Show the picture of cassette player No. 1.*)

	Cassette player 1	*Cassette player 2*
(i) To be used when you are alone		
(ii) To be bought as a gift for someone else and used when alone		
(iii) To be used when you are with other people		
(iv) To be bought as a gift and to be used with other people		

4b I'd like you to do the same with this cassette (*pointing at cassette player No. 2*). How would you expect it to perform if it is for use in each situation. (*Read the situations.*)

5 Here are some attributes of mini-cassettes that people I have spoken to have mentioned. How well do you think each cassette would perform on each attribute separately in each of the following situations? Please use the same scale. (*Show card No. 3.*)

5a Let's start with this cassette. (*Show the picture of cassette player No. 1.*) In the situation:

(i) To be used when you are alone
(ii) To be bought as a gift for someone else and used when alone
(iii) To be used when you are with other people
(iv) To be bought as a gift and to be used with other people

how do you expect (*read attribute 1–4 from the table below*) the cassette will perform?

5b I'd like you to do the same with this cassette. (*Show the picture of cassette player No. 2.*) (*Repeat 5a.*)

	Situation A Cassette player 1 2	Situation B Cassette player 1 2	Situation C Cassette player 1 2	Situation D Cassette player 1 2
Attribute				
1 Sound quality				
2 Convenience in carrying				
3 Sufficient functions for the situation				
4 Prestigiously pretty				

6 (*Take the pictures back from the respondent and take out the mini-cassette players from the bag.*) Here are the mini-cassettes which were shown in the pictures. Please try them. (*Give them to the respondent, and let him/her examine and try them for a while.*)

Do you want to know any other information about the products?

Yes   1   (*Answer the following question*)
No   2   (*Go to Question 6a*)

If yes, what do you want to know? (*Answer the respondent's questions with reference to the fact sheet.*)

6a Now let us see what you feel about the products. Imagine that you have purchased the cassette, and have used it in the previously mentioned situations. Here is a six-point scale. No. 1 means that the cassette is not very good for a situation, and 6 means that the cassette is expected to perform excellently in a situation. (*Show card No. 3 and point to the cassette no. 1.*) If the cassette continued to perform as it does now for at least six months, what would be your opinion about it then? (*Read the situations in turn.*)

	Cassette player 1	Cassette player 2
(i) To be used when you are alone		
(ii) To be bought as gift for someone else and used when alone		
(iii) To be used when you are with other people		
(iv) To be bought as a gift and to be used with other people		

6b I'd like you to do the same with this cassette (*Pointing at cassette player No. 2*). How would you expect it to perform if it is for use in each situation? (*Read the situations in turn.*)

6c Now, let us see how you perceive the performance of the cassette with respect to its attributes. Using the same scale, how do you perceive the performance of this cassette (*pointing at cassette player No. 1*) with respect to its (*read the attributes in turn*)?

Cassette player 1   *Cassette player 2*

1 Sound quality
2 Convenience in carrying
3 Sufficient functions for
  the situation
4 Prestigiously pretty

6d I'd like you to do the same with this cassette (*pointing at cassette player No. 2*). How would you expect it to perform with respect to this attribute? (*Read the attributes in rotation.*)

7 Now, I'd like you to tell me how your expectation regarding the performance of the cassette is confirmed under different situations.

Here is a six-point scale. No. 1 represents your overall expectations regarding the performance of the cassette as too high, that is to say, the cassette was worse than you thought it would be, 6 represents your overall expectations regarding the performance of the cassette as too low, that is to say, the cassette was better than you thought it would be. (*Show card No. 4.*)

7a (*Pointing at cassette No. 1*) Please tell me your overall expectation regarding the performance of the cassette when (*read each situation in turn*):

Cassette player 1   *Cassette player 2*

(i) To be used when you
    are alone
(ii) To be bought as a gift
    for someone else and
    used when alone
(iii) To be used when you
    are with other people
(iv) To be bought as a gift
    and to be used with
    other people

7b I'd like you to do the same with this cassette (*Pointing at cassette player No. 2*). What is your overall expectation of the performance of the cassette when (*read the situations in turn*)?

7c I'd like to know your overall expectations of the performance of each attribute separately in each of the following situations. Please use the same scale. (*Show card No. 3*).

Let's start with this cassette. (*Show the picture of cassette player No. 1.*) In the situation:

(i) To be used when you are alone
(ii) To be bought as a gift for someone else and used when alone

(iii) To be used when you are with other people
(iv) To be bought as a gift and to be used with other people

what is your expectation regarding the performance of (*read attributes 1–4 from the table below*) of the cassette?

7d   I'd like you to do the same with this cassette. (*Show the picture of cassette player No. 2*) (*Repeat 5a*).

	Situation A		Situation B		Situation C		Situation D	
	Cassette player		Cassette player		Cassette player		Cassette player	
Attribute	1	2	1	2	1	2	1	2
1 Sound quality								
2 Convenience in carrying								
3 Sufficient functions for the situation								
4 Prestigiously pretty								

8   Now, I'd like you to tell me how satisfied you are after trying the cassette. This time we use the same six-point scale. But 1 represents you are completely dissatisfied with the cassette and 6 represents you are completely satisfied with it. (*Show Card No. 5.*)

8a   (*Pointing at cassette No. 1*) Please tell me how satisfied you are when the cassette is (*read each situation in turn*)

	Cassette player 1	Cassette player 2
(i) To be used when you are alone		
(ii) To be bought as a gift for someone else and used when alone		
(iii) To be used when you are with other people		
(iv) To be bought as a gift and to be used with other people		

8b   I'd like you to do the same with this cassette (*pointing at cassette player No. 2*). Please tell me how satisfied you are when it is (*read the situations in turn*) . . .

8c   I'd like to do the same with each attribute of the cassette in the following situations. Please use the same scale. (*Show card No. 3.*)

Let's start with this cassette. (*Show the picture of cassette player No. 1.*) In the situation:

(i) To be used when you are alone
(ii) To be bought as a gift for someone else and used when alone
(iii) To be used when you are with other people
(iv) To be bought as a gift and to be used with other people

how satisfied are you with the performance (*read attributes 1–4 from the table below*) of the cassette?

8d I'd like you to do the same with this cassette. (*Show the picture of cassette player No. 2.*) (*Repeat 5a.*)

	Situation A Cassette player 1 2	Situation B Cassette player 1 2	Situation C Cassette player 1 2	Situation D Cassette player 1 2
Attribute				
1 Sound quality				
2 Convenience in carrying				
3 Sufficient functions for the situation				
4 Prestigiously pretty				

9 Now I'd like you to tell me your intention to purchase the cassettes, if they are available in the market with the same prices shown on pictures. Again, we use a six-point scale. No 1 represents that you would definitely not buy it; and 6 represents that you would definitely buy it.

9a How likely it is that you would purchase this cassette (*pointing at cassette No. 1*) for the situation? (*Read each situation in turn.*)

Cassette player 1   Cassette player 2

(i) To be used when you are alone

(ii) To be bought as a gift for someone else and used when alone

(iii) To be used when you are with other people

(iv) To be bought as a gift and to be used with other people

9b I'd like you to do the same with this cassette (*pointing at cassette player No. 2*). (*Repeat question No. 9a.*)

Section 3. Experiences

10a Have you ever bought or had a mini-cassette player?

Yes   1   (Answer 10b)
No   2

10b When did you buy or have it? _____

10c For the following few questions, we will use another six-point scale. On this scale, No. 1 represents that you have never experienced the case before, 6 represents that you experience the case very often. (*Show card No. 7.*)

	Never				Very often

Now, please tell me, how often do you buy cassettes which you find yourself dissatisfied with?   1 2 3 4 5 6

11 How often do you encounter purchases of products which you find you are dissatisfied with?   1 2 3 4 5 6

12	How often do you encounter purchases of electronic audio equipment which you find you are dissatisfied with?	1	2	3	4	5	6
13a	How often do you warn your family, your friends and neighbours not to buy, or decide to stop buying when you find yourself dissatisfied with some products?	1	2	3	4	5	6
13b	How often do you take actions like seeking redress from the firm, manufacturers, consumers, council, or legal action when you find yourself dissatisfied with some products	1	2	2	4	5	6
13c	How often do you think it is your fault in choosing products which you are dissatisfied with?	1	2	3	4	5	6
13d	How often do you think it is your fate that you choose products which you are dissatisfied with?	1	2	3	4	5	6

Section 4. Personal data

In order to help with the analysis of data, please give the following information about yourself. The information will be in strict confidence.

14   Sex

Male	1	☐
Female	2	☐

15   How old are you?

18–20	1	☐
21–25	2	☐
26–30	3	☐
35–40	4	☐
41–45	5	☐
46–50	6	☐
51–55	7	☐
56–65	8	☐
Above 65	9	☐

16   What is the highest level of education you have achieved?

No education	1	☐
Lower than primary	2	☐
Primary	3	☐
Some secondary	4	☐
Secondary	5	☐
Matriculation	6	☐
University and above	7	☐

17   What is your marital status?

Single	1	☐
Married	2	☐
Other	3	☐

18　How much do you earn each month?

20,000 and above	1	7,999–7,000	1
19,000–17,500	2	6,999–6,000	2
17,499–15,000	3	5,999–5,000	3
14,999–12,500	4	4,999–4,000	4
12,499–10,000	5	3,999–3,000	5
9,999– 9,000	6	2,999–2,000	6
8,999– 8,000	7	Under 2,000	7
		None	8

19　Geographical area

　　　　Hong Kong Island　1
　　　　　　　　Kowloon　2
　　　　　New Kowloon　3
　　　　New Territories　4

20　Housing type

　　　　　　　　Private　1
　　　　　Government　2
　　　　　　　Squatter　3
　　　Temporary housing　4

QUESTIONNAIRE FOR THE BALL-PEN SAMPLE

Recruitment starts here
Good morning/afternoon/evening, I am an interviewer of Marketing Strategy Decisions Company. We are now conducting a survey on consumer satisfaction for the Department of Marketing, the Chinese University of Hong Kong. Here is the sample letter which we sent to you some time ago. I hope that you have received it and were expecting our coming.

Would you please tell me which members of your family, who are over 18, ever buy ball-pens? Who is the oldest? Next. (*Record the name, sex, and age of the member in the table below. Repeat for all members.*)

Name	*Sex*	*Age*	1	2	3	4	5	6	7	8
1			1	2	1	3	4	2	6	7
2			1	2	2	1	2	5	5	1
3			1	1	3	2	3	4	7	4
4			1	1	2	4	1	6	4	6
5			1	2	1	1	5	6	2	5
6			1	1	2	4	5	3	1	3
7			1	1	3	3	3	1	7	2
8			1	2	1	2	1	4	3	8

Interviewer: select the right respondent and talk to him/her.
Good morning/afternoon/evening, I am an interviewer of Marketing Strategy Decisions Company, and am now conducting a survey for the Chinese University. Thank you for your interview.

1a Have you ever bought a ball-pen?
   Yes   1   (*Go to 1b*)
   No   2   (*Stop the interview*)
1b What was the brand you bought? _____
1c When did you buy or have it? _____

Section 1. The Chinese cultural values

Here are some common sayings which are in everyday use. I would like you to think about how much you agree or disagree with them. There is no right or wrong answer to these common sayings. You will find some of them that you agree with and some of them that you disagree with. Here is a scale ranging from 1 to 6. (*Show card No. 1.*) No. 1 stands for completely disagree, and 6 stands for completely agree. In other words, the greater the number, the more you agree with the saying.

	Strongly disagree			Strongly agree		
	1	2	3	4	5	6
1 A family will be prosperous if it is in harmony	1	2	3	4	5	6
2 Haughtiness invites ruin; humility receives benefits	1	2	3	4	5	6
3 The best strategy to deal with changes is not to	1	2	3	4	5	6
change at all	1	2	3	4	5	6
4 Children should report everything to their parents						
5 Reflect on our faults when we take a rest	1	2	3	4	5	6
6 The new generation is worse than the old	1	2	3	4	5	6
7 I will treat my teacher as my father even though	1	2	3	4	5	6
he has bought me for one day						
8 Reject an old man's advice and you'll soon pay	1	2	3	4	5	6
for it						
9 An eye for an eye	1	2	3	4	5	6
10 Live as it is predestined	1	2	3	4	5	6
11 He who submits to Heaven shall live; he who	1	2	3	4	5	6
rebels against Heaven shall perish						
12 Do all that is humanly possible and leave the rest	1	2	3	4	5	6
to the will of providence						
13 When in Rome, do as the Romans do	1	2	3	4	5	6
14 Blessings abound in a family that perseveres in	1	2	3	4	5	6
good deeds						
15 Life and death are fated; wealth and honours	1	2	3	4	5	6
hinge on the will of providence						
16 A family has its rules as a state has its laws	1	2	3	4	5	6
17 Forgive others whenever you can	1	2	3	4	5	6
18 At a different time and in a different place we will	1	2	3	4	5	6
meet again						
19 To have a son for old age is to stock provision for	1	2	3	4	5	6
a rainy day						
20 Children have to respect the decisions of their	1	2	3	4	5	6
parents						
21 Talk to people in their own language	1	2	3	4	5	6

22 Fate is predestined	1	2	3	4	5	6
23 Those against the laws should be punished	1	2	3	4	5	6
24 Live with your parents after marriage	1	2	3	4	5	6
25 Endure and you will find everything all right; retreat and you will find yourself happy	1	2	3	4	5	6
26 A man depends on his parents at home	1	2	3	4	5	6
27 Beyond a mountain, yet a higher one	1	2	3	4	5	6
28 Man can communicate with Nature and exist in harmony	1	2	3	4	5	6
29 If you honour me a linear foot, I should in return honour you ten feet	1	2	3	4	5	6
30 There is deceit in excessive courtesy	1	2	3	4	5	6
31 Shameful affairs of the family should not be spoken of outside	1	2	3	4	5	6
32 Unmarried children should make their parents well and strong	1	2	3	4	5	6
33 I won't offend others unless I am offended	1	2	3	4	5	6
34 If we want to criticize others, criticize ourselves first	1	2	3	4	5	6
35 Of the three practices of unfilial piety, having no son is the greatest	1	2	3	4	5	6
36 Old parents are just like a treasure in your house when living with	1	2	3	4	5	6
37 A man who can survive in hardship is the man of men	1	2	3	4	5	6
38 Better bend than break	1	2	3	4	5	6
39 To please someone without a cause is either adulterous or greedy	1	2	3	4	5	6
40 Never forget what others have done to you	1	2	3	4	5	6
41 Face is honoured by others; shame is sought by ourselves	1	2	3	4	5	6
42 No matter what you are doing, don't go too far	1	2	3	4	5	6
43 It is more urgent to pay back favours than debts	1	2	3	4	5	6
44 Help each other whenever in need	1	2	3	4	5	6
45 I will return favours and take revenge as well	1	2	3	4	5	6

Section 2. Ball-pen

3 Now, we would like you to do a simple experiment. Here are two pictures each showing a ball-pen and with a message about it. Please have a look at the pictures. (*Hand the pictures to the respondent. Wait for one or two minutes until he/she has finished reading it.*) Now, I'd like to ask you a few questions about these two pens.

3a First, I would like to know how suitable this pen (*Show the picture of pen No. 1*) will be for use in the following situations.

Here is a six-point scale. If you think the pen is completely appropriate for a situation, give a rating of 1; if you think the pen is completely inappropriate for a situation, give a rating of 6. (*Show card No. 2*)

Now, tell me how appropriate is the pen to be used

                                                          Pen 1   *Pen 2*

1 Quality in writing
2 Prestige
3 Good Appearance

3b I would like you to do the same with this pen. (*Show the picture of pen No. 2.*) Tell me how appropriate the pen is for use in each situation.
4 Now I'd like to know your overall expectations about the pen in different situations. Here is a scale ranging from 1 to 6. No. 1 means that the pen is not very good for a situation, and 6 means that the pen is expected to perform excellently in a situation. (*Show card No. 3.3*)
4a How would you expect this pen to perform if it is for use in each situation? (*Show the picture of pen No. 1.*)

                                                          Pen 1   *Pen 2*

   (i) To be used when you are alone
   (ii) To be bought as gift for someone else and
        used when alone
   (iii) To be used when you are with other people
   (iv) To be bought as a gift and to be used with
        other people

4b I'd like you to do the same with this pen (*pointing at pen No. 2*). How would you expect it to perform if it is for use in each situation? (*Read the situations.*)
5 Here are some attributes of ball-pens that people I have spoken to have mentioned. How well do you think each pen would perform on each attribute separately in each of the following situations? Please use the same scale. (*Show card No. 3.*)
5a Let's start with this pen. (*Show the picture of pen No. 1.*) In the situation:

   (i) To be used when you are alone
   (ii) To be bought as a gift for someone else and used when alone
   (iii) To be used when you are with other people
   (iv) To be bought as a gift and to be used with other people

   how do you expect (*read attributes 1–4 from the table below*) the pen will perform?
5b I'd like you to do the same with this pen. (*Show the picture of pen No. 2.*) (*Repeat 5a.*)

	Situation A		*Situation B*		*Situation C*		*Situation D*	
	Pen		*Pen*		*Pen*		*Pen*	
Attribute	*1*	*2*	*1*	*2*	*1*	*2*	*1*	*2*
1 Quality in writing								
2 Perestige								
3 Good appearance								

6   (*Take the pictures back from the respondent and take out the pens from the bag.*) Here are the ball-pens which were shown in the pictures. Please try them. (*Give them to the respondent, and let him/her examine and try them for a while.*)
    Do you want to know any other information about the products?

Yes   (*Answer the following question.*)
No   (*Go to Question 6a.*)

If yes, what do you want to know? (*Answer the respondent's questions with reference to the fact sheet.*)

6a Now let us see what you feel about the products. Imagine that you have purchased the pen, and have used it in the previously mentioned situations. Here is a six-point scale. No. 1 means that the pen is not very good for a situation, and 6 means that the pen is expected to perform excellently in a situation. (*Show card No. 3 and point to pen No. 1.*) If the pen continued to perform as it does now for at least six months, what would be your opinion about it then? (*Read the situations in turn.*)

	Pen 1	Pen 2

(i)   To be used when you are alone
(ii) To be bought as a gift for someone else and used when alone
(iii) To be used when you are with other people
(iv) To be bought as a gift and to be used with other people

6b I'd like you to do the same with this pen (*pointing at pen No. 2*). How would you expect it to perform if it is for use in each situation? (*Read the situations in turn.*)

6c Now, let us see how you perceive the performance of the pen with respect to its attributes. Using the same scale, how do you perceive the performance of this pen (*pointing at pen No. 1*) with respect to its (*read the attributes in rotation*)?

	Pen 1	Pen 2

1 Quality in writing
2 Prestige
3 Good appearance

6d I'd like to do the same with this pen (*pointing at pen No. 2*). How would you expect it to perform with respect to this attribute? (*Read the attributes in rotation.*)

7   Now, I'd like you to tell me how your expectation regarding the performance of the pen is confirmed under different situations.
    Here is a six-point scale. No. 1 represents your overall expectations regarding the performance of the pen as too high, that is to say, the pen was worse than you thought it would be, 6 represents your overall expectations regarding the performance of the pen as too low, that is to say, the pen was better than you thought it would be. (*Show card No. 4.*)

7a (*Pointing at pen No. 1.*) Please tell me your overall expectation regarding the performance of the pen when (*read each situation in rotation*):

	Pen 1	Pen 2

    (i) To be used when you are alone
    (ii) To be bought as a gift for someone else and
    used when alone
    (iii) To be used when you are with other people
    (iv) To be bought as a gift and to be used with
    other people

7b I'd like you to do the same with this pen (*pointing at pen No. 2*). What is your overall expectation of the performance of the pen when (*read the situations in turn*)?

7c I'd like to know your overall expectations of the performance of each attribute separately in each of the following situations. Please use the same scale. (*Show card No. 3.*)
Let's start with this pen. (*Show the picture of pen No. 1.*) In the situation:

    (i) To be used when you are alone
    (ii) To be bought as gift for someone else and used when alone
    (iii) To be used when you are with other people
    (iv) To be bought as a gift and to be used with other people

What is your expectation regarding the performance (*read attributes 1–4 from the table below*) of the pen?

7d I'd like you to do the same with this pen. (*Show the picture of pen No. 2.*) (*Repeat 5a.*)

Attribute	Situation A Pen 1 2	Situation B Pen 1 2	Situation C Pen 1 2	Situation D Pen 1 2
1 Quality in writing				
2 Prestige				
3 Good appearance				

8 Now, I'd like you to tell me how satisfied you are after trying the pen. This time we use the same six-point scale. But 1 represents you are completely dissatisfied with the pen and 6 represents you are completely satisfied with it. (*Show card No. 5.*)

8a (*Pointing at pen No. 1*) Please tell me how satisfied you are when the pen is (*read each situation in turn*):

	Pen 1	Pen 2

    (i) To be used when you are alone
    (ii) To be bought as a gift for someone else and
    used when alone
    (iii) To be used when you are with other people
    (iv) To be bought as a gift and to be used with
    other people

8b I'd like you to do the same with this pen (*pointing at pen No. 2*). Please tell me how satisfied you are when it is (*read the situations in turn*)...

8c I'd like you to do the same with each attribute of the pen in the following situations. Please use the same scale. (*Show card No. 3.*)

Let's start with this pen. (*Show the picture of pen No. 1.*) In the situation:

   (i) To be used when you are alone
   (ii) To be bought as a gift for someone else and used when alone
   (iii) To be used when you are with other people
   (iv) To be bought as a gift and to be used with other people

how satisfied are you with the performance (*read attributes 1–4 from the table below*) of the pen?

8d I'd like you to do the same with this pen. (*Show the picture of pen No. 2.*) (*Repeat 5a.*)

Attribute	Situation A Pen 1 2	Situation B Pen 1 2	Situation C Pen 1 2	Situation D Pen 1 2
1 Quality in writing				
2 Prestige				
3 Good appearance				

9 Now I'd like you to tell me your intention to purchase the pens, if they are available on the market with the same prices shown on pictures. Again, we use a six-point scale. No. 1 represents that you would definitely not buy it; and 6 represents that you would definitely buy it.

9a How likely it is that you would purchase this pen (*pointing at pen No. 1*) for the situation? (*Read each situation in turn.*).

	Pen 1	Pen 2
(i) To be used when you are alone		
(ii) To be bought as a gift for someone else and used when alone		
(iii) To be used when you are with other people		
(iv) To be bought as a gift and to be used with other people		

9b I'd like you to do the same with this pen (*pointing at pen No. 2*). (*Repeat question No. 9a.*)

Section 3. Experiences

10a Have you ever bought or had a ball-pen?

   Yes   1   (Answer 10b.)
   No   2

10b When did you buy or have it? _____

10c For the following few questions, we will use another six-point scale. On this scale, No. 1 represents that you have never experienced the case before, 6 represents that you experience the case very often. (*Show card No. 7*)

		Never				Very often	
	Now, please tell me, how often do you buy pens which you find yourself dissatisfied with?	1	2	3	4	5	6
11	How often do you encounter purchases of products which you find you are dissatisfied with?	1	2	3	4	5	6
12	How often do you encounter purchases of writing equipment which you find you are dissatisfied with?	1	2	3	4	5	6
13a	How often do you warn your family, your friends and neighbours not to buy, or decide to stop buying when you find yourself dissatisfied with some products?	1	2	3	4	5	6
13b	How often do you take actions like seeking redress from the firm, manufacturers, consumers' council, or legal action when you find yourself dissatisfied with some products?	1	2	3	4	5	6
13c	How often do you think it is your fault in choosing products which you are dissatisfied with?	1	2	3	4	5	6
13d	How often do you think it is your fate that you choose products which you are dissatisfied with?	1	2	3	4	5	6

Section 4. Personal data

In order to help with the analysis of data, please give the following information about yourself. The information will be kept in strict confidence.

14 Sex

| | Male | 1 |
| | Female | 2 |

15 How old are you?

	18–20	1
	21–25	2
	26–30	3
	35–40	4
	41–45	5
	46–50	6
	51–55	7
	56–65	8
	Above 65	9

16 What is the highest level of education you have achieved?

No education	1
Lower than primary	2
Primary	3
Some secondary	4
Secondary	6
Matriculation	6
University and above	7

17 What is your marital status?

Single	1
Married	2
Other	3

17 How much do you earn each month?

20,000 and above	1	7,999–7,000	1
19,000–17,500	2	6,999–6,000	2
17,499–15,000	3	5,999–5,000	3
14,999–12,500	4	4,999–4,000	4
12,499–10,000	5	3,999–3,000	5
9,999–9,000	6	2,999–2,000	6
8,999–8,000	7	Under 2,000	7
		None	8

19 Geographical area

Hong Kong Island	1
Kowloon	2
New Kowloon	3
New Territories	4

20 Housing type

Private	1
Government	2
Squatter	3
Temporary housing	4

Appendix B

Letter of notification

A translation into English of the original letter of notification in Chinese.

Dear Tenant,

Re: Consumer Satisfaction Research Project

I am writing to ask for your help with a research project currently being undertaken by the Department of Marketing and International Business, the Chinese University of Hong Kong. The objective of the research is to understand the determinants of consumer satisfaction. It is hoped that consumers may be benefited from the research as companies at large have more understanding about the behaviour of consumers.

The study entails personal interviews of households carefully selected from sub-samples of the census. Within two weeks' time, an interviewer of the Market Decision Research Co. will visit your household. He/She will wear a badge which identifies him/her as a member of the company, and carry a copy of this letter for identification purposes. In order to give the results more practical value, I very much need your co-operation in this project. If you have any queries, please contact me at 0-6352828, or Mr Lam at 0-6352824.

Again, I appreciate very much your co-operation.

Yours faithfully,

Oliver H.M. Yau
Department of Marketing and International Business.

Appendix C
The determination of the optimal sample size

Tull and Hawkins (1984: 410–14) have suggested several ways to determine the sample size of a research. The formula that is used to determine the size of the sample of the study is shown as follows:

$$n = (Z\delta)^2/e^2$$

where Z is the number of standard errors required to give a percentage level of confidence, e is the allowable error and is the standard deviation. From the formula, it is obvious that three kinds of specifications have to be made before the sample size necessary to estimate the population mean can be determined:

1 Specification of error (e) that can be allowed;
2 Specification of confidence coefficient; and
3 Estimate of the standard deviation.

If allowable error is to be set in relation to the mean rather than in absolute terms, allowable error has to be converted to relative allowable error as follows:

$$R = e/M$$

where M is the absolute mean.
    The standard deviation may also be expressed in terms of the mean. The relative standard error is called the *coefficient of variation*, denoted by the letter C. Hence, the equation for optimal sample size can be expressed as follows:

$$n = Z^2C^2/R^2$$

Now the standard error is set to be equal to 2.58, which is required to give a 99.5 per cent level of confidence. And the relative allowable error is 0.05 of the mean. In order to find out the third parameter of the equation, a pilot survey was conducted. (The sampling procedures and the results of the pilot survey are discussed at pp. 112–117.) Table 4.2 shows the mean satisfaction scores for ball-pens and mini-cassette players under four different situations. Since the values of Z and R are fixed, the coefficient of variation is the variable left to determine the sample size. The greater the coefficient of variation, the larger the sample size will be. For the ball-pen sub-sample, it was conservative that the greatest coefficient of variation, which is 0.348, was selected. Therefore, the sample size for the ball-pen sub-sample is

$$n = Z^2C^2/R^2$$
$$= (2.38)^2(0.349)^2/(0.5)^2$$
$$= 320$$

Similarly, the sample size for the mini-cassette player sub-sample is 318.

Appendix D

Correlations among multi-item measures of constructs: the ball-pen sample

Expectations

	Pen 1 attribute		Pen 2 attribute	
	1	*2*	*1*	*2*
Situation 1				
Attribute 2	0.520		0.533	
3	0.474	0.627	0.390	0.750
Situation 2				
Attribute 2	0.542		0.602	
3	0.348	0.720	0.450	0.783
Situation 3				
Attribute 2	0.517		0.613	
3	0.413	0.636	0.521	0.821
Situation 4				
Attribute 2	0.513		0.640	
3	0.394	0.741	0.616	0.833

Disconfirmation

	Pen 1 attribute		Pen 2 attribute	
	1	*2*	*1*	*2*
Situation 1				
Attribute 2	0.421		0.540	
3	0.324	0.653	0.498	0.807
Situation 2				
Attribute 2	0.440		0.605	
3	0.313	0.715	0.504	0.799
Situation 3				
Attribute 2	0.486		0.543	
3	0.362	0.738	0.460	0.830
Situation 4				
Attribute 2	0.401		0.639	
3	0.312	0.754	0.549	0.882

Satisfaction

Situation 1				
Attribute 2	0.546		0.603	
3	0.380	0.323	0.538	0.855
Situation 2				
Attribute 2	0.562		0.577	
3	0.374	0.717	0.571	0.861
Situation 3				
Attribute 2	0.539		0.590	
3	0.416	0.740	0.601	0.871
Situation 4				
Attribute 2	0.472		0.679	
3	0.421	0.815	0.630	0.892

Consumption experiences

		Scale	
		1	2
Scale	2	0.367	
	3	0.491	0.530

Appendix E
Correlations among multi-item measures of constructs: the mini-cassette player sample

Expectations

	Cassette player 1 Attribute			Cassette player 2 Attribute		
	1	*2*	*3*	*1*	*2*	*3*
Situation 1						
Attribute 2	0.418			0.412		
3	0.457	0.402		0.569	0.400	
4	0.500	0.466	0.535	0.475	0.488	0.573
Situation 2						
Attribute 2	0.478			0.453		
3	0.593	0.542		0.552	0.536	
4	0.492	0.528	0.605	0.496	0.524	0.599
Situation 3						
Attribute 2	0.514			0.497		
3	0.530	0.518		0.521	0.418	
4	0.557	0.539	0.598	0.530	0.473	0.581
Situation 4						
Attribute 2	0.511			0.477		
3	0.581	0.536		0.562	0.536	
4	0.587	0.609	0.700	0.512	0.470	0.592

Disconfirmation

	1	*2*	*3*	*1*	*2*	*3*
Situation 1						
Attribute 2	0.448			0.477		
3	0.540	0.549		0.636	0.527	
4	0.480	0.549	0.606	0.490	0.609	0.603
Situation 2						
Attribute 2	0.456			0.480		
3	0.547	0.501		0.625	0.568	
4	0.486	0.567	0.637	0.541	0.662	0.642

252 Consumer behaviour in China

Situation 3

Attribute						
2	0.492			0.528		
3	0.575	0.432		0.665	0.542	
4	0.503	0.544	0.629	0.530	0.671	0.648

Situation 4

Attribute						
2	0.487			0.497		
3	0.539	0.496		0.637	0.567	
4	0.497	0.576	0.653	0.590	0.658	0.675

Satisfaction

Situation 1

Attribute						
2	0.414			0.508		
3	0.571	0.498		0.550	0.609	
4	0.518	0.558	0.667	0.481	0.618	0.667

Situation 2

Attribute						
2	0.509			0.516		
3	0.595	0.652		0.559	0.611	
4	0.570	0.598	0.715	0.537	0.681	0.655

Situation 3

Attribute						
2	0.527			0.514		
3	0.599	0.601		0.563	0.610	
4	0.556	0.584	0.730	0.521	0.675	0.650

Situation 4

Attribute						
2	0.542			0.501		
3	0.620	0.623		0.569	0.598	
4	0.546	0.642	0.680	0.520	0.645	0.647

Consumption experiences

		Scale	
		1	2
Scale	2	0.319	
Scale	3	0.468	0.384

References

AAKER, D.A. *and* DAY, G.S. (1971), *Consumerism: Search for the Consumer Interest.* New York: Free Press.

ADAMS, J.S. (1963), 'Toward an understanding of Inequity', *Journal of Abnormal Social Psychology*, 67, pp. 422–36.

ADLER, R.D. *and* ROBINSON, L.M. (1980), 'A Consumer Satisfaction Model Based on Job Satisfaction Theory', in H. Keith Hunt and Ralph L. Day (eds), *Refining Concepts and Measures of Consumer Satisfaction and Complaining Behaviour.* Bloomington: Indiana University, pp. 19–22.

ADORNO, T.W. *et al.* (1950), *Authoritarian Personality.* New York: Harper & Brothers, p. 618.

AIELLO, A. *and* CZEPIEL, J.A. (1979), 'Customer Satisfaction in a Catalog-type Retail Store: Explaining the Effect of Product', in Ralph L. Day and H. Keith Hunt (eds) *New Dimensions of Consumer Satisfaction and Complaining Behaviour.* Bloomington: Indiana University, pp. 129–35.

AIELLO, A., CZEPIEL, J.A. *and* ROSENBERG, L.J. (1977), 'Scaling the heights of consumer satisfaction', in Ralph L. Day (ed.), *Consumer Satisfaction, Dissatisfaction and Complaining Behaviour.* Bloomington: Division of Research, School of Business, Indiana University, pp. 43–50.

AJZEN, I. *and* FISHBEIN, M. (1980), *Understanding Attitude and Predicting Social Behaviour.* Englewood Cliffs, N.J.: Prentice Hall.

ALLEN, V.L. (1965), 'Situational Factors in Conformity', in L. Berkowitz (ed.), *Advances in Experimental Social Psychology,* 2. New York: Academic Press.

ALLISON, N.K. (1977), *Consumer Alienation from the Marketplace: Scale Construction and Application.* Unpublished Ph.D. Dissertation, University of Texas at Austin.

ALLPORT, G.W. *and* VERNON, P.E. (1931), *The Study of Values.* Boston: Houghton Mifflin.

ANDERSON, R.E. (1973), 'Consumer Dissatisfaction: The Effect of Disconfirmed Expectancy on Perceived Product Performance', *Journal of Marketing Research,* 10 (February), pp. 38–44.

ANDREASEN, A.R. (1973), 'Consumer Dissatisfaction as a Measure of Market Performance', *Business Horizons*, 16, 4, pp. 30–8.

254   Consumer behaviour in China

—— (1977), 'A Taxonomy of Consumer Satisfaction/Dissatisfaction Measures', in H. Keith Hunt (ed.), *Conceptualisation and Measurement of Consumer Satisfaction and Dissatisfaction*. Cambridge Mass.: Marketing Science Institute (May), pp. 11–35.

—— (1979), 'Consumerism and Health Care Marketing', *California Management Review*, 2 (winter), pp. 89–94.

ASCH, S.E. (1956), 'Studies of Independence and Submission to Group Pressure: Minority of One against a Unanimous Majority', *Psychological Monograph*, 70 (9), Whole.

ASH, S.B. (1977), 'A Comprehensive Study of Consumer Satisfaction with Durable Products', in H. Keith Hunt (ed.), *Advances in Consumer Research*. Ann Arbor: Association for Consumer Research, pp. 254–62.

ASH, S.B. *and* QUELCH, J. (1980), 'Consumer Satisfaction, Dissatisfaction and Consumer Behaviour: A Comprehensive Study of Rentals, Public Transportation and Utilities', in H. Keith Hunt and Ralph L. Day (eds), *Refining Concepts and Measures of Consumer Satisfaction and Complaining Behaviour*. Bloomington: Indiana University, pp. 19–22.

ASH, S.B., GARDINER, D.F *and* QUELCH, J.A. (1982), 'Consumer Satisfaction and Dissatisfaction in the Elderly Market', in Ralph L. Day and H. Keith Hunt (eds), *New Findings on Consumer Satisfaction and Complaining*, Bloomington: Indiana University, pp. 86–96.

ASH, S.B, KENNEDY, J.R. *and* THIRKELL, P.C. (1980), 'Consumer Satisfaction with Product Warranties: A Study of Canadian Automobiles and Appliance owners', in H. Keith Hunt and Ralph L. Day (eds), *Refining Concepts and Measures of Consumer Satisfaction and Complaining Behaviour*. Bloomington: Indiana University, pp. 131–40.

AUSTIN, W. *and* WALSTER, E. (1974), 'Reactions to Confirmation and Disconfirmation of Expectations of Equity and Inequity', *Journal of Personality and Social Psychology*, 30, pp. 208–16.

BAGOZZI, R.P. (1978), *Toward a General Theory for the Explanation of the Performance of Salespeople*. Unpublished Ph.D. Dissertation, Northwestern University.

—— (1980), *Causal Models in Marketing*. New York: John Wiley & Sons Inc.

BANDURA, A. (1969), *Principle of Modification Behaviour*. New York: Holt, Rinehart & Winston.

—— (1970), *Aggression: A Social Learning Analysis*. Englewood Cliffs, N.J.: Prentice Hall Inc.

—— (1977), *Social Learning Theory*. Englewood Cliffs, N.J.: Prentice Hall, Inc.

BARKSDALE, H.C. *and* DARDEN, W.R. (1972), 'Consumer Attitudes toward Marketing and Consumerism', *Journal of Marketing*, 30 (October), pp. 28–35.

BARRON, F. (1953), 'An Ego Strength Scale which Predicts Response to Psychotherapy', *Journal of Consulting Psychology*, 17, pp. 327–33.

BEARDEN, W.D., *and* MASON, J.B. (1977), 'Consumer Satisfaction with Utilities', *ACCI*, 23rd Conference, April.

BEARDEN, W.D. *and* TEEL, J.E. (1983), 'Selected Determinants of Consumer Satisfaction and Complaint Reports', *Journal of Marketing Research,* 20 (February), pp. 21–8.

BEARDEN, W.D. *and* WOODSIDE, A.G. (1976a), 'Commentaries on Belk, 'Situational Variables and Consumer Behaviour', *Journal of Consumer Research,* 2 (December), p. 165.

—— (1976b), 'Interactions of Consumption Situations and Brand Attitudes', *Journal of Applied Psychology,* 61, (6), pp. 764–9.

BEARDEN, W.D., CROCKETT, M. *and* GRAHAM, S. (1980), 'Consumers' Propensity-to-Complain and Dissatisfaction with Automobile Repairs', in H. Keith Hunt and Ralph, L. Day (eds), *Refining Concepts and Measures of Consumer Satisfaction and Complaining Behaviour,* Bloomington: Indiana University.

BEARDEN, W.D., SHARMA, S. *and* TEEL, J.E. (1982), 'Sample Size Effects on Chi Square and Other Statistics Used in Evaluating Causal Models', *Journal of Marketing Research,* 19 (November), pp. 425–30.

BECHTEL, G.G. (1977), 'A Model for Monitoring Consumer Satisfaction', in H. Keith Hunt (ed.), *Conceptualisation and Measurement of Consumer Satisfaction and Dissatisfaction,* Cambridge, Mass.: Marketing Science Institute (May), pp. 187–214.

BELK, W.R. (1974), 'An Exploratory Assessment of Situational Effect in Buying Behaviour', *Journal of Marketing Research,* 11 (May), pp. 156–63.

—— (1975), 'Situational Variables and Consumer Behaviour', *Journal of Consumer Research,* 2 (December), pp. 157–167.

BEM, D.J. *and* ALLEN, A. (1974), 'On Predicting Some of the People Some of the Time: The Search for Cross-situational Consistencies in Behaviour', *Psychological Review,* 81, pp. 506–20.

BENTLER, P.M. (1980), 'Multivariate Analyses with Latent Variables: Causal Modelling', *Annual Review of Psychology,* 31, pp. 419–56.

BENTLER, P.M *and* BONETT, D.G. (1980), 'Significance Tests and Goodness of Fit in the Analysis of Covariance Structure', *Psychological Bulletin,* 88 (3), pp. 588–606.

BERG, J.A. *and* COLLIER, J.S. (1953), 'Personality and Group Differences in Extreme Response Sets', *Educational and Psychological Measurement,* 13 (February), pp. 164–9.

BERKOWITZ, L.N., GINTER, J.L. *and* TALARZYK, W.W. (1977), 'An Investigation of the Effects of Specific Usage Situations on the Prediction of Consumer Choice Behaviour', in B. Greenberg and D. Bellenger (eds), *Contemporary Marketing Thought.* Chicago: American Marketing Association, pp. 909–14.

BERNACCHI, E.N., KONO, J.L. *and* WILLETTE, W.W. (1980a), 'An Investigation of the Effects of Specific Usage Situations in the Prediction of Consumer Choice Behaviour', *Advances in Consumer Research,* 10, pp. 90–4.

—— (1980b), 'The Analysis of Automobiles Warranty Services Dissatisfaction', in H. Keith Hunt and Ralph L. Day (eds), *Refining Concepts and Measures of Consumer Satisfaction and Complaining Behaviour.* Bloomington: Indiana University, pp. 141–3.

BEST, A. *and* ANDREASEN, A.R. (1976), *Talking Back to Business: Voiced and Unvoiced Consumer Complaints.* Washington, D.C.: Centre for Study of Responsive Law.

BLALOCK, H.M., Jr. (1969), 'Multiple Indicators and the Causal Approach to Measurement Error', *American Journal of Sociology,* 75, pp. 264–72.

—— (1971), *Causal Models in the Social Sciences.* Chicago: Aldine Publishing Co.

BMDP (1977), *Biomedical Computer Programs P-series,* Berkeley, California: University of California Press.

BOND, M. (1985), personal communications.

BOOTE, A.S. (1975), 'Market Segmentation by Personal Values and Salient Product Attributes', *Journal of Advertising Research,* 21 (February, 1), pp. 29–35.

BOWERS, K.S. (1973), 'Situationism in Psychology: An Analysis and a Critique', *Psychological Review,* 80 (September), pp. 307–36.

BRADEN, J.L. (1977), 'Measuring Consumer Satisfaction with Automobile Repairs', in Ralph L. Day (ed.), *Consumer Satisfaction, Dissatisfaction and Complaining Behaviour.* Bloomington: Indiana University, p. 172.

—— (1979), 'Consumer Dissatisfaction Measurement Using Conjoint Analysis', in Ralph L. Day and H. Keith Hunt (eds), *New Dimensions of Consumer Satisfaction/Dissatisfaction and Complaining Behaviour.* Bloomington: Indiana University, pp. 62–8.

BRICKMAN, P. *and* BRYAN, J.H. (1975), 'Evaluation of Theft, Charity and Discontented Transfers that Increase or Decrease Equality', *Journal of Personality and Social Psychology,* 31, pp. 156–61.

BRUNNER CARROL, *and* BURNKRANT, R.E. (1975), 'Attribution Theory in Marketing Research Problems and Prospects', in M.S. Slinger (ed.), *Advances in Consumer Research,* 2, pp. 465–9.

BURKHARDT, V.R. (1955), *Chinese Creeds and Customs.* Hong Kong: The South China Morning Post Ltd.

CAMPBELL, D.R. *and* FISKE, D.W. (1959), 'Convergent and Discriminant Validation by the Multitrait-Multimethod Matrix', *Psychological Bulletin,* 59, pp. 81–105.

CAMPBELL, D.T. (1969), 'Reforms as Experiments', *American Psychologist,* 24 (4), pp. 409–29.

CARDOZO, R. (1964), 'Customer Satisfaction: Laboratory Study and Marketing Action', *Journal of Marketing Research,* 2 (August), pp. 244–9.

—— (1965), 'An Experimental Study of Consumer Effort, Expectations and Satisfaction', *Journal of Marketing Research,* 2 (August).

CAVUSGIL, S.T. *and* KAYNAK, E. (1982), 'A Framework for Cross-cultural Measurement of Consumer Dissatisfaction', in Ralph L. Day and H. Keith Hunt (eds), *New Findings on Consumer Satisfaction and Complaining.* Bloomington: Indiana University, pp. 80–4.

CHAN, W.T. (1963), *The Way of Lao Tsu (Tao-te ching),* New York: The Bobbs-Merrill Co. Inc.

CHEN, T.S. (1973), *1001 Chinese Sayings,* Hong Kong: Chung Chi College, The Chinese University of Hong Kong.

CHU, H.C. (1966), 'Culture, Personality and Persuability', *Sociometry,* 29, pp. 169–74.

CHU, C.L. (1973), 'On the Shame Orientation of the Chinese', in Li, Y.Y. and Yang, K.S. (eds) *Symposium on the Character of the Chinese: An Interdisciplinary Approach.* Taipei, Taiwan: Institute of Ethnology Academia SINICA, pp. 85–126. (In Chinese).

CHURCHILL, G.A., Jr. (1979), 'A Paradigm for Developing Better Measures of Marketing Construct', *Journal of Marketing Research,* 16 (February), pp. 64–73.

CHURCHILL, G.A. *and* SURPRENANT, C. (1982), 'An Investigation into the Determinants of Customer Satisfaction', *Journal of Marketing Research,* 19 (November), pp. 491–504

CLABAUGH, M. (1978), *Consumer Alienation: An Attribute of Consumer Dissatisfaction and its Influence on Complaint Behaviour.* Unpublished Doctoral Dissertation, University of Alabama.

CLABAUGH, M.G., MASON, J.B. *and* BEARDEN, W.O. (1979), 'Consumer Alienation and Causal Attribution as Moderators of Consumer Satisfaction/Dissatisfaction', in Ralph L. Day and H. Keith Hunt (eds), *New Dimensions of Consumer Satisfaction and Complaining Behaviour.* Bloomington: Indiana University, pp. 2–10.

CLARK, J.P. (1959), 'Measuring Alienation within a Social System', *American Sociological Review,* December, p. 849.

CLAWSON, G.J. *and* VINSON, D.E. (1978), 'Human Values: A Historical and Interdisciplinary Analysis', in H. Keith Hunt (ed.), *Advances in Consumer Research 5.* Ann Arbor: Association for Consumer Research, pp. 396–402.

CRONBACH, L.J. (1970), *Essentials of Psychological Testing.* 3rd ed., New York: Harper & Row.

CRONBACH, L.J. *and* MEEHL, P.E. (1955), 'Construct Validity in Psychological Tests', *Psychological Bulletin,* 52 (May), pp. 282–302.

CROW, C. (1937), *Four Hundred Million Customers.* London: Hamish Hamilton.

CROWNE, D.P. *and* MARLOWE, D. (1960), 'A New Scale of Social Desirability, Independent of Psychopathology', *Journal of Consulting Psychology,* 24 (August), pp. 349–54.

CZEPIEL, J.A. *and* ROSENBERG, L.J. (1977a), 'The Study of Consumer Satisfaction: Addressing the "So What" Question', in H. Keith Hunt (ed.), *Conceptualisation and Measurement of Consumer Satisfaction and Dissatisfaction,* Cambridge, Mass.: Marketing Science Institute (May), pp. 92–119.

—— (1977b), 'Consumer Satisfaction: Concept and Measurement', *Journal of Academy of Marketing Science,* 5 (fall, 4), pp. 403–11.

CZEPIEL, J.A., ROSENBERG, L.J. *and* AKERALE, A. (1975), 'Perspectives on Consumer Satisfaction', in R.C. Curhan, (ed.) *Combined Proceedings,* Chicago: American Marketing Association, pp. 51–5.

DAY, R.L. (1975), 'Consumer Satisfaction/Dissatisfaction with Services and Intangible Products', *Proceedings of the Marketing Research Seminar,* Marseille: Institut d'Ad des Entreprises, Université d'Aix.

—— (1977), 'Toward a Process Model of Consumer Satisfaction', in H. Keith Hunt (ed.), *Conceptualisation and Measurement of Consumer Satisfaction and Dissatisfaction,* Cambridge, Mass.: Marketing Science Institute (May), pp. 153–86.

—— (1978), 'Extending the Conception of Consumer Satisfaction', in W.D. Perreault, Jr. (ed.) *Advances in Consumer Research,* 6. Ann Arbor: Association for Consumer Research, pp. 149–54.

DAY, R.L. *and* ASH, S.B. (1978), 'Consumer Response to Dissatisfaction with Durable Products', pp. 438–48.

—— (1979), 'Comparison of Patterns of Satisfaction/Dissatisfaction and Complaining Behaviour for Durables, Nondurables and Services', in Ralph L. Day and H. Keith Hunt (eds), *New Dimensions of Consumer Satisfaction and Complaining Behaviour.* Bloomington: Indiana University, pp. 190–5.

DAY, R.L. *and* BODUR, M. (1977), 'A Comprehensive Study of Satisfaction with Consumer Services', in Ralph L. Day (ed.), *Consumer Satisfaction, Dissatisfaction and Complaining Behaviour,* Bloomington: Indiana University, pp. 64–74.

—— (1978), 'Consumer Response to Dissatisfaction with Services and Intangibles', in H. Keith Hunt (ed.), *Advances in Consumer Research,* 5. Ann Arbor: Association for Consumer Research, pp. 263–72.

—— (1979), 'Analysis of Average Satisfaction Scores of Individuals over Product Categories', in Ralph L. Day and H. Keith Hunt (eds), *New Dimensions of Consumer Satisfaction and Complaining Behaviour,* Bloomington: Indiana University, pp. 184–9.

DAY, R.L. *and* LONDON, E.L., Jr., (1977) 'Toward a Theory of Consumer Complaining Behaviour', in Woodside, A.G., Sheth, J.N. and Bennet, P.D. (eds), *Consumer and Industrial Buying Behaviour,* Amsterdam, Netherlands: North-Holland Publishing Co., pp. 425–38.

DAY, R.L. *and* QUELCH, J.A. (1977), 'A Comprehensive Study of Satisfaction with Consumer Services', Ralph L. Day (ed.), *Consumer Satisfaction, Dissatisfaction and Complaining Behaviour,* Bloomington: Indiana University, pp. 64–74.

DEAN, D.G. (1960), 'Alienation and Political Apathy', *Social Forces,* 38 (March), pp. 185–9.

—— (1961), 'Alienation: Its Meaning and Measurement', *American Sociological Review,* 26 (October), pp. 753–8.

DEMING, W.E. (1960), *Sampling Design in Business Research.* New York: John Wiley.

DESHPANDE, R. *and* ZALTMAN, G. (1979), 'The Satisfaction of Consumer Complainers with Consumer Protection Agencies', in Ralph L. Day and H. Keith Hunt (eds), *New Dimensions of Consumer Satisfaction and Complaining Behaviour,* Bloomington: Indiana University, pp. 145–52.

DILLON, W.R., *and* GOLDSTEIN, M. (1984), *Multivariate Analysis: Methods and Applications.* New York: Wiley.

DOHRENDWEND, B.S. (1965), 'Some Effects of Open and Closed Questions', *Human Organisation* (summer), pp. 175–84.

DUNCAN, O.D. (1969a), 'Contingencies in Constructing Causal Models', in E. F. Borgatta (ed.), *Sociological Methodology.* San Francisco: Jossey-Bass, pp. 74–117.

—— (1969b), 'Some Linear Models for Two Waves, Two Variables Panel Analysis', *Psychological Bulletin,* 72, pp. 177–82.

—— (1975), *Introduction to Structural Equation Models.* New York: Academic Press.

EDWARDS, A.L. (1957), *Techniques of Attitude Scale Construction.* New York: Appleton-Century-Crofts.

ENGEL, J.F. (1985a), Keynote Address in the International Conference entitled Historical and International Perspectives of Consumer Research jointly organized by the National University of Singapore and the Association for Consumer Research, Singapore, 18–20 July.

—— (1985b), 'Toward the Contextualisation of Consumer Behaviour', in J.N. Sheth, and T.C. Tan (eds), *Historical and International Perspectives of Consumer Research: Proceedings of International Conference in Singapore.* Singapore: National University of Singapore and Association for Consumer Research, pp. 1–4.

ENGEL, J.F., KOLLAT, D.T. *and* BLACKWELL, R.D (1968), *Consumer Behaviour.* New York: Holt, Rinehart & Winston Inc.

—— (1983), *Consumer Behaviour,* 3rd. ed. New York: The Dryden Press.

ENGLAND, G.W. (1975), *The Manager and his Values.* Cambridge Mass.: Ballinger.

FAIRCY, J.U. *and* MAGIZ, M.B. (1975), 'Personality and Consumer Dissatisfaction: A Multidimensional Approach', in E.M. Mazze (ed.), *Combined Proceedings,* Chicago: American Marketing Association, pp. 202–5.

FARLEY, J.U., HOWARD, J.A. *and* RING, L.W. (1974), *Consumer Behavior: Theory and Application,* Boston: Allyn & Bacon, Inc.

FESTINGER, L. (1957), *A Theory of Cognitive Dissonance,* New York: Harper & Row.

FISHBEIN, M. *and* AJZEN, I. (1975), *Belief, Attitude, Intention and Behaviour: An Introduction to Theory and Research,* Reading, Mass.: Addison Wesley.

FISHBURN, P.C. (1967), *Readings in Attitude Theory and Measurement.* New York: John Wiley.

—— (1968), *Utility Theory for Decision Making.* New York: John Wiley, p. 340.

FLETCHER, C. (1942), 'Homeostasis as an Exploratory Principle in Psychology', *Psychological Review,* 49, pp. 80–7.

FORNELL, C. (1976), *Consumer Input for Marketing Decisions: A Study of Corporate Departments for Consumer Affairs.* New York: Praeger.

—— (ed.) (1982), *A Second Generation of Multivariate Analysis,* New York: Praeger.

FOXALL, G. (1983), *Consumer Choice.* London: Macmillan.

—— (1984), 'Consumers' Intentions and Behaviour: A Note on Research and a Challenge to Researchers', *Journal of the Market Research Society,* 26, 3, pp. 231–41.

—— (1985), 'The Behavioural Analysis of Consumer Choice', in *Proceedings of Second World Marketing Congress.* Stirling: University of Stirling, pp. 406–18.

FULOP, C. (1979), *The Consumer Movement and the Consumer.* London: Advertising Association.

GOLDBERGER, A.S. *and* DUNCAN, O.D. (1973), *Structural Equation Models in the Social Sciences.* New York: Seminar Press.

GOLDBERGER, A.S. *and* KLEIN, L.R. (1964), *Econometric Model of the U.S.* New York: North-Holland.

260   *Consumer behaviour in China*

GREEN, P.E. *and* RAO, V.R. (1975), *Applied Multidimensional Scaling: A Comparison of Approach and Algorithms*. New York: Holt, Rinehart & Winston.
GREEN, P.E. *and* TULL, D. (1972), *Research for Marketing Decisions*. Englewood Cliffs, N.J.: Prentice Hall.
GREEN, P.E. *and* WIND, Y. (1975), 'New Way to Measure Consumers' judgments', *Harvard Business Review*. 53 (July–August), pp 107–17.
GREYSER, S.A. *and* DIAMOND, S.L. (1974), 'Business is Adapting to Consumerism', *Harvard Business Review*, 52, 5 (September–October), pp. 38–40.
GRONHAUG, K. (1972), 'Buying Situation and Buyers' Information Behaviour', *European Marketing Research Review*, 9 (February), pp. 65–8.
—— (1977), 'Exploring Complaining Behaviour: A Model and Some Empirical Results', *Advances in Consumer Research*, 4. Ann Arbor: Association for Consumer Research, pp. 159–63.
GRONHAUG, K. *and* ARNDT, J. (1980) 'Consumer Dissatisfaction and Complaining Behaviour as Feedback: A Comparative Analysis of Public and Private Delivery Systems', in J.C. Olson (ed.), *Advances in Consumer Behaviour*, 7. Ann Arbor: Association for Consumer Research, pp. 324–8.
GUTMAN, J. *and* VINSON, D.E. (1979), 'Value Structures and Consumer Behaviour', in W.L. Wilkie (ed.) *Advances in Consumer Research*, 6. Ann Arbor: Association for Consumer Research, pp. 335–9.
HAGER, C.J. *and* HANDY, C.R. (1979), 'Consumer Satisfaction and Prices', in Ralph L. Day and H. Keith Hunt (eds), *New Dimensions of Consumer Satisfaction and Complaining Behaviour*. Bloomington: Indiana University, pp. 72–8.
HAGGLUND, G. (1982), 'Factor Analysis by Instrumental Variable Methods', *Psychometrika*, 47 (2), pp. 209–22.
HAINES, G.H., Jr. (1979), 'Three Papers on Consumer Satisfaction/ Dissatisfaction: A Comment', in W.L. Wilkie (ed.), *Advances in Consumer Research*, 6. Ann Arbor: Association for Consumer Research, pp. 450–5.
HAJDA, J. (1961), 'Alienation and Integration of Student Intellectuals', *American Sociological Review*, 26 (May), pp. 758–77.
HANDY, C.R. (1977), 'Indexes of Consumer Satisfaction with Food Products: 1974 and 1976 Survey Results', in Ralph L. Day (ed.), *Consumer Satisfaction, Dissatisfaction, and Complaining Behaviour*. Bloomington: Indiana University, pp. 51–63.
HARMAN, H. (1967), *Modern Factor Analysis*. Chicago: University of Chicago Press.
HARRE, R. *and* SECORD, P.F. (1972), *The Explanation of Social Behaviour*. Oxford: Blackwell.
HARVEY, J.H., ICKES, W. *and* KIDD, R.F. (1978), *New Directions in Attribution Research*, 2. Hillsdale, N.J.: LEA.
HAWES, D.K. *and* ARNDT, J. (1979), 'Determining Consumer Satisfaction through Benefit Profiling', *European Journal of Marketing*, 13 (8), pp. 284–95.
HAWKINS, D.I., CONEY, K.A., *and* BEST, R.J. (1980), *Consumer Behavior: Implications for Marketing Strategy*. Dallas: Business Publications Inc.

HCHU, H.Y. *and* YANG, K.S. (1972), 'Individual modernity and psychogenic needs', in Y.Y. Li and K.S. Yang (eds), *Symposium on the Character of the Chinese,* Taipei: Inst. Ethnol. Academic Sinica, pp. 381–410 (in Chinese).

HEISE, D.R. (1969), 'Problems in Path Analysis and Causal Inference', in E.F. Borgatte (ed.) *Sociological Methodology,* San Francisco: Jossey-Bass, pp. 38–73.

—— (1975), *Causal Analysis,* New York: John Wiley & Sons Inc.

HELSEN, H. (1964), *Adaptation-level Theory: An Experimental and Systematic Approach to Behavior,* New York: Harper & Row.

HENRY, W.A. (1976), 'Cultural Values do Correlate with Consumer Behaviour', *Journal of Marketing Research,* 8 (May), pp. 121–7.

HMSO (1981), *A Year Book of the Commonwealth.* London: HMSO, p. 454.

HO, D.Y.F. (1972), 'On the Concept of Face', *American Journal of Sociology,* 81 (4), pp. 72–8.

HO, Ping-ti *and* TSOU, Tang (eds) (1972), *China in Crisis,* 2. Chicago: University of Chicago Press.

HOFSTEDE, Geert (1980), *Cultural Consequences: International Differences in Work-related Values.* Beverly Hills: Sage Publications.

HOLLANDER, E.P. (1967), *Principles and Methods of Social Psychology.* New York: Oxford University Press.

HONG KONG CONSUMER COUNCIL (1977), *Annual Report.* Hong Kong: Hong Kong Government Press.

—— (1979), *Annual Report.* Hong Kong: Hong Kong Government Press.

HONG KONG NEWS DIGEST (1984), Hong Kong: Hong Kong Government Press, 15 December, p. 5 (in Chinese).

HOWARD, J.A. (1977), *Consumer Behaviour: Application of Theory.* New York: McGraw-Hill.

HOWARD, J.A. *and* SHETH, J.N. (1969), *The Theory of Buyer Behaviour.* New York: John Wiley & Sons Inc.

HSU, F.L.K. (1947), *Under the Ancestors' Shadow: Kinship, Personality, and Social Mobility in China.* Stanford: Stanford University Press.

—— (1963), *Clan, Caste, and Club.* Princeton, N.J.: Van Nostrand Co.

—— (1968), 'Psychological Anthropology: An Essential Defect and its Remedy.' Paper presented at the 1968 annual meeting of the American Anthropological Association, Seattle, Wash.

—— (1970), *Americans and Chinese: Passage to Differences,* 3rd ed. Honolulu: The University Press of Hawaii.

—— (1971), 'Psycho-social Homeostasis and Jen: Conceptual Tools for Advancing Psychological Anthropology', *American Anthropologist,* 73, pp. 23–44.

—— (1972) 'Chinese Kinship and Chinese Behaviour', in P.T. Ho and T. Tsou (eds), *China in Crisis,* 2. Chicago: University of Chicago Press.

HU, H.C. (1944), 'The Chinese Concept of Face', *American Anthropologist,* 46 (January–March), pp. 45–64.

HUBER, J. (1976), 'Ideal Point Models of Preference', in *Combined Proceedings.* Chicago: American Marketing Association, pp. 138–42.

262 Consumer behaviour in China

HUGHES, D.A. (1977a), 'An Investigation of the Relation of Selected Factors to Consumer Satisfaction', in H. Keith Hunt (ed.), *Conceptualisation and Measurement of Consumer Satisfaction and Dissatisfaction*. Cambridge Mass.: Marketing Science Institute (May), pp. 300–32.

—— (1977b), 'CS/D Related to Price Paid', in R.L. Day (ed.), *Consumer Satisfaction, Dissatisfaction and Complaining Behaviour*. Bloomington: Indiana University.

HULL, C.H. *and* NIE, N.H. (1981), *SPSS Update 7–9: New Procedures and Faculties for Releases 7–9*. New York: McGraw-Hill.

HUNG, K.C. *and* LEUNG, D.Y. (1977), 'Consumerism in Hong Kong.' Research Monograph. Hong Kong: Chung Chi College, The Chinese University of Hong Kong.

HUNT, H.K. (1977), 'CS/D – Overview and Future Research Directions', in H. Keith Hunt (ed.), *Conceptualisation and Measurement of Consumer Satisfaction and Dissatisfaction*. Cambridge Mass.: Marketing Science Institute (May), pp. 455–88.

HUNT, J.M. (1980), 'Consumer Responses to Inequitable Economic Exchanges: An Attribution Theoretical Analysis', in H. Keith Hunt and Ralph L. Day (eds), *Refining Concepts and Measures of Consumer Satisfaction and Complaining Behaviour*. Bloomington: Indiana University, pp. 23–8.

HUPPERTZ, J.W. (1979), 'Measuring Components of Equity in the Marketplace: Perceptions of Inputs and Outcomes by Satisfied and Dissatisfied Consumers', in Ralph L. Day and H. Keith Hunt (eds), *New Dimensions of Consumer Satisfaction and Complaining Behaviour*. Bloomington: Indiana University, pp. 140–3.

HUSTAD, T.P. *and* PESSEMIER, E.A. (1973), 'Will the Real Consumer Activist Please Stand Up? An Examination of Consumers' Opinions about Marketing Practices', *Journal of Marketing Research*, 10 (August), pp. 319–24.

INKELES, A. *and* LEVINSON, D.L. (1954), 'National Character: The Study of Modal Personality and Socio-cultural System', in G. Lindzey (ed.), *Handbook of Social Psychology*, 4. Reading, Mass.: Addison Wesley.

JACO, E.G. (1954), 'The Social Isolation Hypothesis and Schizophrenia', *American Sociological Review*, 19 (October), pp. 567–77.

JARVIE, I.C. *and* AGASSI, J. (1969), *Hong Kong: A Society in Transition*. London: Routledge & Kegan Paul.

JOHNSTON, J. (1972). *Econometric Models*, New York: McGraw-Hill.

JONES, E.E., *et al* (1972), *Attribution: Perceiving the Causes of Behavior*. Morristown, N.J.: General Learning Press.

JONES, M.G. (1975), 'Consumer Interest: The Role of Business', in Ferrel, O.C. and La Garce, Raymond (eds), *Public Policy Issues in Marketing*, Lexington, Mass.: Lexington Books.

JONES, M.G. *and* GARDNER, D.M. (1976), *Consumerism: A New Force in Society*. Lexington Mass.: D.C. Heath, Lexington Books.

JORESKOG, K.G. (1969), 'A General Approach to Confirmatory Maximum Likelihood Factor Analysis', *Psychometrika*, 34 (June), pp. 183–202.

—— (1970), 'A General Method for Analysis of Covariance Structure', *Biometrika*, 57 (2), pp. 229–51.

—— (1979), *Advances in Factor Analysis and Structural Equation Models.* New York: Abt Books.

JORESKOG, K.G. *and* SORBOM, D. (1982), 'Recent Developments in Structural Equation Modelling', *Journal of Marketing Research,* 19 (November), pp. 440–56.

—— (1985), *Analysis of Linear Structural Relationships by the Method of Maximum Likelihood: Lisrel VI.* Chicago: National Education Resources.

KAKKAR, P. *and* LUTZ, R.J. (1975), 'Toward a Taxonomy of Consumption Situations', *Proceedings of American Marketing Association.* Chicago: American Marketing Association, pp. 206–10.

—— (1981), 'Situational Influence on Consumer Behaviour: A Review', in H.H. Kassarjian and T.S. Robertson (eds), *Perspectives in Consumer Behaviour,* second edition. Glenview: Scott Foresman, pp. 204–15.

KASMAR, J. (1970), 'The Development of a Usable Lexicon of Environmental Descriptors', *Environment Behaviour,* 2, pp. 153–69.

KASSARJIAN, H.H. (1971), 'Personality and Consumer Behaviour: A Review', *Journal of Marketing Research,* 8 (November), pp. 409–18.

KASSARJIAN, H.H. *and* ROBERTSON, T.S. (eds) (1978), *Perspectives in Consumer Behaviour,* second edition. Glenview: Scott Foresman & Co.

KELLEY, H. (1967), 'Attribution Theory in Social Psychology', in David Levine (ed.), *Nebraska Symposium on Motivation,* Lincoln: University of Nebraska Press.

KENNEDY, J.R. *and* THIRKELL, P.C. (1980), 'The Effect of Automobiles Product Experience on Attribute Disconfirmation and Importance', in Ralph L. Day (ed.), *New Findings in Consumer Satisfaction and Complaining Behaviour,* Bloomington: Indiana University, pp. 2–10.

KINDLE, I. (1982), 'A Partial Theory of Chinese Consumer Behaviour: Marketing Strategy Implications', *Hong Kong Journal of Business Management,* 1, pp. 97–109.

—— (1985), 'Chinese Consumer Behaviour: Historical Perspective plus an Update on Communication Hypotheses', in J. Sheth and C.T. Tan (eds), *Historical Perspective of Consumer Research.* Singapore: National University of Singapore and Association for Consumer Research, pp. 186–90.

KING, A.U.C. *and* MYERS, J.R. (1977), 'Shame as an Incomplete Conception of Chinese Culture: A Study of Face', Research Monograph. Hong Kong: Social Research Institute, The Chinese University of Hong Kong.

KINNEAR, T.C. *and* TAYLOR, J.R. (1983), *Marketing Research: An Applied Approach,* 2nd ed. New York: McGraw-Hill.

KINNEAR, T.C., TAYLOR, J.R. *and* AHMED, S.A. (1974), 'Ecologically Concerned Consumers: Who Are they?', *Journal of Marketing,* 38 (April), pp. 20–4.

KISH, L. (1965), Survey Sampling, New York: John Wiley.

KLUCKHOHN, C. (1951), 'Values and Value-Orientations in the Theory of Action: An Exploration in Definition and Classification', in T. Parsons and E.A. Shils (eds), *Toward a General Theory of Action,* New York: Harper & Row, pp. 388–432.

KLUCKHOHN, C. (1954), 'Culture and Behaviour', in G. Lindzey (ed.), *Handbook of Social Psychology,* Reading, Mass.: Addison Wesley, pp. 921–76.

264   *Consumer behaviour in China*

KLUCKHOHN, F.R. *and* STRODTBECK, F.L. (1961), *Variations in Value Orientations.* Evanston, Ill: Row-Peterson.
KRAFT, F.B. (1977), 'Characteristics of Consumer Complainers and Complaint and Repatronage Behaviour', in Ralph L. Day (ed.), *Consumer Satisfaction, Dissatisfaction, and Complaining Behaviour,* Bloomington: Indiana University, pp. 79–84.
KRISHNAN, S. *and* VALLE, V.A. (1978), 'Dissatisfaction Attributions and Consumer Complaining Behaviour', in *Proceedings of American Marketing Association.* Chicago: American Marketing Association, pp. 445–9.
KROEBER, A.L. *and* KLUCKHOHN, F.R. (1952), 'Culture: a Critical Review of Concepts and Definitions', *Peabody Museum,* Cambridge Mass.: 7, 1, p. 27.
KROEBER, A.L. *and* PARSONS, T. (1958), 'The Concept of Culture and Social System', *American Sociological Review,* 23, pp. 582–3.
LA BARRE, W. (1946), 'Some Observations on Character Structure in the Orient', *Psychiatry,* 9, pp. 375–95.
LAI, T.C. (1970), *Selected Chinese Sayings,* Hong Kong: University Book Store.
LAMBERT, Z.V. (1976), 'Consumer Alienation: Some Correlates of Discontent'. Working Paper, College of Business Administration, The University of Florida, September.
LAMBERT, Z.V. *and* KIFFIN, F.W. (1975), 'Consumer Discontent: A Social Perspective', *California Management Review,* 18 (fall, 1), pp. 36–44.
LASTOVICKA, J.L. *and* GARDNER, D.M. (1977), 'Components of Involvement', in Maloney, J.C. (ed.), *Attitude Research Plays for High Stakes.* Chicago, ILL.: American Marketing Association.
LA TOUR, S.A. *and* PEAT, N.C. (1979), 'Conceptual and Methodological Issues in Consumer Satisfaction Research', in W. L. Wilkie, (ed.), *Advances in Consumer Research.* Chicago: Association for Consumer Research, pp. 432–7.
LEAVITT, Clark (1977), 'Consumer Satisfaction and Dissatisfaction: Bipolar or Independent', in H. Keith Hunt (ed.), *Conceptualisation and Measurement of Consumer Satisfaction and Dissatisfaction,* Cambridge, Mass.: Marketing Science Institute (May), pp. 132–52.
LEGGE, J. (1960), *The Chinese Classics,* 1. Hong Kong: Hong Kong University Press.
—— (1970), *The Works of Mencius.* New York: Dover Publications, Inc.
LEIGH, T.W. *and* DAY, R.L. (1979), 'Satisfaction/Dissatisfaction, Complaining Behaviour with Non-durable Products', in Ralph L. Day and H. Keith Hunt (eds), *New Dimensions of Consumer Satisfaction and Complaining Behaviour,* Bloomington: Indiana University, pp. 170–83.
LESSIG, V.P. (1973), 'Consumer Values and Brand Preference', *AIDS Proceedings, 1973,* American Institute for Decision Sciences, pp. 1–3.
—— (1975), 'Measurement of Dependencies between Values and other Levels of Consumers' Belief Space', *Journal of Business Research,* 3, (83), pp. 227–41.
LESSIG, V.P. *and* TOLLEFSON, J.O. (1973), 'Prediction of Buying Behaviour from Personal Characteristics', *European Research,* 1, September, pp. 184–9.

LEVY, S.J. *and* CZEPIEL, J.A. (1974), 'Marketing and Aesthetics'. Paper Presented at American Marketing Association Educators Conference, Portland, Oregon (August).

LIEFELD, J.P., EDGECOMBE, F.H.C. *and* WOLFE, L. (1975), 'Demographic Characteristics of Canadian Consumer Complainers', *Journal of Consumer Affairs,* 9 (summer), pp. 73–80.

LIN, W.T. (1966), 'Chinese Value Orientations in Hong Kong', *Sociological Analysis,* 27, pp. 53–66.

LIN, Yutang (1949), *The Wisdom of China,* London: Michael Joseph.

LINGOES, J.C. and PFAFF, M. (1972), 'The Index of Consumer Satisfaction Methodology', *Proceedings of Association for Consumer Research,* Provo, Utah: ACR, pp. 689–712.

LINTON, R. (1945), *The Cultural Background of Personality.* New York: Appleton-Century-Crofts.

LONG, J.S. (1981), 'Estimation and Hypothesis Testing in Linear Models Containing Measurement Error', in P.V. Marsden (ed.), *Linear Models in Social Research.* Beverly Hills: Sage Publications, pp. 209–56.

LUNDSTROM, W.J. (1974), *The Development of a Scale to Measure Consumer Discontent.* Unpublished Ph.D. Dissertation, The University of Colorado.

LUNDSTROM, W.J. *and* KERIN, R. (1976), 'Psychological and Demographic Correlates of Consumer Discontent', in H.C. Schneider (ed.), *AIDS Proceedings 1976,* American Institute for Decision Science, p. 488.

LUNDSTROM, W.J. *and* LAMONT, L.M. (1976), 'The Development of a Scale to Measure Consumer Discontent', *Journal of Marketing Research,* 8 (November), pp. 373–81.

LUNDSTROM, W.J., SKELLY, G.U. *and* SCIGLIMPAGLIA, D. (1979), 'How Deep Are the Roots of Consumer Discontent? A Study of Rural Consumers', in Ralph L. Day and H. Keith Hunt (eds), *New Dimensions of Consumer Satisfaction and Complaining Behaviour.* Bloomington: Indiana University, pp. 153–6.

LUTZ, R.J. *and* KAKKAR, P. (1974), 'The Psychological Situation as a Determinant of Consumer Behaviour', in M.J. Schlinger (ed.), *Advances in Consumer Research,* 2. Ann Arbor: Association of Consumer Research, pp. 439–54

—— (1976), 'Situational Influences in Interpersonal Persuasion', in B.B. Anderson (ed.), *Advances in Consumer Research,* 3. Ann Arbor: Association for Consumer Research, pp. 370–8.

MACIVER, R. (1950), *The Ramparts We Guard.* New York: Macmillan, pp. 84–7.

MADDOX, R.N. (1977), 'Consumer Satisfaction with Supermarkets: A Factor Analytic Study', in Ralph L. Day (ed.), *Consumer Satisfaction, Dissatisfaction and Complaining Behaviour.* Bloomington: Indiana University, pp. 163–6.

—— (1981), 'Two Factor Theory and Consumer Satisfaction: Replication and Extension', *Journal of Consumer Research,* 8, 1 (June), pp. 97–102.

MAGNUSSON, D. (1981), *Toward a Psychology of Situation: An Interactional Perspective.* Hillsdale, N.J.: Lawrence Erlbaum.

MAGNUSSON, D. *and* EKEHAMMAR, B.O. (1978), 'Similar Situations – Similar Behaviours?', *Journal of Research in Personality,* 12, pp. 41–8.

266   *Consumer behaviour in China*

MAGNUSSON, D. *and* ENDLER, N.S. (1977a), *Personality at the Cross-roads: Current Issues in Interactional Psychology.* Hillsdale, N.J.: Lawrence Erlbaum.
—— (1977b), *Interactional Psychology: Current Issues and Future Prospects.* Hillsdale, N.J.: Lawrence Erlbaum.
MAGNUSSON, D. *and* STATTIN, H. (1978), 'Threatening Situations: A Conceptual and Empirical Analysis', Manuscript, Department of Psychology, University of Stockholm.
MALINVAUD, A. (1970), *Statistical Methods in Econometrics.* New York: North Holland/Elsevier.
MARKET DECISION RESEARCH COMPANY (1985) internal research report, Hong Kong: Market Decision Research Company.
MARKIN, J., Jr. (1974), *Consumer Behavior: A Cognitive Orientation.* New York: Macmillan Publishing Co.
MARSDEN, P.V. (ed.) (1981), *Linear Models in Social Research.* Beverley Hills: Sage Publications.
MASON, J.B. *and* BEARDEN, W.O. (1979), 'Satisfaction/Dissatisfaction with Food Shopping among Elderly Consumers', *Journal of Consumer Affairs,* 13, 2 (winter), pp. 359–69.
MASON, J.B. *and* HIMES, S.H., Jr. (1973), 'An Exploratory Behavioural and Socio-economic Profile of Consumer Action about Dissatisfaction with Selected Household Appliances', *Journal of Consumer Affairs,* 2, 7, 2, pp. 119–27.
MASON, J.B., BEARDEN, W.O. *and* M. CROKETTE (1982), 'Comparative Study of Elderly Marketplace Satisfaction', in Ralph L. Day and H. Keith Hunt (eds), *New Findings on Consumer Satisfaction and Complaining Behaviour.* Bloomington: Indiana University, pp. 103–10.
MATTSON, B.E. (1982), 'Situational Influences on Store Choice', *Journal of Retailing,* 3 (fall), pp. 46–58.
MCNEAL, J.U. (1969), 'Consumer Satisfaction: The Measure of Marketing Effectiveness', *MSU Business Topics,* 17, 3 (summer), pp. 31–5.
MEHRABIAN, A. *and* RUSSELL, J.A. (1974), *An Approach to Environmental Psychology.* Cambridge, Mass.: MIT Press.
MILLER, J.A. (1970), 'Who is the Discontented Consumer?' in T.V. Greer, (ed.), *Combined Proceedings,* Chicago: American Marketing Association, pp. 486–90.
—— (1976), 'Store Satisfaction and Aspiration Theory: A Conceptual Basis for Studying Consumer Discontent', *Journal of Retailing,* 52 (fall, 3), pp. 65–84
—— (1977), 'Exploring Satisfaction Modifying Models, Eliciting Expectations, Posing Problems, and Making Meaningful Measurements', in H. Keith Hunt (ed.), *Conceptualisation and Measurement of Consumer Satisfaction and Dissatisfaction,* Cambridge, Mass.: Marketing Science Institute (May), pp. 72–91.
MIZERSKI, R.W. (1982), 'An Attribution Explanation of the Disproportionate Influence of Unfavourable Information', *Journal of Consumer Research,* 9, 3 (December), pp. 301–10.
MORRIS, C. (1956), *Varieties of Human Value.* Chicago: University of Chicago Press.

MORRIS, E.W., WINTER, M. *and* CRULL, S.R. (1979), 'Transformation and Weighting of Items in the Measurement of Satisfaction', in H. Keith Hunt and Ralph L. Day (eds), *Refining Concepts and Measures of Consumer Satisfaction and Complaining Behaviour,* Bloomington: Indiana University, pp. 81–5.

MOSER, C.A. *and* KALTON, G. (1971), *Survey Methods in Social Investigation,* 2nd ed. London: Heinemann Educational Books.

MUN, K.C. *and* YAU, O.H.M. (1979), *Marketing Research: Basic Methods.* Hong Kong: The Chinese University Press. (In Chinese.)

MUNSON, J.M. *and* MCINTYRE, S.H. (1978), 'Personal Values: A Cross-cultural Assessment of Self-values and Values Attributed to a Distant Cultural Stereotype', *Advances in Consumer Research,* 5, pp. 160–6.

NETTLER, G. (1957), 'A Measure of Alienation', *American Sociological Review,* 22 (December), pp. 870–7.

NICOSIA, F.M. (1966), *Consumer Decision Processes.* Englewood Cliffs, N.J.: Prentice Hall, Inc.

NICOSIA, F.M. *and* MAYER, R.N. (1976), 'Toward a Sociology of Consumption', *Journal of Consumer Research,* 3, pp. 65–77.

NIE, N. *and* HULL, C.H. (1976), *SPSS: Statistical Package for Social Sciences,* New York: McGraw-Hill.

NUNNALLY, J.C. (1967), *Psychometric Theory,* New York: McGraw-Hill, p. 87.

—— (1978), *Psychometric Theory,* 2nd ed. New York: McGraw-Hill.

OLANDER, F. (1977a), 'Consumer Satisfaction – a Skeptic's View', in H. Keith Hunt (ed.), *Conceptualisation and Measurement of Consumer Satisfaction and Dissatisfaction.* Cambridge Mass.: Marketing Science Institute (May), pp. 409–54.

—— (1977b), 'Can Consumer Dissatisfaction and Complaints Guide Public Consumer Policy?', *Journal of Consumer Policy,* 11 (2), pp. 125–37.

OLIVER, Richard (1977), 'A Theoretical Reinterpretation of Expectation and Disconfirmation Effects on Posterior Product Evaluation: Experiences in the Field', in Ralph Day (ed.), *Consumer Satisfaction, Dissatisfaction and Complaining Behaviour,* Bloomington: Indiana University, pp. 2–9.

—— (1979), 'Product Satisfaction as a Function of Prior Expectation and Subsequent Disconfirmation: New Evidence', in Ralph Day and H. Keith Hunt, (eds), *New Dimensions of Consumer Satisfaction and Complaining Behaviour,* Bloomington: Indiana University, pp. 66–71.

—— (1980a), 'Theoretical Bases of Consumer Satisfaction Research: Review, Critique, and Future Direction'. Paper presented at the American Marketing Association Second Special Conference on Marketing Theory.

—— (1980b), 'A Cognitive Model of the Antecedents and Consequences of Satisfaction Decisions', *Journal of Marketing Research,* 17 (November), pp. 460–9.

—— (1981), 'Measurement and Evaluation of Satisfaction Process in Retail Settings', *Journal of Retailing,* 57 (fall), pp. 25–48.

OLSHASKY, R.W. *and* MILLER, J.A. (1972), 'Consumer Expectation, Product Performance and Perceived Product Quality', *Journal of Marketing Research* 9 (February).

OLSON, J.C. *and* DOVER, P. (1976), 'Effects of Expectations, Product Performance, and Disconfirmation on Belief Elements of Cognitive Structures', in B.B. Anderson (ed.), *Advances in Consumer Research, 3.* Ann Arbor: Association for Consumer Research, pp. 168–75.

—— (1979a), 'Effects of Expectation Creation and Disconfirmation on Belief Elements of Cognitive Structure', in B.B. Anderson (ed.), *Advances in Consumer Research*, Ann Arbor: Association for Consumer Research. pp. 168–75.

—— (1979b), 'Disconfirmation of Consumer Expectations through Product Trial', *Journal of Applied Psychology,* 64 (2), pp. 179–89.

OPPENHEIM, A.N. (1966), *Questionnaire Design and Attitude Measurement.* London: Heinemann.

ORTINAU, D.J. (1979), 'Conceptual Model of Consumers' Post-purchase Satisfaction/Dissatisfaction Decision Process', in Ralph L. Day and H. Keith Hunt (eds), *New Dimensions of Consumer Satisfaction and Complaining Behaviour,* Bloomington: Indiana University, pp. 35–40.

—— (1982), 'Testing the Influence of Time/Usage Experience on Consumers' Perceived, Expected, and Actual Satisfaction Attitudes toward Automobiles', in Ralph L Day and H.K. Hunt (eds), *New Findings on Consumer Satisfaction and Complaining Behaviour.* Bloomington: Indiana University, pp. 23–8.

PARSONS, J.E. (1983), 'Expectancies, Values, and Academic Behaviours', in J.T. Spence (ed.), *Achievement and Achievement Motives,* San Francisco: W.H. Freeman, pp. 75–146.

PARSONS, T. *and* SHILS, E.A. (1951), 'Values, Motives, and Systems of Action', in T. Parsons and E.A. Shils (eds), *Toward a General Theory of Action.* New York: Harper & Row, pp. 147–234.

PATCHEN, M. (1961), *The Choice of Wage Comparison*, N.J.: Prentice Hall.

PAYNE, S.L. (1965), 'Are Open-ended Questions Worth the Effort?', *Journal of Marketing Research,* 2 (November), pp. 417–18.

PFAFF, A.B. (1972), 'An Index of Consumer Satisfaction, *Proceedings of the Third Annual Conference,* Ann Arbor: Association for Consumer Research (November), pp. 713–37.

PFAFF, Martin (1977), 'The Index of Consumer Satisfaction: Measurement Problems and Opportunities', in H. Keith Hunt (ed.), *Conceptualisation and Measurement of Consumer Satisfaction and Dissatisfaction,* Cambridge, Mass.: Marketing Science Institute (May), pp. 36–71.

PFAFF, A.B., LINGOES, J.C., *and* BLIVICE, S. (1972), *The Index of Consumer Satisfaction (ICS): Some Results of the Pilot Test,* Interim Report prepared for the U.S. Department of Agriculture, Washington D.C.

PFAFF, A.B., LINGOES, J.C., *and* BLIVICE, S. (1975), *The Index of Consumer Satisfaction with Food products: Results of the Main Study,* Final Report prepared for the U.S. Department of Agriculture, Washington D.C.

PITTS, R.E. (1981), 'Value-group Analysis of Cultural Values in Heterogeneous Populations', *Journal of Social Psychology,* 115, pp. 109–24.

PITTS, R.E. *and* WOODSIDE, A.G. (1983), 'Personal Value Influences on Consumer Product Class and Brand Preferences', *Journal of Social Psychology,* 119, pp. 37–53.

PLUMER, J.T. (1977), 'Life Style, Social, and Economic Trends Influencing Consumer Satisfaction', in H. Keith Hunt (ed.), *Conceptualisation and Measurement of Consumer Satisfaction and Dissatisfaction.* Cambridge Mass.: Marketing Science Institute (May), pp. 382–408.
POWELL, Elwin H. (1958), 'Occupation, Status, and Suicide: Toward a Redefinition of Anomie', *American Sociological Review,* 23 (April, 2), pp. 131–9.
PRATT, R.W. (1972), 'The Index of Consumer Satisfaction and Corporate Marketing Policy', in M. Venkatean (ed.), *Proceedings of the 3rd Annual Conference.* Chicago: Association for Consumer Research, pp. 742–5.
REICH, C.A. (1970), *The Greening of America,* New York: Random House, p. 7.
RENOUX, Y. (1973), 'Consumer Dissatisfaction and Public Policy', in Fred C. Allvine (ed.), *Public Policy and Marketing Practices.* Chicago: American Marketing Association, pp. 53–65.
RICHINS, M.L. (1979), 'Consumer Complaining Processes: A Comprehensive Model', in Ralph L. Day and H. Keith Hunt (eds), *New Dimensions of Consumer Satisfaction and Complaining Behaviour,* Bloomington: Indiana University, pp. 30–4.
—— (1980), 'Consumer Perceptions of Costs and Benefits Associated with Complaining', in H. Keith Hunt and Ralph L. Day, (eds), *Refining Concepts and Measures of Consumer Satisfaction and Complaining.* Bloomington: Indiana University, pp. 50–3.
RODGERS, A.L. *and* SWEENEY, D.J. (1981), 'Satisfaction with Retail Stores as Reflected in Consumers' Opinions', in H. Keith Hunt and Ralph L. Day (eds), *Refining Concepts and Measures of Consumer Satisfaction and Complaining Behaviour.* Bloomington: Indiana University, pp. 153–8.
ROKEACH, M. (1968), *Beliefs, Attitudes, and Values: A Theory of Organisation and Change.* San Francisco: Jossey-Bass Inc., Pub.
—— (1973), *The Nature of Human Values.* New York: Free Press.
ROSENBERG, M. (1951), 'The Measuring of Politics in Mass Society', *Public Opinion Quarterly,* 15 (April), pp. 5–15.
—— (1955), 'The Role of Psychological Situation in Determining the Direction of Human Behaviour', in M.R. Jones (ed.), *Nebraska Symposium on Motivation,* Lincoln: University of Nebraska Press.
ROTTER, J.B. (1966), 'Generalized Expectancies for Internal vs External Control of Reinforcement', *Psychological Monographs,* 80, pp. 1–28.
RUSSEL, B. (1966), *The Problem of China.* London: George Allen & Unwin Ltd.
SALAFF, J.W. (1981), *Working Daughters of Hong Kong: Female Piety or Power in the Family?* London: Cambridge University Press.
SAMPSON, Edward E. (1980), *Introducing Social Psychology.* New York: New Viewpoints.
SAMUELSON, P.A. (1980), *Economics,* 10th ed. New York: McGraw-Hill.
SAMUELSON, P.A. (1980), *Economics,* 11th ed. New York: McGraw-Hill.
SCHIFFMAN, L.G. *and* KANUK, L.L. (1978), *Consumer Behavior.* Englewood Cliffs, N.J.: Prentice Hall.
SCOTT, J.E. *and* LAMONT, L.M. (1973a), 'Relating Consumer Values to Consumer Behaviour: A Model and Method for Investigation', *AMA Proceedings.* Chicago: American Marketing Association, pp. 283–8.

270   *Consumer behaviour in China*

—— (1973b), 'Consumerism: A Theoretical Framework for Analysis', in B.W. Becker and M. Becker (eds), *Combined Proceedings: Marketing Educators and the Real World and Dynamic Marketing in the Changing World*. Chicago: American Marketing Association, pp. 241–8.

SEEMEN, M. (1959), 'On the Meaning of Alienation', *American Sociological Review* (December), pp. 783–91.

SHAW, M. *and* WRIGHT, J.M. (1967), *Scales for the Measurement of Attitude*. New York: McGraw-Hill.

SHERIF, M. *and* HOVLAND, C.I. (1961), *Social Judgment,* New Haven: Yale University Press.

SHETH, J.N. (1971), 'Affect Behavioural Intention and Buying Behaviour as a Function of Evaluative Beliefs', in P.A. Pellemans (ed.), *Insight in Consumer and Marketing Behaviour*. Cerura: Publications of Namaur University.

—— (1972), 'A Field Study of Attitude Structure and Attitude Behaviour Relationship', in J. N. Sheth (ed.) *Model of Buyer Behaviour,* New York: Harper & Row.

—— (1985a), in his Keynote Address to the International Conference entitled *Historical and International Perspectives of Consumer Research* jointly organized by the National University of Singapore and the Association for Consumer Research.

—— (1985b), 'History of Consumer Behaviour: A Marketing Perspective', in J.N. Sheth and T.T. Tan (eds), *Historical and International Perspectives of Consumer Research: Proceedings of International Conference in Singapore*. Singapore: National University of Singapore and Association for Consumer Research, pp. 5–8.

SHETH, J.N., *and* SETHI S.P. (1977), 'A Theory of Cross-cultural Buyer Behavior', in A.G. Woodside, J.N. Sheth, and P.D. Bennett, (eds), *Consumer and Industrial Buying Behavior*. New York: North-Holland, pp. 369–86.

SHIVELY, A.N. *and* SHIVELY, S. (1972), 'Value Changes during a Period of Modernisation: The Case of Hong Kong.' Working Paper, Institute of Social Research, The Chinese University of Hong Kong.

SHORTER OXFORD DICTIONARY, THE (1978), London: Oxford University Press.

SIN, Y.M. *and* YAU, O.H.M. (1984), 'Businessmen's Attitude towards Advertising: A Cross-cultural Study', in C.T. Tan and D. Kujawa (eds), *Proceedings of the Academy of International Business: International Meeting in Singapore*. Singapore: National University of Singapore, pp. 89–99.

SINGER, M. (1968), 'Culture', in D.L. Sills (ed.), *International Encyclopedia of the Social Sciences,* 3. New York.: Macmillan Co., pp. 527–41.

SIRGY, M.J. (1982), 'Towards a Psychological Model of Consumer Satisfaction/Dissatisfaction', in Ralph L. Day and H. Keith Hunt (eds), *New Findings on Consumer Satisfaction and Complaining Behaviour,* Bloomington: Indiana University, pp. 40–7.

SMITH, G. (1982), *The Consumer Interest*. London, England: John Martin Publishing Ltd.

SMITH, M.B. (1949), 'Personal Values as Determinants of a Political Attitude', *Journal of Psychology,* 28, 4, pp. 477–86.

SOLOMON, R.L. *and* CORBIT, J.D. (1974), 'An Opponent–Process Theory of Motivation, I. Temporal Dynamics of Affects', *Psychological Review,* 81 (March), pp. 119–45.

SPECTOR, A.J. (1956), 'Expectations, Fulfillment, and Morale', *Journal of Abnormal and Social Psychology,* 52, (January), pp. 51–6.

STEIN, K. *and* STAMPFL, R. (1981), 'Consumer Values: The Underpinnings of Consumer Issues in a Post-industrial Society', *American Council on Consumer Interests Proceedings,* Cincinnati, Ohio: ACCI, pp. 18–25.

STOGDILL , R.M. (1969), 'Validity for Leader Behaviour Descriptions', *Personnel Psychology,* 22, pp. 53–88.

STOKOLS, D. (1981), 'Group × Place Transaction: Some Neglected Issues: Psychological Research on Settings', in David Magnusson (ed.), *Toward a Psychology of Situations: An Interaction Perspective.* New York: LEA.

STOUFFER, S.A., SUCHMAN, E.A., DEVINNEY, I.C., STAR, S.A. *and* WILLIAMS R.M. Jr. (1949), *The American Soldier: Adjustment during Army Life.* Princeton: Princeton University Press.

SUDMAN, S. (1983), 'Applied Sampling', in P.H. Rossi, J.D. Wright, and A.B. Anderson (eds), *Handbook of Survey Research.* New York: Academic Press.

SUMMER, J.P. *and* GRANBOIS, D.H. (1977), 'Predictive and Normative Explanations of Consumer Dissatisfaction and Complaining Behaviour', in W.D. Perreault, Jr (ed.), *Advances in Consumer Research,* 4. Ann Arbor: Association for Consumer Research, pp. 155–8.

SWAN, J.E. (1977), 'Consumer Satisfaction with a Retail Store Related to its Fulfillment of Expectations on an Initial Shopping Trip', in Ralph L. Day (ed.), *Consumer Satisfaction, Dissatisfaction, and Complaint Behaviour.* Bloomington: Indiana University, pp. 10–17.

SWAN, J.E. *and* CARROLL, M.G. (1981), 'Satisfaction Related to Predictive, Desired Expectations: A Field Study', in Ralph L. Day and H. Keith Hunt (eds), *More Progress in Consumer Satisfaction and Dissatisfaction Research.* Bloomington: Indiana University.

SWAN, J.E. *and* COMBS, L.J. (1976), 'Product Performance and Consumer Satisfaction: A New Concept', *Journal of Marketing,* 40 (April), pp. 25–33.

SWAN, J.E. *and* LONGMAN, D.S. (1972), 'Consumer Satisfaction with Automobile Repair Performance: Attitudes toward the Industry and Government control'. Paper presented at AMA Fall Conference.

SWAN, J.E. *and* TRAWICK, I.F. (1979), 'Testing an Extended Concept of Consumer Satisfaction', in Ralph L. Day and H. Keith Hunt (eds), *New Dimensions of Consumer Satisfaction and Complaining Behaviour.* Bloomington: Indiana University, pp. 56–61.

—— (1980), 'Satisfaction Related to Predictive vs Expectation', in H. Keith Hunt and Ralph L. Day (eds), *Refining Concepts and Measures of Consumer Satisfaction and Complaining Behaviour.* Bloomington: Indiana University, pp. 7–12.

SWAN, J.E., TRAWICK, I.F. *and* CARROLL, M.G. (1982), 'Satisfaction Related to Predictive, Desired Expectations: A Field Study', in Ralph L. Day and H. Keith Hunt (eds) *New Findings on Consumer Satisfaction and Complaining Behaviour.* Bloomington: Indiana University, pp. 15–22.

TECHNICAL ASSISTANCE RESEARCH PROGRAMS (TARP), INC, (1977), *A National Survey of the Complaint-Handling Procedures Used by Consumers.* Washington, D.C.: White House Office of Consumer Affairs.

THOMPSON, J.R. (1972), 'Consumers' Complaints and Cognition'. Paper Presented at the Southwestern Social Science Association, San Antonia, Texas, March.

THORELLI, H.B. (1982), 'China: Consumer Voice and Exit', in Ralph L. Day and H. Keith Hunt (eds), *International Fare in Consumer Satisfaction and Complaining.* Knoxville, Tennessee: The University of Tennessee, pp. 105–10.

TRAWICK, I.F. *and* SWAN, J.E. (1980), 'Inferred and Perceived Disconfirmation in Consumer Satisfaction', in *Marketing in the 80s,* Proceedings of the American Marketing Association Educators' Conference, Chicago: American Marketing Association, pp. 97–101.

TRIANDIS, H.C. (1971), *Attitude and Attitude Change.* New York: John Wiley & Sons.

—— (1973), 'Subjective Culture and Economic Development', *International Journal of Psychology,* 8, pp. 163–80.

—— (1974), 'Major Theoretical and Methodological Issues in Cross-cultural Psychology', in J.L. Dawson and W.J. Lonner (eds), *Readings in Cross-cultural Psychology: Proceedings of the Inaugural Meeting of the International Association for Cross-cultural Psychology held in Hong Kong, August, 1972.* Hong Kong: Hong Kong University Press.

TRIANDIS, H.C., VASSILIOU, S.G., VASSILIOU, V., TANAKA, Y. *and* SHANMUGAM, A. (1972), *The Analysis of Subjective Culture.* New York: John Wiley & Sons.

TSE, K.C. (1980), 'Directions and Opportunities of Consumer Satisfaction/ Dissatisfaction.' Unpublished working paper.

TSE, K.C. *and* WILTON, P.C. (1985), 'An Empirical Comparison of Alternative Consumer Satisfaction Level Models'. Working Paper, University of California, Berkeley.

TSENG, W.H. (1972), 'The Chinese National Character from the Viewpoint of Personality Development', in Y.Y. Li and K.S. Yang (eds), *Symposium on the character of the Chinese,* Taipei: Inst. Ethnol. Academic Sinica.

TULL, D.S. *and* HAWKINS, D.I. (1980), *Marketing Research: Measurement and Method,* 2nd ed. New York: Macmillan Publishing Co. Inc.

—— (1984), *Marketing Research: Measurement and Method,* 3rd ed. New York: Macmillan Publishing Co. Inc.

ULLMAN, L.P. (1965), *Research in Behaviour Modification: New Directions and Implications*, New York: Holt, Rinehart & Winston.

VALLE, V.A. *and* WALLENDORF, M. (1977), 'Consumer Attributions of the Cause of their Product Satisfaction and Dissatisfaction', in Ralph L. Day (ed.), *Consumer Satisfaction, Dissatisfaction and Complaining Behaviour.* Bloomington: Indiana University, pp. 26–30.

VAN DE VIJVER, Fons, Jr. (1982), 'Cross-cultural Generalisation and Universality', *Journal of Cross-cultural Psychology,* 13 (4, December).

VAN OORT, H.A. (1970), 'Chinese Culture Values Past and Present', *Chinese Culture,* Taipei: The China Academy, 11 (March, 1), pp. 1–10.

VINSON, D.E. (1977), 'Personal Values as a Dimensional of Consumer Content', in B. Greenberg and D. Bellenger (eds), *Contemporary Marketing Thought*. Chicago: American Marketing Association, p. 505.

VINSON, D.E. *and* GUTMAN, J. (1978), 'Personal Values and Consumer Discontent'. *AIDS Proceedings*, 2, American Institute of Decision Sciences, pp. 201–3.

VINSON, D.E. *and* NAKANISHI, M. (1976), 'The Structural Composition of Consumer Value-attitude System'. Working Paper. College of Business, University of Southern California.

VINSON, D.E. *and* YANG, C.F. (1979), 'Personal Values and Consumer Discontent'. Unpublished working paper. The University of Southern California.

VINSON, D.E., MUNSON, J.M. *and* NAKANISHI, M. (1977), 'An Investigation of the Rokeach Value Survey for Consumer Research Applications', in W.D. Perreault, Jr (ed.), *Advances in Consumer Research*, 4. Ann Arbor: Association for Consumer Research, pp. 247–52.

VINSON, D.E., SCOTT, J.E. *and* LAMONT, L.M. (1977), 'The Role of Personal Values in Marketing and Consumer Behaviour', *Journal of Marketing*, 3 (April), pp. 44–59.

WALDIE, K.F. (1980) 'Management – Western Ways and Eastern needs: a cultural comparison', *Hong Kong Manager*, June, p. 19.

WALDIE, K.F. (1981), 'Management: Western Ways and Eastern Needs – A Cultural Comparison', *The Hong Kong Manager,* 17 (June), p. 19.

WALL, W.M., DICKEY, L.E. *and* TALARZYK, W.W. (1977), 'Predicting and Profiling Consumer Satisfaction and Propensity to Complain', in Ralph, L. Day (ed.), *Consumer Satisfaction, Dissatisfaction and Consumer Complaining*, Bloomington: Indiana University, pp. 91–101.

—— (1978), 'Correlates of Satisfaction and Dissatisfaction with Clothing Performance', *Journal of Consumer Affairs,* (summer), pp. 104–15.

WALLACE, A.F.C. (1970), *Culture and Personality,* 2nd ed. New York: Random House.

WALTERS, C.G. (1978), *Consumer Behavior: Theory and Practice,* 3rd ed. Homewood, Ill.: Richard D. Irwin Inc.

WARD, S. *and* ROBERTSON, T.S. (1973), *Consumer Behaviour: Theoretical Sources.* Englewood Cliffs, N.J.: Prentice Hall Inc.

WARLAND, R.H., HERMANN, R.O. *and* WILLITS, J. (1977), 'Dissatisfied Consumers: Who gets Upset and Who takes Action', *Journal of Consumer Affairs,* 9 (fall), pp. 152–62.

WEAVER, D. *and* BRICKMAN, P. (1974), 'Expectancy, Feedback and Disconfirmation as Independent Factors in Outcome Satisfaction', *Journal of Personality and Social Psychology,* 30 (March), pp. 420–28.

WEBER, M. (1964), *The Religion of China: Confucianism and Taoism.* New York: Macmillan Co.

WEI, C.T. (1980), *The Wisdom of China.* Taipei: Cowboy Publishing Co.

WEINER, H., HECKHAUSEN, H., MEYER, W.V. *and* COOK, R.E. (1972), 'Causal Ascriptions and Achievement Motivation: A Conceptual Analysis of Effort and Reanalysis of Locus of Control', *Journal of Personality and Social Psychology,* 21, pp. 239–48.

WEINER, B., KUKEA, I.F.A., REED, L., REST, S. *and* ROSENBAUM, R.M. (1978), *Perceiving the Causes of Success and Failure,* New York: General Learning Press.

WESTBROOK, R.A. (1977), 'A Study of Consumer Dissatisfaction before Purchase', *Advances in Consumer Research,* 4, pp. 155–8.

―― (1978), 'Consumer Satisfaction as a Function of Personal Competence/Efficacy', *Journal of the Academy of Marketing Science,* 8 (fall, 4), pp. 7–12.

―― (1980a), 'A Rating Scale for Measuring Product/Service Satisfaction', *Journal of Marketing,* 44 (February), pp. 68–72.

―― (1980b), 'Intrapersonal Affective Influences on Consumer Satisfaction with Products', *Journal of Consumer Research,* 7 (June).

―― (1980c), 'Pre-purchases, Information Search and Post-purchase Product Satisfaction', in H. Keith Hunt and Ralph L. Day (eds), *Refining Concepts and Measures of Consumer Satisfaction and Complaining Behaviour,* Bloomington: Indiana University.

WESTBROOK, R.A. *and* NEWMAN, J.W. (1978), 'An Analysis of Shopper Dissatisfaction for Major Household Appliances', *Journal of Marketing Research,* 15 (August), pp. 456–66.

WESTBROOK, R.A., NEWMAN, J.W. *and* TAYLOR, J.R. (1978), 'Consumer Dissatisfaction in the Purchase Decision Process', *Journal of Marketing,* 15 (October), pp. 54–60.

WIKSTROM, S. (1981), 'Consumer Dissatisfaction: Scope and Policy Implications', working paper, Department of Business Administration, University of Lund, pp. 1–11.

WILSON, R.W. *and* PUSEY, A.W. (1982), 'Achievement Motivation and Small-business Relationship Patterns in Chinese Society', in S.L. Greenblatt, R.W. Wilson and A.A. Wilson (eds), *Social Interaction in Chinese Society.* New York: Praeger, pp. 195–208.

WILTON, P.C. *and* TSE, K.C. (1983), 'A Model of Consumer Response to Communication and Product Experiences'. Working Paper. Berkeley: University of California.

WINTER, M. *and* Morris, E.W. (1979), 'Satisfaction as an Intervening Variable', in R.L. Day and H.K. Hunt (eds), *New Dimensions of Consumer Satisfaction and Complaining Behaviour.* Bloomington: Indiana University, pp. 15–25.

WITHEY, S. (1977), 'Integrating some Models about Consumer Satisfaction', in H. Keith Hunt (ed.), *Conceptualisation and Measurement of Consumer Satisfaction and Dissatisfaction.* Cambridge, Mass.: Marketing Science Institute (May), pp. 120–31.

WONNACOTT, R.J. *and* T.H. (1978), *Economics.* New York: John Wiley & Sons.

WOODRUFF, R.B., CADOTTE, E.R. *and* JENKINS, R.L. (1983), 'Modelling Consumer Satisfaction Processes Using Experience-based Norms', *Journal of Marketing Research,* 20 (August) p. 296.

WORTRUBA, T.R. *and* DUNCAN, P.L. (1975), 'Are Consumers Really Satisfied?' *Business Horizons,* 18 (February, 9), pp. 85–90.

WRIGHT, B.R. (1964), 'Social Aspects of Change in the Chinese Family Pattern in Hong Kong', *Journal of Social Psychology,* 63, pp. 31–9.

YANG, K.S. (1972), 'Expressed Values of Chinese College Students', in Yang, K.S. and Li, Y.Y. (eds), *Symposium on the Character of the Chinese: An Interdisciplinary Approach.* Taipei, Taiwan: Institute of Ethnology Academia Sinica, pp. 257–312.

—— (1979), 'Research on Chinese National Character in Modern Psychology', in Chung I. Wen *et al.* (eds), *Modernisation and Change of Value,* Taiwan: Thought and Word Association. (In Chinese.)

—— (1981), 'Social Orientation and Individual Modernity among Chinese Students in Taiwan', *Journal of Social Psychology,* 113, pp. 159–70.

YANG, K.S. *and* BOND, M. (1980), 'Ethnic Affirmation by Chinese Bilinguals', *Journal of Cross-cultural Psychology,* 11 (December, 4) pp. 411–25.

YANG, K.S. *and* HWANG, K.K. (1991), *The Psychology and Behaviour of the Chinese.* Taipei, Taiwan: Kwai Kwun Publishing Co. Ltd, p. viii.

YAU, O.H.M., LO, T. *and* LI, Y.C. (1985), 'Marketing and Marketing Research in PRC: Some Observations on the Distribution System and Problems of Conducting Marketing Research'. Paper presented at the Conference on *The Enterprise and Management in East Asia,* Hong Kong, 6–9 January, 1985.

ZAICHKOWSKY, J. *and* LIEFELD, J. (1977) 'Personality Profiles of Consumer Complaint Letter Writers', in Ralph L. Day (ed.), *Consumer Satisfaction, Dissatisfaction, and Consumer Behaviour.* Bloomington: Indiana University, pp. 124–9.

ZENSEN, M.J. *and* HAMMER, L.Z. (1978), 'Value Measurement and Existential Wholeness: A Critique of the Rokeachean Approach to Value Research', *Journal of Value Enquiry*, 11 (spring), pp. 142–56.

ZINKHAN, G.M. *and* WALLENDORF, M. (1982), 'A Product Set Approach to Consumer Satisfaction/Dissatisfaction', in Ralph L. Day and H. Keith Hunt (eds), *New Findings on Consumer Satisfaction and Complaining Behaviour.* Bloomington: Indiana University, pp. 33–9.

Index

purchase intention (*continued*)
186–7, 189–90, 201, 203, 210,
218, 219, 221
purposelessness 31
Pusey, A.W. 76

quality, expectations of 1
Quelch, J. 37, 38, 40
questionnaires: length of 95;
modifications to 117–18;
structure of 96–8; text of 228–45
questions in research 99–102,
117–18
queueing 72

reciprocity 73
reference groups and brand loyalty
78
Reich, C.A. 31
reinforcement 87
relational orientation in Chinese
cultural values 72–8
reliability: affective experience
measures 207, 210, 213, 224;
Chinese cultural values scale
147–9, 213–14; consumer
experience measures 202–4, 210,
224; disconfirmation measures
208; multi-item measures 139–45,
212–13, 220; of scales 134–6
Renoux, Y. 32
repurchase
satisfaction/dissatisfaction 32, 33
research: design and methodology
94–127; future 224–6
respect for authority 72–3
response to survey: analysis of
128–34; levels 94, 95, 118–19
retailers, satisfaction/dissatisfaction
with 38, 43
ridged coefficients of Chinese
cultural values scale 160, 162,
214–15
risk and uncertainty, cultural values
of 51, 79, 82
Robertson, T.S. 48, 55
Robinson, L.M. 22, 59
Rodgers, A.L. 38
Rokeach, M. 45, 46, 53, 54, 214,
222

Rosenberg, L.J. 3, 12, 13, 36
Rosenberg, M. 30
Rotter, J.B. 42, 69
Russell, J.A. 55, 56, 81

Salaff, J.W. 76
samples: selection of 108–15; size
247–8
sampling, convenience 6
Samuelson, P.A. 23, 24
satisfaction *see* consumer
satisfaction/dissatisfaction
scales in research 101; construction
145–54; reliability and validity
134–45
Scott, J.E. 45, 47
Secord, P.F. 58
Seemen, M. 30
self-conception and cultural values
50
self-control 81
self-effacement 71
self-orientation and action 49
self-reliance 70
selling: aggressive 72; relationships
with buyer 223–4
service satisfaction/dissatisfaction
32, 36
services marketing 72
Sethi, S.P. 47
shame 75
Sherif, M. 17
Sheth, J.N. 5, 10, 11, 44, 47, 48,
55, 85, 90, 108, 212
Shils, E.A. 50, 51
Shively, A.N. and S. 64, 66, 67, 71
shopping-system dissatisfaction 32
shops *see* retailers
significance of cultural values 51
Singapore: Chinese cultural values
82
Sin, Y.M. 95
Sirgy, M.J. 4, 57
situation/situation effects 195–6,
220, 223; and consumer
expectations 85, 210; and
consumer
satisfaction/dissatisfaction 84–6,
202, 203, 205, 208, 210; LISREL
analysis 120–7